Syntactic Analysis and Description

Open Linguistics Series

Series Editor
Robin Fawcett, Cardiff University

This series is 'open' in two related ways. First, it is not confined to works associated with any one school of linguistics. For almost two decades the series has played a significant role in establishing and maintaining the present climate of 'openness' in linguistics, and we intend to maintain this tradition. However, we particularly welcome works which explore the nature and use of language through modelling its potential for use in social contexts, or through a cognitive model of language – or indeed a combination of the two.

The series is also 'open' in the sense that it welcomes works that open out 'core' linguistics in various ways: to give a central place to the description of natural texts and the use of corpora; to encompass discourse 'above the sentence'; to relate language to other semiotic systems; to apply linguistics in fields such as education, language pathology and law; and to explore the areas that lie between linguistics and its neighbouring disciplines such as semiotics, psychology, sociology, philosophy, and cultural and literary studies.

Continuum also publishes a series that offers a forum for primarily functional descriptions of languages or parts of languages – *Functional Descriptions of Language*. Relations between linguistics and computing are covered in the *Communication in Artificial Intelligence* series, two series, *Advances in Applied Linguistics* and *Communication in Public Life*, publish books in applied linguistics and the series *Modern Pragmatics in Theory and Practice* publishes both social and cognitive perspectives on the making of meaning in language use. We also publish a range of introductory textbooks on topics in linguistics, semiotics and deaf studies.

Recent titles in this series

Construing Experience through Meaning: A Language-based Approach to Cognition, M.A.K. Halliday and Christian M.I.M. Matthiessen

Culturally Speaking: Managing Rapport through Talk across Cultures, Helen Spencer-Oatey (ed.)

Educating Eve: The 'Language Instinct' Debate, Geoffrey Sampson

Empirical Linguistics, Geoffrey Sampson

The Intonation Systems of English, Paul Tench

Genre and Institutions: Social Processes in the Workplace and School, Frances Christie and J. R. Martin (eds)

Language Policy in Britain and France: The Processes of Policy, Dennis Ager

Language Relations across Bering Strait: Reappraising the Archaeological and Linguistic Evidence, Michael Fortescue

Learning through Language in Early Childhood, Clare Painter

Pedagogy and the Shaping of Consciousness: Linguistic and Social Processes, Frances Christie (ed.)

Register Analysis: Theory and Practice, Mohsen Ghadessy (ed.)

Relations and Functions within and around Language, Peter H. Fries, Michael Cummings, David G. Lockwood and William Spruiell (eds)

Researching Language in Schools and Communities: Functional Linguistic Perspectives, Len Unsworth (ed.)

Summary Justice: Judges Address Juries, Paul Robertshaw

Thematic Developments in English Texts, Mohsen Ghadessy (ed.)

Ways of Saying: Ways of Meaning. Selected Papers of Ruqaiya Hasan, Carmen Cloran, David Butt and Geoffrey Williams (eds)

Words, Meaning and Vocabulary: An Introduction to Modern English Lexicology, Howard Jackson and Etienne Zé Amvela

Syntactic Analysis and Description

A constructional approach

DAVID G. LOCKWOOD

continuum
LONDON • NEW YORK

Continuum
The Tower Building, 11 York Road, London, SE1 7NX
370 Lexington Avenue, New York, NY 10017-6503

First published 2002

British Library Cataloguing-in-Publication Data
A catalogue record for this book is available from the British Library.

ISBN 0-8264-5521-2 (hardback)
   0-8264-5522-0 (paperback)

Library of Congress Cataloging-in-Publication Data
Lockwood, David G.
   Syntactic analysis and description: a constructional approach/David G. Lockwood.
      p. cm. – (Open linguistics series)
   Includes bibliographical references and index.
   ISBN 0-8264-5521-2 (hbk.) – ISBN 0-8264-5522-0 (pbk.)
   1. Grammar, Comparative and general–Syntax. 2. Linguistics analysis (Linguistics) I. Title.
   II. Series.

   P291 .L63 2002
   415–dc21   2001054273

Typeset by BookEns Ltd, Royston, Herts
Printed and bound by MPG Books, Bodmin, Cornwall

Contents

Dedicated to the memory of

Kenneth Lee Pike

Pioneer in Function-based Syntactic Description

June 9, 1912–December 31, 2000

Preface

As its title implies, this book focuses on how to analyse and describe the phenomena of syntax. It concentrates on ways to go from data to description rather than on questions of how syntax is learned or acquired, on its organization more than its explanation. It uses an eclectic model which has been drawn primarily from three frameworks: (1) the stratificational model of Sydney M. Lamb; (2) the tagmemic model originated by the late Kenneth L. Pike, and refined by others such as Robert E. Longacre; and (3) the systemic model of M. A. K. Halliday. It is centered around the notion of the syntactic construction, a notion found in most models of syntax, and it characterizes a construction in a fashion that focuses attention on the distinction between a functional position and the class of manifestations associated with that position. This notion is particularly associated with the tagmemic model, but it is also important in the systemic and stratificational views.

While English is usually used (when possible) to begin the discussion of a topic, the book uses a broad geographical, genetic, and typological range of languages to illustrate its points. Most of the data sets presented in the various chapters have been assembled with the aid of published textbooks, reference grammars, and articles. When data items are represented in italic letters, orthography (or a conventional Roman transliteration) is being used. Other examples are in classical phonemic transcription. Where feasible, there has been an attempt to check the data sets presented with native speakers and specialized linguists, but this was not always possible, and it was considered better to illustrate points more broadly rather than confine the data to languages that could be more thoroughly checked. The reader is therefore cautioned against using these data sets to support special theoretical points without checking them personally with speakers or experienced linguists. This seems to be good advice in any case.

Each of the 15 chapters of the book concludes with a set of exercises intended to give the student practice in applying the concepts and notations in the chapter. These include not only the traditional data sets found in linguistics texts, requiring one to proceed from data to description, but also some interpretation problems, designed to give practice in going from a formalized description to a partly analysed representation of the data. An excellent source of additional material of the traditional type is Merrifield et al. (eds) (1987), which includes problems in both morphology and syntax from a wide range of languages.

The book is designed to present both the basics of syntax and some more special topics such as the treatment of clitics (Chapter 8), negation (Chapter 9), and alternative forms of clausal organization (Chapter 10). It presents only the fundamentals of these topics, because syntax is far too complex a subject to be totally covered in a single work of this length.

Thanks are due especially to two colleagues who read and offered their comments on earlier drafts of significant parts of the book: Mayrene Bentley, formerly of Michigan State, who read original versions of Chapters 1–4, and William J. Sullivan of the University of Florida, who read and commented on earlier versions of all 15 chapters. Thanks are also due to the following experts on some of the languages used in illustrations and exercises:

Amharic	Dr. Grover M. Hudson (Michigan State University)
Chinese	Dr. Yen-Hwei Lin (Michigan State University)
German	Dr. Victoria and Mr. Thoralf Hoelzer-Maddox (East Lansing, Michigan)

Hebrew	Ms. Ellen Rothfeld (Michigan State University)
Hindi	Dr. Helen E. Ullrich (New Orleans, Louisiana)
Hungarian	Dr. Miklós Kontra (Hungarian Academy of Sciences)
Japanese	Dr. Mutsuko Endo Hudson (Michigan State University)
Kannada	Dr. Helen E. Ullrich (New Orleans, Louisiana)
Swahili	Dr. Carol Myers-Scotton (University of South Carolina) [Table 7.4]
Welsh	Dr. Toby D. Griffen (Southern Illinois University, Edwardsville)

It is also fitting to remember several linguists now deceased who contributed in various ways to the book. The book as a whole is dedicated to the memory of Kenneth L. Pike, who taught the first course treating syntax in depth that the author took. His emphasis on the distinction between function and class and his interest in a wide range of languages are especially reflected in the book.

Others worthy of special mention include Dr. Seok Choong Song, a native of Korea who grew up bilingual in Korean and Japanese, who helped to refine some Korean and Japanese data sets incorporated in the book. Dr. Michael Eric Bennett was a promising young linguist who received his doctorate at Michigan State in 1986 and contributed the Malagasy data for Chapters 1 and 8. While his premature death at the age of 34 was much to be lamented, he left a collection of language grammars and textbooks which has proven to be a valuable resource for data for this work. The author's independent study of Central Yup'ik Eskimo, finally, was aided and encouraged by Dr. John H. Koo, who had taught at the University of Alaska, Fairbanks, and pursued fieldwork on the language. His sudden death in 1997 cut short a collaboration on a projected handbook of the fascinating morphology of this language, but data from the materials he had provided have nevertheless enriched this book significantly.

1

Constructions, functions, and classes

What is syntax?

According to its Greek etymology, the term "syntax" means "the study of arrangements", and to linguists, this means specifically the study of arrangements in language. Such arrangements need to be studied because they are not automatically predictable: the order of linguistic elements that may seem "natural" to the speakers of one language may not correspond at all to what seems natural to the speakers of another language. This point can easily be demonstrated by comparing the expression *the red book* in English with its equivalent in some other language, for example Italian. The Italian words equivalent to English *the*, *red*, and *book* are *il*, *rosso*, and *libro*, respectively, but they are not properly combined in the English order to give *il rosso libro. Rather, the word meaning RED is put after the word for BOOK to give *il libro rosso*. This example illustrates a minor difference in the patterns of arrangement characteristic of English and Italian, and therefore of the syntax of these languages.

If one looks at the totality of language, it turns out that there are several different kinds of arrangement patterns that need to be studied. In phonology, for example, each language has characteristic arrangements of its basic units, its phonemes. The study of these arrangements is a syntax of the phonology, often called **PHONOTACTICS**.

For many linguists, there is also another area of language called the **SEMOLOGY**, the study of linguistic meanings. This is involved with studying and describing the meaning elements of a language. To those who have seriously examined this area, it appears that each language also has its own syntax of meaningful units (**SEMEMES**), which may be called a **SEMOTACTICS**.

The kind of syntax with which the term is most often associated, however, is neither phonological nor semological. First and foremost, modern usage reserves the term **SYNTAX** for the study and description of how words combine to form particular kinds of language structures. The structures most commonly studied here are known as **PHRASES**, **CLAUSES**, and **SENTENCES**. We can illustrate all three of these terms in connection with the following example:

> *My Aunt Susan is quite ill, and I want to visit her in the hospital.*

As a whole, this example is one sentence, and within it are two clauses:

> (1) *My Aunt Susan is quite ill* and
> (2) *I want to visit her in the hospital.*

These clauses can be termed **INDEPENDENT CLAUSES** because either one could constitute a sentence by itself. Then, by traditional reckoning, the first clause contains two phrases – one is the **NOUN PHRASE** *My Aunt Susan*, and the other is the **ADJECTIVE PHRASE** *quite ill* – and the second clause contains the **INFINITIVE PHRASE** *to visit her* and the **PREPOSITIONAL PHRASE** *in the hospital*. Within the latter phrase, finally, there is another noun phrase, *the hospital*. (Some linguists may view one or more of these matters a bit differently, of course, but one need not be overly concerned with such differences at this point.)

In this work, then, syntax will be understood as involving the study and description of the arrangements of words into phrases, clauses, and sentences in various languages. The study will point out how languages are similar in their syntactic arrangements as well as how they are different. While the major focus will be on the description of the phenomena rather than their explanations, occasional attention will be given to a discussion of possible explanations for syntactic phenomena.

One way of contrasting this kind of syntax with the "syntactic" aspects of phonology and semology is to call it GRAMMATICAL SYNTAX. While such a usage is quite reasonable, it should be pointed out that linguists sometimes use a broader definition of "grammar". According to that broader definition, a "grammar" is a description or characterization of the whole of linguistic knowledge lying behind the language behavior of a speaker, including phonology and semology as well as the structure of words, phrases, clauses, and sentences. According to the narrower view used here, GRAMMAR is one of the three basic subdivisions of linguistic description, along with phonology and semology. In this sense, grammar includes morphology – the internal structure of grammatical words – as well as syntax. In outline form, this view is represented in Figure 1.1.

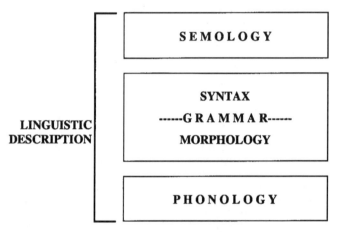

Figure 1.1   Divisions of linguistic structure and description

It should be noted that some languages may not have any morphology, while every language has syntax. Vietnamese and Classical Chinese are often cited as languages without morphology. Among the languages that do have both morphology and syntax – the vast majority – the relative role of each of these subdivisions in the grammar may be proportionately greater or lesser. In English, the role of morphology is, for example, relatively limited. In a language like Eskimo, on the other hand, morphology may do a much larger percentage of the total work of grammar than it does in English or most European languages. This is easily demonstrable when one considers an example from one form of Eskimo, namely Central Alaskan Yup'ik, beside its English translation:

> Yup'ik   /nánvaχpáxtɨŋnáqŋáicuɣnáχcuq/
> English   *He probably won't try to go to the big lake.*

While the English sentence contains at least ten words (and eleven if we treat *won't* as just a reduced form of *will not*), the Eskimo expression really counts as a single word, which is simultaneously a clause and also a sentence. While there are other cases where the number of words in a Yup'ik sentence would be greater, the grammar of this language allows – and indeed requires in many cases – the use of a single word of considerable morphological complexity where English would use many more words, each of them generally less complex, to express the same ideas. For this reason, the burden of morphology in the total grammar of

Yup'ik is much greater, and that of syntax is correspondingly less, in comparison to the relative burdens found in English.

In a language like Vietnamese, on the other hand, the entire burden of the grammar would belong to the syntax, in view of the absence of morphologically complex words.

The construction: an essential element in syntax

According to the approach followed in this book, the most basic concept in syntax is that of the construction. A **CONSTRUCTION** may be defined as a general pattern of combination found in syntax. Evidence for two important constructions in English is shown in Tables 1.1 and 1.3. The evidence is partial, and each construction may in fact be expanded beyond what is shown here, but this material will suffice as a basis for a preliminary discussion.

Table 1.1 Evidence for the noun phrase construction in English

1.	*the book*	7.	*a light box*
2.	*the big book*	8.	*that little box*
3.	*this heavy book*	9.	*a box*
4.	*this box*	10.	*a heavy box*
5.	*that big box*	11.	*the light book*
6.	*that little book*	12.	*this big book*

Considering first the material in Table 1.1, we note that each of the examples begins with one of the four English words *a*, *that*, *the*, *this* and ends with a word of the set *book*, *box*. In between these two parts, the pattern shows that there may be no word at all, or one of the words *big*, *heavy*, *light*, *little*. It is often useful to chart such evidence, as demonstrated in Table 1.2.

Table 1.2 A charting of the English noun-phrase data

POSITION 1 Obligatory	POSITION 2 Optional	POSITION 3 Obligatory
a	*big*	*book*
that	*heavy*	*box*
the	*light*	
this	*little*	

Table 1.3 Evidence for the intransitive clause construction in English

1.	*John works.*	6.	*Mary sits here.*
2.	*Mary sits.*	7.	*John works below.*
3.	*Mary works here.*	8.	*Leslie works.*
4.	*John sits there.*	9.	*John works inside.*
5.	*Leslie sits below.*	10.	*Mary works there.*

Considering next the data in Table 1.3, we see that the first word there is one of the set *John*, *Leslie*, *Mary*, while the second is one of *sits*, *works*. While examples 1, 2, and 8 end with this second word, the others give evidence for a third word, one of the set *below*, *here*, *inside*, *there*. This material can be charted as in Table 1.4. These examples suggest that we can represent the pattern of a construction with an arrangement of positions one after the other, with some positions obligatory and others optional.

Table 1.4 A charting of the English intransitive clause data

POSITION 1 Obligatory	POSITION 2 Optional	POSITION 3 Obligatory
John *Leslie* *Mary*	*sits* *works*	*below* *here* *inside* *there*

Functions within constructions

In the charts shown in Tables 1.2 and 1.4, the parts of each construction have simply been labeled as "positions", numbered from the beginning to the end. It will be better, however, if we can replace these simple position-numbers with linguistically based labels. One way to go about such labeling might be to adopt labels based on the class of words that can occur in each position, reflecting the fact that each of the positions identified so far seems to be manifested by words of a particular sort. So for the parts of the noun phrase, we might use the terms "determining adjective", "descriptive adjective", and "noun" for positions 1 through 3 in Table 1.2. We might similarly adopt the terms "proper noun", "intransitive verb", and "locative adverb" for the corresponding positions of Table 1.4. Some approaches to the matter have proceeded in precisely this way, treating each construction as a sequence of obligatory or optional class-labels. An alternative tradition suggests, however, that it may be more appropriate to label each position according to its FUNCTION – what it does – rather than according to the class of its manifestations. Each function would, in turn, be related to a MANIFESTATION CLASS. According to this tradition, the noun phrase positions would be functionally labeled as DETERMINER, MODIFIER, and HEAD, and those of the intransitive clauses would be SUBJECT, PREDICATOR, and LOCATIONAL. (These specific terms will be further exemplified and discussed in later chapters. The reader should not be preoccupied by the lack of precise definitions for them at this point.) The boxed representations of Figure 1.2 present a more formal representation of the two constructions and their constituent functions. In these representations, the labels for optional functions are placed in square brackets, while those for obligatory ones are unbracketed.

In comparing the approach relating constructions to classes directly with the alternative which brings in function as well, we need to see whether the second alternative is worth the extra complication it seems to involve. The argument that the extra complexity is needed centers on the fact that functions form a part of the meaning of each position that carries a functional label, and that this aspect of the meaning is not going to be adequately treated when

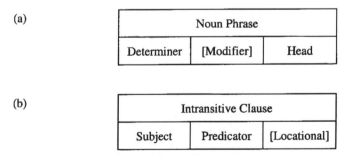

Figure 1.2   Boxed representations of two English constructions

the positions are labeled with class-labels alone. Such a fact can be most easily demonstrated by considering data where the same class is associated with distinct functions, as in the further English data of Table 1.5. Here the same set of nouns can occur in two distinct functions: that of SUBJECT (before the verb), and that of OBJECT (after the verb). If we just referred to the class without the function in treating such examples, these differences would be missed. The construction here with its functions is shown in Figure 1.3, based on the same foundations as the representations of Figure 1.2.

Table 1.5 Evidence for the transitive clause construction in English

1. *Leslie sees John.*
2. *John knows Leslie.*
3. *Mary sees Leslie.*
4. *Leslie knows Mary.*
5. *Mary knows John.*
6. *John sees Leslie.*

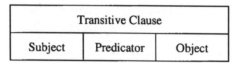

Figure 1.3 Boxed representation of the English transitive clause construction

The manifestation of functions

We have concluded that each construction is characterized by a sequence of optional or obligatory functions. To complete the description, each such function needs to be further related to a class of linguistic units which can serve to manifest it, a manifestation class. In principle, the manifestation class for a given function may consist of single words, other constructions, or a combination of the two. In the simple examples presented so far, words are the only members, though we will soon see evidence for more complex examples.

Figures 1.4 and 1.5 present the complex boxed solutions for the data from Tables 1.1 and 1.5, respectively. Each example includes a CONSTRUCTION BOX presented previously, and each function in one of these is connected by lines to VOCABULARY BOXES listing the words involved.

According to the convention followed here, each vocabulary box is headed by a class-label in the plural. The words in each vocabulary box can conveniently be given in alphabetical order. As is illustrated in Figure 1.5, the same class may manifest more than one function, and in that case it is not necessary to repeat the box that represents that class. The dual (or sometimes multiple) function of a given vocabulary class is indicated in the boxed solution by the fact that different lines connect the vocabulary box to its various functions.

Application to basic clausal data

In order to see how this system can be applied to data from languages other than English, let us consider some evidence for the structure of transitive clauses in three different languages: Turkish (Table 1.6), Thai (Table 1.7), and Welsh (Table 1.8). In examining such data sets from unfamiliar languages, one obviously needs a translation (or GLOSS) for each example if one is to be able to proceed in its analysis. (For the previous English data, glosses were omitted as unnecessary, though they could, of course, have been provided in materials written for speakers of some other language.) The glosses, however, apply to each example as a whole and

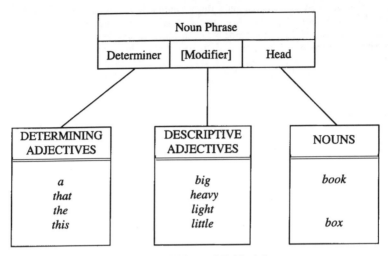

Figure 1.4   Boxed solution to the English data of Table 1.1

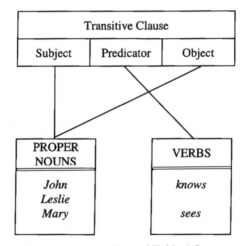

Figure 1.5   Boxed solution to the English data of Table 1.5

Table 1.6 Evidence for the transitive clause construction in Turkish

1.	čiftči köpek gördü	THE FARMER SAW A DOG.
2.	köpek čiftči gördü	THE DOG SAW A FARMER.
3.	köpek adam gördü	THE DOG SAW A MAN.
4.	komšu kedi gördü	THE NEIGHBOR SAW A CAT.
5.	čiftči kedi buldu	THE FARMER FOUND A CAT.
6.	arkadaš köpek istedi	THE FRIEND WANTED A DOG.
7.	kedi komšu duydu	THE CAT HEARD A NEIGHBOR.
8.	adam arkadaš sevdi	THE MAN LIKED A FRIEND.
9.	asker köpek buldu	THE SOLDIER FOUND A DOG.
10.	komšu asker duydu	THE NEIGHBOR HEARD A SOLDIER.

Table 1.7 Evidence for the transitive clause construction in Thai

1.	kʰrǔ· dǔ· pʰû·jǐŋ	THE TEACHER LOOKS AT THE WOMAN.
2.	kʰrǔ· dǔ· dèk	THE TEACHER LOOKS AT THE CHILD.
3.	dèk dǔ· kʰrǔ·	THE CHILD LOOKS AT THE TEACHER.
4.	dèk dǔ· pʰû·jǐŋ	THE CHILD LOOKS AT THE WOMAN.
5.	pʰû·jǐŋ rú·càk dèk	THE WOMAN KNOWS THE CHILD.
6.	dèk rú·càk kʰrǔ·	THE CHILD KNOWS THE TEACHER.
7.	pʰû·jǐŋ rú·càk kʰrǔ·	THE WOMAN KNOWS THE TEACHER.
8.	kʰrǔ· rú·càk dèk	THE TEACHER KNOWS THE CHILD.

Table 1.8 Evidence for the transitive clause construction in Welsh

1.	gweˑl sayr aθro	A CARPENTER SEES A TEACHER.
2.	edwɨn sayr aθro	A CARPENTER KNOWS A TEACHER.
3.	edwɨn sayr šopur	A CARPENTER KNOWS A SHOPKEEPER.
4.	gweˑl aθro sayr	THE TEACHER SEES A CARPENTER.
5.	gweˑl nayn aderɨn	A GRANDMOTHER SEES A BIRD.
6.	gweˑl aderɨn nayn	A BIRD SEES A GRANDMOTHER.
7.	edwɨn šopur says	A SHOPKEEPER KNOWS AN ENGLISHMAN.
8.	edwɨn aθro albanur	A TEACHER KNOWS A SCOTSMAN.
9.	gweˑl says frind	AN ENGLISHMAN SEES A FRIEND.
10.	edwɨn frind šopur	A FRIEND KNOWS A SHOPKEEPER.

do not indicate the meaning of each individual word directly. This has to be deduced by the analyst using a process of comparison between partly similar examples.

Consider first the Turkish data. It seems clear that no single example, taken separately, will permit analysis. Comparison of examples that do not share any words – such as any two of examples 1, 7, and 8 – is also futile. But if we compare items 1 and 2, we see that they share all three words, but the first two words are in a different order in each example. This difference of order corresponds, we can also see, to a difference in the roles of Subject and Object in the two examples. This allows us to guess that /gördü/ is the verb meaning SAW, but it does not tell us whether the two other words are in the order *OBJECT + SUBJECT* or the reverse. Comparing items 2 and 3, however, we see that both have *the dog* as Subject and the word /köpek/ in first position. This sets up the hypothesis that the order in transitive clauses in this language is *SUBJECT + OBJECT + PREDICATOR*, and when we check through the remaining examples, we find this hypothesis confirmed. The analysis of this material is presented in boxed form in Figure 1.6.

When we consider the other two data sets and carry out a similar analysis, we find that Thai is like English in having a *SUBJECT + PREDICATOR + OBJECT* order, while Welsh has the order *PREDICATOR + SUBJECT + OBJECT*. Boxed solutions to these data sets are presented in Figure 1.7 (for Thai) and Figure 1.8 (for Welsh).

In all these data sets, it will be noted, the English glosses include definite and/or indefinite articles which do not correspond to any words in the other language. This situation is quite common, although there are, of course, many other languages that have articles at least roughly similar in usage to the English *the* and *a(n)*. Examples without articles are being used in this preliminary discussion to limit our consideration to just the essentials of clause structure.

Orders of functions in transitive clauses

In examining data from the transitive clause in English and three other languages, we have seen some of the evidence for an important aspect of the syntactic typology of languages. This

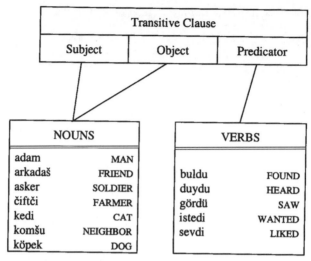

Figure 1.6   Boxed solution to the Turkish clause data of Table 1.6

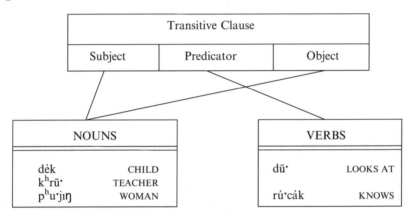

Figure 1.7   Boxed solution to the Thai clause data of Table 1.7

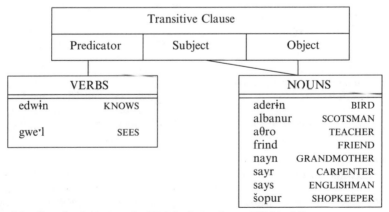

Figure 1.8   Boxed solution to the Welsh clause data of Table 1.8

typology is based on the order of functions in such clauses. As it happens, the orders exemplified in this material, namely *Subject + Predicator + Object*, *Subject + Object + Predicator*, and *Predicator + Subject + Object*, are all quite widely attested in languages. For convenience, they will be represented by initials, as SPO, SOP, and PSO. SPO occurs, for instance, not only in English and Thai, but in most modern European languages, and in many others such as Chinese, Malay, and Swahili. SOP is also very common. Besides Turkish, other languages that have it include Basque, Japanese, Korean, and most languages of modern India. PSO is somewhat rarer than the other two, but it is still fairly frequent. Besides Welsh and its close relatives in the Celtic family, PSO order is found in Classical Arabic and many languages of the Philippines. When we examine the facts more widely, we find that all mathematically possible orders of the functions S, O, and P exist, though the three seen so far account for more than 90 percent of the languages investigated.

As one example of a rarer type, we can consider the Malagasy data of Table 1.9, which exemplifies the POS type. After an analysis based on the comparison of partially identical examples, as before, we can produce the account shown in Figure 1.9.

Table 1.9 Evidence for the transitive clause construction in Malagasy

1.	*mampitahotra zaza alika*	A DOG SCARES A CHILD.
2.	*mampitahotra alika zaza*	A CHILD SCARES A DOG.
3.	*misasa alika zaza*	A CHILD WASHES A DOG.
4.	*miandry zaza sakaiza*	A FRIEND WAITS FOR A CHILD.
5.	*mahita bitro zaza*	A CHILD SEES A RABBIT.
6.	*mampitahotra alika saovaly*	A HORSE SCARES A DOG.
7.	*misasa saovaly sakaiza*	A FRIEND WASHES A HORSE.
8.	*mahita alika sakaiza*	A FRIEND SEES A DOG.
9.	*miandry sakaiza zaza*	A CHILD WAITS FOR A FRIEND.
10.	*mahita saovaly bitro*	A RABBIT SEES A HORSE.

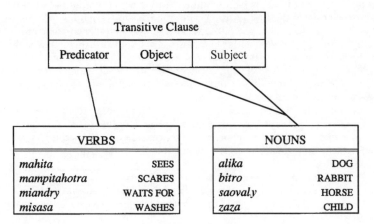

Figure 1.9 Boxed solution to the Malagasy clause data of Table 1.9

The rarest patterns are those that involve an initial object, but a few examples are found among the indigenous languages of South America. The best studied of these is Hixkaryana, a language of the Carib family spoken by about 350 people in an area of northern Brazil. It has an OPS structure, and the other possibility, OSP, is reported for some other languages in the same general area, one of which is the Arawakan language Apurinã.

Of the several ways in which the six possible order types can be subclassified, perhaps the most useful is the one summarized in Table 1.10. This is based on two dimensions:

(1) Position of the Predicator (Final, Medial, or Initial), as shown vertically;
(2) Relative order of Subject and Object (S + O or O + S) as shown horizontally.

This arrangement shows that the three relatively common types share the S + O order, while the rarer ones are O + S. Another somewhat useful classification not captured in Table 1.10 would be based on what is initial. It seems significant that subject-initial languages are overwhelmingly the most common, with predicator-initial languages next, and object-initial languages are by far the rarest.

Table 1.10 Orders of functional elements in the transitive clause

	Subject before Object (common)	Object before Subject (rare)
Predicator – Final	SOP (*Turkish*)	OSP (*Apurinã*)
Predicator – Medial	SPO (*Thai*)	OPS (*Hixkaryana*)
Predicator – Initial	PSO (*Welsh*)	POS (*Malagasy*)

While, on the one hand, we do find that all six logically possible orders of functions occur, the fact that some are rare while others are common calls for some explanation. The best place to look for such an explanation would seem to be in the relative importance of Subjects and Predicators as opposed to Objects. A Subject can usefully be seen as the indication of the person or thing that one is talking about, and a Predicator can be seen as indicating an action or state that pertains to that person or thing. An Object is typically less important, and the frequent association of the first position with importance – a natural relation in many areas outside of language, as in the case of oldest sons in many cultures, for instance – would seem to explain the rarity of object-initial languages. This kind of explanation would seem to be much better than any claim that the orders or order possibilities are something that a person is born with as innate equipment. Even the preference for S + O, which is quite strong, is not an absolute, and claiming that it is would amount to claiming that the speakers of O + S languages are pathological cases.

In connection with this general topic, it should be emphasized that the orders spoken of here as characterizing a language are seldom if ever absolute. They just represent the basic neutral order one would use in reporting a fact outside of any special context of discourse. Even in English, some violation of SPO is possible, as in the OSP examples:

> *That book, I haven't read (but I have studied this one thoroughly).*
> *The report, he left at home (but he did bring a summary of it).*
> *Uncle Joe, we visited last year (but we haven't seen Cousin June in ages).*

Some languages, such as Classical Latin, are sometimes described as having a perfectly free order of their Subjects, Predicators, and Objects. Usually, however, there is a neutral order (in Latin it is S O P) and the other orders all impart further nuances like the above English examples in O S P order. Usually claims like the one traditionally made for Latin simply mean that the order is not needed to allow Subjects to be distinguished from Objects, since the nouns show distinct morphological forms for these functions (like most of the English personal pronouns, where we have *I, he, she, we, they* for Subjects versus *me, him, her, us, them* for Objects). When a language has such morphological markings for nouns in general, it is much easier for it to use element order for other purposes, which are often related very closely to discourse considerations.

Summary of notations introduced

A.   Construction boxes

A		
M	N	[O]

B		
[F]	G	H

1.   A and B are the names of **CONSTRUCTIONS**.
2.   M N O and F G H are functionally based labels for constituents of the constructions, given in the order of their (potential) occurrence.
3.   The constituents whose labels are in square brackets ([O] and [F]) are optional, while others are obligatory in their constructions.

B.   Vocabulary boxes

C	
P	P'
Q	Q'
.	.
.	.
.	.
.	.
Z	Z'

1.   C names a class – it will be in the plural except when the class has just one member.
2. P through Z are vocabulary items, normally listed in alphabetical order.
3. P' through Z' are the glosses for vocabulary items P through Z, respectively. They may be omitted if the language is assumed to be already familiar to the audience at which the description is aimed.

C.   Connections between construction boxes and vocabulary boxes

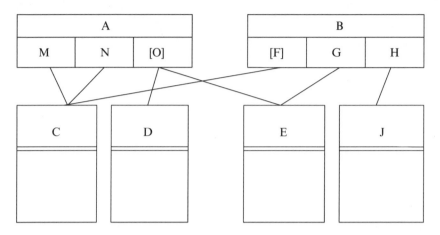

1.   Lines are used to connect each functional constituent of a construction to at least one vocabulary box, representing a class of manifestations of that function.
2.   Some functions (like M N F G H) may connect to just a single vocabulary box, while others (like O) may connect to more than one. The total of vocabulary items a given function connects to is its manifestation class.
3.   A particular vocabulary box may be connected to just one function (as are boxes D and J), or it may connect to two or more alternative functions (as do boxes C and E). The different functions manifested may be in the same construction (like M and N in A), or in different constructions (like O in A and G in B).

(This preliminary summary will require modification as further concepts are introduced in later chapters.)

Exercises

A.   Interpretation problems

1. Mandarin Chinese clauses

On the basis of the diagram of clause structure given below, translate the following English sentences into Mandarin.

1.   THE TEACHER HELPS THE STUDENT.

_____

2.   THE LAWYER INVITES THE FRIEND.

_____

3.   THE DOCTOR RECOGNIZES THE TEACHER.

4.   THE STUDENT LIKES THE DOCTOR.

5.   THE FRIEND MISSES THE LAWYER.

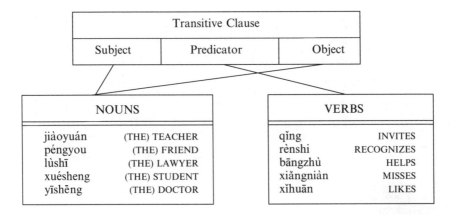

2.   *Maori noun phrases*

Maori is a Polynesian language spoken by the aboriginal inhabitants of New Zealand. On the basis of the diagram of noun phrase structure given below, translate the following English noun phrases into Maori.

1.   THE STRONG MAN

2.   THAT HOUSE OF MINE

3.   YON TALL CHAIR

4.   THIS WOMAN

5.   YON GOOD WOMAN OF YOURS

Noun Phrase			
Determiner	Head	[Modifier]	[Demonstrative]
DETERMINING ADJECTIVES	NOUNS	ADJECTIVES	DEMONSTRATIVE ADJECTIVES

DETERMINING ADJECTIVES		NOUNS		ADJECTIVES		DEMONSTRATIVE ADJECTIVES	
te	*THE	taane	MAN	kaha	STRONG	na	THAT
tooku	MY	tuuru	CHAIR	nui	GREAT	nei	THIS
toona	HIS/HER	wahine	WOMAN	pai	GOOD	ra	YON
toou	YOUR	whare	HOUSE	roa	TALL		

Note: An asterix (*) indicates a word that is not translated when there is a demonstrative in its phrase.

B.   Analysis problems

Use the notational devices presented in this chapter to present analyses of the following data sets.

1.   *Malay transitive clauses*

The following material provides evidence for transitive clauses in Malay, the official language of Malaysia.

1.	kucing kejar burung	THE CAT IS CHASING THE BIRD.
2.	anjing kejar kucing	THE DOG IS CHASING THE CAT.
3.	guru kejar anjing	THE TEACHER IS CHASING THE DOG.
4.	burung lihat kucing	THE BIRD SEES THE CAT.
5.	budak lihat anjing	THE CHILD SEES THE DOG.
6.	bayi lihat guru	THE BABY SEES THE TEACHER.
7.	perempuan basuh bayi	THE WOMAN IS WASHING THE BABY.
8.	budak basuh anjing	THE CHILD IS WASHING THE DOG.
9.	guru basuh kemeja	THE TEACHER IS WASHING THE SHIRT.
10.	kucing suka budak	THE CAT LIKES THE CHILD.
11.	perempuan suka anjing	THE WOMAN LIKES THE DOG.
12.	jiran suka perempuan	THE NEIGHBOR LIKES THE WOMAN.
13.	guru berjumpa budak	THE TEACHER MEETS THE CHILD.
14.	perempuan berjumpa guru	THE WOMAN MEETS THE TEACHER.
15.	kucing berjumpa anjing	THE CAT MEETS THE DOG.

2. *Luiseño noun phrases*

The following data provide evidence for noun phrases in Luiseño, a Uto-Aztecan language of Southern California.

1.	ʔawaal	THE/A DOG
2.	wunaal ʔawaal	THAT DOG
3.	ʔivi ʔawaal ʔoyokval	THE QUIET DOG
4.	yaʔaš ʔoyokval	THE/A QUIET MAN
5.	wunaal ṣuŋaal ʔoyokval	THAT QUIET WOMAN
6.	ʔivi ṣuŋaal	THIS WOMAN
7.	wunaal ʔawaal poloov	THAT GOOD DOG
8.	yaʔaš poloov	A GOOD MAN
9.	ṣuŋaal paapaviš	THE/A THIRSTY WOMAN
10.	ʔivi yaʔaš tavulvuš	THIS TALL MAN
11.	ʔivi nawitmal tavulvuš	THIS TALL GIRL
12.	wunaal qeeŋiš poloov	THAT GOOD SQUIRREL

Terminology

CLAUSE	MORPHOLOGY
INDEPENDENT CLAUSE	
TRANSITIVE CLAUSE	OBJECT
CONSTRUCTION	PHONOLOGY
CONSTRUCTION BOX	PHONOTACTICS
DETERMINER	PHRASE
FUNCTION	PREDICATOR
GLOSS	SEMOLOGY
	SEMOTACTICS
GRAMMAR	SENTENCE
HEAD	SUBJECT
LOCATIONAL	SYNTAX
MANIFESTATION CLASS	VOCABULARY BOX
MODIFIER	

2

Syntax and morphology: pre-editing syntactic data

Inflection in English

While Chapter 1 shows a few of the rudiments of syntactic structure and how to handle them, the material presented there is far too oversimplified to allow us to go very far into syntax without further elaboration. Essentially, it allows us to deal with those aspects of syntax which are strictly matters of word order, but it neglects various further aspects which are also important. In particular, the data used in the first chapter has been restricted so as to exclude some very common phenomena which occur in most languages. Some examples of such phenomena are seen in the English data presented in Table 2.1.

Table 2.1 Further data for the English transitive clause

---

1. *I see your old magazine.*
2. *We saw their books.*
3. *I saw the new pictures.*
4. *They carry my newspapers.*
5. *You carried our big books.*
6. *They bring the magazines.*
7. *We brought the little newspapers.*
8. *You took their new newspapers.*
9. *They take our little book.*
10. *We bring your picture.*

In this material, we see a combination of transitive clauses and noun phrases. Both of these constructions were presented in Chapter 1, but they were treated separately. Our solution to this data set will now have to include both. More important for us at this point, however, is the fact that the nouns and verbs show meaningful differences expressed morphologically, that is, by distinctions within the structure of the grammatical word. These differences involve NUMBER in the noun – *SINGULAR* versus *PLURAL* – and TENSE in the verb – *PRESENT* versus *PAST*. Based on what we did in Chapter 1, we would have to treat each word as a separate item. This would mean that *see* and *saw*, for example, would not be any more closely related than would *take* and *carry*. All of them would simply be members of the class of verbs manifesting the predicator function in these clauses. Similarly, a *SINGULAR/PLURAL* pair like *book/books* would be members of a class of nouns, but so would *picture* and *newspapers*. An account based on these assumptions is presented in Figure 2.1.

Such a solution would not be considered very satisfactory by the typical linguist, who would point out first and foremost its failure to deal with the relationships between pairs of present- and past-tense verbs and singular and plural nouns such as those just mentioned above. It could further be objected that syntax sometimes involves certain relations between such different word forms, even though none of these is in evidence here. To take just one example, English shows different numbers of subject correlated with a further difference of

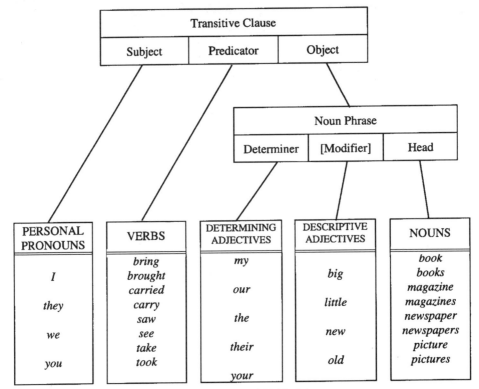

Figure 2.1   A preliminary account of the data of Table 2.1

verb forms, as in *The man arrives* as contrasted with *The men arrive*. Because of such matters as these, it appears that syntax must take account of at least some of the morphological distinctions found in various languages.

The most direct way of doing such a thing would be to ignore the alleged distinction between morphology and syntax altogether, and to treat morphology as simply another subdivision of syntax dealing with the internal structure of words, alongside other subdivisions which would treat the structure of phrases, clauses, and sentences.

Abstracting out morphological details

As it turns out, however, there is an alternative between the extremes of completely ignoring morphology and incorporating it completely into syntax. This involves treating some, but not all, aspects of morphology in relation to syntax, and leaving further details to be handled in the morphology proper.

In relation to English verbs, for instance, it is syntactically important that various verbs have different forms reflecting different tenses, but it is syntactically irrelevant that there are different ways of forming the past tense, as shown in each of the different verbs found in the data of Table 2.1. The nouns in this data set show less difference in plural formation than the verbs, though if phonological forms are considered, *books* has the suffix /s/, while the others have /z/. If further noun pairs like *foot/feet*, *man/men*, *child/children*, and *ox/oxen* are considered, however, we see further morphologically different ways of indicating distinctions of number in nouns. These details can reasonably be left to the morphology, but it will be syntactically important whether an English noun is singular or plural, or whether a verb is in the present or past tense.

In order to reflect such differences while ignoring further details of purely morphological interest, we can edit the data in such a way as to show just the base of the noun or verb, along with the grammatical categories reflected in its morphology. Some examples applied to this data set are presented in Table 2.2. In this analysis, the base is represented by the simple form of the word, and under each of these bases there is a grammatical label representing the morphological category involved. For nouns the labels in English are *SINGULAR* and *PLURAL,* and for the verbs discussed so far they are *PRESENT* and *PAST.* According to this style of editing, we select an overt label for both categorial terms involved in a morphological distinction, even though one of them may not be indicated by an overt affix. Besides abstracting out different manifestations of affixes, this editing also abstracts out the sequences of elements within a word. So if three languages all have a distinction between singular and plural forms, but one uses prefixes, another uses suffixes, and a third shows internal distinctions such as those seen in English *man/men* and *tooth/teeth,* we treat the three examples in exactly the same way with the category labels *SINGULAR* and *PLURAL* placed below the label for each base. In this edited version, such bases and category labels are not in any sequence within each word. Rather, they are treated as simultaneous, as represented by writing the categories below the base label rather than as before or after it.

Table 2.2 Edited versions of selected examples from Table 2.1

1.	*I*	*see*	*your old magazine*
		PRESENT	*SINGULAR*
2.	*We saw*	*their books*	
	PAST	*PLURAL*	
4.	*They carry*	*my newspapers*	
	PRESENT	*PLURAL*	
6.	*They bring*	*the magazines*	
	PRESENT	*PLURAL*	
8.	*You took*	*their new newspapers*	
	PAST	*SINGULAR*	
9.	*They take*	*our little book*	
	PRESENT	*SINGULAR*	

When we edit for morphology in this way, we can prepare a boxed solution for the edited data rather than for the original. For the version sampled in Table 2.2, this would look like Figure 2.2. In its treatment of the transitive clause and noun phrase constructions, it is identical to what is seen in Figure 2.1. In order to handle the edited versions of nouns and verbs, however, we need to relate the Predicator and Head functions to additional constructions for words rather than relating them directly to whole words in vocabulary boxes. In these additional construction boxes, we want to represent the simple association of categories and bases rather than the detailed sequences that would be needed in a full morphological treatment. To represent these differences, we use a different variety of construction box, which depicts the functional constituents as simply associated in the word rather than laid out in a specific sequence in the manner of the clause- and phrase-constructions. This difference is graphically represented by the symbol

used in place of

to separate the constituents in the lower part of a construction box. So while the representation

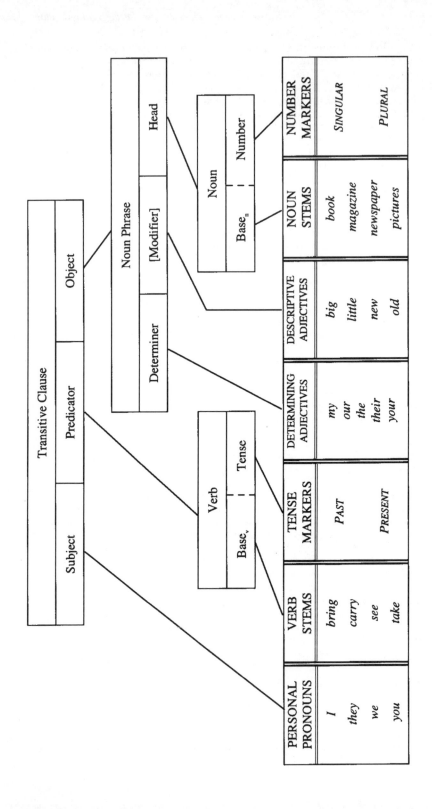

Figure 2.2 A revised account of Table 2.1 (after editing)

A	B	C

is distinct from both

B	C	A

and

C	A	B

in the construction boxes used up to this point for clause- and phrase-constructions, the representations

| A | B | C |, | B | C | A | and | C | A | B |

or any other possible order of constituents are completely equivalent, because they symbolize only simple association rather than linear sequence.

In order to see an example of a more complex word-construction than we can find in English, we can consider the Central Alaskan Yup'ik data in Table 2.3. As already mentioned in Chapter 1, this language puts a much greater burden on its morphology than does English. This morphological richness is evident in both nouns and verbs, but is particularly striking in the latter. As a minimum, the English glosses presented for these items involve three words, while the Yup'ik data items have two words as a maximum. How can this be explained?

Table 2.3 Syntactic data from Central Alaskan Yup'ik

1. taŋχaa	HE SEES HIM.
2. mani taŋχaa	HE SEES HIM HERE.
3. yaani taŋχaaŋa	HE SEES ME THERE.
4. taŋχaatɨn	HE SEES YOU.
5. taŋɨnʙitaa	HE DOESN'T SEE HIM.
6. taŋɨnʙitaqa	I DON'T SEE HIM.
7. mani taŋɨɬχuatɨn	HE SAW YOU HERE.
8. yaani taŋɨɬχunʙitamkɨn	I DIDN'T SEE YOU THERE.
9. kiuɣaqa	I ANSWER HIM.
10. mani kiuɣan	YOU ANSWER HIM HERE.
11. yaani kiuɬχuaχpɨŋa	YOU ANSWERED ME THERE.
12. kiunʙitan	YOU DON'T ANSWER HIM HERE.
13. kiuɬχunʙitaqa	I DIDN'T ANSWER HIM.
14. yaani taŋɨχciqaa	HE WILL SEE HIM THERE.
15. mani kiuŋaitaaŋa	HE WON'T ANSWER ME HERE.
16. taʙiŋaa	HE UNDERSTANDS HIM.
17. yaani taʙiŋɨɬχunʙitaχpɨŋa	YOU DIDN'T UNDERSTAND ME THERE.
18. mani taʙiŋɨŋaitaŋa	HE WON'T UNDERSTAND ME HERE.
19. taʙiŋɨciqaqa	I WILL UNDERSTAND HIM.
20. yaani taʙiŋɨɬχuan	YOU UNDERSTOOD HIM THERE.
21. mani taʙiŋɨciqamkɨn	I WILL UNDERSTAND YOU HERE.
22. taʙiŋɨnʙitaaqa	I DON'T UNDERSTAND HIM.
23. yanni taʙiŋɨɬχuan	YOU UNDERSTOOD HIM THERE.
24. mani taʙiŋɨciqaaŋa	HE WILL UNDERSTAND ME HERE.

By the kinds of comparison illustrated previously, it is possible to deduce that the two-word examples begin with a locative adverb fulfilling a Locational function, which is optional in the clause (here involving either /mani/HERE or /yaani/THERE), and that all the rest of the meaning is contained in the second word (the only word in the examples without a Locational). While the English translations of these remainders involve subject- and object-pronouns as well as verbs, and sometimes other words as well, Yup'ik is an example of a language where all of this is included in the morphological structure of the verb itself. Students of some European languages will be familiar with the idea of expressing the person of the subject and also the tense within the verb, but this Yup'ik data illustrates the expression of additional information within the verb, namely the person of the object and the polarity (*AFFIRMATIVE/NEGATIVE*) of the statement. We find that verbs reflect person, then, for both the subject and the object, as translated into English via personal pronouns. We also see that the tenses indicated within the verb include not just *PRESENT* and *PAST*, as in English, but also the *FUTURE* (which in English is expressed syntactically via the separate modal auxiliary verb *will*). Finally, we see that negation, expressed in English by a separate word *not*, is just another part of the verb in Yup'ik.

The edited versions of a representative selection of the Yup'ik verbs in the data set are presented in Table 2.4. Here the labels for the bases are shown for each example with a total of four categorial labels, one from each of the following sets:

(1)	TENSE	*PRESENT//PAST//FUTURE*
(2)	POLARITY	*AFFIRMATIVE//NEGATIVE*
(3)	SUBJECT-PERSON	*FIRST-SUBJECT//SECOND-SUBJECT//THIRD-SUBJECT*
(4)	OBJECT-PERSON	*FIRST-OBJECT//SECOND-OBJECT//THIRD-OBJECT*

Table 2.4 Edited versions of selected Yup'ik verbs from Table 2.3

1. taŋχ *PRESENT* *AFFIRMATIVE* *THIRD-SUBJECT* *THIRD-OBJECT*	3. taŋχ *PRESENT* *AFFIRMATIVE* *THIRD-SUBJECT* *FIRST-OBJECT*	4. taŋχ *PRESENT* *AFFIRMATIVE* *THIRD-SUBJECT* *SECOND-OBJECT*
5. taŋχ *PRESENT* *NEGATIVE* *THIRD-SUBJECT* *THIRD-OBJECT*	6. taŋχ *PRESENT* *NEGATIVE* *FIRST-SUBJECT* *THIRD-OBJECT*	7. taŋχ *PAST* *AFFIRMATIVE* *THIRD-SUBJECT* *SECOND-OBJECT*
8. taŋχ *PAST* *NEGATIVE* *FIRST-SUBJECT* *SECOND-OBJECT*	10. kiu *PRESENT* *AFFIRMATIVE* *SECOND-SUBJECT* *THIRD-OBJECT*	11. kiu *PAST* *AFFIRMATIVE* *SECOND-SUBJECT* *FIRST-OBJECT*
12. kiu *PRESENT* *NEGATIVE* *SECOND-SUBJECT* *THIRD-OBJECT*	13. kiu *PAST* *NEGATIVE* *FIRST-SUBJECT* *THIRD-OBJECT*	15. kiu *FUTURE* *NEGATIVE* *THIRD-SUBJECT* *FIRST-OBJECT*
18. taʙiŋɨ *FUTURE* *NEGATIVE* *THIRD-SUBJECT* *FIRST-OBJECT*	23. taʙiŋɨ *PAST* *AFFIRMATIVE* *SECOND-SUBJECT* *THIRD-OBJECT*	24. taʙiŋɨ *FUTURE* *AFFIRMATIVE* *THIRD-SUBJECT* *FIRST-OBJECT*

In editing such data for syntactic analysis, it should be noted, we do not have to perform a complete morphological analysis. We only have to penetrate the morphology enough to see what is expressed in it. We can then replace the morphological markers (all matters of suffixation in this set of examples) with categorial labels, relegating the further details to the chapter on morphology.

Figure 2.3 presents the syntactic analysis of the edited Yup'ik data along the same lines as was done for the English material in Figure 2.2. Since there are four sets of inflectional category choices, the word-construction box for the verb must show four functional constituents in addition to the base, for a total of five. Apart from this, we simply need the clause construction with its optional Locational and obligatory Predicator.

It should be noted that, although the English translations of the Yup'ik examples contain subject- and object-functions manifested by pronouns, there are no such clause constituents (Subject or Object) recognized for this Yup'ik material. We must realize that languages may differ in this respect, and we must base our treatment on what we find in each particular language we examine. The data considered here shows no evidence for a syntactic Subject or Object in Yup'ik, but it shows the corresponding meanings expressed in the morphology of the verb rather than in the syntax. This is therefore what we represent in our description.

If we were to examine more data from this language, we would find that there are in fact Subject and Object functions, but they are optional and are not normally used for a Subject or object that is expressible by a pronoun. This kind of practice is quite reasonable in a language like Yup'ik, since the verb forms, as we have seen, regularly express the person of the Subject and Object (and further data would also show that the number of both Subject and Object are also expressed in the verb). In general, we find that there are languages like English, where pronoun Subjects and Objects generally have to be expressed, and other languages like Yup'ik where this is not necessary. In various European languages like Spanish and Italian, furthermore, pronoun Subjects are optional, but pronoun Objects are usually obligatory (at least those referring to animates).

It should be noted, finally, that a syntactic description based on construction boxes and vocabulary boxes can be viewed as a device for producing descriptions of the data items on which they are based. It can be seen as a kind of **GENERATING DEVICE**. In this role, it should produce descriptions not only of data items, but of further combinations assumed to be possible because they fit the general patterns observed in the data. So from the English solution in Figure 2.2, we could generate the following example:

you	bring	our	old	picture
	PRESENT			*PLURAL*

This is simply an edited version of the actual English sentence *You bring our old pictures,* which is possible even though it is not in the data considered. (It is predicted, in this case quite accurately, from the patterns in the data that has been considered.) Similarly, with the Yup'ik solution in Figure 2.3 we can project such unattested examples as the following:

(1)	mani	kiu	(2)	yaani	taŋχ
		FUTURE			*PAST*
		NEGATIVE			*AFFIRMATIVE*
		FIRST-SUBJECT			*SECOND-SUBJECT*
		SECOND-OBJECT			*THIRD-OBJECT*

Item (1) would mean I WON'T ANSWER YOU HERE, while (2) would mean YOU SAW HIM THERE. These examples are certainly possible, as can be confirmed by consultation with a speaker of the language. When such a projection proves to be impossible, of course, one will have to investigate the reason for this and revise the description accordingly.

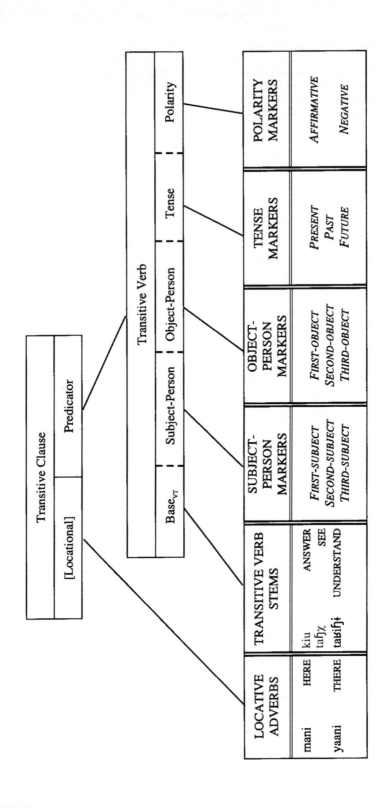

Figure 2.3 Boxed solution for the Yup'ik data of Table 2.3, as edited

Patterns of pre-editing

So far, we have seen some rather simple examples of noun and verb inflection in English and some more complex material from the Yup'ik verb. In this section, a variety of examples of inflectional morphology will be presented to illustrate the possible complications one might find in this area. The data considered here will be presented in morphological data sets. When one is working on syntax, however, it will typically be necessary to extract the morphological data from its fuller syntactic context. With most examples considered in this section, it will be assumed that this has already been done. At the end of the discussion, however, one example will be presented in full form, starting with the relatively raw syntactic data and proceeding through the extraction and editing of the morphological data and the ultimate solution to the edited data.

A first set of morphological data for editing is presented in Table 2.5, from the Aztec dialect of Veracruz in Mexico. The editing of this data set is summarized in Table 2.6. Part (a) of that summary shows one representative verb from the data in all its forms (using the base that means CRY) arranged along two dimensions, one for person (*FIRST* versus *SECOND*) and the other for tense (*PAST* versus *FUTURE*). Once the arrangement is done, one can simply replace each individual inflectional affix with a label, as shown in part (b) of Table 2.6. Part (c) summarizes the labels used in part (b) in relation to the affixes in the full forms. Each of the other verb forms can be edited in an analogous way.

Table 2.5 Morphological data from the Aztec dialect of Veracruz

1.	ničoka?	I CRIED.
2.	tičoka?	YOU CRIED.
3.	ničokas	I WILL CRY.
4.	tičokas	YOU WILL CRY.
5.	nitehkawi?	I CLIMBED.
6.	titehkawi?	YOU CLIMBED.
7.	nitehkawis	I WILL CLIMB.
8.	titehkawis	YOU WILL CLIMB.
9.	nimayana?	I WAS HUNGRY.
10.	timayana?	YOU WERE HUNGRY.
11.	nimayanas	I WILL BE HUNGRY.
12.	timayanas	YOU WILL BE HUNGRY.

Table 2.6 Editing of the morphological data of Table 2.5

		Tense	
Person	(a) *FIRST*	*PAST* ničoka?	*FUTURE* ničokas
	SECOND	tičoka?	tičokas
	(b)	čoka *FIRST* *PAST*	čoka *FIRST* *FUTURE*
		čoka *SECOND* *PAST*	čoka *SECOND* *FUTURE*
	(c)	*FIRST* = ni *SECOND* = ti	*PAST* = ? *FUTURE* = s

A somewhat different situation is shown in the Turkish data of Table 2.7. The analysis of this is given in Table 2.8. Although the expression of categories here is quite straightforward, just as in the Aztec, there are some categories that have no overt expression, but are simply recognized by the fact that they lack an affix of a particular sort. This phenomenon can be termed ZERO EXPRESSION. So the category *SINGULAR* is recognized by the absence of the suffix /lar/ for the contrasting *PLURAL*, and the category *ABSOLUTE* is recognized by the absence of a suffix for case – either /a/ for *DATIVE* or /dan/ for *ABLATIVE*.

Table 2.7 Morphological data from Turkish

1.	adam	A MAN
2.	adama	TO A MAN
3.	adamdan	FROM A MAN
4.	adamlar	MEN
5.	adamlara	TO MEN
6.	adamlardan	FROM MEN
7.	mum	A CANDLE
8.	muma	TO A CANDLE
9.	mumdan	FROM A CANDLE
10.	mumlar	CANDLES
11.	mumlara	TO CANDLES
12.	mumlardan	FROM CANDLES
13.	kol	AN ARM
14.	kola	TO AN ARM
15.	koldan	FROM AN ARM
16.	kollar	ARMS
17.	kollara	TO ARMS
18.	kollardan	FROM ARMS

Table 2.8 Editing of the morphological data of Table 2.7

			Number	
	(a)		*SINGULAR*	*PLURAL*
	ABSOLUTE		adam	adamlar
Case	*DATIVE*		adama	adamlara
	ABLATIVE		adamdan	adamlardan
	(b)		adam	adam
			SINGULAR	*PLURAL*
			ABSOLUTE	*ABSOLUTE*
			adam	adam
			SINGULAR	*PLURAL*
			DATIVE	*DATIVE*
			adam	adam
			SINGULAR	*PLURAL*
			ABLATIVE	*ABLATIVE*
	(c)		*ABSOLUTE* = Ø	*SINGULAR* = Ø
			DATIVE = a	
			ABLATIVE = dan	*PLURAL* = lar

We next see some Czech data in Table 2.9, with its editing shown in Table 2.10. This material can be arranged in a similar fashion to the Turkish, with dimensions applying to both case and number (see part (a) of Table 2.10), and its editing in part (b) proceeds similarly. The difference is seen clearly, however, when it comes to part (c), because in Czech the various suffixes do not indicate case and number separately the way those in Turkish do. Rather, each suffix indicates a combination of case and number. This phenomenon may be termed FUSED EXPRESSION (or alternatively PORTMANTEAU EXPRESSION). While this difference between Czech and Turkish would obviously have to be reflected in the morphological analysis of each language, it is not important as far as the syntax is concerned, so the edited versions of the two are very similar. It is appropriate to always separate case and number categories for syntactic purposes, in fact, because they generally represent independent variables in the syntax of any language where they occur.

Table 2.9 Morphological data from Czech

1.	žena	A WOMAN
2.	ženě	TO A WOMAN
3.	ženou	BY A WOMAN
4.	ženy	WOMEN
5.	ženám	TO WOMEN
6.	ženami	BY WOMEN
7.	ryba	A FISH
8.	rybě	TO A FISH
9.	rybou	BY A FISH
10.	ryby	FISH
11.	rybám	TO FISH
12.	rybami	BY FISH
13.	voda	WATER
14.	vodě	TO WATER
15.	vodou	BY WATER
16.	vody	WATERS
17.	vodám	TO WATERS
18.	vodami	BY WATERS

Table 2.10 Editing of the morphological data of Table 2.9

		Number	
	(a)	*SINGULAR*	*PLURAL*
	NOMINATIVE	žena	ženy
Case	*DATIVE*	ženě	ženám
	INSTRUMENTAL	ženou	ženami
	(b)	žen	žen
		SINGULAR	*PLURAL*
		NOMINATIVE	*NOMINATIVE*
		žen	žen
		SINGULAR	*PLURAL*
		DATIVE	*DATIVE*
		žen	žen
		SINGULAR	*PLURAL*
		INSTRUMENTAL	*INSTRUMENTAL*
	(c)	*SINGULAR* + *NOMINATIVE* = Ø	*PLURAL* + *NOMINATIVE* = y
		SINGULAR + *DATIVE* = ě	*PLURAL* + *DATIVE* = ám
		SINGULAR + *INSTRUMENTAL* = ou	*PLURAL* + *INSTRUMENTAL* = ami

A further very common complication is seen in Russian, as presented in the data of Table 2.11. Here the same categories of case are expressed in different ways in different words. Like the different ways of indicating plurals or past tenses in English, these instances of **DIVERSIFICATION** or **DIVERSIFIED EXPRESSION** are morphological details which should be edited out. The existence of these alternatives is indicated in part (c) of the analysis presented in Table 2.12 by the fact that alternative expressions are shown, separated by commas.

Table 2.11 Morphological data from Russian

1.	visatá	HEIGHT
2.	visatí	OF HEIGHT
3.	visatój	BY HEIGHT
4.	travá	GRASS
5.	traví	OF GRASS
6.	travój	BY GRASS
7.	s^{y}iló	A VILLAGE
8.	s^{y}ilá	OF A VILLAGE
9.	s^{y}ilóm	BY A VILLAGE
10.	gn^{y}izdó	A NEST
11.	gn^{y}izdá	OF A NEST
12.	gn^{y}izdóm	BY A NEST

Table 2.12 Editing of the morphological data of Table 2.11

			Nouns	
Case	(a)	*NOMINATIVE*	visatá	s^{y}iló
		GENITIVE	visatí	s^{y}ilá
		INSTRUMENTAL	visatój	s^{y}ilóm
	(b)		visat	s^{y}il
			NOMINATIVE	*NOMINATIVE*
			visat	s^{y}il
			GENITIVE	*GENITIVE*
			visat	s^{y}il
			INSTRUMENTAL	*INSTRUMENTAL*
	(c)		*NOMINATIVE* = á, ó	
			GENITIVE = í, á	
			INSTRUMENTAL = ój, óm	

The Polish data in Table 2.13 shows another complication: while the genitive case forms always have the suffix /a/ and the nominatives (used for subjects) always have no suffix, the forms used for objects (accusatives) are either with or without a suffix. These accusative forms coincide with the nominative for /kluč/KEY and /fotel/ARMCHAIR, while in the nouns /kot/CAT and /papjeros/CIGARETTE they coincide with the genitive. Even though none of these nouns shows three distinct forms, we nevertheless recognize three rather than two cases when we edit this material. When two forms partly coincide, it is traditional to speak of **SYNCRETISM**. In this instance it seems appropriate to speak more specifically of **DIFFERENTIAL SYNCRETISM**, meaning that the syncretism sometimes goes one way (accusative like nominative) and sometimes the other (accusative like genitive). If we failed to edit this material properly, in the

Table 2.13 Morphological data from Polish

1.	kot	A CAT (SUBJECT)
2.	kota	A CAT (OBJECT)
3.	kota	OF A CAT
4.	papjeros	A CIGARETTE (SUBJECT)
5.	papjerosa	A CIGARETTE (OBJECT)
6.	papjerosa	OF A CIGARETTE
7.	kluč	A KEY (SUBJECT)
8.	kluč	A KEY (OBJECT)
9.	kluča	OF A KEY
10.	fotel	AN ARMCHAIR (SUBJECT)
11.	fotel	AN ARMCHAIR (OBJECT)
12.	fotela	OF AN ARMCHAIR

Table 2.14 Editing of the morphological data of Table 2.13

			Nouns	
Case	(a)	*NOMINATIVE*	kot	kluč
		ACCUSATIVE	kota	kluč
		GENITIVE	kota	kluča
	(b)		kot	kluč
			NOMINATIVE	*NOMINATIVE*
			kot	kluč
			ACCUSATIVE	*ACCUSATIVE*
			kot	kluč
			GENITIVE	*GENITIVE*
	(c)		*NOMINATIVE* = Ø	
			ACCUSATIVE = a, Ø	
			GENITIVE = a	

fashion summarized in Table 2.14, it would unnecessarily complicate our syntactic description, requiring us to have the object in the "nominative" for /kluč/ and /fotel/, but in the "genitive" for the other two nouns /kot/ and /papjeros/.

The next set of data comes from Classical Latin, as shown in Table 2.15. Here we see nouns in four cases and two numbers. The patterns found here combine several phenomena already observed in previous data sets. These include the ZERO EXPRESSION previously seen in the Turkish data of Table 2.7 (found here for the nominative singular), the FUSED EXPRESSION seen in the Czech data of Table 2.9 (seen for case in combination with number here as before), and the DIVERSIFIED EXPRESSION seen in the Russian data of Table 2.11. This new data also shows several examples of the syncretism seen in the Polish data just considered in connection with Table 2.13 involving (1) the nominative and accusative cases in both numbers of the nouns /opus/ and /tempus/ and (2) the dative and ablative cases in the singular of the nouns /vir/ and /puer/ and in the plural of all nouns. In addition, two of the noun bases show another variety of diversified expression, which can be termed BASE DIFFERENTIATION (or STEM DIFFERENTIATION). The editing of this data is summarized in Table 2.16.

The selection of a label for an alternating base like /opus/ ~ /oper-/or/tempus/ ~ /tempor-/ is a fairly arbitrary matter which should not detain the analyst unduly. Here the shapes that

Table 2.15 Morphological data from Classical Latin

1.	vir	A MAN (SUBJECT)		17.	opus	A WORK (SUBJECT)
2.	virum	A MAN (OBJECT)		18.	opus	A WORK (OBJECT)
3.	viro˙	TO A MAN		19.	operi˙	TO A WORK
4.	viro˙	BY A MAN		20.	opere	BY A WORK
5.	viri˙	MEN (SUBJECT)		21.	opera	WORKS (SUBJECT)
6.	viro˙s	MEN (OBJECT)		22.	opera	WORKS (OBJECT)
7.	viri˙s	TO MEN		23.	operibus	TO WORKS
8.	viri˙s	BY MEN		24.	operibus	BY WORKS
9.	puer	A BOY (SUBJECT)		25.	tempus	A TIME (SUBJECT)
10.	puerum	A BOY (OBJECT)		26.	tempus	A TIME (OBJECT)
11.	puero˙	TO A BOY		27.	tempori˙	TO A TIME
12.	puero˙	BY A BOY		28.	tempore	BY A TIME
13.	peuri˙	BOYS (SUBJECT)		29.	tempora	TIMES (SUBJECT)
14.	puero˙s	BOYS (OBJECT)		30.	tempora	TIMES (OBJECT)
15.	pueri˙s	TO BOYS		31.	temporibus	TO TIMES
16.	pueri˙s	BY BOYS		32.	temporibus	BY TIMES

Table 2.16 Editing of the morphological data of Table 2.15

			Number			
	(a)		*SINGULAR*		*PLURAL*	
		NOMINATIVE	vir	opus	viri˙	opera
		ACCUSATIVE	virum	opus	viro˙s	opera
Case		*DATIVE*	viro˙	operi˙	viri˙s	operibus
		ABLATIVE	viro˙	opere	viri˙s	operibus
	(b)		vir	oper	vir	oper
			SINGULAR	*SNGULAR*	*PLURAL*	*PLURAL*
			NOMINATIVE	*NOMINATIVE*	*NOMINATIVE*	*NOMINATIVE*
			vir	oper	vir	oper
			SINGULAR	*SINGULAR*	*PLURAL*	*PLURAL*
			ACCUSATIVE	*ACCUSATIVE*	*ACCUSATIVE*	*ACCUSATIVE*
			vir	oper	vir	oper
			SINGULAR	*SINGULAR*	*PLURAL*	*PLURAL*
			DATIVE	*DATIVE*	*DATIVE*	*DATIVE*
			vir	oper	vir	oper
			SINGULAR	*SINGULAR*	*PLURAL*	*PLURAL*
			ABLATIVE	*ABLATIVE*	*ABLATIVE*	*ABLATIVE*

(c)

NOMINATIVE + *SINGULAR* = Ø
NOMINATIVE + *PLURAL* = i˙, a
ACCUSATIVE + *SINGULAR* = um, Ø
ACCUSATIVE + *PLURAL* = o˙s, a
DATIVE + *SINGULAR* = o˙, i˙
DATIVE + *PLURAL*, *ABLATIVE* + *PLURAL* = i˙s, ibus
ABLATIVE + *SINGULAR* = o˙, e

occur in more inflectional forms of the word have been used. Alternatively, the labels "opus" and "tempus", based on the nominative singular, could have been selected – this is what is traditionally done in Latin dictionaries – or it would even be possible in this case to use what the alternating shapes have in common and come up with "op" and "temp". The only essential thing is that each base be assigned a distinct and unambiguous label. (In the case of homonymy it may be necessary to assign some subscript letter or number to keep elements distinct.) It is also normal, of course, to base this label on the actual forms in some fashion or other, and to treat parallel cases in a parallel way.

Still another example is seen in the German verbal data of Table 2.17 and its edited version in Table 2.18. This material shows many of the same phenomena also observed in the Latin, including zero expression (sometimes seen for the first and third persons in the singular), fused expression (of persons with numbers), diversified expression (particularly of the past tense), and partial syncretism (of first-singular and third-singular in the past tense, of third-singular and second-plural in some present-tense forms, and of first-plural and third-plural in both tenses). In addition, it exhibits vowel distinctions in the verbs /verf/THROW and /lauf/RUN. These differences of vowel are actually of two different sorts: (1) the alternate forms with /au/ or /e/ versus /oi/ or /i/ are used in the present tense to set off the bases of singular verbs outside the first person from the rest; (2) in the past tense, the vowel differences seen in /li·f/ and /varf/ effectively mark the tense category, occurring in place of the suffixes /te/ or /ete/ seen in the other verbs. In other words, in this latter case the internal distinction of vocalic nucleus is in alternation with a suffix as an indicator of the past tense. The distinctions between /verf/ and /virf/ and /lauf/ and /loif/, on the other hand, are not meaningful by themselves, and therefore can be treated as cases of base differentiation like those in some of the Latin bases.

Table 2.17 Morphological data from Modern Standard German

1.	rauxe	(I) SMOKE	1a.	rauxte	(I) SMOKED
2.	rauxst	(YOU SgFm) SMOKE	2a.	rauxtest	(YOU SgFm) SMOKED
3.	rauxt	(HE/SHE/IT) SMOKES	3a.	rauxte	(HE/SHE/IT) SMOKED
4.	rauxen	(WE) SMOKE	4a.	rauxten	(WE) SMOKED
5.	rauxt	(YOU PlFm) SMOKE	5a.	rauxtet	(YOU PlFm) SMOKED
6.	rauxen	(THEY/YOU Po) SMOKE	6a.	rauxten	(THEY/YOU Po) SMOKED
7.	arbaite	(I) WORK	7a.	arbaitete	(I) WORKED
8.	arbaitest	(YOU SgFm) WORK	8a.	arbaitetest	(YOU SgFm) WORKED
9.	arbaitet	(HE/SHE/IT) WORKS	9a.	arbaitete	(HE/SHE/IT) WORKED
10.	arbaiten	(WE) WORK	10a.	arbaiteten	(WE) WORKED
11.	arbaitet	(YOU PlFm) WORK	11a.	arbaitetet	(YOU PlFm) WORKED
12.	arbaiten	(THEY/YOU Po) WORK	12a.	arbaiteten	(THEY/YOU Po) WORKED
13.	laufe	(I) RUN	13a.	li·f	(I) RAN
14.	loifst	(YOU SgFm) RUN	14a.	li·fst	(YOU SgFm) RAN
15.	loift	(HE/SHE/IT) RUNS	15a.	li·f	(HE/SHE/IT) RAN
16.	laufen	(WE) RUN	16a.	li·fen	(WE) RAN
17.	lauft	(YOU PlFm) RUN	17a.	li·ft	(YOU PlFm) RAN
18.	laufen	(THEY/YOU Po) RUN	18a.	li·fen	(THEY/YOU Po) RAN
19.	verfe	(I) THROW	19a.	varf	(I) THREW
20.	virfst	(YOU SgFm) THROW	20a.	varfst	(YOU SgFm) THREW
21.	virft	(HE/SHE/IT) THROWS	21a.	varf	(HE/SHE/IT) THREW
22.	verfen	(WE) THROW	22a.	varfen	(WE) THREW
23.	verft	(YOU PlFm) THROW	23a.	varft	(YOU PlFm) THREW
24.	verfen	(THEY/YOU Po) THROW	24a.	varfen	(THEY/YOU Po) THREW

Note: Parenthesized pronouns are included in these glosses to indicate the persons with which the verb forms are used, though German, like English, normally uses the pronouns even in non-emphatic situations. Special abbreviations used are: Fm = Familiar, Pl = Plural, Po = Polite, Sg = Singular.

Table 2.18 Editing of the morphological data of Table 2.17

			Number			
			SINGULAR		*PLURAL*	
(a)		Person *FIRST*	rauxe	verfe	rauxen	verfen
Tense	*PRESENT*	*SECOND*	rauxst	virfst	rauxt	verft
		THIRD	rauxt	virft	rauxen	verfen
		FIRST	rauxte	varf	rauxten	varfen
	PAST	*SECOND*	rauxtest	varst	rauxtet	varft
		THIRD	rauxtet	varf	rauxten	varfen
(b)			raux *PRESENT* *FIRST* *SINGULAR*	verf *PRESENT* *FIRST* *SINGULAR*	raux *PRESENT* *FIRST* *SINGULAR*	verf *PRESENT* *FIRST* *SINGULAR*
			raux *PRESENT* *SECOND* *SINGULAR*	verf *PRESENT* *SECOND* *SINGULAR*	raux *PRESENT* *SECOND* *SINGULAR*	verf *PRESENT* *SECOND* *SINGULAR*
			raux *PRESENT* *THIRD* *SINGULAR*	verf *PRESENT* *THIRD* *SINGULAR*	raux *PRESENT* *THIRD* *SINGULAR*	verf *PRESENT* *THIRD* *SINGULAR*
			raux *PAST* *FIRST* *SINGULAR*	verf *PAST* *FIRST* *SINGULAR*	raux *PAST* *FIRST* *SINGULAR*	verf *PAST* *FIRST* *SINGULAR*
			raux *PAST* *SECOND* *SINGULAR*	verf *PAST* *SECOND* *SINGULAR*	raux *PAST* *SECOND* *SINGULAR*	verf *PAST* *SECOND* *SINGULAR*
			raux *PAST* *THIRD* *SINGULAR*	verf *PAST* *THIRD* *SINGULAR*	raux *PAST* *THIRD* *SINGULAR*	verf *PAST* *THIRD* *SINGULAR*
(c)	*PRESENT* = Ø			*PAST* = te, ete, (a), (i˙)		
	FIRST + *SINGULAR* = e, Ø			*FIRST* + *PLURAL* = en, n		
	SECOND + *SINGULAR* = est, st			*SECOND* + *PLURAL* = et, t		
	THIRD + *SINGULAR* = et, t, Ø			*THIRD* + *PLURAL* = en, n		

As a final example, let us consider a fuller syntactic data set from the Mexican language Otomí as presented in Table 2.19. This will serve as a fuller demonstration of the processes of editing and solving involved with data of this general kind. In treating this material, it is easy to discover that the initial word in each example is a verb, inflectable for tense. The editing of these verbs is summarized in Table 2.20. The rest of the data involves nouns and adjectives. The adjectives are uninflected as far as we can see. The nouns, however, are inflected and therefore require editing, as summarized in Table 2.21. It should be noted that this inflection seems to involve several semantic dimensions which might, in the last analysis, require separate treatment. Only further data not given here could clarify their status. The only dimension familiar from our previous discussion is number, in that *PLURAL* is involved. Rather than a simple singular in contrast, however, we find three different ones, labeled

DEFINITE (glossed THE), *PROXIMAL* (THIS), and *THIRD-POSSESSIVE* (HIS). In this tentative treatment, all four are put along a single dimension termed DETERMINATION. This is done because there is no clear evidence that we can get more than one categorial term on the same noun, since each noun appears to carry one and only one of the four, expressed as a prefix. We could, and of course should, amend this treatment if further data makes this necessary by providing evidence for the morphological independence of the different categories.

Table 2.19 Data for the transitive clause in Otomí

1.	bihyoni karphani karʔñëhë	THE MAN HUNTED FOR THE HORSE.
2.	bihohki karhnuni karʔbæhñã	THE WOMAN FIXED THE MEAL.
3.	biʔïni karphani karʔñëhë	THE MAN HURT THE HORSE.
4.	biza karʔnʌehʌe karphani	THE HORSE BIT THE MAN.
5.	bime karbayo karʔbæhñã ranoho	THE BIG WOMAN WOVE THE SHAWL.
6.	bimeni karbayo ranoho karʔbæh	THE WOMAN WASHED THE BIG SHAWL.
7.	biʔïni karphani ranthæni karbãhci	THE CHILD HURT THE RED HORSE.
8.	bihohki karhñuni karʔbæhñã čičʔï	THE LITTLE WOMAN FIXED THE MEAL.
9.	bihyoni kárphani karʔñëhë	THE MAN HUNTED FOR HIS HORSE.
10.	dahyoni kïphani nurʔnëhë	THIS MAN WILL HUNT FOR THE HORSES.
11.	damɔʔti nurbãhci karʔyo ranthæni	THE RED DOG WILL KILL THIS CHILD.
12.	daʔïni kárʔyo nurʔñëhë	THIS MAN WILL HURT HIS DOG.
13.	daza kïbãhci nurʔyo ranoho	THIS BIG DOG WILL BITE THE CHILDREN.
14.	bimɔʔti kïʔyo čičʔï nurphani ranoho	THE BIG HORSE KILLED THE LITTLE DOGS.
15.	biza kïʔnëhë nurʔyo čičʔï	THIS LITTLE DOG BIT THE MEN.
16.	dameni kïbayo nurʔbæhñã	THIS WOMAN WILL WASH THE SHAWLS.
17.	dahohki kárhñuni kárʔbæhñã	HIS WIFE WILL FIX HIS MEAL.
18.	dame nurbayo nurʔbæhñã	THIS WOMAN WILL WEAVE THIS SHAWL.

Table 2.20 Editing of verbs from the Otomí data

			Verbs		
Tense	(a)	*PAST*	bihohki	bimeni	biza
		FUTURE	dahohki	dameni	daza
	(b)		hohki	meni	za
			PAST	*PAST*	*PAST*
			hohki	meni	za
			FUTURE	*FUTURE*	*FUTURE*
	(c)	*PAST* = bi			
		FUTURE = da			

Table 2.21 Editing of nouns from the Otomí data

			Nouns	
	(a)	*DEFINITE*	karphani	kar?yo
Determination		*PROXIMAL*	nurhani	nur?yo
		PLURAL	kïphani	kï?yo
		THIRD-POSSESSIVE	kárphani	kár?yo
	(b)		phani	?yo
			DEFINITE	*DEFINITE*
			phani	?yo
			PROXIMAL	*PROXIMAL*
			phani	?yo
			PLURAL	*PLURAL*
			phani	?yo
			THIRD-POSSESSIVE	*THIRD-POSSESSIVE*
	(c)		*DEFINITE* = kar	
			PROXIMAL = nur	
			PLURAL = kï	
			THIRD-POSSESSIVE = kár	

The completed data set edited along the lines given here is presented in Table 2.22, while the solution to the edited data is given in Figure 2.4.

Table 2.22 Edited version of the data set in Table 2.19

1.	hyoni	phani	?ñëhë		
	PAST	*DEFINITE*	*DEFINITE*		
2.	hohki	hñuni	?bæhñã		
	PAST	*DEFINITE*	*DEFINITE*		
3.	?ini	pahni	?ñëhë		
	PAST	*DEFINITE*	*DEFINITE*		
4.	za	?ñëhë	phani		
	PAST	*DEFINITE*	*DEFINITE*		
5.	me	bayo	?bæhñã	ranoho	
	PAST	*DEFINITE*	*DEFINITE*		
6.	meni	bayo	ranoho	?bæhñã	
	PAST	*DEFINITE*		*DEFINITE*	
7.	?ini	phani	ranthæni	bãhci	
	PAST	*DEFINITE*		*DEFINITE*	
8.	hohki	hñuni	?bæhñã	čič?ï	
	PAST	*DEFINITE*	*DEFINITE*		
9.	hyoni	phani	?ñëhë		
	PAST	*THIRD-POSSESSIVE*	*DEFINITE*		
10.	hyoni	phani	?ñëhë		
	FUTURE	*PLURAL*	*PROXIMAL*		
11.	mɔ?ti	bãhci	?yo	ranthæni	
	FUTURE	*PLURAL*	*DEFINITE*		
12.	?ini	?yo	?ñëhë		
	FUTURE	*THIRD-POSSESSIVE*	*PROXIMAL*		
13.	za	bãhci	?yo	ranoho	
	FUTURE	*PLURAL*	*PROXIMAL*		
14.	mɔ?ti	?yo	čič?ï	phani	ranoho
	PAST	*PLURAL*		*PROXIMAL*	

15.	za	ʔn̈ëhë	ʔyo	čičʔï
	PAST	*PLURAL*	*PROXIMAL*	
16.	meni	bayo	ʔbæhñã	
	FUTURE	*PLURAL*	*PROXIMAL*	
17.	hohki	hñuni	ʔbæhñã	
	FUTURE	*THIRD-POSSESSIVE*	*THIRD-POSSESSIVE*	
18.	me	bayo	ʔbæhñã	
	FUTURE	*PROXIMAL*	*PROXIMAL*	

Summary of inflectional categories

Table 2.23 summarizes the most widespread inflectional categories in languages of the world, and indicates the kinds of words in which they most frequently occur. Some of these have been exemplified earlier in this chapter. For further discussion of inflection and the categories it involves, see pages 71–88 in Lockwood's book *Morphological Analysis and Description: A Realizational Approach* (1993).

Table 2.23 Some common inflectional categorial dimensions and terms

Dimension	Terms	Typical Application
NUMBER	*SINGULAR/(DUAL/TRIAL/PAUCAL/)PLURAL*	Noun Pronoun Adjective Verb
GENDER	*MASCULINE/(NEUTER/) FEMININE*	Noun Pronoun Adjective Verb
	ANIMATE/INANIMATE	
	RATIONAL/IRRATIONAL (etc.)	
CASE	*NOMINATIVE/ACCUSATIVE/GENITIVE/DATIVE*	Noun Pronoun Adjective
	ABSOLUTIVE/ERGATIVE/INSTRUMENTAL/	
	COMITATIVE/ABESSIVE/PERLATIVE ...	
	LOCATIVE: INESSIVE/ADESSIVE/SUPERESSIVE	
	ILLATIVE/ALLATIVE/SUBLATIVE	
	ELATIVE/ABLATIVE/DELATIVE (etc.)	
DEFINITENESS	*DEFINITE/INDEFINITE*	Noun Adjective Verb
DEIXIS	*PROXIMAL/(INTERMEDIATE/)DISTAL*	Noun Adjective
POSSESSION	*UNPOSSESSED/POSSESSED*	Noun Adjective
	± PERSON AND NUMBER OF POSSESSOR	
PERSON	*FIRST/SECOND/THIRD*	Verb
OBVIATION	*OBVIATIVE/NON-OBVIATIVE*	(w *THIRD*)
INCLUSION	*INCLUSIVE/EXCLUSIVE*	(W *FIRST NON-SG*)
TENSE	*PAST/PRESENT/FUTURE*	Verb
DISTANCE	*REMOTE ... NEAR*	*(w PAST* and/or *FUTURE)*
ASPECT	*PERFECTIVE/(AORIST/)DURATIVE*	Verb
	INCEPTIVE/CESSATIVE	
	ITERATIVE/SEMELFACTIVE (etc.)	
MOOD	*INDICATIVE/SUBJUNCTIVE/CONDITIONAL/*	Verb
	OPTATIVE/DESIDERATIVE/INTENTIVE/	
	DUBITATIVE (etc.)	
MODE	*DECLARATIVE/INTERROGATIVE/IMPERATIVE*	Verb
VOICE	*ACTIVE/(MIDDLE/)PASSIVE*	Verb
	CAUSATIVE/BENEFACTIVE (etc.)	
POLARITY	*AFFIMATIVE/NEGATIVE*	Verb

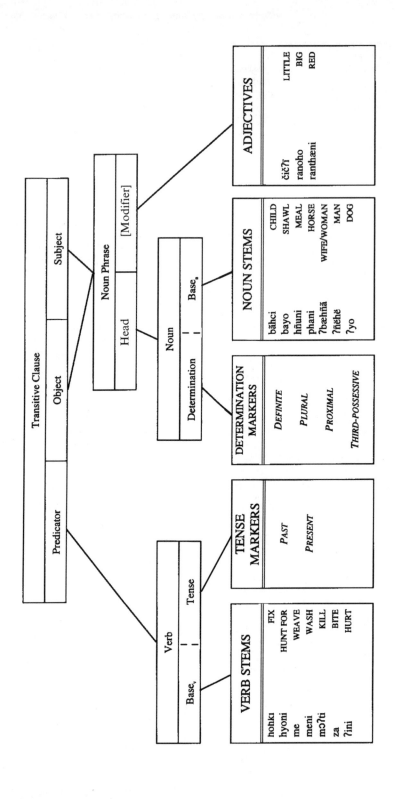

Figure 2.4 Solution to the edited data of Table 2.22

Summary of new notations

Word-construction box

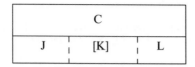

1. Constructions, their constituents, and optionality are indicated in the same way as before.
2. Whereas constituents separated by solid bars (as in Chapter 1) are in linear order, constituents separated by broken vertical lines, as shown here, are viewed as simply ASSOCIATED – having no linear order as far as the syntax is concerned.
3. This kind of construction box is used only for the constituents of word-constructions.
4. All constituents of a construction must show the same sort of arrangement – either with linear order or simply associated. Rather than mixing these types in a single box, we use more than one box. So example (1) below would be ill-formed, and the configuration in example (2) would be used instead:

Example (1)   Ill-formed Construction Box

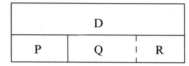

Example (2)   Well-formed alternative to example (1)

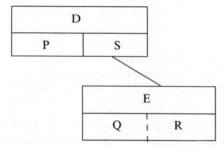

5. Word-construction boxes connect to vocabulary boxes just as before, but in vocabulary boxes for inflectional categories, it is usually preferable to substitute a categorial term label for the actual expressions, which can be varied, such as *SINGULAR*, *PLURAL*, *PAST*, *PRESENT*, *FUTURE*, *MASCULINE*, *FEMININE*, *NEUTER*, *NOMINATIVE*, *ACCUSATIVE*, *GENITIVE*, and so on. Each of these can potentially be manifested in various ways in the language, but details of this are not part of the syntax. They can be left to a separate chapter on the morphology of the language being described.

Exercises

A.   Editing from morphological paradigms

The following data sets from Yup'ik Eskimo and Italian should be subjected to editing in the same fashion as that in Tables 2.5/7/9/11/13/15/17/19 and written up on the model of Tables 2.6/8/10/12/14/16/18/20/21.

1.   Nouns in Central Alaskan Yup'ik Eskimo

Note that the abbreviation (ABS) stands for *ABSOLUTIVE*, a case used for intransitive subjects and intransitive objects, while (REL) stands for *RELATIVE*, a contrasting case used for transitive subjects and possessors.

qayaq	KAYAK (*ABS*)	qimuxta	DOG (*ABS*)
qayam	KAYAK (*REL*)	qimuxtɨm	DOG (*REL*)
qayami	IN A KAYAK	qimuxtɨmi	IN A DOG
qayamun	TO A KAYAK	qimuxtɨmun	TO A DOG
qayamɨk	FROM A KAYAK	qimuxtɨmɨk	FROM A DOG
qayakun	BY KAYAK	qimuxtɨkun	BY A DOG
qayatun	LIKE A KAYAK	qimuxtɨtun	LIKE A DOG
qayaqa	MY KAYAK (*ABS*)	qimuxtɨka	MY DOG (*ABS*)
qayama	MY KAYAK (*REL*)	qimuxtɨma	MY DOG (*REL*)
qayamni	IN MY KAYAK	qimuxtɨmni	IN MY DOG
qayamnun	TO MY KAYAK	qimuxtɨmnun	TO MY DOG
qayamnɨk	FROM MY KAYAK	qimuxtɨmnɨk	FROM MY DOG
qayamkun	BY MY KAYAK	qimuxtɨmkun	BY MY DOG
qayamtun	LIKE MY KAYAK	qimuxtɨmtun	LIKE MY DOG
qayan	YOUR KAYAK (*ABS*)	qimuxtɨn	YOUR DOG (*ABS*)
qayavɨt	YOUR KAYAK (*REL*)	qimuxtɨvɨt	YOUR DOG (*REL*)
qayavni	IN YOUR KAYAK	qimuxtɨvni	IN YOUR DOG
qayavnun	TO YOUR KAYAK	qimuxtɨvnun	TO YOUR DOG
qayavnɨk	FROM YOUR KAYAK	qimuxtɨvnɨk	FROM YOUR DOG
qayafkun	BY YOUR KAYAK	qimuxtɨfkun	BY YOUR DOG
qayaftun	LIKE YOUR KAYAK	qimuxtɨftun	LIKE YOUR DOG
tuntu	CARIBOU (*ABS*)	atkuk	PARKA (*ABS*)
tuntum	CARIBOU (*REL*)	atkuum	PARKA (*REL*)
tuntumi	IN A CARIBOU	atkuɣmi	IN A PARKA
tuntumun	TO A CARIBOU	atkuɣmun	TO A PARKA
tuntumɨk	FROM A CARIBOU	atkuɣmɨk	FROM A PARKA
tuntukun	BY A CARIBOU	atkuxkun	BY A PARKA
tuntutun	LIKE A CARIBOU	atkuxtun	LIKE A PARKA
tuntuka	MY CARIBOU (*ABS*)	atkuka	MY PARKA (*ABS*)
tuntuma	MY CARIBOU (*REL*)	atkuma	MY PARKA (*REL*)
tuntumni	IN MY CARIBOU	atkumni	IN MY PARKA
tuntumnun	TO MY CARIBOU	atkumnun	TO MY PARKA
tuntumnɨk	FROM MY CARIBOU	atkumnɨk	FROM MY PARKA
tuntumkun	BY MY CARIBOU	atkumkun	BY MY PARKA
tuntumtun	LIKE MY CARIBOU	atkumtun	LIKE MY PARKA

tuntun	YOUR CARIBOU (*ABS*)	atkuun	YOUR PARKA (*ABS*)
tuntuvɨt	YOUR CARIBOU (*REL*)	atkuvɨt	YOUR PARKA (*REL*)
tuntuvni	IN YOUR CARIBOU	atkuvni	IN YOUR PARKA
tuntuvnun	TO YOUR CARIBOU	atkuvnun	TO YOUR PARKA
tuntuvnɨk	FROM YOUR CARIBOU	atkuvnɨk	FROM YOUR PARKA
tuntuʃkun	BY YOUR CARIBOU	atkuʃkun	BY YOUR PARKA
tuntuftun	LIKE YOUR CARIBOU	atkuftun	LIKE YOUR PARKA

2. Verbs in Italian

Phonemic accent has been omitted; apart from this, phonemic transcription is used.

parlo	I SPEAK	parto	I LEAVE
parli	YOU (*SG*) SPEAK	parti	YOU (*SG*) LEAVE
parla	HE SPEAKS	parte	HE LEAVES
parliamo	WE SPEAK	partiamo	WE LEAVE
parlate	YOU (*PL*) SPEAK	partite	YOU (*PL*) LEAVE
parlano	THEY SPEAK	partono	THEY LEAVE
parlavo	I SPOKE	partivo	I LEFT
parlavi	YOU (*SG*) SPOKE	partivi	YOU (*SG*) LEFT
parlava	HE SPOKE	partiva	HE LEFT
parlavamo	WE SPOKE	partivamo	WE LEFT
parlavate	YOU (*PL*) SPOKE	partivate	YOU (*PL*) LEFT
parlavano	THEY SPOKE	partivano	THEY LEFT
parlero	I WILL SPEAK	partiro	I WILL LEAVE
parlerai	YOU (*SG*) WILL SPEAK	partirai	YOU (*SG*) WILL LEAVE
parlera	HE WILL SPEAK	partira	HE WILL LEAVE
parleremo	WE WILL SPEAK	partiremo	WE WILL LEAVE
parlerete	YOU (*PL*) WILL SPEAK	partirete	YOU (*PL*) WILL LEAVE
parleranno	THEY WILL SPEAK	partiranno	THEY WILL LEAVE
finisko	I FINISH	kredo	I BELIEVE
finiʃi	YOU (*SG*) FINISH	kredi	YOU (*SG*) BELIEVE
finiʃe	HE FINISHES	krede	HE BELIEVES
finiamo	WE FINISH	krediamo	WE BELIEVE
finite	YOU (*PL*) FINISH	kredete	YOU (*PL*) BELIEVE
finiskono	THEY FINISH	kredono	THEY BELIEVE
finivo	I FINISHED	kredevo	I BELIEVED
finivi	YOU (*SG*) FINISHED	kredevi	YOU (*SG*) BELIEVED
finiva	HE FINISHED	kredeva	HE BELIEVED
finivamo	WE FINISHED	kredevamo	WE BELIEVED
finivate	YOU (*PL*) FINISHED	kredevate	YOU (*PL*) BELIEVED
finivano	THEY FINISHED	kredevano	THEY BELIEVED
finiro	I WILL FINISH	kredero	I WILL BELIEVE
finirai	YOU (*SG*) WILL FINISH	krederai	YOU (*SG*) WILL BELIEVE
finira	HE WILL FINISH	kredera	HE WILL BELIEVE
finiremo	WE WILL FINISH	krederemo	WE WILL BELIEVE
finirete	YOU (*PL*) WILL FINISH	krederete	YOU (*PL*) WILL BELIEVE
finiranno	THEY WILL FINISH	krederanno	THEY WILL BELIEVE

B.   Editing from syntactic data

The following data sets from Latvian and Lithuanian are more realistic than those in part A, in that they require abstraction of the morphological paradigms from syntactic contexts. They require solution on the model of the treatment presented for the Otomí data given in Table 2.19. As a first step in solving each one, paradigms should be extracted for each inflected word. Next an analysis (analogous to what is presented in Tables 2.20–21) should be presented. Then the data should be given in an edited form (analogous to Table 2.22). In this case, only the particular forms suggested in the directions will require an explicit editing in the write-up, but you should be able to do it for the entire set.

1.   Noun phrases in Latvian

Solution should include the edited versions of items 1, 2a, 7, 8a, 13a, 14, 19a, and 20.

1.	laps tirgus	A GOOD MARKET (SUBJ)	1a.	labais tirgus	THE GOOD MARKET (SUBJ)
2.	labu tirgu	A GOOD MARKET (OBJ)	2a.	labo tirgu	THE GOOD MARKET (OBJ)
3.	labi tirgi	GOOD MARKETS (SUBJ)	3a.	labie tirgi	THE GOOD MARKETS (SUBJ)
4.	labus tirgus	GOOD MARKETS (OBJ)	4a.	labos tirgus	THE GOOD MARKETS (OBJ)
5.	liels bra:lis	A BIG BROTHER (SUBJ)	5a.	lielais bra:lis	THE BIG BROTHER (SUBJ)
6.	lielu bra:li	A BIG BROTHER (OBJ)	6a.	lielo bra:li	THE BIG BROTHER (OBJ)
7.	lieli bra:l^{y}i	BIG BROTHERS (SUBJ)	7a.	lielie bra:l^{y}i	THE BIG BROTHERS (SUBJ)
8.	lielus bra:l^{y}us	BIG BROTHERS (OBJ)	8a.	lielos bra:l^{y}us	THE BIG BROTHERS (OBJ)
9.	laps cel^{y}š	A GOOD ROAD (SUBJ)	9a.	labais cel^{y}š	THE GOOD ROAD (SUBJ)
10.	labu cel^{y}u	A GOOD ROAD (OBJ)	10a.	labo cel^{y}u	THE GOOD ROAD (OBJ)
11.	labi cel^{y}i	GOOD ROADS (SUBJ)	11a.	labie cel^{y}i	THE GOOD ROADS (SUBJ)
12.	labus cel^{y}us	GOOD ROADS (OBJ)	12a.	labos cel^{y}us	THE GOOD ROADS (OBJ)
13.	jauks cel^{y}š	A NICE ROAD (SUBJ)	13a.	jaukais cel^{y}š	THE NICE ROAD (SUBJ)
14.	jauku cel^{y}u	A NICE ROAD (OBJ)	14a.	jauko cel^{y}u	THE NICE ROAD (OBJ)
15.	jauki cel^{y}i	NICE ROADS (SUBJ)	15a.	jaukie cel^{y}i	THE NICE ROADS (SUBJ)
16.	jaukus cel^{y}us	NICE ROADS (OBJ)	16a.	jaukos cel^{y}us	THE NICE ROADS (OBJ)
17.	liels lauks	A BIG FIELD (SUBJ)	17a.	lielais lauks	THE BIG FIELD (SUBJ)
18.	lielu lauku	A BIG FIELD (OBJ)	18a.	lielo lauku	THE BIG FIELD (OBJ)
19.	lieli lauki	BIG FIELDS (SUBJ)	19a.	lielie lauki	THE BIG FIELDS (SUBJ)
20.	lielus laukus	BIG FIELDS (OBJ)	20a.	lielos laukus	THE BIG FIELDS (OBJ)

2.   Intransitive clauses in Lithuanian

This solution should include edited versions of data items 1, 3, 4, and 5. Also prepare a full account of the data as edited.

1.	svečias nedirba	THE GUEST IS NOT WORKING.
2.	duktė dirba	THE DAUGHTER IS WORKING.
3.	vyras dirbo	THE MAN WORKED.
4.	vyrai moko	THE MEN ARE TEACHING.
5.	dukterys nedirbo	THE DAUGHTERS DID NOT WORK.
6.	svečiai mokė	THE GUESTS TAUGHT.
7.	arklys bėgo	THE HORSE RAN.
8.	arkliai nebėga	THE HORSES ARE NOT RUNNING.
9.	brolis sėdi	THE BROTHER IS SITTING.
10.	broliai nesėdėjo	THE BROTHERS DID NOT SIT.
11.	sūnus nešoka	THE SON IS NOT JUMPING.
12.	sūnus šoko	THE SONS JUMPED.
13.	vyrai sėdėjo	THE MEN SAT.
14.	duktė nemokė	THE DAUGHTER DID NOT TEACH.
15.	svečias nebėgo	THE GUEST DID NOT RUN.
16.	arkliai nešoko	THE HORSES DID NOT JUMP.
17.	sūnūs nemoko	THE SONS DO NOT TEACH.
18.	vyras nesėdi	THE MAN IS NOT SITTING.

Terminology

ASPECT	MOOD
CASE	NUMBER
DEFINITENESS	PERSON
DEGREE	POLARITY
DEIXIS	POSSESSION
DISTANCE	TENSE
GENDER	VOICE
INCLUSION	WORD-CONSTRUCTION
	WORD-CONSTRUCTION BOX
MODE	

3

Types of phrase constructions

The noun phrase: a typical endocentric phrase

If we consider such English sentences as numbers 1 and 2 from Table 3.1, we see the typical SPO structures of English transitive clauses. Ordinarily, we say that each of the clause functions is manifested by a single word: Subject and Object by a noun, and Predicator by a verb. In examples 3–6, however, we see the "noun" functions manifested by phrases – combinations of words such as we have already seen to some extent in earlier chapters.

Table 3.1 Some English transitive clauses

1.	*Dogs chase cats.*
2.	*Exercise promotes health.*
3.	*All dogs chase cats.*
4.	*Dogs chase all those cats.*
5.	*My three dogs chase all your young cats.*
6.	*Vigorous exercise promotes your good health.*

The first point to be made about this data is that it is convenient, though it goes against earlier tradition, to consider single nouns in Subject or Object function like *dogs*, *cats*, *exercise*, and *health* in examples 1–4 to be special cases of the noun phrase. If we do this, we do not have to say that these functions are manifested either by a noun or by a noun phrase. Instead, we can say that a noun phrase is the manifestation in every instance, with the noun alone as just a special case of this phrase. In general, we can see any single noun as subject to expansion by the use of "modifying" words which we will term **ADJUNCTS**. A single noun in such a function as Subject or Object is simply a phrase in which the option to take such adjuncts as are possible has not been exercised. Table 3.2 gives more examples of the use of adjuncts with the noun *dogs*, showing that there can be several adjuncts in the same phrase, and that some of them precede the word *dogs*, while others follow it.

In all these examples, we can divide the noun phrases first of all into the essential part, traditionally called the **HEAD** of the phrase, and the marginal parts serving in various adjunct functions. When multiple adjuncts occur in a language, there are generally syntactic patterns governing their occurrence, and these patterns can be formalized in a syntactic construction, just as we have seen in the previous chapters.

Table 3.2 Some English noun phrases

1.	*all three dogs*
2.	*his five big dogs*
3.	*all my dogs*
4.	*all those ten dogs over there*
5.	*these little dogs from across the street*
6.	*the two dogs in the story*
7.	*all John's large dogs that I can see*

Table 3.3 A charting based on the English noun phrase data

POSITION 1 Optional	POSITION 2 Optional	POSITION 3 Optional	POSITION 4 Optional	POSITION 5 Obligatory	POSITION 6 Optional
A_{del} (delimiting adjunct)	A_{det} (determining adjunct)	A_{qnt} (quantifying adjunct)	A_{mod} (modifying adjunct)	$Head_n$ (nominal head)	A_q (qualifying adjunct)
Delimiter	Determiner	Quantifier	Modifier		Qualifier
all	*his* *my* *those* *the* *John's*	*three* *five* *ten*	*big* *little* *large*	*dogs* *cats*	*over there* *from across* *the street* *in the story* *that I can see*

Altogether, the phrasal data in Tables 3.1 and 3.2 provides evidence for five syntactically different kinds of adjuncts, as charted along with the head in Table 3.3. In addition to positional labels, this charting provides two alternative kinds of labels for the various adjuncts. Figure 3.1 is a boxed diagram for this structure according to the same model that was used in previous chapters.

In this figure, as in the earlier chapters, each position is associated with a functional label. Here one-word labels have been used, as in earlier chapters, but it would also be possible to use the compound labels A_{del} and so on, which have the advantage of pointing out explicitly that they are all kinds of A (adjunct). The labels Determiner and Modifier repeat the

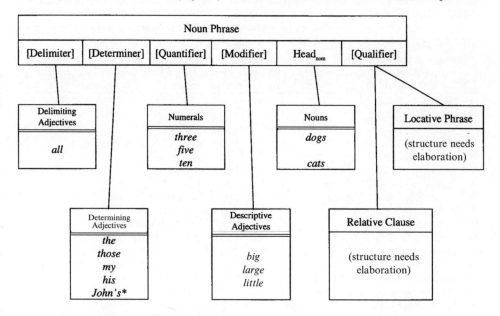

Note: *This "word" is really an example of a postpositional phrase in English. It is listed under the determining adjectives purely for the convenience of this preliminary description.

Figure 3.1 Boxed representation based on the data of Table 3.2

conventions already used in Chapter 1. The label Head$_N$ stands for "nominal head", and this is used instead of simply "Head" to remind us that there can be other sorts of heads in other sorts of phrases. The additional functions seen in this more elaborate data are **DELIMITER** (manifested by *all*), QUANTIFIER (manifested here by a numeral, though less specific quantifying words like *several*, *few*, or *many* can also occur in the same position), and QUALIFIER (used for a post-head function which can be manifested by various kinds of phrases and subordinate clauses, as suggested by the examples).

These English examples provide a useful approach to the structure of noun phrases in general, but it is worthwhile to supplement this beginning by proceeding next to another language, one with a somewhat different structure for its noun phrases. For this purpose, we can consider the Italian data in Table 3.4. This data can be charted as in Table 3.5, and these results can then be converted into the boxed representation of Figure 3.2.

Although we have not yet seen enough data to provide all the details about the full noun-phrase constructions of either language, we do have enough to make some significant comparisons between such phrases in English and Italian. The clearest and most striking differences between the workings of these two constructions concern (1) the positioning of ordinary descriptive adjectives, and (2) the treatment of possessives in relation to the Determiner function.

In Italian, ordinary descriptive adjectives are more likely to follow the head rather than to precede it, although some adjectives like *bella* PRETTY, *nuova* NEW, and *povera* POOR in this material may occur in either position with some subtle difference in their meaning signaled by their positioning. With *nuova* and *povera*, the respective meanings in the pre-head position are NEW in the sense of DIFFERENT and POOR in the sense of UNFORTUNATE. In post-head position, the same adjectives mean NEW in the sense of BRAND-NEW and POOR in the sense of PENNILESS or POVERTY-STRICKEN. With the third example, *bella* PRETTY, the difference is still more subtle, similar to what would be conveyed by a difference of stress-position in English. To treat these facts, we need to recognize two modifier positions, one directly before the head and the other immediately after it. There are also two classes of adjectives associated with these positions. The smaller one, consisting of a fairly short list of common adjectives, may occur in either position, while the other, rather open-ended, class can occur only in the post-head position. The meaning differences mentioned would be further associated with the different syntactic positions.

Table 3.4 Some Italian noun phrases

1.	*la macchina*	THE CAR
2.	*la nostra macchina*	OUR CAR
3.	*una nostra macchina*	A CAR OF OURS
4.	*una nuova macchina*	A NEW [RECENTLY ACQUIRED] CAR
5.	*una mia nuova macchina*	A NEW CAR OF MINE
6.	*la loro macchina bianca*	THEIR WHITE CAR
7.	*questa macchina di Giovanni*	THIS CAR OF GIOVANNI'S
8.	*questa tua macchina rossa*	THIS RED CAR OF YOURS
9.	*tutta la città*	THE WHOLE CITY
10.	*tutta quella mia città*	THAT WHOLE CITY OF MINE
11.	*quella bella città di Silvana*	THAT PRETTY CITY OF SILVANA'S
12.	*quella macchina nuova*	THAT NEW [NEWLY MADE] CAR
13.	*tutta questa bella città italiana*	THIS WHOLE PRETTY ITALIAN CITY
14.	*tutta la loro bella macchina americana*	THEIR WHOLE PRETTY AMERICAN CAR
15.	*una macchina nuova di Paolo*	A NEW CAR OF PAOLO'S
16.	*la macchina bella*	THE PRETTY CAR
17.	*una povera ragazza*	A POOR [UNFORTUNATE] GIRL
18.	*la ragazza povera*	THE POOR [PENNILESS] GIRL
19.	*quella bella ragazza povera*	THAT PRETTY, POOR [PENNILESS] GIRL
20.	*la macchina rossa di Paolo*	PAOLO'S RED CAR

Table 3.5 A charting based on the Italian noun phrase data

Position 1 Optional		Position 2 Optional	Position 3 Optional	Position 4 Optional	Position 5 Obligatory	Position 6 Optional	Position 7 Optional
A_{del}		A_{det}	A_{pos} (possessive adjunct)	A_{prm} (premodifying adjunct)	Head$_n$	A_{ptm} (post-modifying adjunct)	A_q
Delimiter		Determiner	Possessor	Premodifier		Postmodifier	Qualifier
tutta	ALL	la THE	mia MY	bella PRETTY	città CITY	americana AMERICAN	di Giovanni (OF) GIOVANNI'S
	THE	una A(N)	tua YOUR	nuova NEW	macchina CAR	bella PRETTY	di Paolo (OF) PAOLO'S
	WHOLE	questa THIS	nostra OUR	povera POOR	ragazza GIRL	bianca WHITE	di Silvana (OF) SILVANA'S
		quella THAT	loro THEIR			italiana ITALIAN	
						nuova NEW	
						povera POOR	
						rossa RED	

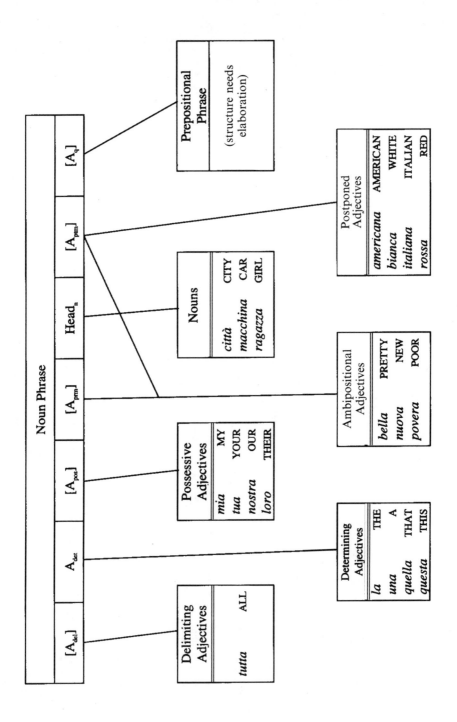

Figure 3.2 Boxed representation of the Italian data of Table 3.5

With regard to possessives, we find that in Italian there is a specific adjunct position devoted to the possessive adjectives, whereas in English the corresponding possessives are just a semantically definable subset of the determining adjectives relatable to the Determiner position. So in English the potential manifestations of the Determiner function include the articles *the* and *a*, the demonstratives (*this* and *that* and their respective plurals *these* and *those*), as well as the possessives and some further possibilities. In Italian, on the other hand, possessive adjectives – the ones in this data and a few others – occur only in an optional position following the Determiner.

Another difference is that the English possessives that can occur in the Determiner position are an open class, because they include not just the short list of pronoun-based possessive adjectives but also instances of the -'s construction with noun phrases. There is no precisely similar construction in Italian, but as shown by examples like numbers 7, 11, 15, and 19 in Table 3.4, the Italian equivalent in meaning is a prepositional phrase with *di* OF, which comes in the Qualifier position.

Since there are different functional syntactic positions for determining and possessive adjectives in Italian, we find that we can and regularly will get some kind of Italian determiner with a possessive. Consider the examples in Table 3.6, items 1–4, which show *mia* MY and *macchina* CAR preceded by any of the four determiners identifiable in the previous Italian data. The "literal" English translations in the second column are asterisked because they are not acceptable in English, because English allows just one of its determining adjectives, which include the possessive adjectives, to occur in a given noun phrase. The freer glosses in the last column show what English speakers have to do to express the same ideas. The simple possessive in the Determiner position is generally construed to be definite, so we do not need *the* in most cases. We can, however, say *the red car of mine*, but would normally do so only with some further post-head adjunct, as in *the red car of Giovanni's that I bought yesterday*. When English speakers want to express indefiniteness or demonstrative meaning along with possession, however, we put the demonstrative or article in the Determiner position, and use a different expression of the possession after the Head, as in *this red car of mine*.

Table 3.6 Determiners and possessive expressions in Italian

Italian phrase	Overly literal translation	Standard English equivalents
1. *la mia macchina*	*THE MY CAR	*MY CAR//THE CAR OF MINE*
2. *una mia macchina*	*A MY CAR	*A CAR OF MINE*
3. *questa mia macchina*	*THIS MY CAR	*THIS CAR OF MINE*
4. *quella mia macchina*	*THAT MY CAR	*THAT CAR OF MINE*
5. *la macchina di Giovanni*	*THE GIOVANNI'S CAR	*GIOVANNI'S CAR// THE CAR OF GIOVANNI'S*
6. *una macchina di Giovanni*	*A GIOVANNI'S CAR	*A CAR OF GIOVANNI'S*
7. *questa macchina di Giovanni*	*THIS GIOVANNI'S CAR	*THIS CAR OF GIOVANNI'S*
8. *quella macchina di Giovanni*	*THAT GIOVANNI'S CAR	*THAT CAR OF GIOVANNI'S*

Examples 5–8 in Table 3.6 then show the situation when the possessor is the referent of a noun rather than a pronoun. Here Italian can only use an expression with the preposition *di*, and this must come in Qualifier position, after the Head. It should be noted that the asterisked "literal" translations are not as totally ungrammatical as the ones in examples 1–4 were. They are ungrammatical only in the sense indicated here, where **this Giovanni's car* would mean THIS CAR BELONGING TO GIOVANNI rather than THE CAR BELONGING TO THIS GIOVANNI.

Another apparent difference between these two noun-phrase constructions concerns the treatment of the function of Determiner (Determining Adjunct) as either optional (as in English) or obligatory (as in Italian). This is because Italian, like many continental European languages, regularly uses the definite article for plurals and abstract/mass nouns used in a generic sense. So with a mass noun like *carne* MEAT one would say, for instance, *Mi piace la carne* (with the definite article *la*) to mean either the specific I LIKE THE MEAT or the generic I LIKE MEAT. (More literally this example means THIS MEAT PLEASES ME.) Similarly, the example *Mi piaciono le macchine* ("THE CARS PLEASE ME") can mean either I LIKE CARS or I LIKE THE CARS. Just like English, however, Italian normally omits the article with proper names applying to persons, like *Giovanni*, *Paolo*, and *Silvana* or to places such as *Roma* ROME, *Venezia* VENICE, *Italia* ITALY, or *Spagna* SPAIN. In either language, this phenomenon could be viewed as some kind of a zero variant of the definite rather than the indefinite article. This would be true because the referent of a proper noun is semantically specific (or unique), and so presumably grammatically definite.

In this comparison of noun phrases in English and Italian, we have seen that such phrases in different languages may have different numbers of functional constituents, and that the order of adjuncts in relation to the Head may vary from one language to another. In these two languages, the variation of order is actually quite limited, in that each of them has some adjuncts before the Head and some after it. In some languages, all adjuncts either precede or follow the Head. The following example shows a noun phrase in Japanese, which is a **HEAD-FINAL** language, with all adjuncts before the Head:

kono	watasi no	nihiki no	kuroi	neko
THIS	MY	TWO	BLACK	CAT

THESE TWO BLACK CATS OF MINE

In other languages like Thai, however, we may find the opposite situation, with all adjuncts after the Head, in a **HEAD-INITIAL** pattern:

mǽ·w	dām	kʰǒ·n pʰǒm	sǒ·ŋ tūa	ní·
CAT	BLACK	MY	TWO	THIS

THESE TWO BLACK CATS OF MINE

In comparison with these head-final and head-initial types, English and Italian noun phrases show a **HEAD-MEDIAL** pattern. The differences between these latter two, as already discussed, show that there can be further differences in noun-phrase structure involving details. The three types based on the general position of the head in the phrase are the most basic ones.

These various kinds of noun phrases have in common, of course, the fact that each of them has an obligatory central constituent, the Head, which may combine with various other constituents, most commonly optional, which are the adjuncts, making the meaning of the Head more specific in one or more ways. Such phrases can be expected in any language and they are in general termed **ENDOCENTRIC PHRASES**. This term means that they contain a "center" (the Head) within them.

Other endocentric phrases

In addition to noun phrases, languages typically have other phrases with an endocentric structure. Among the most commonly found phrases of this sort are those illustrated by the data in Table 3.7. In this table, examples A.1–5 are typical English adjective phrases, containing a Head (double-underlined) and a preceding adjunct (single underlined). The examples in B.1–5 are adverbial phrases, with Heads and adjuncts similarly underlined. Example B.5 shows a postposed adjunct as well as a preposed one.

The occurrence of such adjective phrases as those in this table demonstrates that the modifier function in the English noun phrase is manifested by an adjective phrase rather than simply by an adjective, and a similar argument applies to adverb phrases. Other elements of the noun phrase that are manifested by phrases rather than simply by words include the

Table 3.7 Illustrations of adjective and adverb phrases in English

A.1 *a very beautiful lamp*
A.2 *this extremely serious proposal*
A.3 *the quite tasteless remark*
A.4 *a completely unexpected visit*
A.5 *that less regular occurrence*
B.1 *The storm arrived quite suddenly.*
B.2 *We stopped right there.*
B.3 *They visit us less often nowadays.*
B.4 *He can run very fast.*
B.5 *She finished more quickly than I expected.*

Table 3.8 Further examples of phrases as noun-phrase adjuncts

A.1 *absolutely all the new people*
A.2 *almost all the books*
A.3 *nearly all my relatives*
B.1 *exactly two American students*
B.2 *about seventy-five faculty members*
B.3 *very few Canadian universities*
B.4 *surprisingly many young Mexican bridegrooms*

Delimiter and the Quantifier, as shown by the examples in Table 3.8. Examples A.1–3 illustrate delimiting-adjective phrases headed by *all*, and examples B.1–3 show quantifying phrases with an adjunct + Head structure. Actually the latter examples are of two types, since those headed by numerals (B.1–2) take different kinds of adjuncts than those headed by less definite quantifiers like *few* and *many* (B.3–4).

Also, in a language like English, it is necessary to treat the Pronoun Phrase as a separate construction from the Noun Phrase. Although English personal pronouns can take adjuncts to a limited extent, they cannot properly be considered as just varieties of nouns, as has been done in some traditions. We cannot, for instance, substitute a plural personal pronoun like *we, us, you, they,* or *them* for the plural noun *dogs* in any of the examples in Table 3.2 and get an acceptable phrase. Adjuncts in pronoun phrases are pretty much limited to Modifiers and Qualifiers of the sort that occur in noun phrases, as in examples like *Poor me! I always miss the chances of a lifetime!* or *They, coming from across the street.* The lumping of pronouns as types of nouns and pronoun phrases as just types of noun phrases comes from the fact that the two kinds of phrases tend to have virtually identical FUNCTIONS in larger structures. Also, in some other languages pronouns seem to be substitutable for nouns much more regularly than in English and most European languages. So one should not automatically assume that nouns and pronouns and their associated phrases will be distinct – it is necessary to examine the facts of the language at hand before deciding the question.

The problem of the verb phrase

Our survey of endocentric phrase types has not yet discussed the use of adjuncts in phrases headed by verbs. This is not because such phrases do not exist, but because the term "verb phrase" in traditional usage presents so many problems as to require more extended discussion. This discussion can begin with the various bracketed examples in Table 3.9, whose

Table 3.9 Candidates for the status of "verb phrase"

A.1   (*They*) [gave Aunt Elvira the prize].
A.2   (*They*) [established a new college].
A.3   (*They*) [are his best friends].
B.1   (*They*) [live across the street].
B.2   (*They*) [traveled over the desert].
B.3   (*They*) [came from eastern Europe].
C.1   (*They*) [arrived yesterday].
C.2   (*They*) [visited on Thursday].
C.3   (*They*) [left last week].
D.1   (*They*) [work efficiently].
D.2   (*They*) [speak carefully].
D.3   (*They*) [play happily].
E.1   (*They*) [could work].
E.2   (*They*) [might come].
E.3   (*They*) [have arrived].
E.4   (*They*) [are fighting].
F.1   (*They*) [never interrupt].
F.2   [Do] (*they*) [never interrupt]?
F.3   [Don't] (*they*) [ever interrupt]?
F.4   (*They*) [were never working].
F.5   [Were] (*they*) [never working]?
F.6   [Weren't] (*they*) [ever working]?
F.7   (*They*) [cannot study].
F.8   [Can] (*they*) [not study]?
F.9   [Can't] (*they*) [study]?
F.10 (*They*) [had not surrendered].
F.11 [Had] (*they*) [not surrendered]?
F.12 [Hadn't] (*they*) [surrendered]?

---

sections A–F reflect several different cases which need separate consideration. All of the phrases enclosed in square brackets are viewed as verb phrases in at least some traditions.

According to a fairly well-known and widely adopted tradition, the term "verb phrase" is applied to what traditional grammar calls the "complete predicate". Following this approach, all of the bracketed sections in the examples from the table would be verb phrases. In the examples in A, however, the parts following the verb are noun phrases in roles which are loosely termed "complements". A.1 shows an indirect object followed by a direct object, A.2 has a direct object alone, and A.3 has a "predicate nominal". According to the approach used in this book, these noun phrases all manifest functions at clause rank, and therefore are not parts of the verb phrase, which in all these examples consists of the verb alone.

We can next consider the examples in parts B and C of the table, which all involve elements that can be seen as adjuncts more clearly than the complements in part A. In traditional grammar, indeed, they would all be considered kinds of adverbs or adverbial phrases. Those in B are various Locationals (Locatives) while those in C are Temporals. In these contexts, all these seem to be good candidates for the status of postposed verbal adjuncts, but some additional kinds of data present some problems for this hypothesis. Consider the examples in Table 3.10. These show the use of two of the adjuncts from the relevant sections of Table 3.9 in combination with a transitive verb. They show that in English such expressions occur either at the end of the clause, after the object, or at the beginning, before the subject. They cannot, in fact, occur directly adjacent to the verb itself in any standard form of English. These considerations suggest that these Locationals and Temporals are better treated as clausal constituents rather than as constituents of a verb phrase. If we make the assumption, as we have here, that co-constituents must be contiguous, the postposed ones could be seen as part

Table 3.10 Data on the position of Locationals and Temporals

A.1	*They sent packages from eastern Europe.*
A.2	*From eastern Europe, they sent packages.*
B.1	*They received the books yesterday.*
B.2	*Yesterday, they received the books.*

of the verb phrase, but only if the Objects were similarly treated. The preposed ones create even more problems, since they are not next to the verb phrase in any construal of that term, and could be interpreted as constituents of that phrase only if phrases are allowed to be discontinuous. In the approach adopted in this book, discontinuous syntactic phrases are not allowed. It is recognized that non-contiguous words or phrases may have special semantic relations, but it is not assumed that syntactic relations always mirror these directly.

With the examples in D the situation is similar overall to that of the Locationals and Temporals, though different in some details. As can be seen from the examples in Table 3.11, such adverbs of manner can also occur in positions not adjacent to the verb, though unlike the Locationals and Temporals of Table 3.10, they can also immediately precede the verb itself. Adverbs of this type are usually related to corresponding adjectives and differentiated from them by the suffix *-ly* in English morphology.

Table 3.11 Positional data for adjuncts of manner

A.1	*Efficiently, they finished the work.*
A.2	*They efficiently finished the work.*
A.3	*They finished the work efficiently.*
B.1	*Happily, they play games.*
B.2	*They happily play games.*
B.3	*They play games happily.*
C.1	*Carefully, they pronounced the words.*
C.2	*They carefully pronounced the words.*
C.3	*They pronounced the words carefully.*

In view of their various positions, such adjuncts as those in B through D in Table 3.9 are better viewed as clausal adjuncts rather than as parts of a verb phrase. They can be assigned such labels as L (for Locational) T (for Temporal) and M (for Manner).

We see a rather different situation in the examples at E in Table 3.9. They involve combinations of two words generally acknowledged to be verbs. In traditional grammars of English and other languages which use them similarly, the first verb in each of these structures is termed an AUXILIARY and the second is called the "main verb", which will here be called the PRINCIPAL. In such a combination, the Principal carries the essential lexical meaning of the verb, while the Auxiliary, sometimes in combination with the inflectional form taken by the Principal, signals such grammatical categories as tense, aspect, voice, person, and number, which might, in another language, be purely a matter of verb inflection. The use of Auxiliaries is common in most modern European languages, though these languages certainly differ in the extent to which they use them. Such usages are also found in languages from various other parts of the world, and some languages, such as Hindi, make an even greater use of auxiliaries than the typical European language does.

Given the examples in part E of Table 3.9, it would appear that Auxiliaries and Principals in English form some kind of construction that could possibly be termed a verb phrase. Consideration of the use of objects with transitive verbs would not change this conclusion, as demonstrated by the examples in part A of Table 3.12, where the objects all follow the

Table 3.12 Further examples of Auxiliaries and Principals

A.1	(*They*) [could finish] *the job.*
A.2	(*They*) [might surprise] *everyone.*
A.3	(*They*) [have read] *all the assignments.*
A.4	(*They*) [are giving] *us presents.*
B.1	[Could] (*they*) [work]?
B.2	[Might] (*they*) [come]?
B.3	[Have] (*they*) [arrived]?
B.4	[Are] (*they*) [fighting]?

complex of Auxiliary plus Principal. The hypothesis that this combination is a unified syntactic construction in English runs into trouble, however, when interrogative forms are considered. The forms in part B of Table 3.12 are the normal interrogative counterparts to the sentences in part E of Table 3.9, and these all show that the Subject intervenes between the Auxiliary and the Principal in the interrogative, effectively breaking up the tentative constructions. In view of such data, the idea that Auxiliaries and Principals form a kind of verb phrase in English is rejected. Most European languages with Auxiliaries have similar interrogatives, which would similarly invalidate their status as phrasal constructions for these languages. This does not mean, however, that the idea is universally invalid, so if a combination of Auxiliary and Principal (in either order) is not interrupted in this fashion in certain languages, they may be reasonably analysed as constituting a kind of verb phrase.

The last remaining candidates for the status of adjuncts in an English verb phrase are the negative adverbs *not* and *never*, as illustrated in part F of Table 3.9. Each of these examples is shown with two interrogative forms, which differ in the assignment of the negative element. The implication to be drawn for all the interrogative examples is that there are in fact two sorts of verb phrases: an auxiliary verb phrase and a principal verb phrase with optional negative adjuncts. Of all the candidates considered for English, these seem to be the only ones that consistently show adjuncts next to verbs, so that the adjuncts can be considered elements of a verb phrase rather than of a clause.

In the analysis of another language, it is reasonable to treat such adverbs as occur contiguous to the verb as verbal modifiers, and that kind of analysis may be followed for a whole language if such a pattern of distribution is maintained throughout that language. In doing exercises for class preparation or homework, adverbial expressions (though not objects or other nominal complements) should be treated as verbal adjuncts as long as none of the data shows them in non-adjacent positions. It should not be surprising, however, when further data overturns a preliminary analysis, as it has for so many of the candidates for the status of verb-phrase adjunct in English.

As noted previously, we could treat some or all of the traditional adverbs and adverbial expressions, as well as auxiliaries, as constituents of a verb phrase if we allowed syntactic constructions to be discontinuous. In general, this book is laid out, however, on the assumption that syntactic constructions must be continuous. To be sure, the idea that such adjuncts do indeed in some way "modify" the verb is not totally senseless. The traditional notion, however, is more an analysis of semantic relationships than of syntactic arrangements. The approach followed here recognizes that syntax, while it does in part mirror semantic relationships, may have patterns of its own which do not directly mirror meaning. So adjuncts which are excluded from syntactic verb phrases on the grounds of potential discontinuity may still be seen as manifestations of semological units more closely relatable to the "verbal" units.

Exocentric phrases

The best-known kind of English phrase not yet discussed is the prepositional phrase, as illustrated in the data of Table 3.13. Each such phrase begins with a word of the class called "prepositions", and this is followed by a noun phrase (or pronoun phrase) in a role which traditional grammar terms the "object of the preposition".

Table 3.13 Examples of English prepositional phrases

1. <u>of</u> *the old woman*
2. <u>about</u> *the renowned novelist*
3. <u>from</u> *those high mountains*
4. <u>to</u> *our new home over there*
5. <u>under</u> *the child's bed*
6. <u>above</u> *our city*
7. <u>behind</u> *the horse barn*
8. <u>without</u> *some hope of success*

While in the endocentric phrases previously treated one could pick out one constituent as the Head and see any others as adjuncts, usually optional, it is not reasonable to attempt a similar analysis in the case of prepositional phrases. Generally speaking, a true Head can occur without any adjuncts in the same role in clause- or phrase-structure as can the fuller phrase of which it is the Head. Prepositions as such, however, cannot occur alone, and their roles in larger structures (Locational, Temporal, Possessive, and others) are not filled by simple noun phrases either.

Despite these facts, there has been one fairly influential tradition in recent years (the so-called X-bar theory) which presents prepositions as Heads of prepositional phrases, and sees the traditional "objects" of such phrases as kinds of adjuncts. This kind of view takes advantage of the fact that some English prepositions coincide in form with words traditionally viewed as adverbs. Compare the examples in A.1–3 in Table 3.14 with their counterparts at B.1–3. Examples like these seem to make it reasonable to claim that the "objects" are adjuncts to the prepositions, but they are not the whole story. Within English, we should consider the use of further prepositional phrases, as seen in the examples at A.4–6. The attempt to construct objectless parallels to B.1–3, as in B.4–6, results in ungrammatical sequences. The traditional view, which treats the underlined words in B.1–3 as adverbs homophonous with (though obviously related in meaning to) the prepositions in A.1–3, seems to be the correct one. Some English prepositions do have such corresponding adverbs, while others do not.

Table 3.14 Occurrence of prepositions vs. adverbs in English

A.1   *The otter dove <u>under the boat</u>.*
A.2   *She walked <u>across the street</u>.*
A.3   *They fell <u>behind their friends</u>.*
A.4   *We discussed the idea <u>of surrender</u>.*
A.5   *You are going <u>to Paris</u>.*
A.6   *He arrived <u>from Russia</u>.*
B.1   *The otter dove <u>under</u>.*
B.2   *She walked <u>across</u>.*
B.3   *They fell <u>behind</u>.*
B.4   **We discussed the idea <u>of</u>*
B.5   **You are going <u>to</u>*
B.6   **He arrived <u>from</u>*

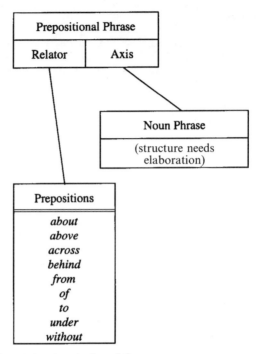

Figure 3.3 Prepositional phrase structure in boxed form

When we look beyond English, furthermore, it is often even harder to make a case for prepositions (or adpositions more generally) as heads of such phrases. Examples like A/B.1–3 are not common in the languages of continental Europe, for example.

In view of these considerations, we should see the prepositional phrase as a construction without a Head. In the same terminology that calls constructions with Heads endocentric, constructions without heads are called **EXOCENTRIC**. This term means "externally centered", implying that none of its constituents is a "center" or head. The structure of the English examples considered above is displayed in boxed form in Figure 3.3. The functional terms for the parts of this phrase are **RELATOR** for the role filled by the preposition and **AXIS** for that filled by the noun or noun phrase (the traditional "object of the preposition").

From some further data, as shown in part A of Table 3.15, an argument might be made that a preposition could be treated as the head of a smaller phrase: such adverbs as *just*, *right*, *well*, *directly*, *completely* and *about*, as illustrated there, could be treated as adjuncts to the prepositions which follow them, so we could see the Relator functions in these exocentric prepositional phrases as manifested by an endocentric "preposition phrase" with the preposition in the role of Head and the adverb as its Modifier. Before we accept such an idea as accurate, however, we need to consider some roughly similar uses of the same adverbs, as in part B of the table. Crucially, these examples show the same adverbs as adjuncts to simple adverbs, and the whole prepositional phrases, rather than just the prepositions themselves, can be seen as heading the phrases. These examples appear to demonstrate that the Heads in the A examples have the whole prepositional phrase as their manifestations. Since the functions of such prepositional phrases are often described as "adverbial", this analysis seems to make a good deal of sense.

Although most European languages, both classical and modern, generally have prepositions and associated prepositional phrases, the use of such words is by no means universal. One deviation from the European norm is found in languages like Hindi, as exemplified by the data of Table 3.16. Here the words translating the English prepositions (*se*

Table 3.15 Adjuncts with prepositional phrases and related expressions

A.1	*just after the meeting*
A.2	*right across the avenue*
A.3	*well behind the others*
A.4	*directly over Paris*
A.5	*completely without hope for improvement*
A.6	*about to the river*
B.1	*just now*
B.2	*right here*
B.3	*well afterward*
B.4	*directly below*
B.5	*completely desperately*
B.6	*about there*

Table 3.16 Postpositional phrases in Hindi

1.	vo [mez se] a·ta· hɛ	THAT ONE COMES FROM THE TABLE.
2.	ye [mez par] bɛtʰa· hɛ	THIS ONE IS SITTING ON THE TABLE.
3.	ye [kursi· par] bɛtʰa· hɛ	THIS ONE IS SITTING ON THE CHAIR.
4.	vo [šahar mẽ] rahta· hɛ	THAT ONE LIVES IN THE CITY.
5.	ye [gã·v mẽ] rahta· hɛ	THIS ONE LIVES IN THE VILLAGE.
6.	vo [kamre se] a·ta· hɛ	THAT ONE COMES FROM THE ROOM.
7.	ye [maka·n tak] calta· hɛ	THIS ONE GOES AS FAR AS THE HOUSE.
8.	vo [maka·n ko] calta· hɛ	THAT ONE GOES TO THE HOUSE.
9.	ye [gã·v ko] a·ta· hɛ	THIS ONE COMES TO THE VILLAGE.
10.	vo [šahar tak] calta· hɛ	THAT ONE GOES AS FAR AS THE CITY.

FROM, *par* ON, *mẽ* IN, *tak* AS FAR AS, *ko* TO) come after the Axis instead of before it. Since the word "preposition" does not refer to either the meaning or the function of the words involved, but rather to their placement ("what is put before"), it is not appropriate to term these Hindi words "prepositions". In keeping with their use in Hindi, they are instead called **POSTPOSITIONS**. Apart from position, however, postpositions in a language such as Hindi work much like the prepositions of European languages. It seems desirable to have a more general term to use when one wants to speak of this general sort of vocabulary item without being specific about its position. To fulfill this need, modern linguists have coined the term **ADPOSITION**, covering both prepositions and postpositions as special cases. So this term will be used in general statements about such words.

Prepositions, then, are not true language universals, but can one justly say that every language would have adpositions – prepositions, postpositions, or some of each? Actually, about all we can say is that every language can be expected to have a means of expressing the kinds of relational ideas which are often expressed by adpositions. As an example of a language with no adpositions, consider the Yup'ik Eskimo data in Table 3.17. This material illustrates two different ways to express the ideas commonly associated with adpositions without any words of such a class.

In all these examples, the last word is a verb in the third-person singular of the present tense, translated into English by a verb with its subject. The one or two words preceding this verb are the expressions glossed in English with prepositional phrases. In each of the examples 1 through 4, a single Yup'ik word is involved, specifically a case-form of the noun *nuna* VILLAGE. The cases involved are the *ALLATIVE* (TO), *LOCATIVE* (IN/AT), *ABLATIVE* (FROM), and *PERLATIVE* (VIA/BY WAY OF). These examples illustrate the use of morphological case in the

Table 3.17 Expression of "prepositional" ideas in Yup'ik Eskimo

1. nunamun taiɣuq	HE IS COMING TO THE VILLAGE.
2. nunami qavaχtuq	HE IS SLEEPING IN THE VILLAGE.
3. nunamɨk taiɣuq	HE IS COMING FROM THE VILLAGE.
4. nunakun taiɣuq	HE IS COMING BY WAY OF THE VILLAGE.
5. aɦyam ciuɦanun ayaxtuq	HE IS GOING TO THE FRONT OF THE BOAT.
6. qayam caniani qavaχtuq	HE IS SLEEPING BESIDE THE KAYAK.
7. yaasiikɨm acianɨk taiɣuq	HE IS COMING FROM UNDER THE CRATE.
8. nunam quliinun tɨɦauχtuq	IT IS FLYING (TO) OVER THE VILLAGE.
9. nunam ɨlatiini aqumɣauq	HE IS SITTING OUTSIDE THE VILLAGE.
10. ɨstuulum qaiɦanɨk kataχtuq	IT IS FALLING FROM THE TABLE.

expression of ideas that might be expressed by adpositions in other languages. In the remaining examples, a broadly locative sense is expressed in a two-word construction. The first word in each of these examples is a noun in another case called the *RELATIVE*, which is characterized in its singular forms by the suffix -*m*. At first glance, the additional words might be thought to be postpositions combining with a preceding noun in the relative. If we examine their morphology more deeply, however, we find that these words are actually nouns in the same cases used in examples 1–3. Rather than postpositions, these words are positional nouns inflected for both an appropriate case and for possession by a third-person singular whose identity is specified by the preceding noun in the relative case. More details of these possibilities are shown in Table 3.18. Edited in the fashion set forth in Chapter 2, example 6, for instance, would be as follows:

qaya	cani	qavaʁ
RELATIVE	*LOCATIVE*	*PRESENT*
SINGULAR	*SINGULAR*	*THIRD-PERSON*
	THIRD-SG POSS	*SINGULAR*
[OF THE KAYAK]	[IN ITS AREA BESIDE]	[HE/SHE/IT SLEEPS]

So, rather than being any kind of adpositional phrase, the locative expression used here consists of a positional noun in the locative case with a further noun in the relative case as its adjunct. The remaining examples in 5–10 of Table 3.17 and the further possibilities outlined in Table 3.18 will be subject to parallel analyses involving the allative, ablative, or locative cases.

Table 3.18 Cases of some positional nouns in Yup'ik Eskimo

Noun root	*ALLATIVE*	*LOCATIVE*	*ABLATIVE*
ciu- AREA IN FRONT OF	ciaŋanun[5]	ciaŋani	ciaŋanɨk
cani- AREA BESIDE	canianun	caniani[6]	canianɨk
aci- AREA UNDER	acianun	aciani	acianɨk[7]
qulɨ- AREA ABOVE	quliinun[8]	quliini	quliinɨk
ɨlatɨ- AREA OUTSIDE	ɨlatiinun	ɨlatiini[9]	ɨlatiinɨk
qai- SURFACE	qaiŋanun	qaiŋani	qaiŋanɨk[10]

Note: Forms from the data of Table 3.17 are underlined and referenced by superscript numbers.

In addition to adpositional phrases, languages commonly have further exocentric constructions on both the rank of the phrase and the rank of the clause. These typically include clause constructions as wholes, and relator-axis constructions in which conjunctions rather than adpositions are the Relators. The latter are treated in greater detail in Chapter 5, and the former will be taken up in Chapter 6.

Summary of phrasal constituents and symbols

Table 3.19 presents a summary of the various syntactic functions discussed in this chapter. Most of the matters shown are quite self-explanatory in connection with this discussion. A few matters, however, require some additional comments.

Table 3.19 Typical syntactic functions at phrase rank

Type	Function	Suggested symbol	Typical manifestation
Head	NOMINAL HEAD	H_N	Noun (Adj, Numeral)
	PRONOMINAL HEAD	H_P	Personal Pronoun
	ADJECTIVAL HEAD	H_A	Adjective
	ADVERBIAL HEAD	H_D	Adverb
	VERBAL HEAD	H_V	Verb
Adjunct	DELIMITING ADJUNCT	Del/A_{del}	Delimiting Adjective
	DETERMINING ADJUNCT	Det/A_{det}	Determining Adjective
	POSSESSIVE ADJUNCT	Po/A_{pos}	Poss. Adjective/Phrase
	DEMONSTRATIVE ADJUNCT	Dem/A_{dem}	Demonstrative Adjective
	QUANTIFYING ADJUNCT	Qnt/A_{qnt}	Numeral/Nonspec. Quant.
	NOMINAL MODIFIER	Mod_N	Ordinary Adjective
	NOMINAL QUALIFIER	Q_Q	Adpositional Phrase/ Relative Clause/Participal Phrase
	ADJECTIVAL MODIFIER	Mod_A/M_{MA}	Adadjectival Adverb
	ADVERBIAL MODIFIER	Mod_D/A_{MD}	Adadverbial Adverb
	PRONOMINAL MODIFIER	Mod_P/A_P	(Like NOMINAL MODIFIER)
	VERBAL MODIFIER	Mod_V/M_V	Adverb Proper
	VERBAL QUALIFIER	Q_V	Adpositional Phrase
Relator	ADPOSITIONAL RELATOR	R_{AP}	Adposition (Pre-/Post-)
Axis	ADPOSITIONAL AXIS	Ax_{AP}	Noun/Pronoun Phrase

Under the manifestation of the Nominal Head, we have only seen examples of nouns. In some languages, including English, in fact, it is possible to have noun phrases whose Head function is manifested by something other than a noun, such as an adjective or a numeral. Examples would be the Subject noun phrases in the following sentences:

> *The __poor__ settled on the edges of the city.*

> *All her __twenty-five__ have arrived.*

For adjuncts, two styles of symbols are offered, following the examples used in the discussion of noun phrases. The relation of Determiners to possessives and demonstratives, it should be noted, can be expected to vary from one language to the next. So English possessives are appropriately treated as kinds of Determiners, while those of Italian are not, and in another language demonstratives might be separate from articles.

Exercises

A.   Interpretation problems

1.   *Japanese postpositional and noun phrases*

The following account shows the structure of some phrases in Japanese.

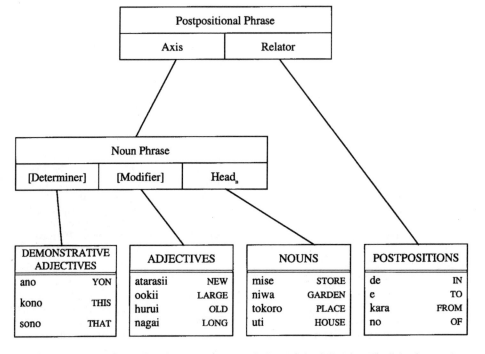

Use this account to determine the Japanese translation of the following English phrases (note that the English indefinite article *a* in item 3 requires no translation):

1.   FROM YON GARDEN

_____

2.   TO THIS NEW STORE

_____

3.   OF A LARGE HOUSE

_____

4.   IN THAT OLD PLACE

For answers 2 and 4, show the phrasal structure assigned by the account in a boxed form. For example, the account for the English original in 3, based on English syntax, is as follows:

Prepositional Phrase			
Relator	Axis		
	Noun Phrase		
	Determiner	Modifier	Head$_a$
Prepositions	Determining Adjectives	Descriptive Adjectives	Nouns
of	a	large	house

2. Thai verb phrase

The following diagram sketches part of the structure of the intransitive verb phrase in Thai (the official language of Thailand in Southeast Asia). Use this account as the basis for answering the questions below.

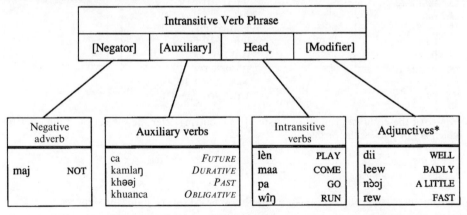

Note: Since these words can be used as nominal modifiers as well as verbal Modifiers, the term "adjunctive", neutral between "adjective" and "adverb", is used for them.

a.   On the basis of the diagram, show the Thai phrases that would have the following meanings. In the English glosses, the absence of an Auxiliary is translated by the simple present; the *DURATIVE* is translated by the *be* ...-*ing* construction and the *OBLIGATIVE* by *should*.

1.   IS RUNNING FAST

_____

2.   SHOULD NOT PLAY

_____

3.   DID NOT GO WELL

_____

4.   DOES NOT COME

_____

5.   WILL RUN A LITTLE

_____

b.   For the phrases in 3 and 5 above, show the complete structure in a boxed diagram.

B.   Analysis problems

1. Bekwarra verb phrases

Based on the following data, prepare an analysis of the verb phrase structure in Bekwarra, a Nigerian language of the South-Central Niger-Congo group.

1. ba fia		WILL PAY
2. fia ma		HAVE PAID
3. ba fia re		WILL NOT PAY
4. fia		PAID
5. ka fia		PAID THEN
6. ka ba fia		WILL PAY THEN
7. fia re		DID NOT PAY
8. fia ma re		HAVE NOT PAID
9. ba fia ma		ARE ABOUT TO PAY
10. ka ba fia re		WILL NOT PAY THEN

Note: All these phrases can be understood as occurring after the subject pronoun /e/ THEY, which is not part of the problem.

2. Latvian noun phrase

Prepare an account of the Latvian noun phrase based on the following data set.

1. puķes	FLOWERS
2. manas puķes	MY FLOWERS
3. ta:s puķes	THOSE FLOWERS
4. skaista:s puķes	THE BEAUTIFUL FLOWERS
5. ta:s skaista:s puķes	THOSE BEAUTIFUL FLOWERS

6. manas skaista:s puķes   MY BEAUTIFUL FLOWERS
7. visas manas puķes   ALL MY FLOWERS
8. visas tavas ma:jas   ALL YOUR HOUSES
9. manas ma:jas   MY HOUSES
10. ša:s skaista:s ma:jas   THESE BEAUTIFUL HOUSES
11. manas jauna:s zivis   MY NEW FISH (*plural*)
12. visas tavas liela:s zivis   ALL YOUR BIG FISH
13. ta:s manas zivis   THOSE FISH OF MINE
14. tavas jauna:s gra:matas   YOUR NEW BOOKS
15. visas ša:s manas liela:s gra:matas   ALL THOSE BIG BOOKS OF MINE

Terminology

ADJUNCT	EXOCENTRIC

ADPOSITION
   POSTPOSITION
   PREPOSITION
	POSITIONAL NOUN
	
	PRINCIPAL

AUXILIARY	QUALIFIER
AXIS	QUANTIFIER
DELIMITER	RELATOR
ENDOCENTRIC	

4

Concord and government in the phrase

Simple concord

In languages that have inflection, we very often observe that some inflectional categories may affect more than one constituent in a phrase construction, especially a noun phrase. English shows this phenomenon only to a very limited extent, as exemplified by the data in Table 4.1. In this material, the data in the first column involves a singular phrase, while that in the second gives the corresponding plural. In edited form, the last group of examples would be as follows:

11.	*this*	*ox*	11a.	*this*	*ox*
	SINGULAR	SINGULAR		PLURAL	PLURAL
12.	*that*	*ox*	12a.	*that*	*ox*
	SINGULAR	SINGULAR		PLURAL	PLURAL

and all the other examples would be edited analogously. Basically, we see that when the SINGULAR/PLURAL selection is made for one constituent, the identical selection must be made for the other as well, meaning that only phrases in which the constituents agree regarding this selection are grammatical, while other combinations like *this oxen* and *those ox* would be ungrammatical in view of the failure of those constituents to agree.

Table 4.1 Number concord in the English noun phrase

1.	*this boy*	1a.	*these boys*
2.	*that boy*	2a.	*those boys*
3.	*this house*	3a.	*these houses*
4.	*that house*	4a.	*those houses*
5.	*this girl*	5a.	*these girls*
6.	*that girl*	6a.	*those girls*
7.	*this table*	7a.	*these tables*
8.	*that table*	8a.	*those tables*
9.	*this dog*	9a.	*these dogs*
10.	*that dog*	10a.	*those dogs*
11.	*this ox*	11a.	*these oxen*
12.	*that ox*	12a.	*those oxen*

When such an inflectional specification as that seen here for number is relevant for two or more co-constituents in a phrase (or other construction) we speak of SIMPLE CONCORD.

According to what we have studied up to now, a boxed account of this case of simple concord would require the recognition of two separate constructions, one for singular noun phrases, and another for plural noun phrases, as depicted in Figure 4.1. Such a presentation may leave us a little dissatisfied, however, because it requires us to repeat a great deal of noun phrase structure, such as the order of constituents and the general types of bases, in order to allow for the consistent difference in inflectional selection. Where there is as little such concord

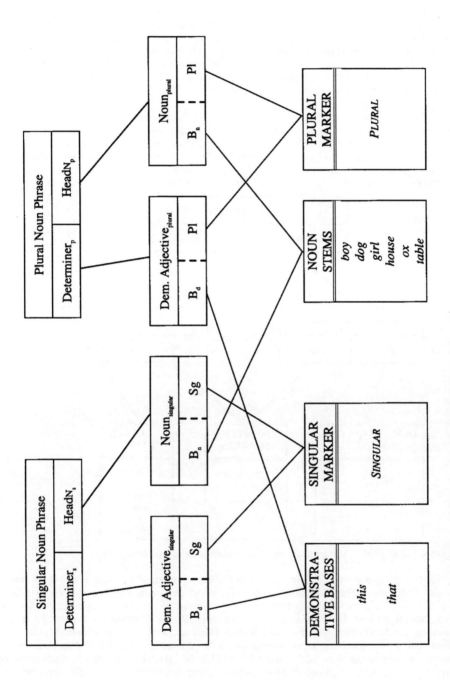

Figure 4.1 Solution to English number concord using two distinct phrase types

as there is in English, it may seem acceptable to allow a few cases like this of repeated structure. When we look at a language with more inflection and more concord, however, it seems clearly less acceptable to allow multiple but essentially parallel constructions in this way. The Old Church Slavic noun phrase, for instance, shows concord in regard to three numbers and seven cases, meaning that we would need not just two or three constructions, but a total of twenty-one different types of noun phrase to deal with the facts adequately, though the constructions would still be largely parallel. It is therefore very desirable to have a more economical way to show simple concord, which would avoid, or at least minimize, this multiplication of constructions.

In Figure 4.2, we see an alternative which seeks just this kind of reduction. If we ignore, for the moment, the superscript labels found in some of the boxes, this account seems to fail, because it seems to allow not only the correct combinations, but also incorrect ones like those cited above, in which co-constituents have different number markers. The superscript numbers, however, are an attempt to augment our model with a device to rule out such incorrect selections. Let us now consider some conventions for their interpretation.

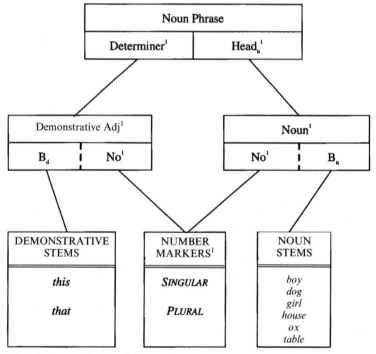

Figure 4.2 Solution to the English number concord using one phrase type

We see the superscript [1] first introduced in the two constituent sub-boxes within the noun-phrase construction. These identical numerical superscripts are intended to indicate that there is some kind of a grammatical tie between these co-constituents. The exact nature of that tie can be seen if we look further down in the structure. We see first that the superscript is also found on the word-level constructions named Demonstrative Adjective[1] and Noun[1], and within each of those boxes it further carries to No[1]. Finally, each of the latter sub-boxes connects to the vocabulary box labeled NUMBER MARKERS[1]. In this and all cases of simple concord, both or all concording co-constituents will eventually connect to a common vocabulary box involving some inflectional categorial dimension. The meaning of the continuing chain of superscripts to this point is always the same: it means that the selection made for one of the co-constituents marked as agreeing by the superscripts must also be taken for the other co-constituents with the same marking. So by this device, only the combinations shown by the data (as edited) are permitted, and others which mix different number markers in the same phrases are disallowed. This device allows us to reduce the number of constructions while still accounting precisely for the data.

Number concord is doubtless the most common kind to be found in noun phrases. Another fairly common sort of concord involves inflection for definiteness in the noun phrase, as seen in combination with number concord in the Israeli Hebrew data shown in Table 4.2. Here, definiteness is signaled by the prefix /ha-/, in contrast to its absence for the indefinite, and the expression of number on both nouns and adjectives involves suffixation. A solution based on an edited version of this data set is presented in Figure 4.3. This account applies further the same essential principles that were used in Figure 4.2, this time using the superscript [1] for definiteness and [2] for number. Since the agreeing modifier here is an optional constituent, it should be noted, the superscripts are placed *inside* the brackets that show the optionality. If the option to omit the modifier is taken, the superscripts on the noun are meaningless, since they will not have a co-constituent with which the concord can apply.

Table 4.2 Definiteness and number concord in the Modern Israeli Hebrew noun phrase

1.	šulxan	A TABLE
2.	šulxanot	TABLES
3.	hašulxan	THE TABLE
4.	hašulxanot	THE TABLES
5.	šulxan xadaš	A NEW TABLE
6.	šulxanot tovim	GOOD TABLES
7.	hašulxan hatov	THE GOOD TABLE
8.	hašulxanot haxadašim	THE NEW TABLES
9.	more	A TEACHER
10.	morim	TEACHERS
11.	hamore	THE TEACHER
12.	hamorim	THE TEACHERS
13.	more raʔ	A BAD TEACHER
14.	morim yafim	HANDSOME TEACHERS
15.	hamore haraʔ	THE BAD TEACHER
16.	hamorim hayafim	THE HANDSOME TEACHERS
17.	hagan haxadaš	THE NEW GARDEN
18.	baxurim raʔim	BAD BOYS
19.	haʔolamot hatovim	THE GOOD WORLDS
20.	haʔaviron hayafe	THE PRETTY AIRPLANE
21.	habaxur hagadol	THE BIG BOY
22.	roš tov	A GOOD HEAD

Still another very common category for noun phrase concord, particularly in Indo-European languages, is case. This is exemplified by the Polish data seen in Table 4.3 and solved in Figure 4.4. This solution applies the same basic principles as the previous ones. The editing of the Polish data, it should be noted, is a little more difficult than for the Hebrew because the expression of case and number is fused in a single suffix in Polish. Once this editing is completed, however, the solutions differ only in details of order and vocabulary peculiar to each language.

Gender concord

Still another inflectional category involved in noun phrase concord in many languages is gender. A simple example of this is seen in the Hindi data of Table 4.4. This gives evidence for

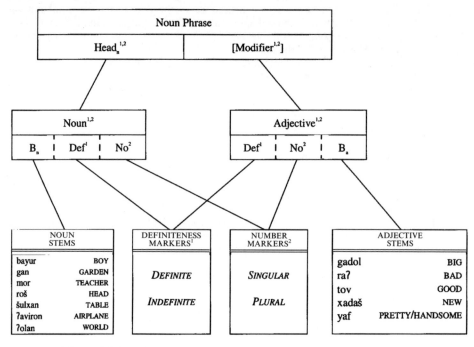

Figure 4.3 Solution to Hebrew definiteness and number concord

Table 4.3 Case and number concord in the Polish noun phrase

1. ta mawa wapa	THIS LITTLE PAW (Subject)
2. te mawõ wape	THIS LITTLE PAW (Object)
3. tej mawej wapy	OF THIS LITTLE PAW
4. te mawe wapy	THESE LITTLE PAWS (Subject/Object)
5. tyx mawyx wap	OF THESE LITTLE PAWS
6. ta śeć	THIS NET (Subject)
7. te śeć	THIS NET (Object)
8. tej śeći	OF THIS NET
9. te śeći	THESE NETS (Subject/Object)
10. tyx śeći	OF THESE NETS
11. pjĕkna stopa	THE/A BEAUTIFUL FOOT (Subject)
12. pjĕknõ stope	THE/A BEAUTIFUL FOOT (Object)
13. pjĕknej stopy	OF THE/A BEAUTIFUL FOOT
14. pjĕkne stopy	(THE) BEAUTIFUL FEET (Subject/Object)
15. pjĕknyx stop	OF (THE) BEAUTIFUL FEET
16. ta nova jama	THIS NEW HOLE (Subject)
17. te novõ jame	THIS NEW HOLE (Object)
18. tej novej jamy	THIS NEW HOLE
19. mawa kość	THE/A LITTLE BONE (Subject)
20. mawõ kość	THE/A LITTLE BONE (Object)
21. mawej kośći	OF THE/A LITTLE BONE
22. stopy	(THE) FEET (Subject/Object)
23. wap	OF (THE) PAWS
24. jame	THE/A HOLE (Object)

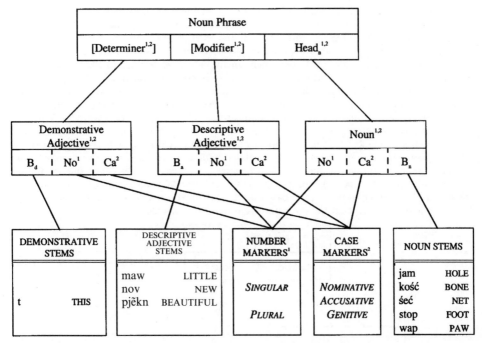

Figure 4.4 Solution to Polish case and number concord

two different genders in Hindi, as reflected in the different forms taken by the adjectives in items 1 through 8. Gender concord, however, does not work in exactly the same manner as the concord for number, definiteness, and case that have already been examined. This is because only the adjunct(s), and not the head, have different inflectional forms representing the genders. Unlike the adjectives, the nouns simply *belong* to a gender class rather than showing different inflectional forms for each gender. In the other examples of concord, we had a choice for the overall phrase reflected typically in both the head and one or more adjuncts, but here a classification applying to the head is reflected in the inflectional forms of the adjuncts only. This is the way gender typically works.

Table 4.4 Examples of gender concord in Hindi

1. acchaˑ kamraˑ	THE/A GOOD ROOM
2. acchiˑ mez	THE/A GOOD TABLE
3. chotaˑ aˑdmiˑ	THE/A SMALL MAN
4. chotiˑ larkiˑ	THE/A SMALL GIRL
5. nayaˑ ghar	THE/A NEW HOUSE
6. nayiˑ pustak	THE/A NEW BOOK
7. baraˑ deš	THE/A BIG COUNTRY
8. bariˑ ciriyaˑ	THE/A BIG BIRD
9. saˑf kamraˑ	THE/A CLEAN ROOM
10. saˑf mez	THE/A CLEAN TABLE
11. sundar deš	THE/A BEAUTIFUL COUNTRY
12. sundar larkiˑ	THE/A BEAUTIFUL GIRL
13. laˑl ghar	THE/A RED HOUSE
14. laˑl pustak	THE/A RED BOOK

An account of this Hindi gender concord is seen in Figure 4.5. In examining this solution, we need to observe several ways in which its treatment of gender concord differs from the previous examples of simple concord. At the initial level of co-constituents, it is the same: the superscript ^{1} stands for the tie of gender concord between the co-constituents. Further down, however, there is a gender word-constituent in the adjective leading to the Masculine and Feminine Gender Markers, but on the nouns there is no inflection in evidence. Instead, the Head relates to two alternative classes of nouns, the Masculine, marked with superscript ^{1M}, and the Feminine, marked with superscript ^{1F}. These superscripts are then repeated on the corresponding inflectional markers for the adjectives (*MASCULINE*^{1M}, *FEMININE* ^{1F}). When the basic numerical superscripts have letters added to them in this fashion, we may speak of **AUGMENTED SUPERSCRIPTS**. It is necessary to use these in treating gender concord, where we find a classification for one constituent correlated with an inflection on one or more agreeing co-constituents in the construction. In such a case, furthermore, we have one of the co-constituents (here the Head) which can be termed the **GOVERNOR**, since it controls the inflection of the other constituent(s) based on its classification. The other constituents whose form is partly dependent on the governor are termed the **GOVERNED**.

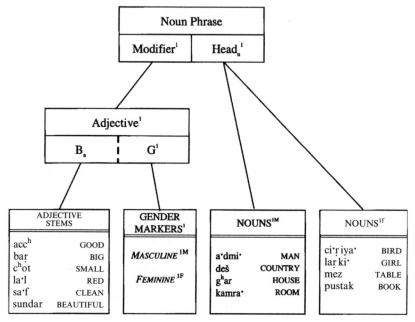

Figure 4.5 Solution to gender concord in Hindi

Several additional remarks about the labeling of classes within gender systems are also appropriate. In treating this Hindi material, first of all, the genders have been given the names that are traditionally used in grammars of the language. The data hints at the appropriateness of these labels by the inclusion of the word for MAN in the masculine class and the word for GIRL in the feminine. In solving this problem, however, the only thing that is really important is to recognize the membership of each of the gender classes found and to assign each of them some kind of distinctive label. We could have used different and indeed quite arbitrary labels for our genders here without affecting the essential correctness and viability of our solution. We could, for example, have labeled them *GENDER-A*^{1A} and *GENDER-B*^{1B}.

Furthermore, when we do use traditional labels like *MASCULINE* and *FEMININE*, we should be sure to remember that we are speaking in linguistics about gender as a purely grammatical concept not tied to a biological concept like sex classification. The fact that the grammar of

Hindi classifies nouns into two genders conventionally named "masculine" and "feminine" does not mean that the culture of the speakers of this language actually causes them to believe that all objects referred to by masculine nouns are "male", while those referred to by feminine nouns are "female". It is just a convention that one naturally picks up when learning the language, and a speaker may master such a convention with no explicit awareness of the "masculine" or "feminine" labels.

It should also be noted that three of the adjectives in the Hindi data (la·l RED, sa·f CLEAN, and sundar BEAUTIFUL) do not show the different gender forms seen in the others. In this syntactic analysis, such differences can be ignored and it can be left to the morphological description to distinguish those adjectives that agree from those that do not, given that they are all alternatives in the same syntactic position. It is similar to the usual way of treating English nouns such as *sheep* and *deer* which do not show overt singular/plural distinctions. In syntax we treat them the same way as more regular nouns, with distinct singular and plural forms, but we set them apart as a special class in the morphology. Since the special classification of these Hindi adjectives as uninflected does not affect the syntax, we classify them together with the other adjectives and thereby simplify the syntactic account.

As an example of gender in combination with number concord, we can consider the Italian data of Table 4.5. This table begins by repeating some of the examples used earlier in Table 3.5 in items 1–4. Items 5–8 then give the plurals of these earlier items, while 9–12 and 13–16 give singulars and corresponding plurals from a second gender. Finally, items 17–19 and 20–22 provide examples (in the singular and plural, respectively) for a third gender.

Table 4.5 Gender and number concord in Italian

1. *la macchina bella*	THE PRETTY CAR
2. *questa tua macchina rossa*	THIS RED CAR OF YOURS
3. *tutta quella mia città*	ALL THAT CITY OF MINE
4. *la ragazza povera*	THE POOR [PENNILESS] GIRL
5. *le macchine belle*	THE PRETTY CARS
6. *queste tue macchine rosse*	THESE RED CARS OF YOURS
7. *tutte quelle mie città*	ALL THOSE CITIES OF MINE
8. *le ragazze povere*	THE POOR [PENNILESS] GIRLS
9. *il libro bello*	THE PRETTY BOOK
10. *questo tuo libro rosso*	THIS RED BOOK OF YOURS
11. *tutto quello mio albergo*	ALL THAT HOTEL OF MINE
12. *il contadino povero*	THE POOR [PENNILESS] PEASANT
13. *i libri belli*	THE PRETTY BOOKS
14. *questi tui libri rossi*	THESE RED BOOKS OF YOURS
15. *tutti quelli miei alberghi*	ALL THOSE HOTELS OF MINE
16. *i contadini poveri*	THE POOR [PENNILESS] PEASANTS
17. *questo muro alto*	THIS HIGH WALL
18. *il mio dito*	MY FINGER
19. *il braccio lungo*	THE LONG ARM
20. *queste mura alte*	THESE HIGH WALLS
21. *le mie dita*	MY FINGERS
22. *le braccia lunghe*	THE LONG ARMS

In the boxed account provided in Figure 4.6, the genders, in the order presented in the table, are identified as *FEMININE*, *MASCULINE*, and *NEUTER*. Besides showing an extra gender, this material goes beyond what we saw in Hindi in showing how gender concord can be readily combined with number concord. Here the superscript [1] is used for gender and the superscript [2] for number. It also shows these two kinds of concord in relation to four different noun-phrase adjuncts. It should be noted that the neuter gender has a special morphological relationship to the other two, as seen in the suffixal forms found in the various adjectives:

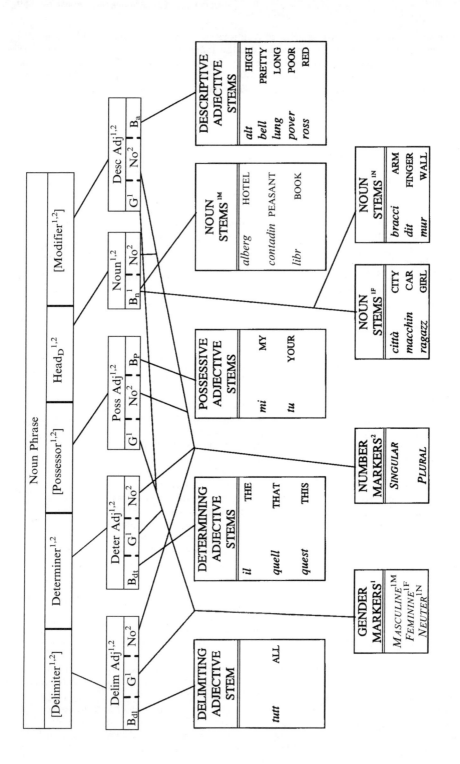

Figure 4.6 Solution to gender and number concord in the Italian noun phrase

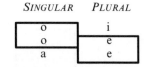

As a result of these relationships, some grammars of Italian insist that the language has only two genders, but that some nouns (here the neuters) are "ambigenic" – masculine in the singular but feminine in the plural. This is essentially a morphological rather than a syntactic view of the matter. From a syntactic point of view, the fact remains that nouns fall into three classes, not just two, and it is of no real consequence whether we choose to label the third class as "neuter" or as "ambigenic". Details in the manifestation of the genders can be left to the morphology, which will have to deal with the coincidence of *MASCULINE* and *NEUTER* in conjunction with *SINGULAR*, and of *FEMININE* and *NEUTER* in conjunction with *PLURAL*.

The examples of gender seen so far have involved inflected languages. In some languages without inflection for gender, however, a case can still be made for the existence of syntactic gender. One example is provided by the Thai data given in Table 4.6. In this material, there is no inflection in any of the words. Still, we see that the noun phrases containing one of the demonstratives /ní·/ THIS or /nán/ THAT contain an additional word between the noun, which functions as Head, and the demonstrative word. The exact form taken by this word, furthermore, is correlated with the noun in the Head position, so the nouns fall into classes much like those involved in the genders previously exemplified. Four different classes are shown in this data, though a deeper examination of Thai would reveal many more. The only essential difference between the situation here and inflectional gender is that the gender distinctions are expressed by separate words instead of affixes. Such words, here /kʰōn/, /tūa/, /kʰān/, and /lû·k/ are commonly called **CLASSIFIERS**. Like gender markers, they show up in conjunction with adjuncts, here the demonstratives, and the one taken depends on a classification of the nouns in the Head position.

Table 4.6 Classifiers with demonstrative in Thai

1.	dèk	THE/A CHILD	7.	càkkrājān	THE/A BICYCLE
1a.	dèk kʰōn ní·	THIS CHILD	7a.	càkkrājān kʰān ní·	THIS BICYCLE
1b.	dèk kʰōn nán	THAT CHILD	7b.	càkkrājān kʰān nán	THAT BICYCLE
2.	kʰrū·	THE/A TEACHER	8.	rót	THE/A CAR
2a.	kʰrū· kōn ní·	THIS TEACHER	8a.	rót kʰān ní·	THIS CAR
2b.	kʰrū· kōn nán	THAT TEACHER	8b.	rót kʰān nán	THAT CAR
3.	pʰŷan	THE/A FRIEND	9.	tʰǽksî·	THE/A TAXI
3a.	pʰŷan kʰōn ní·	THIS FRIEND	9a.	tʰǽksî· kʰān ní·	THIS TAXI
3b.	pʰŷan kʰōn nán	THAT FRIEND	9b.	tʰǽksî· kʰān nán	THAT TAXI
4.	mǎ·	THE/A DOG	10.	klûaj	THE/A BANANA
4a.	mǎ· tūa ní·	THIS DOG	10a.	klûaj lû·k ní·	THIS BANANA
4b.	mǎ· tūa nán	THAT DOG	10b.	klûaj lû·k nán	THAT BANANA
5.	mǽ·w	THE/A CAT	11.	māmûaŋ	THE/A MANGO
5a.	mǽ·w tūa ní·	THIS CAT	11a.	māmûaŋ lû·k ní·	THIS MANGO
5b.	mǽ·w tūa nán	THAT CAT	11b.	māmûaŋ lû·k nán	THAT MANGO
6.	nók	THE/A BIRD	12.	sǒm	THE/AN ORANGE
6a.	nók tūa ní·	THIS BIRD	12a.	sǒm lû·k ní·	THIS ORANGE
6b.	nók tūa nán	THAT BIRD	12b.	sǒm lû·k nán	THAT ORANGE

An account of this data is presented in Figure 4.7. In most details, the treatment is exactly like what would be done for inflectional gender. The differences result entirely from the fact that the classifier is identified as a separate word rather than an affix: we have a **DEMONSTRATIVE PHRASE** rather than a word construction with gender inflection, and the classifiers are spelled out as words in their vocabulary box – since they are not affixes, they are not subject to editing. The letters used for the augmented superscripts could have been

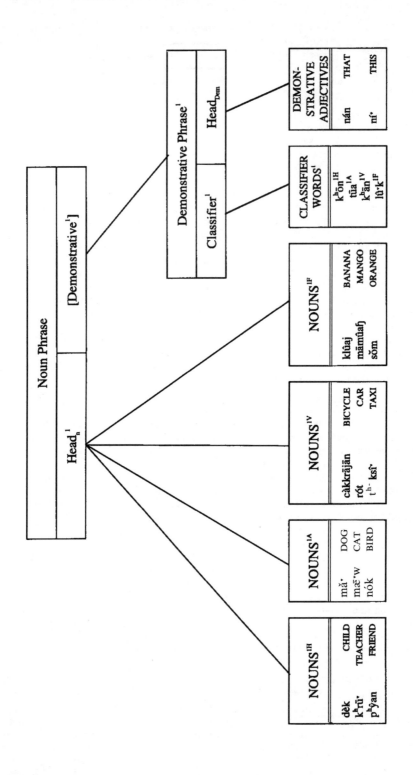

Figure 4.7 Solution to classifiers with demonstratives in Thai

arbitrarily assigned (as ABCD or WXYZ, for instance), but here they are assigned so as to take advantage of an apparent correlation of gender classes with semantic groupings: nouns taking /kʰōn/ generally refer to humans (^{1H}), those taking /tūa/ to animals (^{1A}), those taking /kʰān/ refer to vehicles (^{1V}), and those with /lûˑk/ to fruits (^{1F}).

The occurrence of classifiers is often correlated with numerals (and/or other quantifiers) rather than or in addition to demonstratives. Indonesian is a language that uses classifiers with numerals, but not with demonstratives, as seen in the data of Table 4.7. This data is solved in Figure 4.8, using a NUMERAL PHRASE ending with a classifier. Here the alternative style using arbitrary letters for augmented superscripts is exemplified, although correlations with semantic classes can be observed here too.

Table 4.7 Classifiers with numerals in Indonesian

1. prahoto	A TRUCK
1a. prahoto ini	THE/THIS TRUCK
1b. dua buah prahoto	TWO TRUCKS
1c. sembilan buah prahoto itu	THOSE NINE TRUCKS
2. pikiran	A THOUGHT
2a. pikiran itu	THE/THAT THOUGHT
2b. tiga buah pikiran	THREE THOUGHTS
2c. delapan buah pikiran ini	THESE EIGHT THOUGHTS
3. guru	A TEACHER
3a. guru ini	THE/THIS TEACHER
3b. empat orang guru	FOUR TEACHERS
3c. tujuh orang guru itu	THOSE SEVEN TEACHERS
4. bibi	AN AUNT
4a. bibi itu	THE/THAT AUNT
4b. lima orang bibi	FIVE AUNTS
4c. enam orang bibi ini	THESE SIX AUNTS
5. kera	A MONKEY
5a. kera ini	THE/THIS MONKEY
5b. sembilan ékor kera	NINE MONKEYS
5c. lima ékor kera itu	THOSE FIVE MONKEYS
6. kucing	A CAT
6a. kucing itu	THE/THAT CAT
6b. delapan ékor kucing	EIGHT CATS
6c. tiga ékor kucing ini	THESE THREE CATS
7. kapak	AN AXE
7a. kapak ini	THE/THIS AXE
7b. tujuh bilah kapak	SEVEN AXES
7c. dua bilah kapak itu	THOSE TWO AXES
8. pisau	A KNIFE
8a. pisau itu	THE/THAT KNIFE
8b. enam bilah pisau	SIX KNIVES
8c. empat bilah pisau ini	THESE FOUR KNIVES

In general, we seem to find some degree of semantic correlation and some degree of arbitrariness in all gender systems. The more genders we find, however, the greater the tendency toward semantic correlation rather than arbitrariness. A system with many genders would be difficult to maintain if there were not a strong correlation with facts as interpreted through culture. A system with just two or three genders, on the other hand, can tolerate more arbitrariness, though it will often exhibit a partial correlation with morphology as well as some with meaning, making it less than wholly arbitrary.

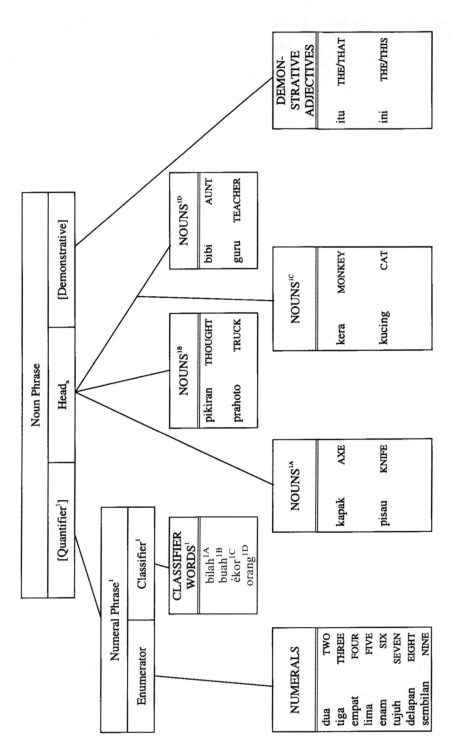

Figure 4.8 Solution to classifiers with numbers in Indonesian

Grammatical government

Still another kind of grammatical tie between phrasal constituents is seen in the Latvian data of Table 4.8. In this material, various nouns are shown in combination with different prepositions. Although details differ from one noun to the next, we observe that each of the nouns shown has three different forms, and these forms depend on a classification of the preposition that precedes the noun. Such a pattern is common in Indo-European languages that have retained case inflection, including virtually all the ancient languages of the family and such modern groups as Baltic (which includes Latvian), Slavic and part of Germanic. Here the different noun forms represent different grammatical CASES, which most typically can also appear in other syntactic functions without prepositions. When a classification applying to adpositions in a Relator function affects the case form assumed by a noun in this way, the adposition is said to GOVERN the particular case, and the grammatical tie that holds between the two is called **GOVERNMENT**.

Table 4.8 Prepositional case government in Latvian

1.	aiz āboles	BEHIND THE APPLE TREE	6.	aiz ledus	BEHIND THE ICE
1a.	ap āboli	ABOUT THE APPLE TREE	6a.	ap ledu	ABOUT THE ICE
1b.	ar āboli	WITH THE APPLE TREE	6b.	ar ledu	WITH THE ICE
1c.	līdz ābolei	AS FAR AS THE APPLE TREE	6c.	līdz ledum	AS FAR AS THE ICE
1d.	pa ābolei	OVER THE APPLE TREE	6d.	pa ledum	OVER THE ICE
1e.	uz āboles	ON THE APPLE TREE	6e.	uz ledus	ON THE ICE
2.	aiz augļa	BEHIND THE FRUIT	7.	aiz mājas	BEHIND THE HOUSE
2a.	ap augli	ABOUT THE FRUIT	7a.	ap māju	ABOUT THE HOUSE
2b.	ar augli	WITH THE FRUIT	7b.	ar māju	WITH THE HOUSE
2c.	līdz auglim	AS FAR AS THE FRUIT	7c.	līdz mājai	AS FAR AS THE HOUSE
2d.	pa auglim	OVER THE FRUIT	7d.	pa mājai	OVER THE HOUSE
2e.	uz augļa	ON THE FRUIT	7e.	uz mājas	ON THE HOUSE
3.	aiz galda	BEHIND THE TABLE	8.	aiz spaiņa	BEHIND THE BUCKET
3a.	ap galdu	ABOUT THE TABLE	8a.	ap spaini	ABOUT THE BUCKET
3b.	ar galdu	WITH THE TABLE	8b.	ar spaini	WITH THE BUCKET
3c.	līdz galdam	AS FAR AS THE TABLE	8c.	līdz spainim	AS FAR AS THE BUCKET
3d.	pa galdam	OVER THE TABLE	8d.	pa spainim	OVER THE BUCKET
3e.	uz galda	ON THE TABLE	8e.	uz spaiņa	ON THE BUCKET
4.	aiz istaba	BEHIND THE ROOM	9.	aiz tirgus	BEHIND THE MARKET
4a.	ap istabu	ABOUT THE ROOM	9a.	ap tirgu	ABOUT THE MARKET
4b.	ar istabu	WITH THE ROOM	9b.	ar tirgu	WITH THE MARKET
4c.	līdz istabai	AS FAR AS THE ROOM	9c.	līdz tirgum	AS FAR AS THE MARKET
4d.	pa istabai	OVER THE ROOM	9d.	pa tirgum	OVER THE MARKET
4e.	uz istabas	ON THE ROOM	9e.	uz tirgus	ON THE MARKET
5.	aiz lauka	BEHIND THE FIELD	10.	aiz upes	BEHIND THE RIVER
5a.	ap lauku	ABOUT THE FIELD	10a.	ap upi	ABOUT THE RIVER
5b.	ar lauku	WITH THE FIELD	10b.	ar upi	WITH THE RIVER
5c.	līdz laukam	AS FAR AS THE FIELD	10c.	līdz upei	AS FAR AS THE RIVER
5d.	pa laukam	OVER THE FIELD	10d.	pa upei	OVER THE RIVER
5e.	uz lauka	ON THE FIELD	10e.	uz upes	ON THE RIVER

A boxed solution to this example of case governed by prepositions is presented in Figure 4.9, which shows a three-way classification applied to the prepositions correlating with the inflection of the nouns in the *ACCUSATIVE, DATIVE*, and *GENITIVE* cases. (These are the usual labels found in grammars of this language; if we did not know them we would substitute more arbitrary labels such as *CASE-A, CASE-B, CASE-C*.) Labeling aside, it should be clear that government is formally very similar to the gender concord discussed in the

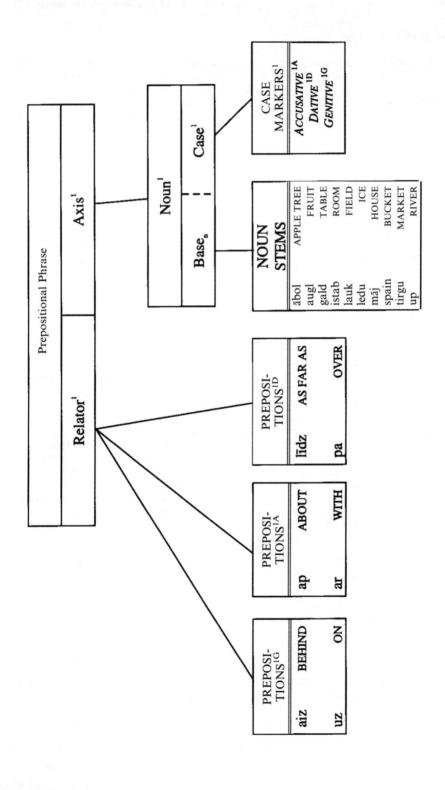

Figure 4.9 Solution to prepositional case government in Latvian

previous section. In both instances, there is a governing word (the preposition or the noun) whose classification correlates with an inflection on the governed word (case in the noun or noun phrase, and gender on adjectives or other adjuncts). More will be said about this comparison when the overall classification of phrase-level congruence is discussed in the next section.

While government involving adpositions in correlation with cases is doubtless the best-known kind of phrase-internal government, there are some other kinds which can appropriately be mentioned and exemplified here. One very frequent type involves the grammatical number of nouns in correlation with numerals and other quantifying words. This phenomenon occurs in English as well as most European languages. Its occurrence in English is exemplified in Table 4.9. This data combines the simple number concord of demonstratives, as seen earlier, with another phenomenon describable as follows: when there is no quantifier, one is free to choose either a *SINGULAR* or a *PLURAL* as long as any demonstrative agrees in number with the noun at Head position; when we select a quantifier, however, we can only select *SINGULAR* with *one*, and only select *PLURAL* with one of the other specific and non-specific quantifiers shown. (It might seem that this is more a semantic notion than a grammatical one, but some languages do not have the same requirement, and some in fact require a *SINGULAR* with any quantifier.)

Table 4.9 Number government and concord in the English noun phrase

1.	*this book*	11.	*these five old boats*
2.	*this one book*	12.	*those two new bushes*
3.	*that house*	13.	*my six aunts*
4.	*that one house*	14.	*your eight little books*
5.	*these houses*	15.	*their nine new cars*
6.	*these four houses*	16.	*his several young nephews*
7.	*those books*	17.	*his one old boat*
8.	*those ten books*	18.	*my one car*
9.	*these seven big men*	19.	*the few stories*
10.	*those three little boys*	20.	*the one good nephew*

A solution to this data is shown in Figure 4.10. When no quantifier is selected, we have simple concord as for the simple data presented in Table 4.1 and solved in Figure 4.2. But when a quantifier is present, its classification as singular or plural governs the selection of number on the other constituents involved. It should be noted that augmented superscripts have been introduced for number (^{1S} and ^{1P}). This must be done when anything beyond simple concord is to be accounted for.

The final example of government at the rank of the phrase is provided by the German noun phrases in Table 4.10. If we look first at items 1–15, we see what appear to be three different genders affecting the inflection of the determiners. In the second half of the data, however, the same nouns and adjectives are used with different determiners, and while the determiners show some gender distinctions, the descriptive adjectives apparently functioning as Modifiers also show gender differences, which seem to be absent when the same adjectives are used in the first half of the data. The differences in adjective inflection here depend on a classification of the words in Determiner position. The definite article and the other determiners seen in items 1–15 belong to one class and require one form of adjective inflection, while the mostly possessive determiners in items 16–30 belong to a different class and require a different adjective inflection, which clearly reflects gender as well. In edited form, some representative examples from this data would be as follows.

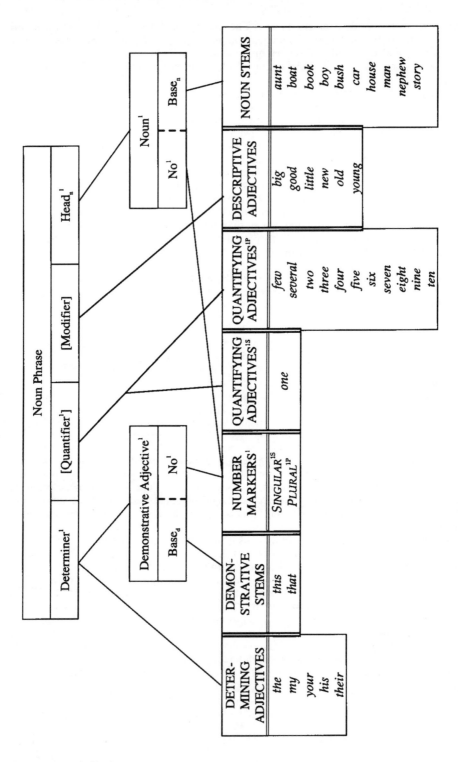

Figure 4.10 Solution to English noun phrases with government and concord for number

1	d	arm	Bruder	16	mein	arm	Bruder
	MASCULINE	MASCULINE DEFINITE			MASCULINE	MASCULINE POSSESSIVE	
6	d	arm	Kind	21	mein	gut	Auge
	NEUTER	NEUTER DEFINITE			NEUTER	NEUTER POSSESSIVE	
11	d	arm	Schwester	26	mein	arm	Schwester
	FEMININE	FEMININE DEFINITE			FEMININE	FEMININE POSSESSIVE	

In this editing, the genders have been named as they traditionally are in German grammars. Traditional descriptions of the adjective forms, though they account for the facts adequately, do not assign terms for the inflectional categories involved here as clearly as might be possible. For that reason, this editing departs from tradition in assigning the terms DEFINITE and POSSESSIVE on a grammatical dimension which will be called GENUS. We then say that the determining adjectives are divided into two classes which govern the genus selected for the descriptive adjective in Modifier position. The form of this latter adjective may also depend on the gender of the noun that occurs in the Head function. (Further German data would also show the relevance of case and number, but these categories are ignored here, since they do not show up in this limited data set.)

Table 4.10 Government for genus in the German noun phrase

1. *der arme Bruder*	THE POOR BROTHER
2. *dieser gute Löffel*	THIS GOOD SPOON
3. *jeder alter Bruder*	EVERY OLD BROTHER
4. *mancher neue Wagen*	MANY A NEW CAR
5. *jener hohe Berg*	THAT HIGH MOUNTAIN
6. *das arme Kind*	THE POOR CHILD
7. *dieses alte Messer*	THIS OLD KNIFE
8. *jedes gute Buch*	EVERY GOOD BOOK
9. *manches alte Haus*	MANY AN OLD HOUSE
10. *jenes schöne Buch*	THAT PRETTY BOOK
11. *die arme Schwester*	THE POOR SISTER
12. *diese gute Katze*	THIS GOOD CAT
13. *jede alte Stadt*	EVERY OLD CITY
14. *manche schöne Frau*	MANY A PRETTY WOMAN
15. *jene neue Gabel*	THAT NEW FORK
16. *mein armer Bruder*	MY POOR BROTHER
17. *unser alter Löffel*	OUR OLD SPOON
18. *sein guter Wagen*	HIS GOOD CAR
19. *ihr neuer Sohn*	HER NEW SON
20. *kein schöner Berg*	NO PRETTY MOUNTAIN
21. *mein gutes Auge*	MY GOOD EYE
22. *unser neues Haus*	OUR NEW HOUSE
23. *sein kleines Messer*	HIS LITTLE KNIFE
24. *ihr altes Buch*	HER OLD BOOK
25. *kein hohes Kind*	NO TALL CHILD
26. *meine arme Schwester*	MY POOR SISTER
27. *unsere alte Gabel*	OUR OLD FORK
28. *seine neue Frau*	HIS NEW WIFE
29. *ihre gute Katze*	HER GOOD CAT
30. *keine schöne Stadt*	NO PRETTY CITY

Note: Though evidence is lacking here, it should be assumed that the modifier position is optional for this problem.

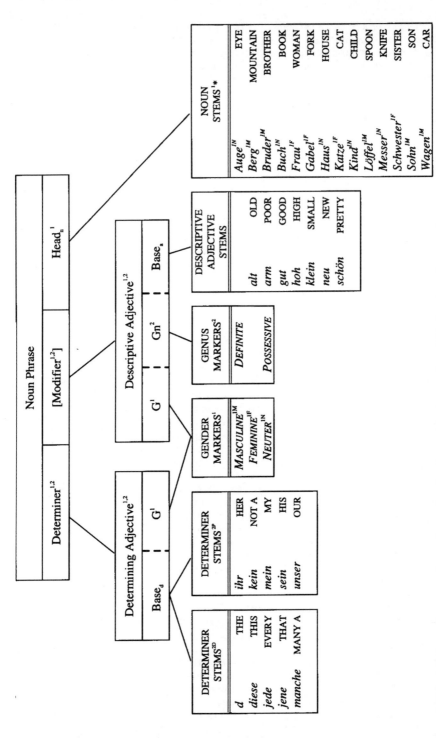

Note: * This solution adopts an alternative style of representing the genders. This involves the use of an augmented superscript indicating the gender of each individual noun rather than a separate box for each gender class. This achieves more economy in terms of the number of boxes used, but requires one to write more explicit superscripts.

Figure 4.11 Solution to gender concord and genus in German noun phrases

An account of these phrases is given in Figure 4.11, which uses the superscript [1] for gender and [2] for genus. In the gender concord, the classification of the Head governs the forms of the two adjuncts, while in the genus government, the classification of the determining adjective governs the genus inflection of the descriptive adjective.

Types of phrasal congruence

According to the titles used for the three previous sections in this chapter, there ought to be three basic types of grammatical ties between constituents at the rank of the phrase: SIMPLE CONCORD, GENDER CONCORD, and GRAMMATICAL GOVERNMENT. Judging from these names, furthermore, they ought to be classified as follows:

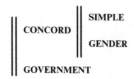

If we consider the more formal treatment of these phenomena, however, we find that gender concord is actually much more like government than it is like simple concord. Many, but not all, linguists have simply overlooked these resemblances in treating the gender phenomenon as a variety of concord rather than a kind of government. Based on these considerations of formalism, however, the classification of these phenomena should look more like this:

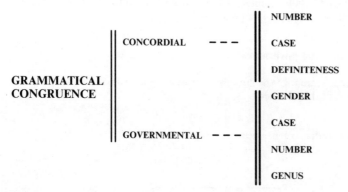

This outline, it should be noted, goes on to specify the grammatical categorial dimensions that may be affected by each of the phenomena, as they have been illustrated in this chapter. In the case of simple concord, now termed CONCORDIAL GRAMMATICAL CONGRUENCE, there is not much we can say beyond the listing of these categories and the fact that all of the phrasal examples we have seen so far occur within the noun phrase.

The other basic variety, GOVERNMENTAL GRAMMATICAL CONGRUENCE, however, can be classified in greater detail if we consider the syntactic function and class of the governors and governed words. Such a classification is summarized in Table 4.11. Here, the more traditional terms for each type are given in the first column. The very traditional term GENDER CONCORD is given the alternative designation GENDER GOVERNMENTAL CONCORD in recognition of the contribution of Charles F. Hockett to the discussion of this question. In a 1958 textbook, Hockett explicitly recognized the similarities between traditional gender concord and government, setting both apart from simple concord, and in this connection he set forth the term GOVERNMENTAL CONCORD to apply to the gender phenomenon. It can be seen from Table 4.11 that this kind of governmental congruence is the only variety in which a head functions as the governor.

Table 4.11 Classification of governmental grammatical congruence

Traditional term	Governor (classified word)		Governed (inflected word)		
	Function	Type	Function	Type	Inflectional category
gender (governmental) concord	Head	Noun	Adjunct(s)	Various Adjectives	gender
adpositional case government	Relator	Adposition	Axis	Noun/ Pronoun Phrase	case
quantifier number government	Quantifier	Numeral/ Qualifying Adjective	Head	Noun	number
determiner genus government	Determiner	Determining Adjective	Modifier	Descriptive Adjective	genus

The present classification is limited, of course, by the fact that only phrase constructions have been considered in this chapter. Further examples of both varieties of grammatical congruence will be found in later chapters, and this classification will be extended and refined as these new examples are identified and discussed.

Notations for concord and government

The following outlines summarize the notations for treating the various kinds of concord and government discussed in this chapter.

A.   Concord (= concordial congruence)

1.   Diagram

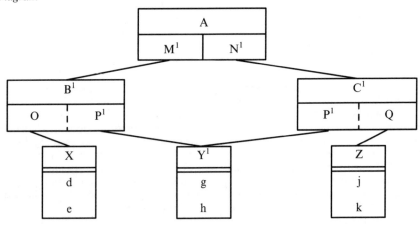

2.   List of well-formed combinations

(d · g) (j · g)	(e · g) (j · g)
(d · g) (k · g)	(e · g) (k · g)
(d · h) (j · h)	(e · h) (j · h)
(d · h) (k · h)	(e · h) (k · h)

3.   Explanation and commentary

a.   A–C are labels for constructions.
b.   M–Q are labels for constituents.
c.   X–Z are labels for vocabulary classes.
d.   Lower case letters are labels for vocabulary items.
e.   The superscript [1] shows that the constituents M and N show CONCORD with respect to the vocabulary selection involved in Y. Intermediate uses of [1] in boxes B, C, and P indicate the continuity of the concord relation. Cf. further point i.
f.   Simple concord can affect two or more constituents of a construction, and each constituent so affected will be assigned the appropriate numerical superscript.
g.   When simple concord applies to more than one selection of categories, each category involved should be assigned its own superscript numeral: [1], [2], [3], ... as necessary.
h.   When a constituent involved in concord is optional in a construction, the appropriate superscript(s) should be placed inside of the square brackets indicating optionality.
i.   The initial indication of concord is essentially a potential: it actually applies only if the further construction or class selected to manifest each involved constituent is itself of a concording type, as indicated by its carrying the appropriate superscript on its constituent label. For example, an alternate manifestation of constituent N in the sample diagram might be construction D, which does not carry a superscript [1]. In such a case, no actual concord would be involved with this constituent, even if some of the further constituents of construction D had the superscripts due to a concord of their own. This explains the necessity of chaining the superscripts through all the constructions, constituents, and classes involved until the vocabulary box is reached.
j.   In the sample, only one layer of additional constructions is shown between the initial concording construction and the vocabulary, but potentially there may be several layers of constructions before the vocabulary boxes are reached.
k.   Concord typically occurs between heads and attributes in endocentric (headed) constructions, or between subjects (and sometimes objects) and predicators in a predicative construction. The latter phenomena will be detailed in Chapter 6.
l.   Concord most often involves such grammatical category selections as NUMBER, CASE, and/or DEFINITENESS.

B.   Governmental congruence

1.   Diagram

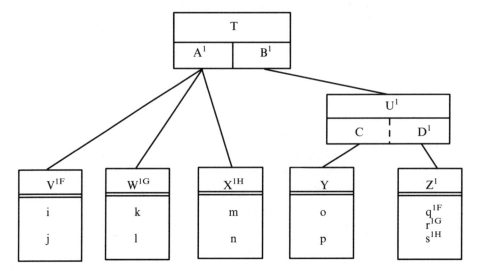

2.   List of well-formed combinations

i (o · q)	k (o · r)	m (o · s)
i (p · q)	k (p · r)	m (p · s)
j (o · q)	l (o · r)	n (o · s)
j (p · q)	l (p · r)	n (p · s)

3. Explanation and commentary

a.   T and U are labels for constructions.
b.   A–D are labels for constituents.
c.   V–Z are labels for classes.
d.   Lower case letters are labels for vocabulary items.
e.   The superscript ^{1} shows that A and B are in a relationship of either GOVERNMENT or GOVERNMENTAL CONCORD according to which the selection of a vocabulary item in class Z (an inflection) is governed by a particular class (V, W, or X) which is selected to manifest constituent A.
f.   A may be termed the GOVERNING CONSTITUENT and B the GOVERNED CONSTITUENT.
g.   Beyond the governed constituent, superscripts are carried through to vocabulary classes in the same manner as for simple concord.
h.   In addition, there are augmented superscripts on each member of class Z, correlated with superscripts on the labels for the different governing classes. In an augmented superscript, the number assigned to the general category selection (gender, case, etc.) is augmented by a small capital letter standing for the particular choice demanded. Here the small capitals F G H show the correlation between classes V, W, X and the inflectional markers q, r, s, respectively.

i.   The ultimate governing items will normally be classes, as shown here, but they could conceivably be different constructions at some level. In either case, superscripts are carried through to the level of the governed items, which will show the corresponding augmented superscripts.

j.   GOVERNMENTAL CONCORD typically occurs either in an endocentric (headed) construction with the head as governing and one or more attributes as governed or else in a predicative construction with the subject or object as governing and the predicated as governed. It typically applies to gender, animateness, or similar classifications.

k.   GOVERNMENT involves the same basic relationship as governmental concord, but applies to situations other than those outlined in (j). In relator-axis constructions, the relator is typically governing and the axis is governed (especially with respect to CASE). In predicative constructions, government typically also affects case, with the predicate as governing and an object as governed.

l.   Like simple concord, governmental concord can affect more than two constituents, in which case one of these is governing and the others are all governed.

m.   When government or governmental concord affects more than one selection of categories, each should be assigned its own number, and these numbers should be further kept distinct from those used for simple concord in the same construction.

n.   Remarks h, i, and j given for simple concord apply equally to government and governmental concord.

Exercises

A.   Interpretation problems

1.   *Gothic noun phrase*

The following diagram sketches the structure of the noun phrase in Gothic (an ancient Germanic language of southeastern Europe). Use this account as the basis for answering the questions below.

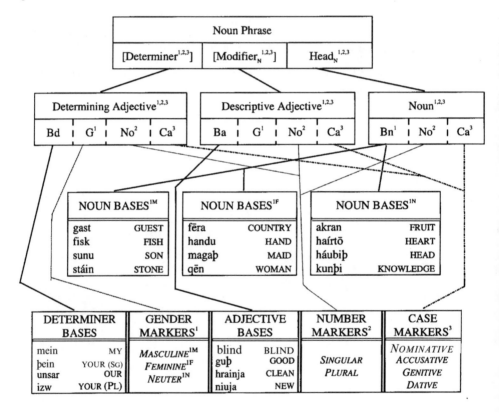

a. On the basis of the diagram, show the (edited) Gothic phrases with following meanings. Show simultaneous properties one above the other. In relation to the case system, assume the Subject glosses imply the *NOMINATIVE*, Object glosses imply the *ACCUSATIVE*, OF implies the *GENITIVE*, and TO the *DATIVE*.

1. MY GUEST (Subject)

    _____

2. OF A GOOD HAND

    _____

3. OUR BLIND FISHES (Object)

    _____

4. TO YOUR (pl) CLEAN FRUIT

    _____

5. OF A NEW MAID

    _____

b. For the phrases in 3 and 5 above, show the complete structure in a boxed diagram.

2.   *Latin prepositional and noun phrases*

The diagram belowsketches some aspects of the structure of the Latin prepositional phrase and the associated noun phrase. Use this account as the basis for answering the following questions.

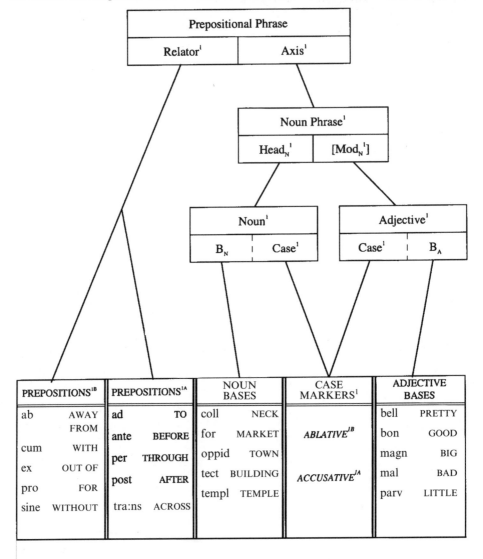

a.   On the basis of the diagram, show the Latin expressions corresponding to the following meanings in edited form, indicating simultaneous properties one above the other as in the previous problem from Gothic. The English articles do not require Latin translations.

1.   WITHOUT A LARGE TEMPLE

2.   TO THE BIG TOWN

                      /

_____

3.   AWAY FROM THE MARKET

_____

4.   THROUGH THE LITTLE NECK

_____

5.   WITH A GOOD BUILDING

_____

b.   For the phrases in 2 and 5 above, show the complete structure in a boxed diagram.

B.   Extension problems

1. Polish

The following data is an extension of what was presented in Table 4.3 and analysed in Figure 4.4. Decide what revisions of the figure are necessary to account for the total set of data. Describe these changes succinctly in prose and then present the revised diagram reflecting them.

25.	ten mawy kot	THIS LITTLE CAT (Subject)
26.	tego mawego kota	THIS LITTLE CAT (Object)/OF THIS LITTLE CAT
27.	te mawe koty	THESE LITTLE CATS (Subject/Object)
28.	tyx mawyx kotuf	OF THESE LITTLE CATS
29.	ten koń	THIS HORSE (Subject)
30.	tego końa	THIS HORSE (Object)/OF THIS HORSE
31.	te końe	THESE HORSES (Subject/Object)
32.	tyx końi	OF THESE HORSES
33.	pjĕkny pjes	THE/A BEAUTIFUL DOG (Subject)
34.	pjĕknego psa	THE/A BEAUTIFUL DOG (Object)/OF THE/A BEAUTIFUL DOG
35.	pjĕkne psy	(THE) BEAUTIFUL DOGS (Subject/Object)
36.	pjĕknyx psuf	OF (THE) BEAUTIFUL DOGS
37.	ten novy koźow	THIS NEW GOAT (Subject)
38.	tego novego kozwa	THIS NEW GOAT (Object)/OF THIS NEW GOAT
39.	te nove kozwy	THESE NEW GOATS (Subject/Object)
40.	tyx novyx kozwuf	OF THESE NEW GOATS
41.	mawy byk	THE/A LITTLE BULL (Subject)
42.	mawego byka	THE/A LITTLE BULL (Object)/OF THE/A LITTLE BULL
43.	mawe ptaki	THE/A LITTLE BIRDS (Subject/Object)
44.	mawyx ptakuf	OF THE/A LITTLE BIRDS
45.	psy	(THE) DOGS (Subject/Object)
46.	kotuf	OF (THE) CATS

47.	końa	THE/A HORSE (Object)/OF THE/A HORSE
48.	to mawe može	THIS LITTLE SEA (Subject/Object)
49.	tego mawego moža	OF THIS LITTLE SEA
50.	te mawe moža	THESE LITTLE SEAS (Subject/Object)
51.	tyx mawyx muš	OF THESE LITTLE SEAS
52.	to śedwo	THIS SADDLE (Subject/Object)
53.	tego śedwa	OF THIS SADDLE
54.	te śedwa	THESE SADDLES (Subject/Object)
55.	tyx śeduw	OF THESE SADDLES
56.	pjĕkne mjasto	THE/A BEAUTIFUL CITY (Subject/Object)
57.	pjĕknego mjasta	OF THE/A BEAUTIFUL CITY
58.	pjĕkne mjasta	(THE) BEAUTIFUL CITIES (Subject/Object)
59.	pjĕknyx mjast	OF (THE) BEAUTIFUL CITIES
60.	ta nove pole	THIS NEW FIELD (Subject/Object)
61.	tego novego pola	OF THIS NEW FIELD
62.	mawe okno	THE/A LITTLE WINDOW (Subject/Object)
63.	mawego okna	OF THE/A LITTLE WINDOW
64.	pola	(THE) FIELDS (Subject/Object)
65.	okjen	OF (THE) WINDOWS
66.	mjasta	(THE) CITIES (Subject/Object)

2. Hindi

Consider the following data as an addition to the Hindi data set in Table 4.4. On the basis of the total material, decide how the solution in Figure 4.5 needs to be modified in order to account for it. Describe the changes succinctly in prose and then present the revised diagram reflecting them.

15.	acc^{h}e kamre	(THE) GOOD ROOMS
16.	acc^{h}i· mezẽ	(THE) GOOD TABLES
17.	c^{h}ote a·dmi·	(THE) SMALL MEN
18.	c^{h}oti· larkiyã·	(THE) SMALL GIRLS
19.	naye g^{h}ar	(THE) NEW HOUSES
20.	nayi· pustakẽ	(THE) NEW BOOKS
21.	bare deš	(THE) BIG COUNTRIES
22.	bari· ciriyã·	(THE) BIG BIRDS
23.	sa·f kamre	(THE) CLEAN ROOMS
24.	sa·f mezẽ	(THE) CLEAN TABLES
25.	sundar deš	(THE) BEAUTIFUL COUNTRIES
26.	sundar larkiyã·	(THE) BEAUTIFUL GIRLS
27.	la·l g^{h}ar	(THE) RED HOUSES
28.	la·l pustakẽ	(THE) RED BOOKS

3. Latvian noun phrases

The following Latvian noun phrase data should be added to that presented for editing in Problem B.1 in Chapter 2. Present a solution to the total data set produced in this way, as edited.

21.	laba istaba	A GOOD ROOM (Subj)	21a.	laba: istaba	THE GOOD ROOM (Subj)
22.	labu istabu	A GOOD ROOM (Obj)	22a.	labo istabu	THE GOOD ROOM (Obj)
23.	labas istabas	GOOD ROOMS (Subj/Obj)	23a.	laba:s istabas	THE GOOD ROOMS (Subj/Obj)
24.	jauka ma:sa	A NICE SISTER (Subj)	24a.	jauka: ma:sa	THE NICE SISTER (Subj)

25.	jauku ma:su	A NICE SISTER (Obj)		25a.	jauko ma:su	THE NICE SISTER (Obj)
26.	jaukas ma:sas	NICE SISTERS (Subj/Obj)		26a.	jauka:s ma:sas	THE NICE SISTERS (Subj/Obj)
27.	liela sirts	A BIG HEART (Subj)		27a.	liela: sirts	THE BIG HEART (Subj)
28.	lielu sirdi	A BIG HEART (Obj)		28a.	lielo sirdi	THE BIG HEART (Obj)
29.	lielas sirdis	BIG HEARTS (Subj/Obj)		29a.	liela:s sirdis	THE BIG HEARTS (Subj/Obj)
30.	laba ma:te	A GOOD MOTHER (Subj)		30a.	laba: ma:te	THE GOOD MOTHER (Subj)
31.	labu ma:ti	A GOOD MOTHER (Obj)		31a.	labo ma:ti	THE GOOD MOTHER (Obj)
32.	labas ma:tes	GOOD MOTHERS (Subj/Obj)		32a.	laba:s ma:tes	THE GOOD MOTHERS (Subj/Obj)
33.	liela govs	A BIG COW (Subj)		33a.	liela: govs	THE BIG COW (Subj)
34.	lielu govi	A BIG COW (Obj)		34a.	lielo govi	THE BIG COW (Obj)
35.	lielas govis	BIG COWS (Subj/Obj)		35a.	liela:s govis	THE BIG COWS (Subj/Obj)
36.	jauka gra:mata	A NICE BOOK (Subj)		36a.	jauka: gra:mata	THE NICE BOOK (Subj)
37.	jauku gra:matu	A NICE BOOK (Obj)		37a.	jauko gra:matu	THE NICE BOOK (Obj)
38.	jaukas gra:matas	NICE BOOKS (Subj/Obj)		38a.	jauka:s gra:matas	THE NICE BOOKS (Subj/Obj)

4. Noun phrases in Modern Israeli Hebrew

Definiteness and number concord in Hebrew was illustrated in Table 4.2 and solved in Figure 4.3. Add the following data to the original set, and revise the figure as necessary to accommodate the additional concord patterns and vocabulary.

1.	šaxen	A NEIGHBOR	1d.	šaxen xaxam	A SMART NEIGHBOR
1a.	šaxenim	NEIGHBORS	1e.	šaxenim xaxamim	SMART NEIGHBORS
1b.	hašaxen	THE NEIGHBOR	1f.	hašaxen haxaxam	THE SMART NEIGHBOR
1c.	hašaxenim	THE NEIGHBORS	1g.	hašaxenim haxaxamim	THE SMART NEIGHBORS
2.	ʔaruxa	A MEAL	2d.	ʔaruxa tova	A GOOD MEAL
2a.	ʔaruxot	MEALS	2e.	ʔaruxot tovot	GOOD MEALS
2b.	haʔaruxa	THE MEAL	2f.	haʔaruxa hatova	THE GOOD MEAL
2c.	haʔaruxot	THE MEALS	2g.	haʔaruxot hatovot	THE GOOD MEALS
3.	šiʔur	A LESSON	3d.	šiʔur kal	AN EASY LESSON
3a.	šiʔurim	LESSONS	3e.	šiʔurim kalim	EASY LESSONS
3b.	haši?ur	THE LESSON	3f.	haši?ur hakal	THE EASY LESSON
3c.	haši?urim	THE LESSONS	3g.	haši?urim hakalim	THE EASY LESSONS
4.	baxura	A GIRL	4d.	baxura nexmada	A NICE GIRL
4a.	baxurot	GIRLS	4e.	baxurot nexmadot	NICE GIRLS
4b.	habaxura	THE GIRL	4f.	habaxura hanexmada	THE NICE GIRL
4c.	habaxurot	THE GIRLS	4g.	habaxurot hanexmadot	THE NICE GIRLS
5.	talmid	A PUPIL	5d.	talmid xadaš	A NEW PUPIL
5a.	talmidim	PUPILS	5e.	talmidim xadašim	NEW PUPILS
5b.	hatalmid	THE PUPIL	5f.	hatalmid haxadaš	THE NEW PUPIL
5c.	hatalmidim	THE PUPILS	5g.	hatalmidim haxadašim	THE NEW PUPILS
6.	šaʔa	AN HOUR	6d.	šaʔa rišona	A FIRST HOUR
6a.	šaʔot	HOURS	6e.	šaʔot rišonot	FIRST HOURS
6b.	hašaʔa	HOUR	6f.	hašaʔa harišona	THE FIRST HOUR
6c.	hašaʔot	HOURS	6g.	hašaʔot harišonot	THE FIRST HOURS
7.	sakin	A KNIFE	7d.	sakin nexmad	A NICE KNIFE
7a.	sakinim	KNIVES	7e.	sakinim nexmadim	NICE KNIVES
7b.	hasakin	THE KNIFE	7f.	hasakin hanexmad	THE NICE KNIFE
7c.	hasakinim	THE KNIVES	7g.	hasakinim hanexmadim	THE NICE KNIVES
8.	mora	A TEACHER (Fem)	8d.	mora xaxama	A SMART TEACHER
8a.	morot	TEACHERS	8e.	morot xaxamot	SMART TEACHERS
8b.	hamora	THE TEACHER	8f.	hamora haxaxama	THE SMART TEACHER
8c.	hamorot	THE TEACHERS	8g.	hamorot haxaxamot	THE SMART TEACHERS

9.	mixtav	A LETTER	9d.	mixtav tov	A GOOD LETTER
9a.	mixtavim	LETTERS	9e.	mixtavim tovim	GOOD LETTERS
9b.	hamixtav	THE LETTER	9f.	hamixtav hatov	THE GOOD LETTER
9c.	hamixtavim	THE LETTERS	9g.	hamixtavim hatovim	THE GOOD LETTERS
10.	hacaga	PLAY	10d.	hacaga kala	AN EASY PLAY
10a.	hacagot	PLAYS	10e.	hacagot kalot	EASY PLAYS
10b.	hahacaga	THE PLAY	10f.	hahacaga hakala	THE EASY PLAY
10c.	hahacagot	THE PLAYS	10g.	hahacagot hakalot	THE EASY PLAYS
11.	xaver	A FRIEND	11d.	xaver rišon	A FIRST FRIEND
11a	xaverim	FRIENDS	11e.	xaverim rišonim	FIRST FRIENDS
11b.	haxaver	THE FRIEND	11f.	haxaver harišon	THE FIRST FRIEND
11c.	haxaverim	THE FRIENDS	11g.	haxaverim harišonim	THE FIRST FRIENDS
12.	para	A COW	12d.	para xadaša	A NEW COW
12a.	parot	COWS	12e.	parot xadašot	NEW COWS
12b.	hapara	THE COW	12f.	hapara haxadaša	THE NEW COW
12c.	haparot	THE COWS	12g.	haparot haxadašot	THE NEW COWS

C.   Additional problems

1.   Noun phrases in Dutch

a   The following data set provides evidence for gender concord in Dutch. Determine the number of genders, edit the data, and prepare a solution.

1.	*de vrouw*	THE WOMAN	17.	*het varken*	THE PIG
2.	*deze vrouw*	THIS WOMAN	18.	*dit varken*	THIS PIG
3.	*die vrouw*	THAT WOMAN	19.	*dat varken*	THAT PIG
4.	*onze vrouw*	OUR WOMAN	20.	*ons varken*	OUR PIG
5.	*de man*	THE MAN	21.	*het brood*	THE BREAD
6.	*deze man*	THIS MAN	22.	*dit brood*	THIS BREAD
7.	*die man*	THAT MAN	23.	*dat brood*	THAT BREAD
8.	*onze man*	OUR MAN	24.	*ons brood*	OUR BREAD
9.	*de pen*	THE PEN	25.	*het vest*	THE WAISTCOAT
10.	*deze jas*	THIS COAT	26.	*dit kantoor*	THIS OFFICE
11.	*die broer*	THAT BROTHER	27.	*dat bord*	THAT PLATE
12.	*onze vriend*	OUR FRIEND	28.	*ons boek*	OUR BOOK
13.	*de deur*	THE DOOR	29.	*het schaap*	THE SHEEP
14.	*deze hond*	THIS DOG	30.	*dit kopje*	THIS CUP
15.	*die vork*	THAT FORK	31.	*dat huis*	THAT HOUSE
16.	*onze moeder*	OUR MOTHER	32.	*ons glas*	OUR GLASS

b   The following data set can be seen as an expansion of the previous problem, in that it adds additional kinds of concord to the gender already illustrated. Determine the number and type of concord categories, edit the data, and prepare a solution encompassing both data sets.

33.	*de man*	THE MAN	57.	*het boek*	THE BOOK
34.	*de goede man*	THE GOOD MAN	58.	*het goede boek*	THE GOOD BOOK
35.	*de mannen*	THE MEN	59.	*de boeken*	THE BOOKS
36.	*de goede mannen*	THE GOOD MEN	60.	*de goede boeken*	THE GOOD BOOKS
37.	*een man*	A MAN	61.	*een boek*	A BOOK
38.	*een goede man*	A GOOD MAN	62.	*een goed boek*	A GOOD BOOK
39.	*mannen*	MEN	63.	*boeken*	BOOKS
40.	*goede mannen*	GOOD MEN	64.	*goede boeken*	GOOD BOOKS

41.	*de oom*	THE UNCLE	65. *het schip*	THE SHIP
42.	*de oude oom*	THE OLD UNCLE	66. *het oude schip*	THE OLD SHIP
43.	*de ooms*	THE UNCLES	67. *de schepen*	THE SHIPS
44.	*de oude ooms*	THE OLD UNCLES	68. *de oude schepen*	THE OLD SHIPS
45.	*een oom*	AN UNCLE	69. *een schip*	A SHIP
46.	*een oude oom*	AN OLD UNCLE	70. *een oud schip*	AN OLD SHIP
47.	*ooms*	UNCLES	71. *schepen*	SHIPS
48.	*oude ooms*	OLD UNCLES	72. *oude schepen*	OLD SHIPS
49.	*de stoel*	THE CHAIR	73. *het kind*	THE CHILD
50.	*de kleine stoel*	THE LITTLE CHAIR	74. *het kleine kind*	THE LITTLE CHILD
51.	*de stoelen*	THE CHAIRS	75. *de kinden*	THE CHILDREN
52.	*de kleine stoelen*	THE LITTLE CHAIRS	76. *de kleine kinden*	THE LITTLE CHILDREN
53.	*een stoel*	A CHAIR	77. *een kind*	A CHILD
54.	*een kleine stoel*	A LITTLE CHAIR	78. *een klein kind*	A LITTLE CHILD
55.	*stoelen*	CHAIRS	79. *kinden*	CHILDREN
56.	*kleine stoelen*	LITTLE CHAIRS	80. *kleine kinden*	LITTLE CHILDREN

2. Modern Greek

This data illustrates the government of nominal case by prepositions in Modern Greek. Determine the number of distinct cases needed, edit the data and prepare a solution.

1.	apó ton potamó	FROM THE RIVER
2.	xorís ton potamó	WITHOUT THE RIVER
3.	enandíon tu potamú	AGAINST THE RIVER
4.	eksetías tu potamú	BECAUSE OF THE RIVER
5.	apó ton ánθropo	FROM THE MAN
6.	xorís ton ánθropo	WITHOUT THE MAN
7.	enandíon tu ánθropu	AGAINST THE MAN
8.	eksetías tu ánθropu	BECAUSE OF THE MAN
9.	apó ton pólemo	FROM THE WAR
10.	xorís ton pólemo	WITHOUT THE WAR
11.	enandíon tu pólemu	AGAINST THE WAR
12.	eksetías tu pólemu	BECAUSE OF THE WAR
13.	apó tin kiría	FROM THE LADY
14.	xorís tin kiría	WITHOUT THE LADY
15.	enandíon tis kirías	AGAINST THE LADY
16.	eksetías tis kirías	BECAUSE OF THE LADY
17.	apó tin θési	FROM THE PLACE
18.	xorís tin θési	WITHOUT THE PLACE
19.	enandíon tis θésis	AGAINST THE PLACE
20.	eksetías tis θésis	BECAUSE OF THE PLACE
21.	apó tin θálassa	FROM THE SEA
22.	xorís tin θálassa	WITHOUT THE SEA
23.	enandíon tis θálassas	AGAINST THE SEA
24.	eksetías tis θálassas	BECAUSE OF THE SEA

Terminology

AUGMENTED SUPERSCRIPT	GOVERNMENT
	= GOVERNMENTAL CONGRUENCE
CLASSIFIER	GOVERNED
	GOVERNOR
CONCORD	
= CONCORDIAL CONGRUENCE	SUPERSCRIPTS
= SIMPLE CONCORD	
GENDER CONCORD	

5

Phrase coordination

Basic varieties of coordination

When two or more phrases or words jointly fulfill some kind of grammatical role in a larger structure, languages commonly have particular grammatical devices to use to join them into a larger unit. Table 5.1 illustrates some common devices of this type as applied to English phrases. As this material shows, English uses special words, termed CONJUNCTIONS in the usual grammatical tradition, to link words and phrases in five different patterns. The conjunction *and*, which indicates a combination, is traditionally called CONJUNCTIVE, in contrast to *or*, which indicates an alternative, and is called DISJUNCTIVE. Beyond these two simple patterns, three others are shown. These are called CORRELATIVE, because they use two different words correlated together, one before the first main phrase and the other before the second. The terms conjunctive and disjunctive are applied to the patterns using *both ... and* and *either ... or*, respectively, and the third correlative pattern, using *neither ... nor*, is simply called NEGATIVE in the terminology suggested. Since it does indeed negate both of its associated terms, it could properly be called NEGATIVE CONJUNCTIVE, though its forms are morphologically related to the correlative disjunctives. The general use of conjunctions or other grammatical devices for joining words, phrases, or other units in a language is termed COORDINATION or CONJOINING.

It has long been recognized that in order to fit into any of these patterns of conjoining, the words or phrases must have functional similarity. This does not necessarily mean that their internal structure will be similar. So, for example, we would think it strange for an English speaker to use *and* to join expressions of different functions, as in an example like *She went yesterday and to the city*, where it seems very odd to join the temporal expression *yesterday* with the locational expression *to the city*. It should be noted that the problem lies in the differences of function rather than the differences of internal structure. So even if the temporal and locational are both expressed by prepositional phrases, it is not any more acceptable: *She went in the spring and to the city* is just as strange as the previous example. A seeming exception to this is seen in *She went then and there*. In this case we are dealing with a special idiom, a set phrase, and its meaning is usually more temporal (IMMEDIATELY) than locational. Another such set phrase is *here and now*, which uses the component expressions in the opposite order. Neither of these is acceptable when used in reverse (no *there and then* or *now and here*) and they cannot serve as models for coordinating other combinations of temporal and locational expressions. *Here and now*, furthermore, most commonly functions as a kind of noun.

In other European languages there are generally similar patterns, but some of them differ in more than just the particular words used. Table 5.2 shows a comparison between the English conjunctions used and their equivalents in a selection of European languages. The most striking differences come in the use of repeated instances of the simple conjunction to translate the correlative cases in English, as generally found in Latin and the Romance and some Slavic languages (represented here by Russian). Modern Greek agrees with these latter regarding the conjunctives and negatives, but is unique in using a different word (/ite/) for the disjunctive "correlatives" than for the simple disjunctive (/i/). Slovenian follows the Romance/Russian pattern only in the negative, and is otherwise close to the German pattern. In the table, the term "correlative" has been put in quotation marks because it is not really appropriate to cases where the same word is used in both positions. In that case the term MULTIPLE (or perhaps REPLICATIVE) would be more appropriate.

Table 5.1 Basic examples of phrase coordination

Simple conjunctive
1. **John and Rob** *manage the store.*
2. *I found* **your cat and my dog** *in the yard.*
3. *The trip was* **relaxing and leisurely.**
4. *Sean* **neatly mowed and thoroughly watered** *the lawn.*

Simple disjunctive
5. *I'll leave the key with* **Aunt Sarah or Uncle Max.**
6. *We don't want a* **large or elaborate** *ceremony.*
7. *They tried not to* **hurt or injure** *anyone.*
8. *It should be done* **quickly or not at all.**

Correlative conjunctive
9. **Both Pat and Lynn** *missed the party.*
10. *We thoroughly searched* **both there and across the street.**
11. *Aunt Matilda can speak* **both French and German.**
12. *It should be completed* **both thoroughly and neatly.**

Correlative disjunctive
13. **Either Marie or Suzanne** *will be there to help you.*
14. *The key will be* **either under the mat or on the ledge.**
15. *He needs to* **either borrow some money or postpone his trip.**
16. *You need* **either a lot of skill or great self-confidence** *to do that.*

Correlative negative
17. **Neither our friends nor their neighbors** *were at home.*
18. *He would* **neither encourage nor tolerate** *that activity.*
19. *We saw it* **neither beside nor behind** *the house.*
20. *They could finish it* **neither quickly nor easily.**

Table 5.2 Comparative table of conjunctions in some European languages

	English	German	Latin	Spanish	Russian	Slovenian	Modern Greek
SIMPLE CONJUNCTIVE	*and*	*und*				*in*	
"CORRELATIVE" CONJUNCTIVE 1	*both*	*sowohl*	*et*	*y (e)*	*i*	*tako*	/ke/
"CORRELATIVE" CONJUNCTIVE 2	*and*	*als*				*kator*	
SIMPLE DISJUNCTIVE	*or*	*oder*				*ali*	/i/
"CORRELATIVE" DISJUNCTIVE 1	*either*	*entweder*	*aut*	*o (u)*	*ili*	*bodisi*	/i/ ~ /ite/
"CORRELATIVE" DISJUNCTIVE 2	*or*	*oder*				*ali*	
"CORRELATIVE" NEGATIVE 1	*neither*	*weder*	*nec*	*ni*	*ni*	*niti*	/mite/ ~
"CORRELATIVE" NEGATIVE 2	*nor*	*noch*					/ute/

In English, it is fairly unusual to coordinate terms without any overt word to mark the relationship, but for simple conjunction this is possible in English and is regularly found much more often in some languages. Coordination marked with an overt word is called SYNDETIC, and the opposite, coordination without an overt marker, is called ASYNDETIC. The one common use of this in English is when giving an incomplete listing, normally at the end of a sentence, as in such an example as *She sells dresses, suits, shoes …*; the selection of this pattern leaves the fairly clear implication that the list is not intended to be exhaustive.

In languages like Mandarin Chinese, asyndetic coordination is used much more regularly, as illustrated by the examples in Table 5.3. This illustrates the coordination of single nouns, pronouns, and noun phrases.

Table 5.3 Asyndetic coordination in Mandarin Chinese

1. Wǒmen yǒu yī ge nǚ'ér	WE HAVE A DAUGHTER.
2. Nǐmen yǒu yī zhī māo	YOU (PL) HAVE A CAT.
3. Tāmen yǒu yī ge nǚ'ér yī zhī māo	THEY HAVE A DAUGHTER AND A CAT.
4. Māo gǒu hěn hǎo	THE CAT AND DOG ARE VERY WELL.
5. Nǐ mǎi bàozhǐ	YOU BUY NEWSPAPERS.
6. Tā mǎi mài shū	HE BUYS AND SELLS BOOKS.
7. Wǒ mài bǐ	I SELL PENS.
8. Tāmen mǎi shū bǐ bàozhǐ	THEY BUY BOOKS, PENS, AND NEWSPAPERS.
9. Nǐ tāmen yǒu shū zázhì	YOU AND THEY HAVE BOOKS AND MAGAZINES.
10. Nǐ mài shū bàozhǐ	YOU SELL BOOKS AND NEWSPAPERS.

Note: In examples 1–3, the word /yī/ is the word for ONE, used here as an indefinite article, and the immediately following words are classifiers appropriate to the nouns which follow.

Position of conjunctions

In all the examples seen so far, single explicit conjunctions come between the first and second of the words or phrases that they join, and in the case of multiple or correlative conjunctions, a conjunction precedes each of the joined items. That this pattern of preposed conjunctions is not universally found, however, is shown by examples like the Yup'ik pattern given in Table 5.4. Here the conjunction meaning AND comes *after* the second word rather than before it. In some languages both patterns are found with different conjunctions, so in Classical Latin we find *et*, functioning about like English *and*, but also *-que*, which works like the Yup'ik conjunction shown.

Table 5.4 Coordination in Central Alaskan Yup'ik Eskimo

1. aŋun	THE MAN
2. aʙnaq	THE WOMAN
3. qimuxta	THE DOG
4. yaqulɨk	THE BIRD
5. aŋun aʙnaq-ɫu	THE MAN AND THE WOMAN
6. aʙnaq qimuxta-ɫu	THE WOMAN AND THE DOG
7. aŋun yaqulɨk-ɫu	THE MAN AND THE BIRD
8. yaqulɨk tuntu-ɫu	THE BIRD AND THE CARIBOU
9. tuntu caʙayak-ɫu	THE CARIBOU AND THE BEAR
10. caʙayak aŋun-ɫu	THE BEAR AND THE MAN
11. iʙniaq aʙnaq-ɫu	THE CHILD AND THE WOMAN
12. kuskaq iʙniaq-ɫu	THE CAT AND THE CHILD

Another possible, but less obvious, case of postposed conjunctions is found in Japanese, as exemplified in Table 5.5. This material illustrates the use of four different conjunctions. The one disjunctive one is /ka/ OR. The other three are conjunctive, and one is specifically used in the multiple (BOTH ... AND) construction. Of the other two, /to/ indicates a complete listing, and may be termed the EXHAUSTIVE conjunctive. In contrast, /ya/, the SELECTIVE conjunctive, indicates that only a partial listing has been given.

Table 5.5 Japanese noun phrase coordination

1. sakana o taberu	HE EATS FISH.
2. hon o yonda	HE READ A BOOK.
3. hon to zassi [to] o yomu	HE READS A BOOK AND A MAGAZINE.
4. sakana to pan [to] o tabeta	HE ATE FISH AND BREAD.
5. pan to sakana to yasai [to] o taberu	HE EATS BREAD, FISH, AND VEGETABLES.
6. sakana ka niku [ka] o kau	HE BUYS FISH OR MEAT.
7. hon ka zassi ka sinbun [ka] o yonda	HE READS A BOOK OR A MAGAZINE OR A NEWSPAPER.
8. sakana mo niku mo tabeta	HE ATE BOTH FISH AND MEAT.
9. pan mo yasai mo tabenai	HE EATS NEITHER BREAD NOR VEGETABLES.
10. zassi ya sinbun o katta	HE BOUGHT MAGAZINES AND* NEWSPAPERS.
11. sinbun ya zassi o yomu	HE READS NEWSPAPERS AND* BOOKS.
12. yasai ya sakana o taberu	HE EATS VEGETABLES AND* FISH.
	*(AMONG OTHER THINGS)

Note: None of the sentences here has an overt subject, so it could be translated into English with any pronoun. The appropriate translation would depend on the linguistic and extra-linguistic context. The single HE is used here purely for convenience.

The conclusion that these various conjunctions are postposed is not immediately obvious in all of the examples. Taken by themselves, examples 10–12, showing the selective conjunctive, seem compatible with the same analysis that would be used for English *and* and *or*. The multiple conjunctive /mo/, however, is repeated **after** each conjoined word, and /to/ and /ka/ may be, though that usage is not obligatory, and is, in fact, uncommon. Another clue to the postposed nature of these items is the fact that they are pronounced within the same phonological contour with the preceding, rather than the following. One pauses, if at all, in other words, after the conjunctions rather than before them. This would not necessarily be decisive, since phonological linkage is not invariably parallel to what we find in grammar. However, given the additional facts about position, the conclusion that we are dealing with postposed conjunctions, parallel in many ways to the postpositions which are also used in Japanese instead of prepositions, seems to be clear. These examples, it should be noted, all involve Direct Objects, and these are normally marked with the postposition /o/, as in most of these examples. Exceptionally, this postposition is omitted after /mo/, as we see in examples 8 and 9.

Formalization of coordination

When it comes to the analysis of coordinate phrases, there are two distinct approaches to the subject. One approach emphasizes the essentially logical fact that if, for instance, two or more noun phrases are coordinated, they equally fulfill whatever larger role the phrase occurs in, whether this is Subject, Direct Object, or whatever. Sometimes this is put in terms of the Head function, saying that each of the coordinated terms is equally the Head of such a phrase. When one is dealing with asyndetic structures, where a simple juxtaposition signals the coordination, this would give a simple structure with two, three, or more heads as the individual case may be. An example is provided in Figure 5.1, for one of the Mandarin Chinese examples in Table 5.3.

This approach works fairly well for examples like this one, but it becomes more problematical when one considers cases where overt conjunctions are used. How can we fit these additional constituents into this kind of model? One answer that has sometimes been suggested is to call them "markers" of the coordination and suggest that they are not full constituents. If we were to try to represent this view in a diagram, some special status for the "markers" would have to be indicated by some sort of special form(s) in that diagram.

Expandable Noun Phrase						
Head$_x$				Head$_x$		
Noun Phrase				Noun Phrase		
Enumerator			Head$_N$	Enumerator		Head$_N$
Enumeration Phrase				Enumeration Phrase		
H$_E$	Cl			H$_E$	Cl	
NUMERAL	CLASSI-FIER		NOUN	NUMERAL	CLASSI-FIER	NOUN
yī	ge		nǚ'ér	yī	zhī	māo

Figure 5.1 Dual-headed structure for a Mandarin coordinate noun phrase

As an alternative to this LOGIC-BASED (or MULTIPLE-CONSTITUENT) APPROACH, however, there is another approach which is perhaps more closely related to what a speaker does in producing such a structure. In speaking, that is, someone first mentions the initial coordinate and can stop there, either finishing the sentence or going on to a different constituent entirely, but alternatively one can choose to take one or more additional coordinate constituents along with the additional structures needed to get a grammatically correct combination. According to this PRODUCTION-BASED (or HIERARCHICAL) APPROACH, the structure of the English example *my book, and paper, and pencil* would be as in Figure 5.2. Instead of treating all the coordinated elements as equal, this approach posits a hierarchy depending on how many there are. So the coordinated Head in Figure 5.2 is broken first into the Initial (manifested by *book*) and the Addition (manifested by the remainder). This latter is then manifested by a Continuation Phrase, consisting of a MAIN followed by a CONTINUATION. The Main is manifested by a Conjunctive Phrase, while the Continuation involves another Continuation Phrase with a Main alone manifested by another Conjunctive Phrase. In both cases, the Conjunctive Phrase is seen to consist of the functional positions of Conjunctive Relator followed by an Axis. This means it is an exocentric construction quite similar to a Prepositional Phrase. An expandable structure allowing noun phrases such as those in Figure 5.2 is given in Figure 5.3. It should be noted that the optional Continuation element in the Continuation Phrase allows one to retake the Continuation Phrase repeatedly, thus getting any number of Conjunctive Phrases, according to what one wants to say, of course.

In the following discussion of other varieties of coordination, the production-based hierarchical approach using conjunctive phrases rather than the logic-based (multiple-head) approach will be assumed. It needs to be applied to the asyndetic examples of the Chinese type, to the postposed conjunctions of Yup'ik Eskimo and Japanese, and to the alternative type that exists in English and many other languages, where one can say, for instance, *my book, paper, and pencil*, using an overt conjunction only before the last coordinate. Since it makes use of just a single conjunction, this latter pattern may be termed MONOSYNDETON as opposed to the POLYSYNDETON exhibited in the examples used in Figure 5.2.

Noun Phrase					
Determiner	Head$_N$				
	Expandable Head Phrase				
	Initial	Addition			
		Continuation Phrase			
		Main		Continuation	
		Conjunctive Phrase		Continuation Phrase	
		Relator$_c$	Axis	Main	
				Conjunctive Phrase	
				Relator$_c$	Axis
DETERMINING ADJECTIVES	NOUNS	CONJUNC-TIONS	NOUNS	CONJUNC-TIONS	NOUNS
my	*book*	*and*	*paper*	*and*	*pencil*

Figure 5.2 Illustration of constituency according to the production-based (hierarchical) approach

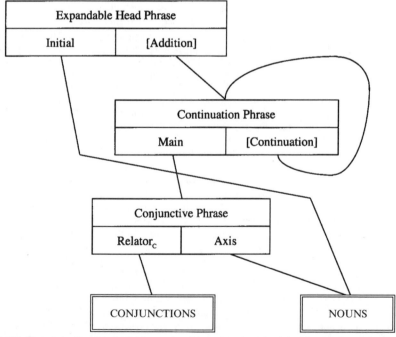

Figure 5.3 Structure for expandable noun-phrase heads using the production-based (hierarchical) view of constituency

Figure 5.4 provides an account of the asyndetic pattern seen in the Mandarin data of Table 5.3. Since there is no overt conjunction involved, it simply allows the nominal phrases to be accessed repeatedly. ("Nominal phrase" is used to imply something broader than simply a noun phrase, including pronouns, for instance.) For the Yup'ik Eskimo situation, we can use the account in Figure 5.5. Apart from the order of the Axis and the Relator in the conjunctive phrase, this is very similar to that seen in the account of English in Figure 5.3.

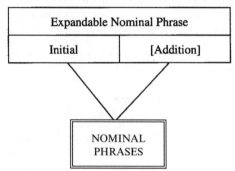

Figure 5.4 Solution to simple asyndetic coordination

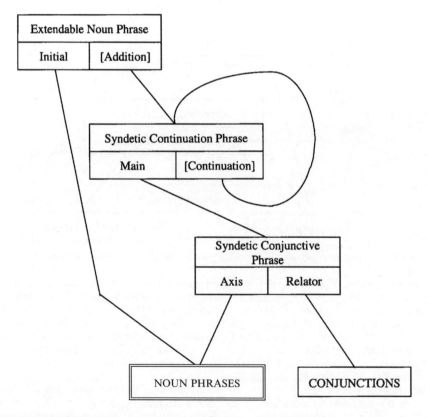

Figure 5.5 Afterbranching schema for polysyndeton with postposed conjunctions, as in Yup'ik Eskimo noun phrases

In order to treat the Japanese patterns seen in Table 5.5, it appears that we need to recognize a pattern according to which additions are made *before* rather than *after* the obligatory part of the extended noun phrase. This pattern, shown in Figure 5.6, is more or less the mirror image of the schema for English Nominal Head coordination presented in Figure 5.3, which has preposed conjunctions with afterbranching. This version will deal with all of the cases where the conjunction is not repeated after the last noun. This means it can be used to handle the selective conjunctive /ya/, and one of the uses of the disjunctive /ka/ and the exhaustive conjunctive /to/. In order to do this properly, however, it is necessary to use a kind of concord to guarantee that the same conjunction will be taken throughout a given use of the construction. To that end, the superscript [1] is placed on the concording constituents and is shown to affect the selection of conjunctions. This is perhaps not an ordinary use of the notion of concord, but the concept as introduced in the previous chapter will be workable for this material.

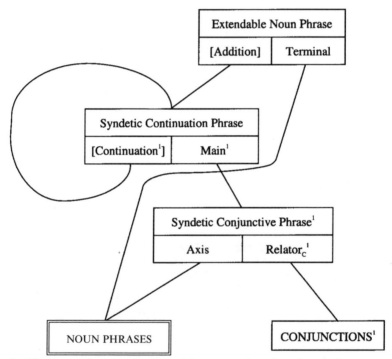

Figure 5.6 Forebranching coordination with postposed conjunctions in Japanese

The next figure, Figure 5.7, shows a somewhat different structure needed to treat the multiple usage which is obligatory with /mo/ and optional with /to/ and /ka/. This differs from the previous structure in that the Terminal as well as the Main connect to the Conjunctive Phrase, so that all uses of the noun phrase in this construction must be followed by a conjunction. The superscripts stipulating the concord also have to be extended up to the top level to guarantee that either /mo/ or /to/ will be used through a given construction. Also, the addition has been made obligatory, rather than optional, since there must be at least two coordinates in a structure like this one.

Before we settle on this as the ultimately correct way to treat the Japanese situation, however, it is necessary to consider how realistic the FOREBRANCHING structure is in providing a system that the speaker can actually use in the way spoken language normally functions. It seems fairly clear that forebranching can work as well as afterbranching in providing a system to *generate* the needed combinations in a quasi-mathematical fashion. Yet any speaker who is

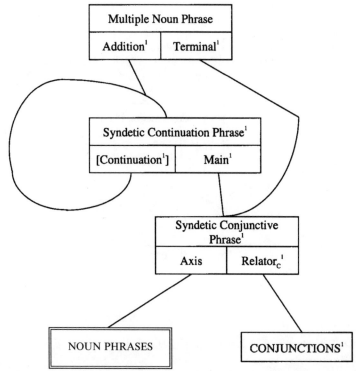

Figure 5.7 Forebranching multiple coordination with postposed conjunctions, as in Japanese

going to use it would have to plan ahead in a way often found in writing or deliberated oration, but not in spontaneous speech, where the speaker may not be sure how a sentence or phrase already begun will end. While a system with AFTERBRANCHING naturally provides various ways allowing one to continue by putting the constituents termed Addition and Continuation after something has been said, a forebranching account requires one to plan ahead and decide to take the Addition before the obligatory Terminal and the Continuation before the obligatory Main. So if one wants an account that is cognitively realistic, the possibility of an afterbranching account of this material needs to be considered. Figure 5.8 shows a way to handle these situations using afterbranching, though recognizing the phonological linkage of the conjunctions to preceding elements. This approach tries to incorporate all of the four Japanese conjunctions considered into a single diagram, relegating differences of detail to the editing summarized in Table 5.6.

Table 5.6 Editing assumptions regarding Japanese conjunctions

Conjunction		Details related to realization
mo	MULTIPLE AND	Object Marker /o/ is automatically realized as zero following it.
ka	OR	Automatically zero in phrase-final position.
to ya	EXHAUSTIVE AND SELECTIVE AND	Optionally zero in phrase-final position (according to unidentified stylistic conditions).

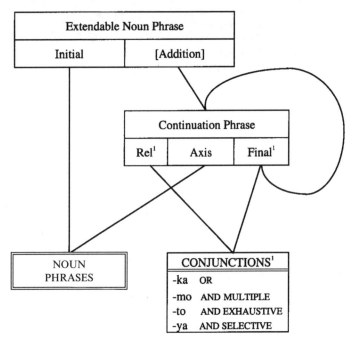

Figure 5.8 Reformulation of Japanese multiple coordination with postposed conjunctions using afterbranching

It will be assumed that, though forebranching can provide a possible account of the facts from a logico-mathematical standpoint, the consideration of cognitive realism makes the seemingly more awkward afterbranching treatment of Figure 5.8 more reasonable. The hyphens inserted before each of the conjunctions are intended to indicate the fact that they belong phonologically with the previous word despite their grammatical status. This notation and its uses will be detailed in Chapter 7.

The final example, in Figure 5.9, provides an account of English noun-phrase coordination, including the choice between the polysyndetic pattern with a conjunction before each added constituent and the alternative monosyndetic pattern, using the conjunction only before the last of the Noun Phrases that is stated.

Structural types of coordination

Since it is based on meaning, the distinction of conjunctive, disjunctive and negative types of coordination can be termed SEMANTIC. Examples in preceding sections partially illustrate another classification of coordination patterns based on syntactic factors such as position and number of correlates. In outline form, this STRUCTURAL TYPOLOGY can be presented as follows:

1.	**Number and occurrence**
1.1	ASYNDETIC COORDINATION: without overt conjunctions
1.2	SYNDETIC COORDINATION: with overt conjunctions
1.2.1	Multiple type: conjunction with each coordinate
1.2.1.1	Correlative subtype: different conjunctions with different coordinates
1.2.1.2	Repetitive subtype: same conjunction with each coordinate
1.2.2	Polysyndetic type: conjunction with each coordinate except the first
1.2.3	Monosyndetic type: one conjunction regardless of number of coordinates

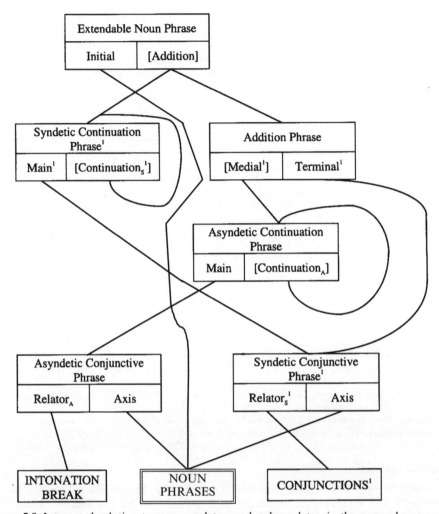

Figure 5.9 Integrated solution to monosyndeton and polysyndeton in the noun phrase

2.   **Sequence**
2.1   RELATOR-INITIAL: conjunction before coordinate
2.2   RELATOR-FINAL: conjunction after coordinate

3.   **Branching pattern**
3.1   Afterbranching: expansion after obligatory initial
3.2   Forebranching: expansion before obligatory final

All of the varieties outlined under part 1 (Number and Occurrence) have been illustrated previously, including asyndetic coordination from Chinese and the others from English or various European languages. The six types there are potentially multiplied by two when part 2 (Sequence) is considered, and by two again when we consider part 3 (Branching pattern), for a total of 24 potential structural types. In practice, this can be reduced to 21, because the differences of sequence and branching pattern can only be applicable to the syndetic types. In the case of sequence, the reason for its inapplicability in the case of asyndeton should be obvious, since the matter cannot be meaningful when there is no overt conjunction to place.

When it comes to branching, previous discussion has led us to question its reality if one moves beyond the logico-mathematical realm into the realm of the cognitive realism. Even without this consideration, afterbranching seems to be found in overwhelmingly many more cases than forebranching. This is fairly understandable, since, as already suggested, when we view the matter from the standpoint of production, it seems more natural to add on extra words *after* rather than *before*.

The total exploration of how many of the remaining 21 categories actually occur would be beyond the scope of this textbook. It seems fairly clear that examples of all five syndetic categories with relator-initial and afterbranching will be numerous, while the others will be rarer, even viewing the matter without consideration of cognitive realism. Some consideration of the way these combine with the semantically based classification involving the categories conjunctive, disjunctive, and negative may also be worth while. It seems probable that asyndeton, for example, will be entirely conjunctive. Even with this restriction, the total typology could involve 61 categories if each of the three semantic types occurs with all 20 of the other structural types. Table 5.7 summarizes the various specific situations formalized in Figures 5.3–5.9.

Table 5.7 Types of coordination illustrated in previous figures

	Number/ occurrence	Sequence	Branching
Figure 5.3	POLYSYNDETIC	RELATOR-INITIAL	AFTERBRANCHING
Figure 5.4	ASYNDETON	RELATOR-INITIAL	AFTERBRANCHING
Figure 5.5	POLYSYNDETIC	RELATOR-FINAL	AFTERBRANCHING
Figure 5.6	POLYSYNDETIC	RELATOR-FINAL	FOREBRANCHING*
Figure 5.7	MULTIPLE POLYSYNDETIC	RELATOR-FINAL	FOREBRANCHING*
Figure 5.8	POLYSYNDETIC	RELATOR-INITIAL AND SEQUENCE-FINAL	AFTERBRANCHING
Figure 5.9	POLYSYNDETIC AND MONOSYNDETIC	RELATOR-INITIAL	AFTERBRANCHING

Note: *Cognitively questionable.

General patterns of coordination

In English, the general patterns formalized in Figure 5.9 are by no means confined to just the coordination of Noun Phrases. Instead they are in wide use in the language as a whole. They may be used, for instance, to coordinate adjectives, verbs, verb + object combinations, and prepositions. The other major pattern found in English is asyndeton, but as was pointed out earlier its use usually implies that a listing is incomplete. One English use of asyndeton without this implication, however, is found with attributive adjectives, those in the role of Modifier, as shown in examples 1–3 of Table 5.8. In the "predicative" position (more precisely when the adjectives involved function as a Complement, to use a term to be introduced in Chapter 6), however, asyndeton may also be used, but there it carries the usual implication of incompleteness. These latter uses are illustrated in examples 4–6 of Table 5.8.

Table 5.8 Asyndetic coordination of English adjectives

1.   *They have a* nice big roomy *house*.
2.   Those *sweet old Irish* songs are my aunt's favorites.
3.   We need to take a *long relaxing* vacation.
4.   Their inspection was *slow, bothersome, sloppy* …
5.   Her work has always been *friendly, efficient, precise* …
6.   That kind of music is *annoying, obnoxious, cacophonous* …

As one examines coordination patterns in different languages, one must be prepared to find more variety of coordination patterns with different types of coordinated words or phrases than are typical of English and most European languages. In Mandarin Chinese, for instance, in addition to the asyndeton exemplified in Table 5.3, there is also a syndetic conjunction /hé/ which can be used for AND when it is a matter of coordinating nominals, such as nouns, pronouns, or noun phrases. But according to standard Chinese grammar, this conjunction may not be used to coordinate verbs or clauses, where asyndeton is generally the only possibility. Similarly, the Japanese conjunctives seen in Table 5.5 are limited to use with nominals.

As a final example of the formalization of coordination, Figure 5.10 shows a modified version of Figure 5.9 which can potentially be used to state a general pattern applicable to the

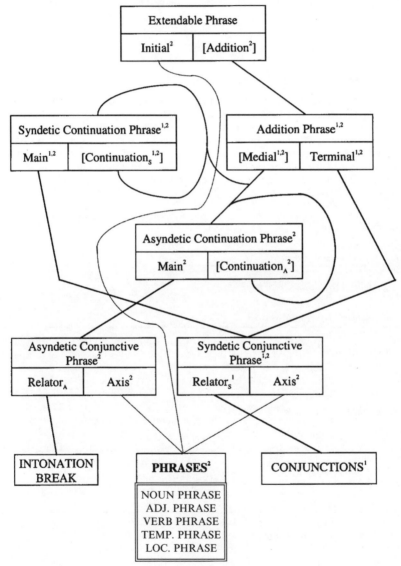

Figure 5.10 Integrated solution to monosyndeton and polysyndeton extended beyond the noun phrase

coordination of a considerable number of different elements, whether nouns, noun phrases, adjectives, verbs or whatever. The account is generalized via a further use of numerical superscripts. Here the superscript [1] has been carried over from Figures 5.8 and 5.9 to guarantee that the same overt conjunction (*and* or *or*) will be used in the case of polysyndeton. Here a second superscript [2] has also been added to guarantee that the phrases subjected to coordination will be of the same functional (not necessarily structural) type. At the bottom of the diagram, it can be seen that superscript [1] relates to relator functions, and ultimately to the selection of conjunctions, while superscript [2] relates to PHRASES, an abbreviation here for different functional types, such as Noun Phrase, Verb Phrase, Temporal Phrase, and so on.

Exercises

A.   Classification and interpretation problems

1.   English phrase coordination

As the chapter shows, one way to classify English coordination involves the five types shown in Table 5.1: SIMPLE CONJUNCTIVE, SIMPLE DISJUNCTIVE, CORRELATIVE CONJUNCTIVE, CORRELATIVE DISJUNCTIVE, and CORRELATIVE NEGATIVE. In addition, we can further classify according to the sort of phrase or other unit subject to coordination. So we can speak of nominal head coordination in *my pots and pans*, as opposed to other types like noun phrase coordination in *either my money or his life*, and verbal head coordination in *neither negotiated nor surrendered*. For each of the following examples, indicate the proper classification in these two ways.

1. *will read or write*

    _____

2. *both Uncle Lloyd and Aunt Ruth*

    _____

3. *under and behind the house*

    _____

4. *neither there nor outside the city*

    _____

5. *either today or next week*

    _____

6. *considerate, kind, and loving [relatives]*

    _____

7. *both quietly and efficiently*

_____

8. *neither above nor beyond*

_____

9. *either four or five [times]*

_____

10. *her large car or his expensive mansion*

_____

2. Structures for English coordinate phrases

Figure 5.10 is admittedly somewhat schematic, but it is designed to cover a wide range of examples of English coordination, both conjunctive and disjunctive, excluding only the correlative types. Using the two samples shown below as a model, show the structure assigned by this figure for each of the following examples.

1. *Christopher Columbus, or John Cabot, or Amerigo Vespucci*
2. *runs, plays, and works*
3. *between the houses and in the streets and under the trees*
4. *dark gray, light beige, or cherry red*

Sample 1: *eats slowly or drinks rapidly*

Extendable Phrase			
Initial	Addition		
PHRASES	Addition Phrase		
	Terminal		
	Syndetic Conjunctive Phrase		
	Relator	Axis	
		PHRASES	
VERB PHRASE	CONJUNCTION	VERB PHRASE	
eats slowly	or	drinks rapidly	

Sample 2: *houses, barns, and other outbuildings*

Extendable Phrase				
Initial	Addition			
	Addition Phrase[1,2]			
	Medial[1,2]		Terminal[1,2]	
	Asyndetic Cont. Phrase[2]		Syndetic Conjunctive Phrase[1,2]	
	Main[2]		Relator$_s$[1]	Axis[2]
	Asyndetic Conj. Phrase[2]			PHRASES
	Relator$_A$	Axis[2]		
NOUN PHRASE	INTONATION BREAK	NOUN PHRASE	CONJUNCTION	NOUN PHRASE
houses	,	*barns*	*and*	*other outbuildings*

B.   Analysis problems

1.   *Phrase coordination in Classical Sanskrit*

The following data set shows some patterns of word (ultimately phrase) coordination in Classical Sanskrit. Provide an accurate account of these patterns using as few distinct constructions as you can.

1.	netā	THE/A LEADER
2.	rājñī	THE/A QUEEN
3.	bālā	THE/A GIRL
4.	pitā	THE/A FATHER
5.	rājñī bālā ca	THE QUEEN AND THE GIRL
6.	jāyā rājā ca	THE WIFE AND THE KING
7.	rājā ca bālā ca	[BOTH] THE KING AND THE GIRL
8.	rājā rājñī netā ca	THE KING, THE QUEEN AND THE LEADER
9.	pitā vā jāyā vā	EITHER A FATHER OR A WIFE
10.	jetā netā vā	A WINNER OR A LEADER
11.	nārī vā bālā vā pitā vā	EITHER A WOMAN OR A GIRL OR A FATHER
12.	bālā nārī rājñī vā	THE GIRL, THE WOMAN, OR THE QUEEN
13.	pibati	[HE/SHE/IT] DRINKS
14.	pibanti	[THEY] DRINK
15.	gacchati	[HE/SHE/IT] GOES
16.	vadanti	[THEY] SPEAK
17.	gacchati ca vadati ca	[HE/SHE/IT] [BOTH] GOES AND SPEAKS
18.	pibanti patanti ca	[THEY] DRINK AND FALL

19. vadanti patanti vā	[THEY] GO OR FALL
20. gacchati vā tisthati vā sidati vā	[HE/SHE/IT] EITHER GOES OR STANDS OR SITS
21. pibati vā pibanti vā	EITHER [HE/SHE/IT] DRINKS OR [THEY] DRINK
22. gacchati patanti ca	[HE/SHE/IT] GOES AND [THEY] FALL
23. gacchanti tisthati vā	[THEY] GO OR [HE/SHE/IT] STANDS
24. pibanti ca vadati ca vadanti ca	[THEY] DRINK AND [HE/SHE/IT] FALLS AND [THEY] GO
25. pibati vā vadanti vā tisthanti vā	EITHER [HE/SHE/IT] DRINKS OR [THEY] GO OR [THEY] STAND

2. Nominal coordination in Korean

The following shows patterns of coordination for nouns in Korean. Edit the data and account for it. Note that some of the suffixes have different phonological forms depending on the way the noun ends. So these differences should be edited out as matters of phonological alternation. They are not dependent on any classification such as gender.

1. chayki	THE BOOK (*SUBJECT*)
2. cepsiga	THE PLATE (*SUBJECT*)
3. uysaga	THE DOCTOR (*SUBJECT*)
4. pyengcengi	THE SOLDIER (*SUBJECT*)
5. sangini	THE MERCHANT (*SUBJECT*)
6. congiga	THE PAPER (*SUBJECT*)
7. yenphili	THE PENCIL (*SUBJECT*)
8. yenphilkwa congiga	THE PENCIL AND THE PAPER (*SUBJECT*)
9. uysawa pyengcengi	THE DOCTOR AND THE SOLDIER (*SUBJECT*)
10. sanginkwa uysaga	THE MERCHANT AND THE DOCTOR (*SUBJECT*)
11. chaykkwa capciga	THE BOOK AND THE MAGAZINE (*SUBJECT*)
12. cepsiwa cani	THE PLATE AND THE CUP (*SUBJECT*)
13. canul	THE CUP *(OBJECT)*
14. cepsilul	THE PLATE *(OBJECT)*
15. cankwa cepsilul	THE CUP AND THE PLATE *(OBJECT)*
16. malwulul	THE FLOOR *(OBJECT)*
17. cangul	THE STORAGE CHEST *(OBJECT)*
18. cangkwa malwulul	THE STORAGE CHEST AND THE FLOOR *(OBJECT)*
19. uysaege	TO THE DOCTOR
20. yecaege	TO THE WOMAN
21. uysawa yecaege	TO THE DOCTOR AND THE WOMAN
22. pyengcengege	TO THE SOLDIER
23. sanginege	TO THE MERCHANT
24. pyengcengkwa sanginege	TO THE SOLDIER AND THE MERCHANT

3. Coordination with stative verbs in Japanese

Japanese has a kind of word appropriately called a stative verb (traditional English-language grammars of Japanese call them "adjectives"). Items 1–16 illustrate such verbs in two tenses. It should be noted that /wa/ does not carry the meaning BE; rather it is a topic marking postposition going with the preceding word. Given this, we can see that the words /yasui/ and /yasukatta/ mean IS CHEAP and WAS CHEAP, respectively. In order to coordinate these in the role of Predicator in a descriptive clause, Japanese uses a different device from those seen with noun phrases in the main part of the chapter. This pattern is illustrated in items 17–30. Edit the verb forms (the rest has no inflection) and prepare an account of the data.

1. kore wa yasui	THIS IS CHEAP.
2. are wa takai	THAT IS EXPENSIVE.
3. kore wa siroi	THIS IS WHITE.
4. are wa kuroi	THAT IS BLACK.
5. kore wa takakatta	THIS WAS EXPENSIVE.
6. are wa sirokatta	THAT WAS WHITE.
7. kore wa kurokatta	THIS WAS BLACK.
8. are wa yasukatta	THAT WAS CHEAP.
9. are wa osoi	THAT IS SLOW.
10. kore wa osokatta	THIS WAS SLOW.
11. kore wa amai	THIS IS SWEET.
12. are wa karukatta	THAT WAS LIGHT.
13. are wa yasasii	THAT IS EASY.
14. kore wa omokatta	THIS WAS HEAVY.
15. kore wa akai	THIS IS RED.
16. are wa aokattta	THAT WAS BLUE.
17. kore wa siroku yasui	THIS IS WHITE AND CHEAP.
18. are wa kuroku yasui	THAT IS BLACK AND CHEAP.
19. kore wa yasuku kuroi	THIS IS CHEAP AND BLACK.
20. are wa siroku kuroi	THAT IS WHITE AND BLACK.
21. are wa yasuku takai	THAT IS CHEAP AND EXPENSIVE.
22. kore wa yasuku omokatta	THIS WAS CHEAP AND HEAVY.
23. are wa osoku amai	THIS IS SLOW AND SWEET.
24. kore wa yasusiku omokatta	THIS WAS EASY AND HEAVY.
25. are wa akaku aoi	THAT IS RED AND BLUE.
26. kore wa karuku sirokatta	THIS WAS LIGHT AND WHITE.
27. kore wa amaku yasukatta	THIS WAS SWEET AND CHEAP.
28. are wa kuroku aokatta	THAT WAS BLACK AND BLUE.
29. are wa aoku amai	THAT IS BLUE AND SWEET.
30. kore wa omoku osokatta	THIS WAS HEAVY AND SLOW.

Terminology

AFTERBRANCHING	MONOSYNDETON = MONOSYNDETIC COORDINATION
ASYNDETIC COORDINATION = ASYNDETON	MULTIPLE COORDINATION
CONJUNCTIVE COORDINATION	NEGATIVE COORDINATION
CONTINUATION	POLYSYNDETON = POLYSYNDETIC COORDINATION
COORDINATION LOGIC-BASED FORMALIZATION PRODUCTION-BASED FORMALIZATION	POSTPOSED CONJUNCTIONS
	PREPOSED CONJUNCTIONS
CORRELATIVE COORDINATION	RELATOR-FINAL CONJUNCTIVE PHRASE
DISJUNCTIVE COORDINATION	RELATOR-INITIAL CONJUNCTIVE PHRASE
EXHAUSTIVE CONJUNCTIVES	
EXTENDABLE PHRASE	REPETITIVE COORDINATION
FOREBRANCHING	SELECTIVE CONJUNCTIVES
MAIN	SYNDETIC COORDINATION

6

Types of basic clause constructions

Verbal clauses and their elements

In Chapter 1 we considered the elements in transitive clauses, recognizing Subjects, Objects, and Predicators. Some further evidence regarding clauses of this kind and others is displayed in Table 6.1. While all examples here contain a Subject and a Predicator, the verbs functioning as Predicators divide into six classes based on (1) how many objects they may take, and (2) which objects are optional versus obligatory. The items in section 1 of the table have Intransitive Predicators manifested by verbs which take no Objects at all. Those in sections 2 and 3 are united by the fact that they may all take a single Object, but in section 2 the Object may be omitted, while in section 3 it seems to be obligatory. The latter type may simply be called a Transitive Predicator, while that in section 2 may be termed Semi-Transitive. In the remaining sections, we can get two objects, what are traditionally divided into the INDIRECT OBJECT (expressing a recipient or beneficiary of the action) and the DIRECT OBJECT. Collectively the Predicators that allow two Objects (at least potentially) in this way may be called BITRANSITIVE. They are, however, divisible into three subtypes: in section 4, we may use no Object at all, just a Direct Object, or one of each type – this type may be termed SEMI-BITRANSITIVE; in section 5, we can get either Object, both of them, or neither – this can be termed the PSEUDO-BITRANSITIVE; in section 6, where only the Indirect Object can be omitted, we can speak of the (simple) bitransitive. This analysis is summarized in the construction boxes displayed in Figure 6.1, which omits details concerning the manifestations of the various functions. In the case of the Semi-Bitransitive, the notation used for optionality is a makeshift

Table 6.1 Evidence for some basic declarative clause types in English

1.1	*She died.*
1.2	*The man slept.*
1.3	*My neighbor wept.*
2.1	*My uncle unpacked [his suitcases].*
2.2	*Some drugs can kill [you].*
2.3	*Her mother washed [all the clothes].*
3.1	*Our friend timed them.*
3.2	*He sealed the letters.*
3.3	*The accident damaged the dishes.*
4.1	*They sang [[us] an old song].*
4.2	*The lawyer read [[the boy] a story].*
4.3	*Our son drew [[me] a picture].*
5.1	*She told [us] [everything].*
5.2	*They served [you] [supper].*
5.3	*My aunt wrote [me] [a letter].*
6.1	*I sent [you] a gift.*
6.2	*My brother brought [me] a book.*
6.3	*She cut [my mother] a bouquet.*

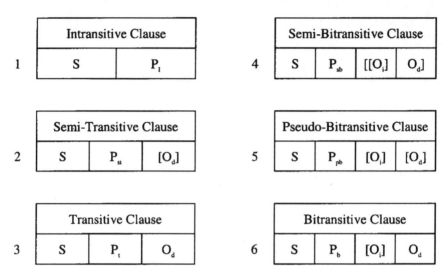

Figure 6.1 General schemas for six basic declarative clause types in English

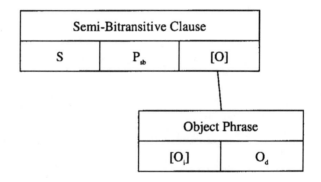

Figure 6.2 A more explicit account of the semi-bitransitive clause

designed to allow a brief indication of the options involved: one may choose to take no objects at all, but if one opts to take objects, the Direct Object (O_d) must be taken, and the Indirect Object (O_i) may be taken or omitted. In a more explicit notation, the Semi-Bitransitive type would be represented as in Figure 6.2.

All these English examples require some kind of explicit Subject (though they generally have imperative counterparts where the second-person Subject is only optional). In some languages, however, the Predicator is the only obligatory function in the clause. Yup'ik Eskimo is such a language, as illustrated by the data in Table 6.2. In this material, subjects as well as objects are only optional, though in most examples a pronoun is supplied in the English translation. Like many languages, Yup'ik has pronouns, but they do not have to be used in many situations. Here, the persons and numbers of notional "subjects" and "direct objects" are signaled by the verbal inflection. (This fact is not clearly evident here, since only third-person singular forms have been used.) Schemas for the three types of clause found in this material are presented in Figure 6.3.

Some further Yup'ik Eskimo data in Table 6.3 provides a good illustration of the need to base one's classification of clause types on the facts of the language under analysis rather than relying too heavily on the translation into English or another language. If we look only at the

Table 6.2 Evidence for some basic clause types in Central Alaskan Yup'ik Eskimo

1.1	ayaxtuq	HE/SHE/IT IS LEAVING.
1.2	qavaχtuq	HE/SHE/IT IS SLEEPING.
1.3	aʙnaq ayaxtuq	THE WOMAN IS LEAVING.
1.4	aŋun qavaχtuq	THE MAN IS SLEEPING.
2.1	taŋχaa	HE/SHE/IT SEES HIM/HER/IT.
2.2	mauʙluum taŋχaa	GRANDMOTHER SEES HIM/HER/IT.
2.3	aŋun taŋχaa	HE/SHE/IT SEES THE MAN.
2.4	qimuxtïm aʙnaq taŋχaa	THE DOG SEES THE WOMAN.
2.5	qacaχtaa	HE/SHE/IT SLAPS HIM/HER/IT.
2.6	anŋam qacaχtaa	THE OLDER BROTHER SLAPS HIM/HER/IT.
2.7	aŋun qacaχtaa	HE/SHE/IT SLAPS THE MAN.
2.8	aŋaɬkum aʙnaq qacaχtaa	THE SHAMAN SLAPS THE WOMAN.
3.1	tunaa	HE/SHE GIVES IT TO SOMEONE.
3.2	anŋam tunaa	THE OLDER BROTHER GIVES IT TO SOMEONE.
3.3	qayaq tunaa	HE/SHE GIVES A KAYAK TO SOMEONE.
3.4	aatamun tunaa	HE/SHE GIVES IT TO FATHER.
3.5	uim aŋyaq tunaa	THE HUSBAND GIVES A BOAT TO SOMEONE.
3.6	aŋaɬkum aanamun tunaa	THE SHAMAN GIVES IT TO MOTHER.
3.7	paniɣmun aŋyaq tunaa	HE/SHE GIVES A BOAT TO THE DAUGHTER.
3.8	anŋam mikïlŋuɣmun qayaq tunaa	THE OLDER BROTHER GIVES A KAYAK TO THE CHILD.

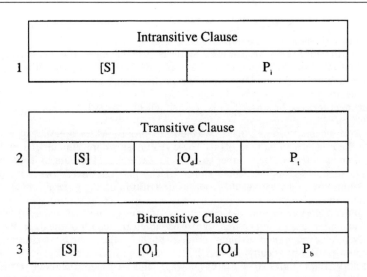

Figure 6.3 General schemas for three basic declarative clause types in Yup'ik Eskimo

glosses here, we would certainly expect to find transitive clauses, since the English verbs *have*, *acquire*, *make*, and *work on* are all transitive. In Yup'ik, however, the verbs used here all have the meaning of the English verb plus the meaning of its Object. This material illustrates some morphological patterns in Yup'ik whereby a nominal root may be suffixed to form an intransitive verb. The specific suffixes seen in this material are /ŋqïχt/ for a possessive verb (HAS), /ŋ/ for an acquisitional verb (ACQUIRES), /li/ for a factitive verb (MAKES) and /liuχt/ for an occupative verb (WORKS ON). So in terms of Yup'ik grammar, this data simply illustrates further instances of the **INTRANSITIVE** verb, just like the verbs meaning LEAVE and SLEEP in Table 6.2, and so they are covered by schema (1) in Figure 6.3.

Table 6.3 Some further examples of intransitive clauses in Central Alaskan Yup'ik Eskimo

1.1	nazauɓluq qayaŋqɨχtuq	THE GIRL HAS A KAYAK.
1.2	aɓnaq caviŋqɨχtuq	THE WOMAN HAS A KNIFE.
1.3	aŋyaŋqɨχtuq	HE/SHE HAS A BOAT.
2.1	aŋun aŋyaŋuq	THE MAN ACQUIRES A BOAT.
2.2	aɓnaq qayaŋuq	THE WOMAN ACQUIRES A KAYAK.
2.3	atkuŋuq	HE/SHE ACQUIRES A PARKA.
3.1	aŋun qayaliuq	THE MAN IS MAKING A KAYAK.
3.2	taŋɣuχaq aŋyaliuq	THE BOY IS MAKING A BOAT.
3.3	atkuliuq	HE/SHE IS MAKING A PARKA.
4.1	aɓnaq atkuliuχtuq	THE WOMAN IS WORKING ON A PARKA.
4.2	nazauɓluq ulualiuχtuq	THE GIRL IS WORKING ON A WOMAN'S KNIFE.
4.3	aŋyaliuχtuq	HE/SHE IS WORKING ON A BOAT.

We can ask, however, why the particular three-way classification in Figure 6.3 is the appropriate one, rather than, for instance, one which combines them all together or, at the other extreme, one which disregards optionality and sets up a different construction based on the actual constituents present. The first of the possibilities mentioned would be representable in a single formula to cover all the data:

$$[S] \qquad [O_i] \qquad [O_d] \qquad P$$

This schema would indeed allow all items in the data to occur, and in the observed order, but it would fail to exclude impossible combinations of some specific verbs with the various kinds of Objects. The intransitive verb, for instance, can never take an Object, but this schema does not provide that information. Similarly, though a transitive verb can appear without an explicit Object, it can take only a Direct Object, and not an Indirect Object. Only a bitransitive verb would be able to take both kinds of Object. So, taken by itself, this formula would be overgeneralizing precisely because it fails to distinguish impossible syntactic combinations from possible ones.

Each general schema in Figure 6.3, by virtue of its provisions for optionality, permits two or more specific schemas to be read off it. These relationships are summarized in Table 6.4, which also includes reference by number to items in Table 6.2. (The data of Table 6.3 would also fit in as instances of general schema number 1.) This material then allows us to address the second question above, why we should base our description on the general schemas in Table 6.4 rather than on the specific ones, giving fourteen construction formulas rather than just three. The general answer is that the optionality of constituents is a reasonable and easy concept to use, and its use permits a much more economical account of the data. Beyond this, some linguists have suggested explicit criteria to help the analyst decide how many constructions to posit. Specifically, Robert E. Longacre outlined a concept which he termed the **DUAL STRUCTURAL CRITERION**. In paraphrase, this criterion suggested that a single difference is not enough to warrant the positing of separate constructions. Rather, he suggested, genuinely different constructions must differ in at least two ways. By this criterion, we are not justified in separating the two specific schemas listed under (1) in Table 6.4 because they show just one difference, and this difference can easily be captured by making the Subject function optional. Specific schemas $S P_i$ and $S P_t$, though they superficially seem to show only one difference, can be separated because the difference in verb class further correlates with the fact that P_t can optionally be preceded by an object, while P_i cannot. (The difference between a transitive and an intransitive verb correlates in this language, incidentally, with a different form of inflection.) A complete application of this criterion to this material gives exactly three constructions, as represented by the general schemas in the table. In any pair of these general schemas that we compare, one difference concerns verb classes, and one other concerns the possibility of objects being included. The intransitive and bitransitive schemas, of course, have

Table 6.4 Relation of general schemas (Figure 6.3) to data (Table 6.2)

General Schema	Specific Schema	Examples from Table 6.2
1. [S] P_i	P_i	1.1, 2
	S P_i	1.3, 4
2. [S] [O_d] P_t	P_t	2.1, 5
	S P_t	2.2, 6
	O_d P_t	2.3, 7
	S O_d P_t	2.4, 8
3. [S] [O_i] [O_d] P_b	P_b	3.1
	S P_b	3.2
	O_d P_b	3.3
	O_i P_b	3.4
	S O_d P_b	3.5
	S O_i P_b	3.6
	O_i O_d P_b	3.7
	S O_i O_d P_b	3.8

three differences altogether – different verb classes and two optional objects in the latter, neither of which is possible in the former.

Basic clause types in English

Table 6.1 and the analysis of it in Figure 6.1 represent a beginning in the discussion of the most basic clause types in English. One way to carry this further is to consider some additional data involving clauses with the verb *to be*, as in Table 6.5.

Table 6.5 Examples of clauses using *be* in English

1.1	*There is a strange man in the yard.*
1.2	*There are some sheep over there.*
1.3	*There were important differences.*
2.1	*His uncle is an academic philosopher.*
2.2	*My cousin is a famous attorney.*
2.3	*John is a friend of mine.*
3.1	*Those people are my friends.*
3.2	*That man is the plumber.*
3.3	*This woman is my favorite aunt.*
4.1	*They are behind the curtain.*
4.2	*My daughter is over there.*
4.3	*The birds are on the roof.*
5.1	*This notebook is mine.*
5.2	*The linens are my mother's.*
5.3	*All the bread is yours.*
6.1	*That issue is very important.*
6.2	*These dogs are too big.*
6.3	*His sister is beautiful.*

The numbering of these examples suggests six different kinds of being. The examples in section 1 all assert the existence of some person(s) or thing(s), so they can be termed EXISTENTIAL. The examples in section 2 all express a classification of a person or thing as a member of some more general category, so they may be called CLASSIFICATORY. Although they are somewhat similar to the examples in 2, the ones in section 3 indicate an equation between the referent of the subject and that of the nominal expression after the verb, and so may be called EQUATIVE. The examples in section 4 all indicate the location of the subject's referent, and so may be termed LOCATIVE. Those in section 5 all express possession, broadly construed, and so may be called POSSESSIVE. Finally, the examples in section 6 use an adjective phrase to describe the referent of the subject, and so may be termed DESCRIPTIVE.

All of these sets of examples, then, are united by the fact that they use forms of the English verb *to be*. But their general characteristics of meaning differ in the ways just outlined. In observing the structure of these examples, we should note first that the existential stands apart from the others in that it is introduced by the word *there*, and by the fact that the Subject (here defined as the nominal that shows concord in number with the verb) comes after the verb. All the other examples, on the other hand, share two essential structural facts: (1) they begin with the Subject, (2) the Subject is followed by a form of *to be*. These examples differ only in what occurs in the last position, after the Subject + *be* sequence.

These examples can be reduced to the schemas shown in Figure 6.4, which follows the dual structural criterion by recognizing just two types, termed the EXISTENTIAL CLAUSE and the COPULAR CLAUSE. The existential clause is characterized by the occurrence of an initial INTRODUCER followed by a COPULAR PREDICATOR, followed in turn by a Subject agreeing in number with the Predicator (if further data is considered, the agreement can be shown to involve person as well). At the end of the construction, the Locational is included as an optional element, since it is found in some of the examples and is very common in this type, though clearly not obligatory. The five remaining varieties in Table 6.5, however, all fit into the Copular Clause, since they differ only in the kind of phrase selected for the final constituent, as the figure shows. A proposal to separate these five semantic types into different clause types would fail the dual structural criterion, since a comparison of any two of them would reveal just a single difference. It should be clear, on the other hand, that the Existential Clause is distinct from the Copular despite the fact that they both share the same type of Predicator, because the two have differences involving (1) the obligatory presence of the Introducer in the Existential, and (2) the difference in order between the Subject and the Predicator in the two types.

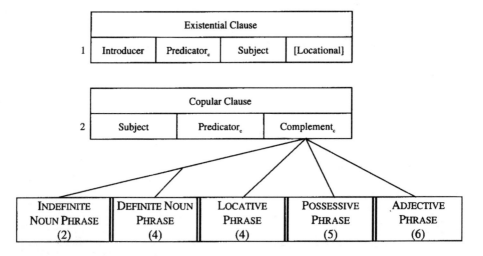

Figure 6.4 English clause types with Copular Predicators

Adding these two to the types already set forth in Figure 6.1, we now have seen evidence for a total of eight basic declarative clause types in English. Table 6.6 shows evidence for a few additional types. In all of these examples, the verb is followed by two expressions, one of which is clearly an Object of the sorts already discussed. In section 1 of the table, we see a Direct Object followed by a locational expression, with an appropriate prepositional phrase, or an adverb. At first glance, the examples in this section seem to be similar to such clauses as *They met her on the street* or *I saw them over there,* which simply add an optional Locational to a basic transitive clause. The difference, however, is that the examples just cited would be complete without the Locational, while those in section 1 of the table would not be. Verbs such as *set, put* and *lay* (in the ordinary senses intended here) simply require a Locational to be complete. Using the dual structural criterion, we can make sense of all of this by positing an additional clause type differing from the ordinary transitive clause in (1) the class of verb and (2) the obligatory Locational.

Table 6.6 Evidence for further types of clauses in English

1.1	*We set the books on the table.*
1.2	*Todd put the dishes here.*
1.3	*They laid the papers on the desk.*
2.1	*Zelda named Todd treasurer.*
2.2	*The governor appointed him judge.*
2.3	*Susan made Todd a good husband.*
3.1	*Susan made Todd a good wife.*
3.2	*Reginald will make Mr. Baxter a fine valet.*
3.3	*He will make us a loyal employee.*

The examples in sections 2 and 3 of the table are all reminiscent of bitransitives in that they have two noun or pronoun phrases after the Predicator. In the type in section 2, however, both of these phrases actually refer to the same individual, and the verb indicates an effect upon the referent of the Direct Object, expressed by the first phrase, such that its referent comes to be whatever is indicated by the following nominal expression. This extra nominal is not an Indirect Object, but what is termed an **OBJECTIVE COMPLEMENT**, so named because it refers to the same individual as the Direct Object. In the type in section 3, which seems to occur exclusively with the verb *make*, the first nominal after the Predicator indicates the beneficiary, and can therefore be termed an Indirect Object. Compare *Susan made Todd a new sweater* with example 3.1. In the former, the final nominal is clearly the Direct Object, but in the latter, as well as in the rest of section 3, it refers to the same person as the Subject, and is therefore called the **SUBJECTIVE COMPLEMENT**.

The structures for these three additional types of clause are schematized in Figure 6.5. It can readily be seen that these three differ from each other and from the roughly similar bitransitives in (1) the classes of verbs associated with the Predicator roles, and (2) the particular functions that follow the Predicator.

To conclude our discussion of basic clause types in English, let us consider the matter of Indirect Objects expressed alternatively with a prepositional phrase, as shown in the data of Table 6.7. In section 1, the examples show six different verbs which have paraphrased Indirect Objects expressed with the preposition *to.* In section 2, six other verbs are shown which have paraphrases using *for* instead of *to.* Finally, in section 3, paraphrases of all three examples in section 3 of Table 6.6 are presented, with the preposition *for* in all cases. For all these examples, we must allow variant orders of Objects and have the Indirect Object in the form of a prepositional phrase when it occurs as the second Object after the Predicator. Expanded schemas for all the four types of clause affected by this revision are shown in Figure 6.6. These all set up special object phrases to deal with differences between the two varieties of Indirect Object, involving both order in the clause and the use of a preposition.

In total, this gives us eleven basic types of declarative clauses, as summarized in Table 6.8.

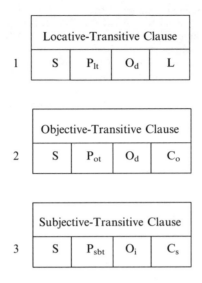

Figure 6.5 General schemas for three additional basic declarative clause types in English

Table 6.7 Paraphrases involving Indirect Objects in English

1.1	*I gave **Jerry** the prize.*	~ *I gave the prize **to Jerry**.*
1.2	*They awarded **Professor Jones** the grant.*	~ *They awarded the grant **to Professor Jones**.*
1.3	*She will tell **the judge** her story.*	~ *She will tell her story **to the judge**.*
1.4	*You can write **your aunt** a letter.*	~ *You can write a letter **to your aunt**.*
1.5	*He can read **the children** a story.*	~ *He can read a story **to the children**.*
1.6	*She brought **us** the dessert.*	~ *She brought the dessert **to us**.*
2.1	*They did **him** a great favor.*	~ *They did a great favor **for him**.*
2.2	*We provided **them** free meals.*	~ *We provided free meals **for them**.*
2.3	*You chose **him** a nice present.*	~ *You chose a nice present **for him**.*
2.4	*They cut **you** a pound of salami.*	~ *They cut a pound of salami **for you**.*
2.5	*She cooked **us** an excellent dinner.*	~ *She cooked an excellent dinner **for us**.*
2.6	*Susan made **Todd** a new sweater.*	~ *Susan made a new sweater **for Todd**.*
3.1	*Susan made a good wife **for Todd**.*	
3.2	*Reginald will make a fine valet **for Mr. Baxter**.*	
3.3	*He will make a loyal employee **for us**.*	

The more detailed schemas are in Figures 6.1 (items 1–3), 6.4 and 6.6. These are just schemas because (1) they generally ignore optional non-essential constituents, known collectively as CIRCUMSTANTIALS, such as Locational, Temporal, Manner, and so on, and (2) they do not attempt to deal with number agreement between Subjects and Predicators, which occurs throughout, nor with the use of *to* versus *for* in the prepositional expression of Indirect Objects. These matters will be considered in more detail in the next chapter.

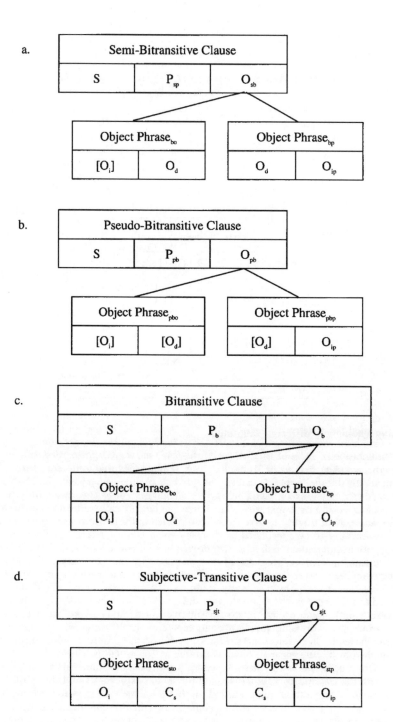

Figure 6.6 Expanded schemas distinguishing ordinary and prepositional-phrase Indirect Objects

Table 6.8 Summary of basic declarative clause types in English

General schema	Type	Formula	Example
Subject 　Predicator	INTRANSITIVE		*She laughed.*
Subject 　Predicator 　　X	SEMI-TRANSITIVE TRANSITIVE COPULAR	$S\ P_{st}\ [O_d]$ $S\ P\ O$ $S\ P\ C$	*I see [it].* *He sealed it.* *He is a teacher.* *He is my friend.* *He is mine.* *He is here.* *He is homely.*
Subject 　Predicator 　　X 　　Y	SEMI-BITRANSITIVE $\sim S\ P_{sb}\ O_d\ O_{ip}$ PSEUDO-BITRANSITIVE BITRANSITIVE LOCATIVE-TRANSITIVE SUBJECTIVE-TRANSITIVE OBJECTIVE-TRANSITIVE	$S\ P_{sb}\ [O_i]\ [O_d]$ $\sim$ *She drew that for me.* $S\ P_{pb}[O_i]\ [O_d]$ $\sim S\ P_{pb}\ O_d\ O_{ip}$ $S\ P_b\ [O_i]\ O_d$ $\sim S\ P_b\ O_d\ O_{ip}$ $S\ P_{lt}\ O_d\ L$ $S\ P_{sjt}\ O_i\ C_s$ $\sim S\ P_{sjt}\ C_s\ O_i$ $S\ P_{ot}\ O_d\ C_o$	*She drew [me] [that].* *They served [you] [that].* $\sim$ *They served that to you.* *He gave [her] that.* $\sim$ *He gave that to her.* *She put it here.* *She made them a fine maid.* $\sim$ *She made a fine maid for them.* *They crowned him king.*
Introducer 　Predicator 　　Subject	EXISTENTIAL	$I\ P_c\ S\ [L]$	*There is a difference [here].*

Expressing "being" in different languages

In our consideration of types of English declarative clauses, we recognized two different types involving the copular verb *to be*, though it was pointed out that different choices in the Complement divide the copular clause into five semantic subtypes. This section will concentrate on expressions of being in further languages, since this is an area in which languages can differ in interesting ways. The languages considered will be compared with one another as well as with English to give the reader an idea of the differences that can be found.

The first language to be considered is Spanish, which is not far removed from English in many ways, but is different enough in this respect to be of interest. Consider first the examples in Table 6.9, which presents expressions of existence and location. (In this presentation, word-for-word glosses are provided along with glosses of the entire clause; this approach allows the various points to be made without so many examples.) The existential types in section 1 show a special word *hay*, glossed as THERE-IS. Further data would show that this word, like a typical Spanish verb, is inflected for tense, so it is reasonable to treat it as a verb. In section 2 of the table, the examples expressing location contain a completely different verb, *está*, which likewise can have different tense inflections. In view of the different verbs and orders of constituents involved, we appear to have two different constructions here.

Before setting up schemas for these, however, let us examine some further Spanish data, beginning with the classificatory, equative, and possessive expressions in Table 6.10. Here all the data is much closer to the English pattern, in that the same verb *es* (a form of the Spanish verb *ser*) is used, and the differences are concentrated in the complements, with a noun (phrase) with no article in the classificatory examples (section 1), a definite noun phrase (marked by either a definite article or a possessive adjective) in the equative examples (section 2), and a possessive expression for the possessive subtype (section 3). Taken together, the

Table 6.9 The expression of existence and location in Spanish

1.1	*Hay*	*peces*	*en*	*el*	*río.*
	THERE-IS	FISH (PL)	IN	THE	RIVER
	THERE ARE FISH IN THE RIVER.				
1.2	*Hay*	*mucha gente*	*en*	*el*	*mercado.*
	THERE-IS	MUCH PEOPLE	IN	THE	MARKET
	THERE ARE MANY PEOPLE IN THE MARKET.				
1.3	*No hay*	*alumnos*	*en*	*la*	*clase.*
	NOT THERE-IS	PUPILS	IN	THE	CLASSROOM
	THERE ARE NO PUPILS IN THE CLASSROOM.				
2.1	*Este libro*	*está*	*en*	*la*	*mesa.*
	THIS BOOK	IS	IN	THE	TABLE
	THIS BOOK IS ON THE TABLE.				
2.2	*Madrid está*	*en*	*España.*		
	MADRID IS	IN	SPAIN		
	MADRID IS IN SPAIN.				
2.3	*El correo*	*está*	*aquí.*		
	THE POST OFFICE	IS	HERE		
	THE POST OFFICE IS HERE.				

Table 6.10 The expression of classificatory, equative, and possessive being in Spanish

1.1	*Juan es*	*médico.*		
	JUAN IS	DOCTOR		
	JUAN IS A DOCTOR.			
1.2	*María es*	*maestra.*		
	MARIA IS	WOMAN-TEACHER		
	MARIA IS A TEACHER.			
1.3	*Mi hermano es*	*soldado.*		
	MY BROTHER IS	SOLDIER		
	MY BROTHER IS A SOLDIER.			
2.1	*Este hombre es*	*el*	*maestro.*	
	THIS MAN IS	THE	TEACHER	
	THIS MAN IS THE TEACHER.			
2.2	*Es la*	*casa*	*del*	*presidente.*
	IS THE	HOUSE	OF-THE	PRESIDENT
	IT IS THE PRESIDENT'S HOUSE.			
2.3	*José es*	*mi*	*amigo.*	
	JOSE IS	MY	FRIEND	
	JOSE IS MY FRIEND.			
3.1	*Este libro es*	*mío.*		
	THIS BOOK IS	MINE		
	THIS BOOK IS MINE.			
3.2	*Aquella casa es*	*de*	*María.*	
	YON HOUSE IS	OF	MARIA	
	THAT HOUSE OVER THERE IS MARIA'S.			
3.3	*Este niño es*	*nuestro.*		
	THIS CHILD IS	OURS		
	THIS CHILD IS OURS.			

examples in this table seem to form an additional type, differing from the locative in having both a difference of verb and a correlated difference in the type of complement used.

Finally, the expression of descriptive being is shown in Table 6.11. Here we see some examples parallel to Table 6.10 (in section 1) and others parallel to the locatives from Table 6.9 (compare section 2 of each table). The descriptive examples in section 1 use the verb *es*, while those in section 2 use *está*. The difference between the two is particularly highlighted by the comparison of examples 1.3 and 2.3, which differ only in the verb used. As suggested by the glosses for each clause, *es* is used if the description involves something more or less inherent, while *está* implies a more or less temporary state. To quote from one Spanish grammar:

> *Ser* [the verb of which *es* is one form] is used ... with an adjective to express an inherent quality or characteristic of the subject ... while *estar* [the verb of which *está* is one form] is used ... with adjectives to indicate a state or condition of the subject which may be temporary, accidental, or variable. (Turk, 1943, pp. 44–5)

This data therefore suggests an analysis of these Spanish expressions of being into a total of four clause types, as displayed in the schemas in Figure 6.7. The existential type differs from all the others in having the verb first, as well as in the fact that a special verb is used. Although all examples here (section 1 of Table 6.9) have a locative expression, the Locational is actually an optional constituent, just as in English, so this fact is reflected in its schema. The remaining three types show greater similarities among themselves, but they are separated by differences involving the class of verbs in the Predicator in correlation with the type of Complement selected. The Subject is shown as optional for all of these three types, because subject pronouns are not always used in Spanish. They occur only where the reference would not be clear without them, or when special emphasis on the Subject is needed.

Table 6.11 The expression of descriptive being in Spanish

1.1	*El*	*parque*	*es*	*muy*	*grande.*
	THE	PARK	IS	VERY	LARGE
	THE PARK IS VERY LARGE.				
1.2	*Esta*	*tiza*	*es*	*blanca.*	
	THIS	CHALK	IS	WHITE	
	THIS CHALK IS WHITE.				
1.3	*Nuestro*	*maestro*	*es*	*pálido.*	
	OUR	TEACHER	IS	PALE	
	OUR TEACHER IS PALE (by nature).				
2.1	*El*	*café*	*está*	*caliente.*	
	THE	COFFEE	IS	HOT	
	THE COFFEE IS HOT.				
2.2	*Mi*	*niño*	*está*	*cansado.*	
	MY	CHILD	IS	TIRED	
	MY CHILD IS TIRED.				
2.3	*Nuestro*	*maestro*	*está*	*pálido.*	
	OUR	TEACHER	IS	PALE	
	OUR TEACHER IS PALE (at the moment).				

A further perspective can be provided by considering the situation in another language, Japanese. We can begin this with the expression of locative and existential being, as shown in Table 6.12. The locational examples are shown in sections 1 and 2, while the rest of the examples are existential. It can be observed that the same verbs are used in both types, but the verb is *aru* for an inanimate subject, and *iru* if the subject is animate. The difference between the simple locatives and the existentials concerns the use of particular adpositions and clause

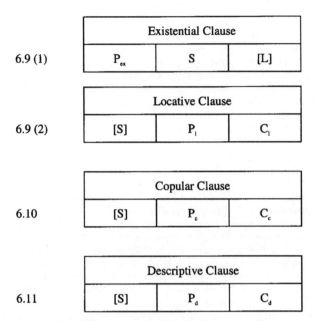

6.9 (1)

Existential Clause		
P_{ex}	S	[L]

6.9 (2)

Locative Clause		
[S]	P_l	C_l

6.10

Copular Clause		
[S]	P_c	C_c

6.11

Descriptive Clause		
[S]	P_d	C_d

Figure 6.7 Schemas for four different types of "being" in Spanish

Table 6.12 The expression of existence and location in Japanese

1.1   *hon*   *wa*   *uti*   *ni*   *aru*
     BOOK   *TOPIC*   HOUSE   *IN*   IS
     THE BOOK IS IN THE HOUSE.

1.2   *uti*   *wa*   *tookyoo*   *ni*   *aru*
     HOUSE   *TOPIC*   TOKYO   *IN*   IS
     THE HOUSE IS IN TOKYO.

1.3   *syoosetu*   *wa*   *tosyokan*   *ni*   *aru*
     NOVEL   *TOPIC*   LIBRARY   *IN*   IS
     THE NOVEL IS IN THE LIBRARY.

2.1   *watasi*   *wa*   *rondon*   *ni*   *iru*
     I   *TOPIC*   LONDON   *IN*   IS
     I AM IN LONDON.

2.2   *kodomo*   *wa*   *tookyoo*   *ni*   *iru*
     CHILD   *TOPIC*   TOKYO   *IN*   IS
     THE CHILD IS IN TOKYO.

2.3   *neko*   *wa*   *uti*   *ni*   *iru*
     CAT   *TOPIC*   HOUSE   *IN*   IS
     THE CAT IS IN THE HOUSE.

3.1   *koko*   *ni*   *hon*   *ga*   *aru*
     HERE   *IN*   BOOK   *SUBJECT*   IS
     THERE IS A BOOK HERE.

3.2   *asoko*   *ni*   *kami*   *ga*   *aru*
     OVER-THERE   *IN*   PAPER   *SUBJECT*   IS
     THERE IS PAPER OVER THERE.

3.3   *tookyoo*   *ni*   *uti*   *ga*   *aru*
     TOKYO   *IN*   HOUSE   *SUBJECT*   IS
     THERE IS A HOUSE IN TOKYO.

table continues

4.1	*tookyoo*	*ni*		*kodomo*	*ga*		*iru*
	TOKYO	IN		CHILD	SUBJECT		IS
	THERE IS A CHILD IN TOKYO.						
4.2	*uti*	*ni*		*neko*	*ga*		*iru*
	HOUSE	IN		CAT	SUBJECT		IS
	THERE IS A CAT IN THE HOUSE.						
4.3	*koko*	*ni*		*musi*	*ga*		*iru*
	HERE	IN		INSECT	SUBJECT		IS
	THERE IS AN INSECT HERE.						

orders. So just as Spanish has a choice of verbs in descriptive clauses, Japanese has a choice for these clause types, based on the animacy of the subject.

The expression of classificatory, equative, and possessive being is illustrated in Table 6.13. These types are characterized by a different verb *da*, generally called the copula in Japanese grammars. The formal difference between classificatory and equative types, as seen in sections 1 and 2, involves using the topical postposition *wa* in the former and the subject postposition *ga* in the latter. It might seem at first glance that these are equivalent to the English indefinite and definite articles, but this is not true. In these types, the basic structure involves Subject plus Complement plus Copular Predicator, with the Complement manifested by a noun phrase unmarked by a postposition. To get the possessive, the same basic structure is used, but a postpositional phrase marked by the possessive postposition *no* is taken in the role of Complement. This latter phrase is the same one that would be used in a noun phrase to indicate a possessive attribute. So the difference between the classificatory and the possessive involves the kind of Complement selected.

Table 6.13 The expression of classificatory, equative, and possessive being in Japanese

1.1	*sono*	*eikokuzin*		*wa*	*sensei*		*da*
	THAT	ENGLISHMAN		TOPIC	TEACHER		IS
	THAT ENGLISHMAN IS A TEACHER.						
1.2	*watasi*	*wa*		*gakusei*			*da*
	I	TOPIC		STUDENT			IS
	I AM A STUDENT.						
1.3	*kare*	*wa*		*amerikazin*			*da*
	HE	TOPIC		AMERICAN			IS
	HE IS AN AMERICAN.						
2.1	*sono*	*eikokuzin*		*ga*	*sensei*		*da*
	THAT	ENGLISHMAN		SUBJECT	TEACHER		IS
	THAT ENGLISHMAN IS THE TEACHER.						
2.2	*watasi*	*ga*		*gakusei*			*da*
	I	SUBJECT		STUDENT			IS
	I AM THE STUDENT.						
2.3	*kare*	*ga*		*amerikazin*			*da*
	HE	SUBJECT		AMERICAN			IS
	HE IS THE AMERICAN.						
3.1	*kono*	*uti*	*wa*	*watasi*	*no*		*da*
	THIS	HOUSE	TOPIC	I	OF		IS
	THIS HOUSE IS MINE.						
3.2	*ano*	*hon*	*wa*	*kare*	*no*		*da*
	YON	BOOK	TOPIC	HE	OF		IS
	THAT BOOK OVER THERE IS HIS.						
3.3	*sono*	*uti*	*wa*	*isya*	*no*		*da*
	THAT	HOUSE	TOPIC	DOCTOR	OF		IS
	THAT HOUSE IS THE DOCTOR'S.						

Finally, we can consider the expression of descriptive being, as illustrated in Table 6.14. It can be observed that, somewhat like those in Spanish, these descriptive clauses fall into two types. The difference between them, however, is purely a matter of grammatical classification, unlike the differences found in Spanish. The examples in section 1 of the table involve STATIVE VERBS (usually called "adjectives" in English-language grammars of Japanese) which as verbs show distinctions of tense and other grammatical categories generally characteristic of Japanese verbs. In section 2, however, the examples use the copula *da* with a complement in the form of what is sometimes termed an ADJECTIVAL NOUN or DESCRIPTIVE NOUN. The examples in the first type, then, would form a separate clause type, which may be called a STATIVE CLAUSE, while the others would simply be further choices of complement in a Copular Clause, along with the examples in Table 6.13.

Table 6.14 The expression of descriptive being in Japanese

1.1	*kono*	*hon*	*wa*	*kuroi*	
	THIS	BOOK	*TOPIC*	IS-BLACK	
	THIS BOOK IS BLACK.				
1.2	*ano*	*neko*	*wa*	*siroi*	
	YON	CAT	*TOPIC*	IS-WHITE	
	THAT CAT OVER THERE IS WHITE.				
1.3	*sono*	*teeburu*	*wa*	*omoi*	
	THAT	TABLE	*TOPIC*	IS-HEAVY	
	THAT TABLE IS HEAVY.				
2.1	*kono*	*hito*	*wa*	*hen*	*da*
	THIS	PERSON	*TOPIC*	STRANGE	IS
	THIS PERSON IS STRANGE.				
2.2	*ano*	*hon*	*wa*	*rippa*	*da*
	YON	BOOK	*TOPIC*	SPLENDID	IS
	THAT BOOK OVER THERE IS SPLENDID.				
2.3	*sono*	*kodomo*	*wa*	*zyoozu*	*da*
	THAT	CHILD	*TOPIC*	SKILLFUL	IS
	THAT CHILD IS SKILLFUL.				

An analysis based on the Japanese data of Tables 6.12–14 is presented in Figure 6.8. Subjects are shown as optional despite their presence in all these examples, because they are in fact able to be omitted in Japanese, just as they are in Spanish. (This is true, incidentally, even though the Japanese verb, unlike the Spanish verb, never shows inflections for either person or number.) It will be noted that the Copular Clause has several varieties, just as in English, based on what is chosen in the role of Complement, though there are fewer basic possibilities here than in English.

For still further useful comparisons, we may now consider the expression of various kinds of being in the Central Alaskan dialect of Yup'ik Eskimo, beginning with locative and existential expressions seen in Table 6.15. Like Yup'ik clauses in general, these all have optional Subjects. Beyond these Subjects, furthermore, these examples contain only a single word, which is always a verb. So, unlike what we saw with locative expressions of being in English, Spanish, and Japanese, we do not have a verb combined syntactically with a locative Complement. Rather, the morphology of the verb itself includes both the verbal and locative meanings. So in Yup'ik there is not one locative verb, or just a couple as in Japanese *iru/aru*, but there is one corresponding to every locative case form of a noun, and the noun can have 30 different locative forms corresponding to different numbers and states of possession. For each of these locative verbs there are inflections for tense, polarity, person, and number. A selection of locative noun and verb forms based on the noun /aŋyaq/ BOAT is presented in Table 6.16. In summary, this language will have thousands of locative verbs, typically 30 for each noun in the language.

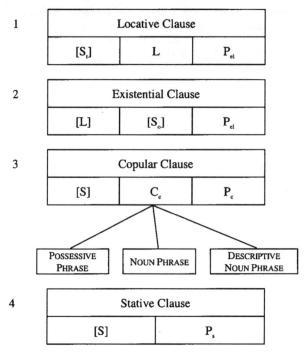

Figure 6.8 Schemas for four different types of "being" in Japanese

Table 6.15 The expression of locative and existential being in Central Alaskan Yup'ik Eskimo

---

1.1 nutɨk   aŋyamɨtuq
    GUN   IS-IN-BOAT
    THE GUN IS IN THE BOAT.
1.2 cavik   atkuɣmɨtuq
    KNIFE   IS-IN-PARKA
    THE KNIFE IS IN THE PARKA.
1.3 aŋun   nɨmmɨtuq
    MAN   IS-IN-HOUSE
    THE MAN IS IN THE HOUSE.
2.1 kuik   nɨqtaŋqɨχtuq
    RIVER   THERE-ARE-FISH
    THERE ARE FISH IN THE RIVER. = THE RIVER HAS FISH IN IT.
2.2 nanvak qayaχtaŋqɨχtuq
    LAKE   THERE-ARE-KAYAKS
    THERE ARE KAYAKS IN THE LAKE. = THE LAKE HAS KAYAKS IN IT.
2.3 tiŋsuutɨtaŋqɨχtuq
    THERE-ARE-AIRPLANES
    THERE ARE AIRPLANES.

Table 6.16 Selected locative case forms with corresponding locative verbs based on the Yup'ik noun /aŋyaq/BOAT

1.	aŋyami	aŋyamɨtut
	IN A/THE BOAT	THEY ARE IN A/THE BOAT.
2.	aŋyani	aŋyanɨtut
	IN (THE) BOATS	THEY ARE IN (THE) BOATS.
3.	aŋyamni	aŋyamnɨtut
	IN MY BOAT(S)	THEY ARE IN MY BOAT(S).
4.	aŋyaχpɨni	aŋyaχpɨnɨtut
	IN YOUR TWO BOATS	THEY ARE IN YOUR TWO BOATS.
5.	aŋyaini	aŋyainɨtut
	IN HIS/HER BOATS	THEY ARE IN HIS/HER BOATS.
6.	aŋyamɨxni	aŋyamɨxnɨtut
	IN THEIR OWN BOATS	THEY ARE IN THEIR OWN BOATS.

The existential examples in section 2 of Table 6.15 similarly show special verbs based on nouns. Grammatically, these verbs are again intransitive, and the subject, when it is expressed, indicates the place involved. There would only be one of these verbs per noun-stem, but there would still be a large number of such verbs in the language.

Table 6.17 The expression of equative, classificatory, and possessive being in Central Alaskan Yup'ik Eskimo

1.1	aataka	aŋaɬkuuɣuq	
	MY-FATHER	IS-SHAMAN	
	MY FATHER IS A/THE SHAMAN.		
1.2	mauluqa	ɨlicaristɨŋuuq	
	MY-GRANDMOTHER	IS-TEACHER	
	MY GRANDMOTHER IS A/THE TEACHER.		
1.3	pista	yupiuɣuq	
	SERVANT	IS-YUP'IK	
	THE SERVANT IS A YUP'IK ESKIMO.		
2.1	aʁnaq	aanakaqa	
	WOMAN	I-HAVE-AS-MOTHER	
	THE WOMAN IS MY MOTHER.		
2.2	tauna	qayaqaa	
	THAT	HE/SHE-HAS-AS-KAYAK	
	THAT IS HIS/HER KAYAK.		
2.3	mikiɬŋuq	qɨtunʁaqan	
	CHILD	YOU-HAVE-AS-SON	
	THE CHILD IS YOUR SON.		
3.1	una	aŋyaq	pikaqa
	THIS	BOAT	I-HAVE-AS-THING
	THIS BOAT IS MINE.		
3.2	tauna	nuusiq	pikaa
	THAT	KNIFE	HE/SHE-HAS-AS-THING
	THAT KNIFE IS HIS/HERS.		
3.3	nutɨk	pikan	
	GUN	YOU-HAVE-AS-THING	
	THE GUN IS YOURS.		

The expression of equative, classificatory, and possessive being is illustrated by the data in Table 6.17. In this language, there is no formal difference between the equative and the classificatory types, which are given in section 1 of the table. In these cases, the Predicator function is filled by yet another kind of verb that can be formed from a Yup'ik noun. This will be termed an **IDENTIFICATIONAL VERB**. Again, there is one for each noun in the language, and they are all intransitive.

From their translations, one would suppose that the examples in section 2 of this table would also be equatives marked for possession, but they have quite a different structure in Yup'ik from the examples in section 1. In essence, these examples involve transitive verbs, while those in section 1 are intransitive. In these particular kinds of transitives, the referent of the Subject is the possessor of the referent of the Object in a role indicated by the noun which serves as the base of the verb. Generally, such a verb can be formed from any Yup'ik noun by the use of a suffix in the shape /k/ or /q/. Such a verb can be termed a **ROLE-POSSESSIVE** since it indicates possession in a particular role. Though these examples are distinct from the equative-classificatory verbs in section 1, they do not form a completely new clause type: they are simply additional transitives.

The examples in section 3 are actually more varieties of the same role-possessive verbs in section 2. Here the verb is based on the semantically general noun base /pi/ THING. So syntactically the Yup'ik examples seen so far fall into two types, intransitives in Table 6.15 and section 1 of Table 6.17, and transitives in sections 2 and 3 of Table 6.17. The further subvarieties are semantic and/or morphological, but not syntactic.

The expression of descriptive being in Yup'ik is exemplified in Table 6.18. All of the examples involve intransitive verbs again, but as the numbering and literal glosses suggest, the examples in sections 1 and 2 are somewhat distinct. Those in section 1 simply use stative verbs, similar to those we saw in Japanese. Those in section 2 are syntactically similar, and can be translated in a parallel way. Morphologically, however, these verbs are based on nouns and are simply more examples of the identificational verbs already seen in section 1 of Table 6.17. Syntactically, then, expressions of being in Yup'ik do not introduce any new clause types at all. They are simply more examples of intransitive and transitive clauses, with verbs differing further in morphological details. The morphological classification of the verbs involved in these examples is summarized in Table 6.19.

Table 6.18 The expression of descriptive being in Central Alaskan Yup'ik Eskimo

---

1.1 tauna   nuusiq   asiχtuq
     THAT   KNIFE   IS-GOOD
     THAT KNIFE IS GOOD.
1.2 una   qayaq   takkuq
     THIS   KAYAK   IS-LONG
     THIS KAYAK IS LONG.
1.3 imna   ɨna   aŋŋuq
     AFOREMENTIONED   HOUSE   IS-LARGE
     THE HOUSE (WE'VE MENTIONED) IS LARGE.
2.1 tauna   qayaq   nutaʁauɣuq
     THAT   KAYAK   IS-NEW-THING
     THAT KAYAK IS NEW.
2.2 una   nutɨk   akkaɬuuɣuq
     THIS   GUN   IS-OLD-THING
     THIS GUN IS OLD.
2.3 tauna   aɬauɣuq
     THAT   IS-DIFFERENT-THING
     THAT ONE IS DIFFERENT.

Table 6.19 Syntactic and morphological classification of Yup'ik expressions of being

GENERAL TYPE (MORPHOLOGICAL/ SYNTACTIC)	SPECIFIC TYPE (MORPHOLOGICAL)	SUFFIX SHAPE	INTERPRETATION	CORRESPONDING ENGLISH TYPE
INTRANSITIVE	LOCATIVE	/ɨt/	BE IN (THE) X	COPULAR: LOCATIVE
	LOCATIVE-EXISTENTIAL	/taŋqɨχt/	THERE IS/ARE X IN (SUBJECT)	EXISTENTIAL
	IDENTIFICATIONAL	/u/ ∼ /ŋu/	BE A/THE X BE (ADJECTIVE)	COPULAR: CLASSIFICATORY/ EQUATIVE/DESCRIPTIVE
	STATIVE	(individual verbs)		COPULAR: DESCRIPTIVE
TRANSITIVE	ROLE-POSSESSIVE	/k/ ∼ /q/	(SUBJECT) HAS (OBJECT) IN ROLE OF X	COPULAR: POSSESSIVE ∼ EQUATIVE: POSSESSIVE

In summary, we have seen that languages can divide up the notion of being in various ways. In English, the matter involves just two special clause types, both of which use the verb *to be*. In Spanish, however, there are four special clause types involving three different verbs of being. Japanese also has four special clause types and three general verbs indicating being, but the existence of individual stative verbs for many categories of descriptive being makes the total of verbs of being in the language rather large. Finally, in Yup'ik, there are no general verbs of being at all. Rather, the typical noun has a corresponding identificational and locative-existential intransitive verb, a role-possessive transitive, and up to 30 locative verbs corresponding to it. In addition, there are many individual stative verbs, as in Japanese.

Non-verbal clauses

Whatever their variety, all of the clauses discussed so far have had a verb in the role of Predicator. While every genuine clause must be seen as having a Predicator, however, some languages have examples in which the Predicator function is manifested by something other than a verb. Standard English is not such a language, but examples of non-verbal Predicators may be observed in a special non-standard spoken style generally understandable by English speakers. This will be termed "pseudo-pidgin" style, as exemplified in the now-proverbial "*Me – Tarzan; you – Jane*". Table 6.20 gives some examples of this style, in which expressions that would be Complements (or existential Subjects) in the standard form of English are used as Predicators. The dashes in these examples are intended to signal intonation breaks, which characteristically occur in this style. Two written styles which have certain similarities to this spoken style are those found in newspaper headlines and in telegrams, as in such possible headlines as *Tax Hike Possible, Triple Murderer Convicted, Crucial Decision Pending*, or *French President in City*.

One of the better-known European languages in which apparently verbless clauses regularly occur is Russian, as shown by the examples in Table 6.21. In full context, however, the analysis of the apparently verbless Predicators of this language as truly verbless is complicated by the fact that overt verbs do occur when these ideas are expressed in other tenses, such as past or future, or even in the present tense when special emphasis is intended. In view of these facts, these Russian examples are perhaps best treated as having a zero allomorph for the non-emphatic present of the otherwise overt verb *byt'* TO BE. In languages without a parallel situation to this, however, genuine non-verbal Predicators may be recognized. The key fact indicating the presence of non-verbal Predicators is a different general behavior from what is observed for verbs in the language. So if a verb is inflected for

Table 6.20 Examples of verbless clauses in the pseudo-pidgin style of spoken English

Type	Example
EQUATIVE	*Me – Tarzan.*
CLASSIFICATORY	*You – doctor.*
LOCATIVE	*His house – over there.*
POSSESSIVE	*This – mine.*
DESCRIPTIVE	*This knife – very dull.*
EXISTENTIAL	*There – bananas.*

tense, person, and number and we see an apparent noun inflected for the same categories in the role of Predicator, it is probably best viewed as an identificational verb such as those in Yup'ik. In a language where neither nouns nor verbs show inflection, we could simply say that a word can function either as a noun or as a verb rather than insisting on nominal Predicators.

Table 6.21 Some apparent verbless clauses in Modern Russian

Type	Example		
EQUATIVE	*On –*	*Gospodin*	*Petrov.*
	HE	MISTER	PETROV
	HE IS MISTER PETROV.		
CLASSIFICATORY	*Ja –*	*inžener.*	
	I	ENGINEER	
	I AM AN ENGINEER.		
LOCATIVE	*Vse*	*zdes'.*	
	ALL	HERE	
	EVERYONE IS HERE.		
POSSESSIVE	*Èta*	*kniga – moja.*	
	THIS	BOOK MY	
	THIS BOOK IS MINE.		
DESCRIPTIVE	*Vaši*	*risunki –*	*krasivy.*
	YOUR	DRAWINGS	BEAUTIFUL
	YOUR DRAWINGS ARE BEAUTIFUL.		
EXISTENTIAL	*Tam*	*xleb.*	
	THERE	BREAD	
	THERE IS BREAD THERE.		

Summary of clausal constituents and symbols

Table 6.22 presents a summary of the various syntactic functions discussed in this chapter. They are divided into three types: Predicators, Participants, and Circumstantials.

As we have seen, Predicators are present in any clause, and are most commonly manifested by verbs, though some languages have other kinds of manifestation. All of the types brought up in this chapter are included, but this listing should by no means be seen as rigid or exhaustive.

PARTICIPANT is suggested as the best generic term for the clausal functions designating the most central persons or things participating in the actions or states designated by clauses. Among linguists heavily influenced by the traditions of philosophical semantics, the term "argument" is most commonly used for what are here termed participants. One should be prepared to meet this alternative term, but it is rejected here as more confusing than informative, since its meaning here has nothing to do with "argument" in the more usual sense

Table 6.22 Typical syntactic functions at clause rank

Type	Function	Suggested symbol	Typical manifestation
PREDICATOR	INTRANSITIVE PREDICATOR	P_i	Intransitive Verb Phrase
	COPULAR PREDICATOR	P_c	Copular Verb Phrase
	LOCATIVE PREDICATOR	P_l	Locative VP/Locative Expression
	EXISTENTIAL-LOCATIVE PREDICATOR	P_{el}	Existential Locative Verb Phrase
	STATIVE PREDICATOR	P_s	Stative Verb Phrase
	DESCRIPTIVE PREDICATOR	P_d	Adjective Phrase
	NOMINAL PREDICATOR	P_n	Noun Phrase/Pronoun Phrase
	TRANSITIVE PREDICATOR	P_t	Transitive Verb Phrase
	SEMITRANSITIVE PREDICATOR	P_{st}	Semitransitive Verb Phrase
	SUBJECTIVE-TRANSITIVE PREDICATOR	P_{sjt}	Subjective-Transitive Verb Phrase
	OBJECTIVE-TRANSITIVE PREDICATOR	P_{ot}	Objective-Transitive Verb Phrase
	LOCATIVE TRANSITIVE PREDICATOR	P_{lt}	Locative-Transitive Verb Phrase
	BITRANSITIVE PREDICATOR	P_b	Bitransitive Verb Phrase
	SEMIBITRANSITIVE PREDICATOR	P_{sb}	Semibitransitive Verb Phrase
	PSEUDOBITRANSITIVE PREDICATOR	P_{pb}	Pseudobitransitive Verb Phrase
PARTICIPANT	SUBJECT	S	Noun Phrase/
	DIRECT OBJECT	O_d	Pronoun Phrase/
	INDIRECT OBJECT	O_i	Adpositional Phrase
	COPULAR COMPLEMENT	C_c	
	SUBJECTIVE COMPLEMENT	C_s	
	OBJECTIVE COMPLEMENT	C_o	
CIRCUMSTANTIAL	LOCATIONAL	L	Locative Adverb/Adpositional Ph.
	TEMPORAL	T	Temporal Adverb/Adpositional Ph.
	INSTRUMENT	In	Noun/Pronoun/Adpositional Phrase
	MANNER	M	Manner Adverb/Adpositional Ph.

of a dispute or verbal discussion. "Participant", on the other hand, correctly suggests that it refers to some one or some thing that *participates* in the action or state in a significant way.

The final grouping, the CIRCUMSTANTIALS, as mentioned previously, designate factors seen as worth mention in connection with an event or state, but they are involved less centrally than the participants. Unlike most participants, furthermore, they are not generally essential to or diagnostic of clause types, but potentially any or all of them could be included in a clause as appropriate. A partial exception is the Locational, particularly as it occurs obligatorily in the English Locative-Transitive Clause.

Exercises

1.   Clause types in Indonesian

Determine the number of clause types in evidence in the following data and account for the data, including any phrasal structures as well as clauses. It should be noted that the verbs are not inflected for tense, so you should not look for evidence of inflection.

1.	orang itu tertawa	THE MAN LAUGHED.
2.	anjing ini menggonggong	THIS DOG BARKED.
3.	anak itu menangis	THE CHILD CRIED.
4.	burung menyanyi	A BIRD IS SINGING.
5.	serdadu itu lelah	THE SOLDIER IS TIRED.
6.	orang pandai ini kuat	THIS CLEVER MAN WAS STRONG.
7.	gadis itu rajin	THE GIRL WAS DILIGENT.
8.	burung itu indah	THE BIRD IS BEAUTIFUL.
9.	serdadu lelah ini menembak harimau	THIS TIRED SOLDIER SHOT A TIGER.
10.	guru itu menangkap pencuri itu	THE TEACHER CAUGHT THE THIEF.
11.	kucing itu makan ikan ini	THE CAT ATE THE FISH.
12.	harimau kuat itu makan anjing	THE TIGER ATE A DOG.
13.	guru muda itu memberi gadis itu buku	THE YOUNG TEACHER GAVE THE GIRL A BOOK.
14.	gadis pandai itu memberi anjing tulang ini	THE CLEVER GIRL GAVE THE DOG THIS BONE.
15.	serdadu itu memberi guru pandai itu méja bagus	THE SOLDIER GAVE THE CLEVER TEACHER A NICE TABLE.
16.	anak nakal memberi pencuri buku bagus	A NAUGHTY CHILD GAVE A THIEF A NICE BOOK.

2.   Clause types in Northern Havyaka Kannada

The following data set illustrates some contrasting clause types in a local variety of Kannada, a major Dravidian language spoken in southwestern India. Determine the number of contrasting clause types, edit the inflected forms, and account for the data.

1.	malukta	HE LIES DOWN/THEY LIE DOWN.
2.	appa malukta	FATHER LIES DOWN.
3.	tamma malukta	THE YOUNGER BROTHER LIES DOWN.
4.	tammandru malukta	THE YOUNGER BROTHERS LIE DOWN.
5.	makḷu malukta	THE CHILDREN LIE DOWN.
6.	malukoṇḍidda	HE/THEY LAY DOWN.
7.	malukoṇḍidda	THE CHILD LAY DOWN.
8.	aṇṇa malukoṇḍidda	THE ELDER BROTHER LAY DOWN.
9.	ho˙gta	HE GOES/THEY GO.

10.	aṇṇandru hoˑgta	THE ELDER BROTHERS GO.
11.	appa hoˑgta	FATHER GOES.
12.	mawa hoˑgta	THE UNCLE GOES.
13.	hoˑgidda	HE/THEY WENT.
14.	mawa hoˑgidda	THE UNCLE WENT.
15.	tammandru hoˑgidda	THE YOUNGER BROTHERS WENT.
16.	mej noˑḍta	HE SEES/THEY SEE THE TABLE(S).
17.	pustaka noˑḍta	HE SEES/THEY SEE THE BOOK(S).
18.	magu pustaka noˑḍta	THE CHILD SEES THE BOOK(S).
19.	mawagaḷu sinema noˑḍta	THE UNCLES SEE THE MOVIE(S).
20.	sinema noḍidda	HE/THEY SAW THE MOVIE(S).
21.	tammandru mej noḍidda	THE YOUNGER BROTHERS SAW THE TABLE(S).
22.	appa magu noḍidda	FATHER SAW THE CHILD.
23.	pustaka barita	HE WRITES/THEY WRITE A BOOK/BOOKS.
24.	aṇṇandru pustaka barita	THE ELDER BROTHERS WRITE A BOOK/BOOKS.
25.	magu kaˑgda barita	THE CHILD WRITES A LETTER/LETTERS.
26.	mawagaḷu kaˑgda barita	THE UNCLES WRITE A LETTER/LETTERS.
27.	kaˑgda baradda	HE/THEY WROTE A LETTER/LETTERS.
28.	appa kaˑgda baradda	FATHER WROTE A LETTER/LETTERS.
29.	tamma pustaka baradda	THE YOUNGER BROTHER WROTE A BOOK/BOOKS.
30.	aṇṇandru pustaka baradda	THE ELDER BROTHERS WROTE A BOOK/BOOKS.

The following data from the same language show some evidence for different types of clauses that involve being. Treat these data in the same way as the previous set.

31.	hatra iddidda	HE WAS/THEY WERE CLOSE BY.
32.	appa hatra iddidda	FATHER WAS CLOSE BY.
33.	manuṣa hatra idda	THE MAN IS CLOSE BY.
34.	alli idda	HE IS/THEY ARE THERE.
35.	tamma alli iddidda	THE YOUNGER BROTHER WAS THERE.
36.	manuṣaru alli idda	THE MEN ARE THERE.
37.	illi idda	HE IS/THEY ARE HERE.
38.	magu illi idda	THE CHILD IS HERE.
39.	aṇṇandru illi iddidda	THE ELDER BROTHERS WERE HERE.
40.	tammandru illi idda	THE YOUNGER BROTHERS ARE HERE.
41.	aˑkaḍe iddidda	HE WAS/THEY WERE OVER THERE.
42.	manuṣa aˑkaḍe iddidda	THE MAN WAS OVER THERE.
43.	appa aˑkaḍe idda	FATHER IS OVER THERE.
44.	sustaˑgi aˑkta	HE/THEY ARE TIRED.
45.	tamma sustaˑgi aˑkta	THE YOUNGER BROTHER IS TIRED.
46.	mawagaḷu sustaˑgi aˑkta	THE UNCLES ARE TIRED.
47.	sustaˑgi aˑgidda	HE/THEY WERE TIRED.
48.	appa sustaˑgi aˑgidda	FATHER WAS TIRED.
49.	manuṣaru sustaˑgi aˑgidda	THE MEN WERE TIRED.
50.	kuṣi aˑkta	HE IS/THEY ARE HAPPY.
51.	magu kuṣi aˑkta	THE CHILD IS HAPPY.
52.	tammandru kuṣi aˑkta	THE YOUNGER BROTHERS ARE HAPPY.
53.	kuṣi aˑgidda	HE WAS/THEY WERE HAPPY.
54.	aṇṇandru kuṣi aˑgidda	THE ELDER BROTHERS WERE HAPPY.
55.	mawa kuṣi aˑgidda	THE UNCLE WAS HAPPY.

3.   Being in Amharic

The following data illustrate the expression of being in Amharic, the traditional national language of Ethiopia. Determine how many clause types need to be recognized and account for the data. For purposes of this solution, it may be assumed that (1) there is inflection for definiteness in the nouns and (2) the expressions of location are all adverbs. (Further data from the language could force different analyses, but are not in evidence here.)

1.   betu tɨllɨk' nəw — THE HOUSE IS BIG.
2.   lɨju k'onjo nəw — THE CHILD IS PRETTY.
3.   lɨju t'əru nəw — THE CHILD IS GOOD.
4.   məs'hafu tɨllɨk' nəw — THE BOOK IS GOOD.
5.   səwu tɨnnɨš nəw — THE MAN IS SMALL.
6.   lɨj ɨzzih allə — A CHILD IS HERE. OR THERE IS A CHILD HERE.
7.   məs'haf ɨkɨfɨr allə — A BOOK IS IN THE CLASSROOM. OR THERE IS A BOOK IN THE CLASSROOM.
8.   wəmbər ɨkɨfɨr allə — A CHAIR IS IN THE CLASSROOM. OR THERE IS A CHAIR IN THE CLASSROOM.
9.   səw ɨzzih allə — A MAN IS HERE. OR THERE IS A MAN HERE.
10.   hakim ɨzziya allə — A DOCTOR IS THERE. OR THERE IS A DOCTOR THERE.
11.   lɨju ɨzzih allə OR lɨju ɨzzih nəw — THE CHILD IS HERE.
12.   məs'hafu ɨkɨfɨr allə OR məs'hafu ɨkɨfɨr nəw — THE BOOK IS IN THE CLASSROOM.
13.   hakimu ɨzziya allə OR hakimu ɨzziya nəw — THE DOCTOR IS THERE.
14.   gʷaddəññaw ɨzzih allə OR gʷaddəññaw ɨzzih nəw — THE FRIEND IS HERE.
15.   təmariw ɨkɨfɨr allə OR təmariw ɨkɨfɨr nəw — THE STUDENT IS IN THE CLASSROOM.
16.   səwu təmari nəw — THE MAN IS A STUDENT.
17.   səwu sərratəñña nəw — THE MAN IS A WORKER.
18.   təmariw lɨj nəw — THE STUDENT IS A CHILD.
19.   gʷaddəññaw hakim nəw — THE FRIEND IS A DOCTOR.
20.   sərratəññaw gʷaddəñña nəw — THE WORKER IS A FRIEND.
21.   gʷaddəññaw hakimu nəw — THE FRIEND IS THE DOCTOR.
22.   əmariw gʷaddəññaw nəw — THE STUDENT IS THE FRIEND.
23.   lɨju təmariw nəw — THE CHILD IS THE STUDENT.
24.   gʷaddəññaw sərratəññaw nəw — THE FRIEND IS THE WORKER.
25.   hakimu lebaw nəw — THE DOCTOR IS THE THIEF.

4.   Syntax of direct objects in Italian

The following data set shows some Italian transitive verbs with noun-phrase and pronoun objects. It should be assumed that the examples in each numbered group 1–8 are paraphrases expressing the same situation, and that underlining in the English glosses shows emphasis. Account for these data, including the gender and number concord within the noun phrase.

1.   *Giovanni vede la donna.* — GIOVANNI SEES THE WOMAN.
1a.   *Giovanni vede lei.* — GIOVANNI SEES HER.
1b.   *Giovanni la vede.* — GIOVANNI SEES HER.

2.   *Silvana prende il bambino.* — SILVANA TAKES THE BABY.
2a.   *Silvana prende lui.* — SILVANA TAKES HIM.

2b.	*Silvana lo prende.*	SILVANA TAKES HIM.
3.	*Luigi prende il ragazzo.*	LUIGI TAKES THE BOY.
3a.	*Luigi prende lui.*	LUIGI TAKES <u>HIM</u>.
3b.	*Luigi lo prende.*	LUIGI TAKES HIM.
4.	*Mariana vede la nonna.*	MARIAN SEES THE GRANDMOTHER.
4a.	*Mariana vede lei.*	MARIAN SEES <u>HER</u>.
4b.	*Mariana la vede.*	MARIAN SEES HER.
5.	*Giulio saluta le donne.*	JULIUS GREETS THE WOMEN.
5a.	*Giulio saluta loro.*	JULIUS GREETS <u>THEM</u>.
5b.	*Giulio le saluta.*	JULIUS GREETS THEM.
6.	*Lucia lava i bambini.*	LUCIA WASHES THE BABIES.
6a.	*Lucia lava loro.*	LUCIA WASHES <u>THEM</u>.
6b.	*Lucia li lava.*	LUCIA WASHES THEM.
7.	*Sergio cerchia i ragazzi.*	SERGIO LOOKS FOR THE BOYS.
7a.	*Sergio cerchia loro.*	SERGIO LOOKS FOR <u>THEM</u>.
7b.	*Sergio li cerchia.*	SERGIO LOOKS FOR THEM.
8.	*Luisa visita le nonne.*	LUISA CALLS ON THE GRANDMOTHERS.
8a.	*Luisa visita loro.*	LUISA CALLS ON <u>THEM</u>.
8b.	*Luisa le visita.*	LUISA CALLS ON THEM.

5. Location and possession in Russian

The following data set shows examples of the expression of location and possession in Russian. Determine how many clause types are required to account for the data and prepare a solution based on an appropriate editing. Note that only the verbs will require editing, though students of Russian will realize that there are inflectional differences not in evidence here that affect other words. Note in particular the word *u*: (1) based on parallels with other words, what kind of word does it seem to be?; (2) how can it be glossed? The answers to these two questions should be reflected in your solution.

1.	*Tam karandaš.*	A PENCIL IS THERE.
2.	*Zdes' byl karandaš.*	A PENCIL WAS HERE.
3.	*Naprotiv budet karandaš.*	A PENCIL WILL BE ACROSS THE WAY.
4.	*Zdes' stul.*	A CHAIR IS HERE.
5.	*Tam byl stul.*	A CHAIR WAS THERE.
6.	*Naprotiv budet stul.*	A CHAIR WILL BE ACROSS THE WAY.
7.	*Naprotiv dom.*	A HOUSE IS ACROSS THE WAY.
8.	*Tam byl gruzovik.*	A TRUCK WAS THERE.
9.	*Zdes' budet stol.*	A TABLE WILL BE HERE.
10.	*Okolo menja budet karandaš.*	I WILL HAVE A PENCIL.
11.	*Okolo vas byl dom.*	NEAR YOU WAS A HOUSE.
12.	*Okolo nego budet stul.*	NEAR HIM WILL BE A CHAIR.
13.	*Okolo nas muzej.*	NEAR US IS A MUSEUM.
14.	*Okolo nix byl nož.*	NEAR THEM WAS A KNIFE.
15.	*Okolo neë budet škaf.*	NEAR HER WILL BE A CUPBOARD.
16.	*U menja nož.*	I HAVE A KNIFE.
17.	*U nas budet muzej.*	WE WILL HAVE A MUSEUM.
18.	*U vas byl stol.*	YOU HAD A TABLE.
19.	*U nego gost'.*	HE HAS A GUEST.
20.	*U neë byl dom.*	SHE HAD A HOUSE.
21.	*U menja budet karandaš.*	I WILL HAVE A PENCIL.

22. *U vas škaf.*	YOU HAVE A CUPBOARD.
23. *U nas byl gost'.*	WE HAD A GUEST.
24. *U nego budet drug.*	HE WILL HAVE A FRIEND.
25. *U neë gruzovik.*	SHE HAS A TRUCK.

Terminology

BITRANSITIVE CLAUSE
   PSEUDO-BITRANSITIVE
     CLAUSE
   SEMI-BITRANSITIVE CLAUSE

CIRCUMSTANTIAL

COPULAR CLAUSE
   DESCRIPTIVE CLAUSE
   EQUATIVE CLAUSE
   IDENTIFICATIONAL CLAUSE
   LOCATIVE CLAUSE
   POSSESSIVE CLAUSE

EXISTENTIAL CLAUSE

INDIRECT OBJECT

INTRANSITIVE CLAUSE

INTRODUCER

PARTICIPANT

STATIVE CLAUSE

TRANSITIVE CLAUSE
   OBJECTIVE-TRANSITIVE
     CLAUSE
   SEMI-TRANSITIVE CLAUSE
   SUBJECTIVE-TRANSITIVE
     CLAUSE

7

Congruence and determination in the clause

Congruence between Subject and Predicator

Various kinds of congruence within the phrase were discussed in Chapter 4. As it happens, many of the general kinds of congruence also apply between clause constituents in many languages. Probably the most frequent of such relations at the rank of the clause involves agreement between the Subject and the Predicator. One common variety of this is illustrated by the Classical Latin data in Table 7.1. In this material, the concord involves the categorial dimensions of person and number. The first- and second-person examples are shown with optional subjects, since personal pronoun subjects are commonly omitted in Latin. The third-person examples shown all have nouns as subjects, but it would also be possible to find Latin examples translated into English with third-person pronouns, either with no explicit subjects and third-person verbs, or with demonstrative pronouns of various types, technically functioning as Nominal Heads in noun phrases which function as Subjects at clause rank. For example, *currit* could constitute a clause translatable into English as *he runs*, *she runs*, or *it runs*, according to context. English *he runs* could also be expressed in Latin as *is currit*, *hic currit*, or *ille currit*, but the explicit Subjects in these examples are THIS/THAT ONE, THIS ONE, and THAT ONE, respectively. Figure 7.1 presents the solution to this data, which introduces no new concepts or notations. It simply extends the notations used for concord previously on the phrase rank to use on the rank of the clause. The number concord shown with the superscript [1] is completely straightforward, as an example of simple concord. The person concord can be argued, however, to be of the governmental type, since it depends on a lexical selection of Subject rather than on any inflection for person in the Subject expressions. When a noun (really a noun phrase, but this data does not provide evidence for phrases) is selected, the augmented superscript [2T] requires the verb to be in the third-person form. Otherwise, the choice of a first- or second-person pronoun will require the corresponding personal inflection in the verb. If there is no explicit Subject taken, of course, the concord will be nullified, and the choice of person and number in the verb will be free. It should be noted that the plural subject pronouns *nōs* WE and *vōs* YOU have been edited as the plurals of their singular counterparts.

In some languages, the concord of Subjects and Predicators may also involve gender, as illustrated by the Israeli Hebrew data in Table 7.2. This material is presented in a partly analysed form, in that the pronouns for various persons, genders, and numbers are lined up with the verb forms for the present and past tenses of the verbs meaning LIVE and WRITE. It can be seen that pronouns, present-tense verbs, and past-tense verbs differ in what they distinguish morphologically. The pronouns have distinct forms for all possibilities, except for their failure to distinguish genders in the first person. Past-tense verbs show this same syncretism, and they also fail to distinguish the genders in the third-person plural. Present-tense verbs, finally, always distinguish both gender and number, but they do not show any distinctions of person. These inconsistencies need to be leveled out in the process of editing, allowing the details about syncretism to be left to the morphology. It should also be noted that the two verbs involved here, representable as /gar/ LIVE and /k t v/ WRITE, differ in the way they express the tense distinctions.

The solution to this data is given in Figure 7.2. Here the gender concord appears to be simple rather than governmental, since the gender of the pronouns seems to be reasonably

Table 7.1 Person/number concord in Classical Latin

1.	*(egō) ambulō*	I WALK.
2.	*(tū) ambulās*	YOU (Sg) WALK.
3.	*dux ambulat*	THE LEADER WALKS.
4.	*(nōs) ambulāmus*	WE WALK.
5.	*(vōs) ambulātis*	YOU (Pl) WALK.
6.	*amīcī ambulant*	THE FRIENDS WALK.
7.	*(egō) currō*	I RUN.
8.	*(tū) curris*	YOU (Sg) RUN.
9.	*mulier currit*	THE WOMAN RUNS.
10.	*(nōs) currimus*	WE RUN.
11.	*(vōs) curritis*	YOU (Pl) RUN.
12.	*puerī currunt*	THE BOYS RUN.
13.	*(egō) sēdeō*	I SIT.
14.	*(tū) sēdēs*	SIT.
15.	*puer sēdet*	THE BOY SITS.
16.	*(nōs) sēdēmus*	WE SIT.
17.	*(vōs) sēdētis*	YOU (Pl) SIT.
18.	*mulierēs sēdent*	THE WOMEN SIT.
19.	*(egō) dormiō*	I SLEEP.
20.	*(tū) dormīs*	YOU (Sg) SLEEP.
21.	*amīcus dormit*	THE FRIEND SLEEPS.
22.	*(nōs) dormīmus*	WE SLEEP.
23.	*(vōs) dormītis*	YOU (Pl) SLEEP.
24.	*agricolae dormiunt*	THE FARMERS SLEEP.

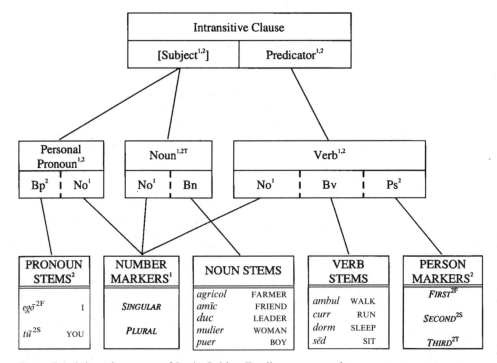

Figure 7.1 A boxed account of Latin Subject/Predicator concord

treatable as inflectional. Hebrew nouns, however, fall into gender classes just like those of other languages with gender systems, so the governmental nature of the gender concord overall would become evident in this further context.

Table 7.2 Pronoun subjects and verbs in Israeli Hebrew

	Pronoun	LIVE(S)	LIVED	WRITE(S)	WROTE
FIRST SINGULAR MASCULINE	ʔaní	gár	gárti	kotév	katávti
FIRST SINGULAR FEMININE		gará		kotévet	
SECOND SINGULAR MASCULINE	ʔatá	gár	gárta	kotév	katávta
SECOND SINGULAR FEMININE	ʔát	gará	gárt	kotévet	katávt
THIRD SINGULAR MASCULINE	hú	gár	gár	kotév	katáv
THIRD SINGULAR FEMININE	hí	gará	gára	kotévet	katvá
FIRST PLURAL MASCULINE	ʔanáxnu	garím	gárnu	kotvím	katávnu
FIRST PLURAL FEMININE		garót		kotvót	
SECOND PLURAL MASCULINE	ʔatém	garím	gártem	kotvím	ktavtém
SECOND PLURAL FEMININE	ʔatén	garót	gárten	kotvót	ktavtén
THIRD PLURAL MASCULINE	hém	garím	gáru	kotvím	katvú
THIRD PLURAL FEMININE	hén	garót		kotvót	

So, in summary, we see that many languages show concord between the Subject and the Predicator with respect to one or more of the inflectional categorial dimensions of person, number, and gender.

Congruence between Predicator and Objects

In some languages, transitive verbs may also agree with one or more of their Objects with respect to any of person, number, and gender. An example is provided by the Yup'ik data in Table 7.3. Some of these examples are similar to those considered in Table 2.3 and analysed in Table 2.4 (Chapter 2).

Table 7.3 Agreement of Predicators with Subjects and Objects

1.	(iɬiin) (iɬii) taŋχaa	HE SEES HIM.
2.	(iɬiin) (wiiŋa) taŋχaaŋa	HE SEES ME.
3.	(iɬiin) (iɬpɨt) taŋχaatɨn	HE SEES YOU.
4.	(iɬiin) (iɬait) taŋχai	HE SEES THEM.
5.	(iɬiin) (waŋkuta) taŋχaakut	HE SEES US.
6.	(iɬiin) (iɬpɨci) taŋχaaci	HE SEES YOU (PL).
7.	(iɬiin) (iɬpɨtɨk) taŋχaatɨk	HE SEES YOU TWO.
8.	(iɬiin) (waŋkuk) taŋχaakuk	HE SEES US TWO.
9.	(iɬiin) (iɬkɨk) taŋχak	HE SEES THEM (TWO).
10.	(iɬpɨt) (wiiŋa) taʁŋapɨŋa	YOU UNDERSTAND ME.
11.	(iɬpɨt) (iɬii) taʁiŋan	YOU UNDERSTAND HIM.
12.	(iɬpɨt) (iɬait) taʁiŋatɨn	YOU UNDERSTAND THEM.
13.	(iɬaita) (iɬpɨt) taʁiŋaatxɨn	THEY UNDERSTAND YOU.
14.	(iɬaita) (waŋkuk) taʁiŋaitkuk	THEY UNDERSTAND US TWO.
15.	(iɬaita) (iɬii) taʁiŋaat	THEY UNDERSTAND HIM.
16.	(wiiŋa) (iɬpɨtɨk) kiuɣamtɨk	I ANSWER YOU TWO.
17.	(wiiŋa) (iɬait) kiuɣanka	I ANSWER THEM.
18.	(wiiŋa) (iɬpɨt) kiuɣamkɨn	I ANSWER YOU.
19.	(iɬpɨtɨk) (waŋkuta) kiuɣaχpɨtɨxkuk	YOU TWO ANSWER US.
20.	(iɬpɨtɨk) (wiiŋa) kiuɣaχpɨtɨɣŋa	YOU TWO ANSWER ME.
21.	(iɬpɨtɨk) (iɬkɨk) kiuɣaxtɨk	YOU TWO ANSWER THEM (TWO).

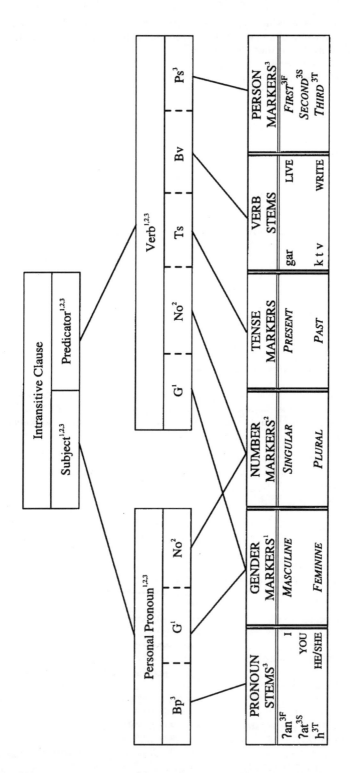

Figure 7.2 Account of gender, number, and person concord in Hebrew clauses

Although it does not give complete paradigms, this material is enough to indicate the general picture: transitive verbs in Yup'ik agree with both Subject and Object with respect to both person (*FIRST, SECOND, THIRD*) and number (*SINGULAR, DUAL, PLURAL*). When this happens, the categorial dimensions of person and number are doubly reflected in each verb, once for the Subject and a second time for the Object. Three possible ways of representing the word structure involved are shown in Figure 7.3. In version (a), the superscript ^{1} is assigned to person and ^{2} to number, much as in the previous treatments. This version is actually unworkable, however, because it carries the incorrect implication that the person and number of the Subject and Object must be the same. One attempt to remedy this problem would be to assign different numbers to the doubly represented categories, depending on whether they refer to the Subject or the Object, thus giving superscripts ^{1} through ^{4}, as in version (b), where odd numbers are used for person and even numbers for number. While this approach would be workable in a way in which (a) is not, it still seems less than ideal, because it does not allow a uniform single category of person together with another one for number, and therefore seems to require separate listings for each category as it applies to the Subject and the Object. The third alternative at (c) recognizes the need to separate the different kinds of person and number while still reflecting their basic similarities. It accomplishes this by using a variety of superscript incorporating decimal points. Before the decimal point ^{1} and ^{2} represent person and number, respectively, just as in version (a), but after the decimal point, ^{1} is used to refer to Subject categories, and ^{2} for Object categories.

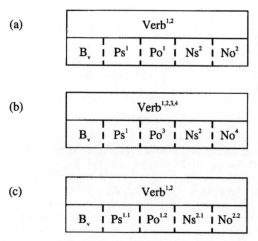

Figure 7.3 Alternative analyses for concording verbs in Yup'ik Eskimo

Figure 7.4 shows the incorporation of this idea into a complete solution for the Yup'ik data. The kinds of superscripts with decimal points will be termed **EXTENDED**, as opposed to SIMPLE ones and also to the **AUGMENTED** superscripts, those with letters after the numbers, as introduced for phrasal congruence in Chapter 4 and applied in the present chapter as well. This account also uses the augmented superscripts (in the vocabulary box for person markers) and uses some superscripts that are both augmented and extended (in the box for pronoun bases). The use of simple superscripts here is actually a form of abbreviation: in the sub-box with P (under Transitive Clause) and in the construction labeled Verb, the notation ^{1,2} abbreviates $^{1.1,1.2,2.1,2.2}$. In vocabulary boxes, a similar abbreviatory convention is used to show alternatives rather than combinations, so the ^{1} after person markers stands for $^{1.1/1.2}$, meaning that it will connect upward to either $^{1.1}$ or $^{1.2}$, and a similar thing can be said of the use of ^{2} for number markers. One can be more explicit if that is preferred, but here it seems quite clear which value the abbreviation has in which context.

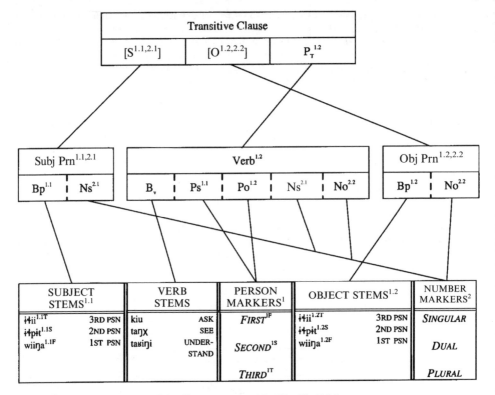

Figure 7.4 Boxed account of Predicator concord in Yup'ik Eskimo

An example involving gender and number is found in the Swahili data of Table 7.4. This material gives evidence for six of the roughly one dozen genders found in Swahili nouns. Further data would show that person is also involved, but gender is relevant only in the third person. The solution to this data is presented in Figure 7.5. The names for the genders used here are based on the data presented, but they are not traditional among the grammarians of Swahili and other Bantu languages, who commonly use an arbitrary numbering system, assigning different numbers to the singular and the corresponding plural.

Table 7.4 Agreement of Predicators with Subjects and Objects in Swahili

1. *Mtu huyu alimshinda mkulima mvivu.*	THIS MAN SURPASSED THE LAZY FARMER.
2. *Watu hawa waliwashinda wakulima wavivu.*	THESE MEN SURPASSED THE LAZY FARMERS.
3. *Mti huu uliushinda mnazi mdogo.*	THIS TREE SURPASSED THE SMALL COCONUT TREE.
4. *Miti hii iliishinda minazi midogo.*	THESE TREES SURPASSED THE SMALL COCONUT TREES.
5. *Nanasi hili lililishinda tunda dogo.*	THIS PINEAPPLE SURPASSED THE SMALL FRUIT.
6. *Mananasi haya yaliyashinda matunda madogo.*	THESE PINEAPPLES SURPASSED THE SMALL FRUITS.
7. *Tunda hhili linalishinda nanasi dogo.*	THIS FRUIT SURPASSES THE SMALL PINEAPPLE.
8. *Matunda haya yanayashinda mananasi madogo.*	THESE FRUITS SURPASS THE SMALL PINEAPPLES.

9. *Kikombe hiki kilikishinda chombo*   THIS CUP SURPASSED THE SMALL VESSEL.
   kidogo.
10. *Vikombe hivi vinavishinda vyombo*   THESE CUPS SURPASS THE SMALL VESSELS.
    vidogo.
11. *Tunda hili linamshinda mtu mdogo.*   THIS FRUIT SURPASSES THE SMALL MAN.
12. *Mti huu unamshinda mtu mdogo.*   THIS TREE SURPASSSES THE SMALL MAN.
13. *Miti hii inamshinda mtu mdogo.*   THESE TREES SURPASS THE SMALL MAN.
14. *Mananasi haya yanamshinda mtu huyu.*   THESE PINEAPPLES SURPASS THIS MAN.
15. *Chombo hiki kinamshinda mtu mdogo.*   THIS VESSEL SURPASSES THE SMALL MAN.
16. *Ndizi hii iliishinda mboga hii.*   THIS COCONUT SURPASSED THIS VEGETABLE.
17. *Ndizi hizi zinazishinda mboga ndogo.* THESE COCONUTS SURPASS THESE VEGETABLES.
18. *Ndizi hii itaishinda ndizi hii.*   THIS COCONUT SURPASSES THE SMALL
                                            VEGETABLES.
19. *Ndizi hizi zilizishinda mboga ndogo.* THESE COCONUTS SURPASS THE SMALL
                                            VEGETABLES.
20. *Mboga hii itaishinda ndizi hii.*   THIS VEGETABLE WILL SURPASS THIS COCONUT.
21. *Ubao huu uliushinda ufagio mdogo.*   THIS PLANK SURPASSES THE SMALL BROOM.
22. *Mbau huu zilizishinda fagio ndogo.*   THESE PLANKS SURPASSED THE SMALL BROOMS.
23. *Watu hawa wanavishinda vyombo*   THESE MEN WILL SURPASS THE SMALL COCONUT
    vidogo.   TREE.
24. *Watu hawa wataushinda nmazi mdogo.*   THESE MEN SURPASS THE SMALL VESSELS.

Examples of concord between Predicator and participants apart from Subjects and Direct Objects are not common, but there is a case of a three-way number concord in Basque, as exemplified by the data in Table 7.5. In this language, it may be observed, Predicators contain an auxiliary inflected for person and number in combination with a main verb inflected for tense. It is the bitransitive auxiliary shown here which reflects the numbers of all three participants as well as the person of both the Subject and the Indirect Object. Figure 7.6 presents an account of this data, organized along the same lines as were seen for the Yup'ik and Swahili data in Figures 7.4 and 7.5, using extended superscripts as necessary.

Table 7.5 Agreement of Predicators with Subjects, Direct Objects, and Indirect Objects in Basque

1. *(nik) (zuri) liburua ematen dizut*   I GIVE YOU THE BOOK.
2. *(nik) (zuri) liburuak ematen dizkizut*   I GIVE YOU THE BOOKS.
3. *(zuk) (niri) liburua emango didazu*   YOU WILL GIVE ME THE BOOK.
4. *(zuk) (niri) liburuak emango dizkidazu*   YOU WILL GIVE ME THE BOOKS.
5. *(hark) (niri) liburua ematen dit*   HE GIVES ME THE BOOK.
6. *(hark) (niri) liburuak emango dizit*   HE WILL GIVE ME THE BOOKS.
7. *(nik) (haiei) liburuak emango diet*   I WILL GIVE THEM THE BOOKS.
8. *(haiek) (zuri) liburuak ematen dizkizute*   THEY GIVE YOU THE BOOKS.
9. *(guk) (hari) liburua erosko diogu*   WE WILL BUY HIM THE BOOK.
10. *(zuek) (guri) liburuak erosten dizkiguzue* YOU (Pl) BUY US THE BOOKS.
11. *(zuk) (hari) liburua erosten diozu*   YOU (Sg) BUY HIM THE BOOK.
12. *(hark) (haiei) liburuak erosko dizkie*   HE WILL BUY THEM THE BOOKS.
13. *(haiek) (hari) liburua erosko diote*   THEY WILL BUY THEM THE BOOK.
14. *(guk) (zuri) liburuak erosten dizugu*   WE BUY YOU THE BOOKS.

This section has shown, then, that Direct Objects, and in some languages Indirect Objects, may show the same kinds of concord with the Predicator that Subjects often show, involving one or more of the categories of person, number, and gender. The concept of extended superscripts has been presented as a notational device to allow a more systematic account of this kind of concord than would otherwise be possible.

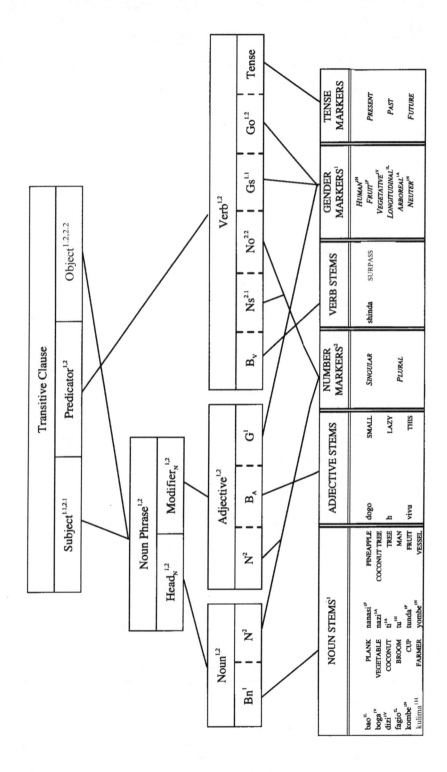

Figure 7.5 Account of concord in gender and number between Predicator and both Subject and Object in Swahili

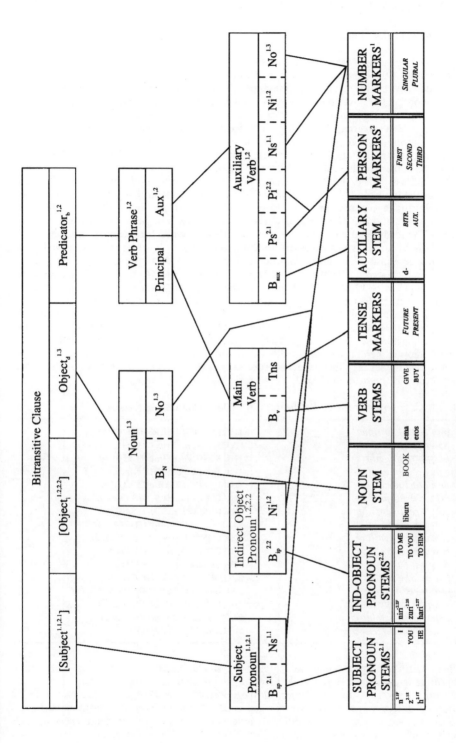

Figure 7.6 Concord of Predicator with Subjects and Objects in Basque

Government in the clause

In investigating government in the phrase, we saw that case government in adpositional phrases is one of the most common kinds, with the case of a noun (or pronoun) phrase in the role of Axis governed by a classification applicable to the adpositions serving as Relators. A very common kind of government between clausal constituents also involves the case of noun/ pronoun phrases as a governed inflection. The governing constituent in this instance is the Predicator, which governs the case of the associated Direct Object, manifested by a noun phrase or a pronoun. A good example of this is seen in the Classical Latin data in Table 7.6. In this example, the nouns are marked by case inflections in the form of suffixes. To make the illustration simpler for those not familiar with Latin, all the nouns used are of the same basic inflectional class (called the "Third Declension" in traditional Latin grammars). It will be noted that the nouns in Object function in 1–4 take *-em*, those in that function in 5–8 take *ī*, those in 9–12 take *-e* and those in 13–16 take *-is*. These suffixes signal different Latin cases, and the classification of the verbs determines which case will be involved for each given instance. The traditional name of each case will be mentioned here; though, as indicated in previous discussion, it is not necessary to know these names in order to make an adequate editing and description. As reflected in the solution presented in Figure 7.7, the verbs in 1–4 (like the vast majority of Latin verbs) require the *ACCUSATIVE*; those in 5–8 require the *DATIVE*, those in 9–12 the *ABLATIVE*, and the rest the *GENITIVE*. This solution treats governmental phenomena in the same general way as phrasal government was treated in Chapter 4, just applying the notational devices at clause rank. (In traditional grammars of Latin, it may be noted, only the verbs that govern the accusative for Objects are called "transitive", while the others are considered special types of "intransitive" verbs. In the approach adopted here, it is considered better to term all verbs that take Objects "transitive". The various subtypes may then be called **ACCUSATIVE-TRANSITIVE**, **DATIVE-TRANSITIVE**, and so on, according to the case involved.)

Table 7.6 Case government by Predicators in Classical Latin

1.	*dux cōnsulem timet*	THE LEADER FEARS THE CONSUL.
2.	*pater pontem videt*	FATHER SEES THE BRIDGE.
3.	*rēx patrem laedit*	THE KING HARMS FATHER.
4.	*canis rēgem amat*	THE DOG LOVES THE KING.
5.	*dux patrī nocet*	THE LEADER HARMS FATHER.
6.	*urbs cōnsulī placet*	THE CITY PLEASES THE CONSUL.
7.	*māter rēgī cōnfīdit*	MOTHER TRUSTS THE KING.
8.	*pater mātrī favet*	FATHER FAVORS MOTHER.
9.	*cōnsul ponte ūtitur*	THE CONSUL USES THE BRIDGE.
10.	*rēx duce caret*	THE KING LACKS A LEADER.
11.	*dux pisce fruitur*	THE LEADER ENJOYS FISH.
12.	*frāter urbe potitur*	BROTHER SEIZES THE CITY.
13.	*dux rēgis memeinit*	THE LEADER REMEMBERS THE KING.
14.	*rēx patris oblīvīscitur*	THE KING FORGETS FATHER.
15.	*pater urbis reminiscitur*	FATHER REMEMBERS THE CITY.
16.	*māter frātris miserētur*	MOTHER PITIES BROTHER.

These Latin examples could be matched by similar examples in various other Indo-European languages, including Greek, German, Lithuanian, and Russian. They all show the Predicator as governor and the Object as the governed. The Hungarian data in Table 7.7 illustrates a different variety of governor/governed relation between its constituents. In this language, transitive verbs have a different inflection according to the definiteness of their associated objects. So in this present data, an object marked with the definite article /a/ will call forth a definite inflection, whereas one with the indefinite article /eʒ/ will require an

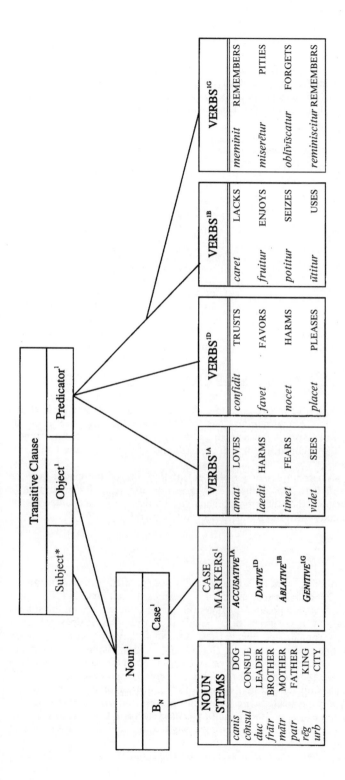

Note: *This account is incomplete in regard to the grammatical form of the noun that appears in Subject function. This matter will be clarified in the section on DETERMINATION.

Figure 7.7 Account of case government by Predicators in Latin

indefinite verb form. (Besides a noun phrase with a definite article, a definite object may be (1) a proper noun; (2) a third-person pronoun; (3) a demonstrative pronoun; (4) an object clause; (5) a noun inflected for possession; or (6) an infinitive with a definite object (paraphrased from pages 112–13 in *Learn Hungarian* by Zoltán Bánhidi, Zoltán Jókay, and Dénes Szabó, Budapest, 1965).) When no overt object is present, furthermore, the definite verb implies the existence of a definite, though unexpressed, object, while the indefinite implies no specific object.

Table 7.7 Hungarian examples of definiteness government by Objects

1.	a tanaˑr išmeri a ȝereket	THE TEACHER KNOWS THE CHILD.
2.	a ȝerek išmer eȝ tanaˑrt	THE CHILD KNOWS A TEACHER.
3.	eȝ mačka laˑćća a madarat	A CAT SEES THE BIRD.
4.	a madaˑr laˑt eȝ mačkaˑt	THE BIRD SEES A CAT.
5.	a kuća laˑćća a tanaˑrt	THE DOG SEES THE TEACHER.
6.	a taˑrš hiˑv eȝ munkaˑšt	THE COMPANION CALLS A WORKER.
7.	eȝ munkaˑš hiˑvi a baraˑtot	THE WORKER CALLS THE FRIEND.
8.	eȝ kuća kereš eȝ mačkaˑt	A DOG LOOKS AT A CAT.
9.	a ȝerek kereši a kučaˑt	THE CHILD LOOKS AT THE DOG.
10.	a naȝ kuća kerešt a laˑñt	THE BIG DOG LOOKED AT A GIRL.
11.	a laˑñ hifta a baraˑtot	THE GIRL CALLED THE FRIEND.
12.	a kiči laˑñ hivott eȝ ȝereket	THE LITTLE GIRL CALLED A CHILD.
13.	a naȝ munkaˑš išmert eȝ kiči ȝereket	THE BIG WORKER KNEW A LITTLE CHILD.
14.	a ȝerek išmerta a naȝ kućaˑt	THE CHILD KNEW THE BIG DOG.
15.	a baraˑt laˑtotta a ferfit	THE FRIEND SAW THE MAN.
16.	a kiči ferfi laˑtott eȝ taˑršat	THE LITTLE MAN SAW A COMPANION.

Figure 7.8 presents a solution to this data, using [1] for the tie of definiteness between the Object and the Predicator. Since Hungarian also has something like the case government by Predicators, such as we saw in Latin, it can be seen as having some examples of government where the Object governs the Predicator (for definiteness) and others where the Predicator governs the Object (for case).

In summary, we have seen examples of government at the rank of the clause between Predicator and Object, both with the Predicator as governor and with the Predicator as governed. We have further seen that these phenomena can be reasonably accounted for by devices similar to those already introduced for phrases in Chapter 4.

Determination

When it comes to case, we often see that a particular case is not specified by a co-constituent, as it is with government by either Predicators or adpositional Relators, but is simply associated with a particular syntactic position or function. While some writers on the subject have tried to extend the notion of government to include these examples, it does not really make sense to speak of government (as other writers have in fact recognized) when some particular case is the only one that is possible in that function. So in English, for example, personal pronouns in any of the functions Direct Object, Indirect Object, or Axis in a prepositional phrase will be in the accusative case: *They saw **him**, He gave **me** the report, We talked about **her***. Here we can simply associate the case with the function involved and say that that function rather than any particular co-constituent specifies the use of this case. No standard term for this relation exists, but the name **DETERMINATION** will be adopted here as a useful and appropriate one. So in such instances, we will say that the function (Axis or Direct or Indirect Object) determines the *ACCUSATIVE*.

A further example of case determination is seen in the Hindi data of Table 7.8. Here the

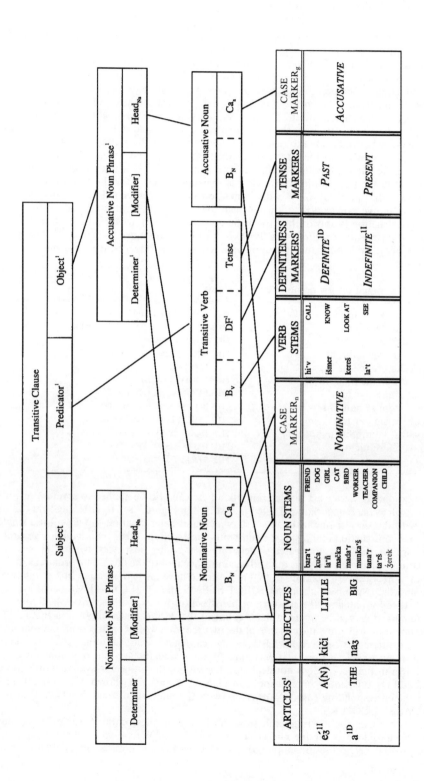

Figure 7.8 Definiteness government of Hungarian Predicators by their Objects

initial nouns are Subjects and the next word in each example is another noun serving as the Axis in a postpositional phrase. The case of the Subject is known in Hindi grammar as the *DIRECT* case, and that of the AXIS is the *OBLIQUE* case. Since Subjects and Axes generally occur only in these cases, there is no government. The cases are simply determined by the syntactic functions of the noun phrases. Up to now, we would have needed a separate word-box (and ultimately also a phrase-box, when data of just slightly greater complexity is considered) for each of the different cases. But we can use a reasonable extension of the superscripting system to represent the determination as illustrated in Figure 7.9. Specifically, we show the superscript devoted to case (here ^{1}) with an augmenting letter indicating the case. This in its turn connects to the augmented superscripts in the vocabulary box for the case categories, so the Subject function in the clause is shown with ^{1D} for the Direct case, and the Axis function in the postpositional phrase has the superscript ^{1O} for the Oblique case. The boxes between the specification of a determination and the associated vocabulary box for case have the simple superscript ^{1} allowing them to carry case determination along. So when the noun construction is approached from the Subject function, it will be determined as ^{1D}, but when it is instead approached from the Axis, it will be determined instead as ^{1O}. This gives us an easy way to handle this phenomenon without an unnecessary multiplication of constructions.

Table 7.8 Determination for nominal case in Hindi

1.	beṭa· gʰoṛe par hɛ	THE SON IS ON THE HORSE.
2.	gʰoṛa· ra·ste mẽ	THE HORSE IS NOT IN THE STREET.
3.	ta·la· darva·ze se hɛ	THE LOCK IS FROM THE DOOR.
4.	kuã· a·gre mẽ nahĩ· hɛ	THE WELL IS NOT IN AGRA.
5.	gʰaṛa· kamre mẽ hɛ	THE JAR IS IN THE ROOM.
6.	kʰa·na· kŭe mẽ nahĩ· hɛ	THE FOOD IS NOT IN THE WELL.
7.	patta· piñjre par hɛ	THE LEAF IS ON THE CAGE.
8.	laṛka· a·gre se nahĩ· hɛ	THE BOY IS NOT FROM AGRA.
9.	bacca· ra·ste par hɛ	THE CHILD IS ON THE STREET.
10.	darva·za· kamre mẽ nahĩ· hɛ	THE DOOR IS NOT IN THE ROOM.
11.	gʰoṛa· piñjre mẽ hɛ	THE HORSE IS IN THE CAGE.
12.	ra·sta· a·gre mẽ nahĩ· hɛ	THE STREET IS NOT IN AGRA.

The notational devices used for determination here can also be applied to several previous examples, such as the Hungarian in Table 7.7 as solved in Figure 7.8. The latter account can be replaced with the simpler one in Figure 7.10, which uses determination to allow just a single noun-phrase construction and a single noun-word construction rather than having a separate construction for each of the cases. There are also other instances where the use of determination will allow a simpler, but still accurate, account of the facts. The pronouns in the account of Yup'ik transitive clauses in Figure 7.4 could have the two pronoun boxes collapsed into one and the two boxes labeled SUBJECT STEMS and OBJECT STEMS could also be collapsed, thereby reducing the number of construction boxes to three instead of four. A similar simplification can be made in the account of the Basque material given in Figure 7.6: case determination will allow the collapse of the two pronoun word-constructions into one and eliminate the differences between the bases, though case must be added to the pronoun (and in the end to noun phrases as well). It was already noted that the account of Latin transitive clauses shown in Figure 7.7 does not deal with the case of the Subject. Given determination, we could add an augmented superscript ^{1N} in place of the asterisk shown after Subject, and then add the corresponding case NOMINATIVE (with the same augmented superscript) in the box for CASE MARKERS.

Some further uses for determination show up in the Japanese data of Table 7.9. In this language, postpositions occur for Object, Topic, and so on. We would need three separate, though highly similar, postpositional-phrase constructions if we did not recognize determination.

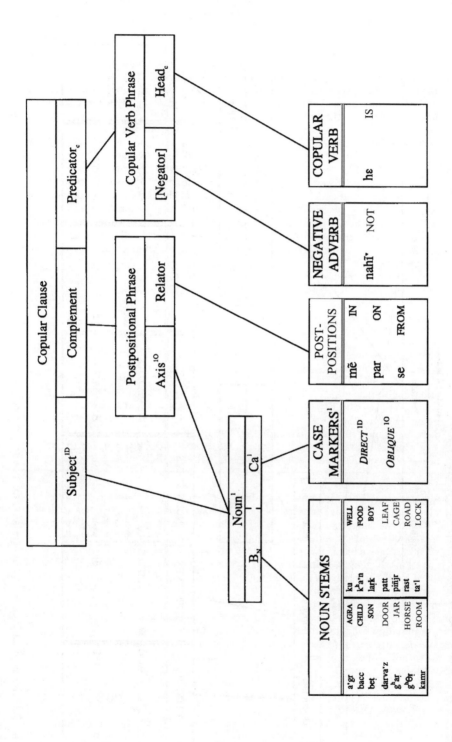

Figure 7.9 Account of determination for nominal case in Hindi

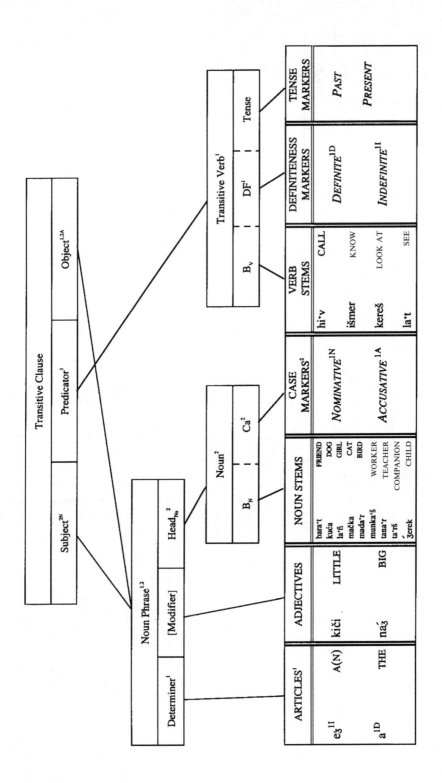

Figure 7.10 Revision of Figure 7.8 (Hungarian) incorporating determination

Table 7.9 Determination for selection of postpositions and verbs in Japanese

1.	gakusei wa gakkoo de kami o tukau	THE STUDENT USED PAPER AT SCHOOL.
2.	sensei wa depaato de tukatta	THE TEACHER USED IT IN THE DEPARTMENT STORE.
3.	kodomo wa isu o miru	THE CHILD SEES THE CHAIR.
4.	kodomo wa niwa de gakusei o mitta	THE CHILD SAW THE STUDENT IN THE GARDEN.
5.	sensei wa tookyoo de kodomo o matu	THE TEACHER WAITS FOR THE CHILD IN TOKYO.
6.	gakkoo de sensei o matta	(SOMEONE) WAITED FOR THE TEACHER AT SCHOOL.
7.	kau	(SOMEONE) BUYS IT.
8.	isya wa depaato de hon o katta	THE DOCTOR BOUGHT A BOOK AT THE DEPARTMENT STORE.
9.	tomodati wa rondon de ringo o uru	THE FRIEND SELLS APPLES IN LONDON.
10.	teeburu o utta	(SOMEONE) SOLD THE TABLE.
11.	gakusei wa rondon de oyogu	THE STUDENT SWIMS IN LONDON.
12.	tomodati wa oyoida	THE FRIEND SWAM.
13.	sensei wa tookyoo de hataraku	THE TEACHER WORKS IN TOKYO.
14.	gakkoo de hataraita	(SOMEONE) WORKED AT THE SCHOOL.
15.	kodomo wa gakkoo de korobu	THE CHILD FALLS IN SCHOOL.
16.	koronda	(SOMEONE) FELL.
17.	kodomo wa niwa de asobu	THE CHILD PLAYS IN THE GARDEN.
18.	depaato de asonda	(SOMEONE) PLAYED IN THE DEPARTMENT STORE.
19.	tomodati wa gakkoo de odoru	THE FRIEND DANCES IN SCHOOL.
20.	gakusei wa odotta	THE STUDENT DANCED.

With determination, however, we can easily show the selection of postpositions, and therefore use a single postpositional-phrase construction. The same thing applies to the verbs in this material, and the data shows that both are inflected for tense. We must insure, however, that transitive stems go with transitive clauses and intransitive stems with intransitive clauses. Without determination, this would require separate, but highly similar, word-constructions, but with determination we can use the simpler account shown in Figure 7.11.

In view of the simplifications possible via the use of congruence and determination, some further discussion of the dual structural criterion introduced in Chapter 6 is necessary. The two differences involved should be seen as **necessary** to allow the use of separate constructions, but not always **sufficient** to justify their separation. The two differences are not sufficient, to be specific, when such devices as congruence (concord or government) and determination allow the easy combination of otherwise separate constructions. So, in general, we can see the results of the application of the criterion as giving us preliminary, tentative constructions. Then the concepts of congruence and determination can be brought in to allow partly similar constructions to be combined to some degree, so the final list of distinct constructions can be decided only after attempts at reasonable combination have been carried out.

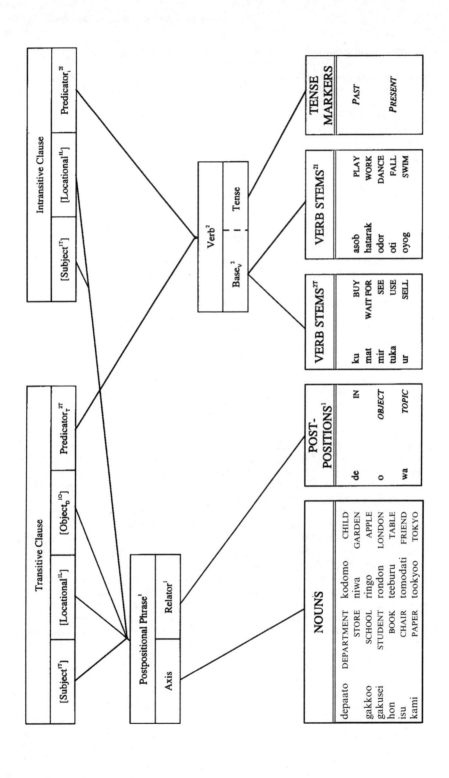

Figure 7.11 Account of determination for postpositions and verbs in Japanese

Summary of new notations

The following outline deals with determination as an addition to the summaries of notational conventions introduced in Chapters 1–4.

A sample of determination

1. Diagram

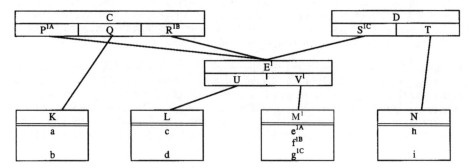

2. List of well-formed combinations

(a) From Construction C

(c·e) a (c·f)	(d·e) a (c·f)
(c·e) b (c·f)	(d·e) b (c·f)
(c·e) a (d·f)	(d·e) a (d·f)
(c·e) b (d·f)	(d·e) b (d·f)

(b) From Construction D

(c·g) h	(d·g) h
(c·g) i	(d·g) i

3. The discussion on this diagram is as follows:

a. C–E are labels for constructions.
b. P–V are labels for constituents.
c. K–N are labels for classes.
d. Lower case letters are labels for vocabulary items.
e. The augmented superscripts ^{1A}, ^{1B}, ^{1C} on constituents P, R, and S determine the selections within class M for any instance of E which occurs in the function of P, R, or S: any E manifesting P will show e, any E manifesting R will show f, and any E manifesting S will show g. The use of such augmented superscripts on constituent labels always indicates this phenomenon.
f. Determination is pertinent only if the construction selected for the manifestation of a constituent carrying an augmented superscript carries the corresponding unaugmented version. Similarly, all further constituents, constructions, and classes selected would have

to bear this (unaugmented) superscript in order for the determination to apply. A specified determination is nullified, in other words, if any constituent, construction, or class lacking the corresponding superscript is reached, or if such a superscript occurs only on an optional constituent which happens not to be taken in a given instance.

g.   Determination is recognized when two or more clause-, phrase-, or word-constructions sharing the same overall structure, but differing in specifics, would otherwise have to be recognized. The differences typically involve specific cases, moods, adpositional selections, etc. correlated with specific functions in larger structures. The recognition of this phenomenon simplifies the description by eliminating the need for multiple constructions with minor differences between them.

h.   Sometimes the extension of determination to its logical extreme may tend to obscure rather than clarify the structure to the reader of a syntactic description. A degree of judgement is necessary in such cases to decide whether a logically defensible use of the determination system should actually be made in a given case.

In addition, it should also be noted that the possibility of extended superscripts including decimal points was introduced in this chapter to allow a convenient treatment of those cases where a Predicator agrees with respect to the same categorial dimensions (such as person, gender, or number) with more than one of its co-constituents. In such a case, the number before the decimal point would refer to the general category, while that after it would refer to its relation to a particular constituent. A sample of a rather complete application would be as follows.

1.1	for NUMBER in the Subject
1.2	for NUMBER in the Direct Object
1.3	for NUMBER in the Indirect Object
2.1	for PERSON in the Subject
2.2	for PERSON in the Direct Object
2.3	for PERSON in the Indirect Object
3.1	for GENDER in the Subject
3.2	for GENDER in the Direct Object
3.3	for GENDER in the Indirect Object

The particular assignment of number to categories in participants here is only intended as a suggestion. It is not meant to stipulate that particular numbers should always be reserved for the particular functions illustrated here.

Exercises

A.   Interpretation problems

1.   *Transitive clauses in Ivatan*

The following account is based on data from Ivatan, a Philippine language.

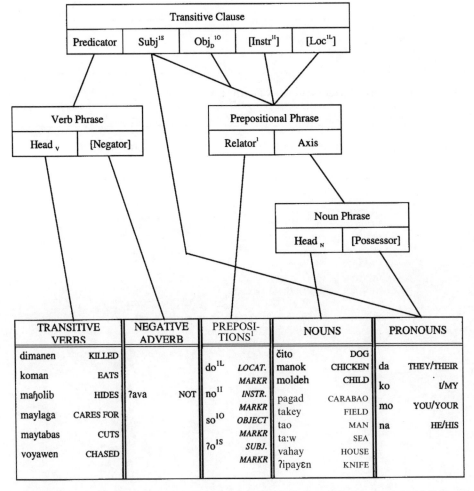

Use this account to produce the translations of the English sentences shown, giving full boxed representations of items 3 and 6. Since this language lacks articles, no translation is needed for "THE".

1. THE MAN CHASED THEIR CHILD IN THE FIELD.

   _____

2. HIS CHILD DID NOT KILL THE CARABAO WITH MY KNIFE.

   _____

3. THE DOG EATS THE CHICKEN IN YOUR HOUSE.

   _____

4. HE CARES FOR MY CHILD IN THE FIELD.

   _____

5. YOUR CARABAO CHASED THE MAN IN THE SEA.

   _____

6. MY CHILD DID NOT CUT THE CHICKEN WITH YOUR KNIFE IN THEIR HOUSE.

   _____

2. Hindi intransitive clauses

The following diagram presents some Hindi structures in a stylistic variant of the presentations used earlier. This involves connecting the various functions simply to the class labels characteristic of vocabulary boxes. A listing on the next page then enumerates the members of each class. This approach is convenient when there are too many classes and/or too many class-members to allow the listing of all details on a single page. When necessary, the listing of the class-members may be expanded to an indefinite number of following pages.

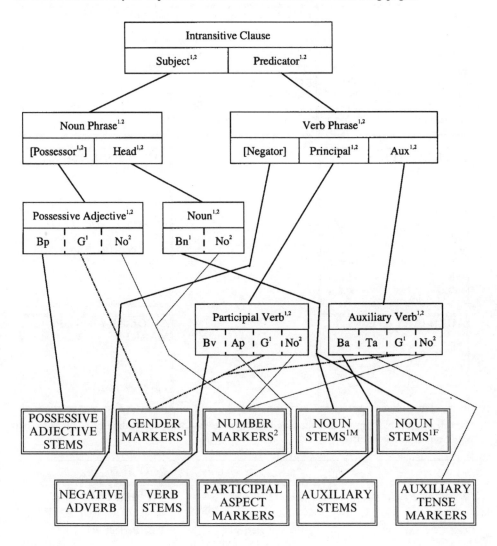

POSSESSIVE ADJECTIVE STEMS		GENDER MARKERS[1]	NUMBER MARKERS[2]	
mer	MY	*MASCULINE*[1M]	*SINGULAR*	
hama·r	OUR			
ter	YOUR	*FEMININE*[1F]	*PLURAL*	

NOUN STEMS[1M]		NOUN STEMS[1F]		NEGATIVE ADVERB	
a·dmi·	MAN	bahin	SISTER		
dost	FRIEND	beṭi·	DAUGHTER	nahĩ·	NOT
gʰora·	HORSE	ga·y	COW		
ha·tʰi·	ELEPHANT	laṛki·	GIRL		
mantri·	SECRETARY	patni·	WIFE		
vidyartʰi·	STUDENT	sava·ri·	PASSENGER		

INTRANSITIVE VERB STEMS		PARTICIPIAL ASPECT MARKERS	
a·	COME		
bol	SPEAK	*PERFECT-PARTICIPLE*	
cal	GO		
ga·	SING	*IMPERFECT-PARTICIPLE*	
pi·	DRINK		
rah	STAY		
so·	SLEEP		

AUXILIARY STEM		AUXILIARY TENSE MARKERS	
h	*AUXILIARY*	*PAST-TENSE*	
		PRESENT-TENSE	

The following table summarizes the English translation of various combinations of participial aspect and auxiliary tense.

	PRESENT AUXILIARY	*PAST AUXILIARY*
IMPERFECT PARTICIPLE	General Present GO(ES)	Past (Habitual) WENT/USED TO GO
PERFECT PARTICIPLE	Present Perfect HAS/HAVE GONE	Past Perfect HAD GONE

Based on this information and the understanding that Hindi has no equivalents for the English definite and indefinite articles (*the/a(n)*), show the equivalents of the following English sentences, writing abstracted categorial labels below the associated base. Include the full boxed representations for items 3 and 6.

1.   MY SISTERS DID NOT STAY.

_____

2.   THE STUDENTS HAD COME.

_____

3.   YOUR DAUGHTER USED TO SING.

_____

4.   OUR ELEPHANT HAS NOT SLEPT.

_____

5.   THE PASSENGERS HAVE GONE.

_____

6.   MY FRIEND HAD NOT DRUNK.

_____

B.   Analysis problems

1. English clauses

Use determination and concord as necessary to account for the following English data as succinctly as possible. For purposes of this exercise, treat a verb as **TRANSITIVE** or **INTRANSITIVE** only on the basis of the examples given. Your editing of the morphology should extract case and number from the pronouns and tense and number for the verbs.

1. *He sees them.*	13. *He ran.*
2. *She likes him.*	14. *She runs.*
3. *They saw her.*	15. *They walk.*
4. *She liked them.*	16. *He disappeared.*
5. *He surprised them.*	17. *They disappear.*
6. *They surprise him.*	18. *She walks.*
7. *He pardoned her.*	19. *She works.*
8. *She pardons him.*	20. *He worked.*
9. *They call him.*	21. *They played.*
10. *He called him.*	22. *She plays.*
11. *She excused her.*	23. *He swam.*
12. *They excuse them.*	24. *They swim.*

2. Polish clause concord

After an appropriate editing of the examples, account for the following Polish data, including especially the concord between Subject and Predicator.

1. xwopjec piše   THE BOY IS WRITING.   1a. xwopcy pišõ   THE BOYS ARE WRITING.
2. kobjeta piše   THE WOMAN IS WRITING.   2a. kobjety pišõ   THE WOMEN ARE
                                                                    WRITING.
3. měščyzna pisaw   THE MAN WAS WRITING.   3a. měščyźńi pisali THE MEN WERE WRITING.
4. ćotka pisawa   THE AUNT WAS WRITING.   4a. ćotki pisawy   THE AUNTS WERE
                                                                    WRITING.
5. měščyzna śpi   THE MAN IS SLEEPING.   5a. měščyźńi śpjõ   THE MEN ARE SLEEPING.
6. krova śpi   THE COW IS SLEEPING.   6a. krovy śpjõ   THE COWS ARE SLEEPING.
7. vuj spaw   THE UNCLE WAS   7a. vujovje spali   THE UNCLES WERE
                     SLEEPING.   SLEEPING.
8. kobjeta spawa   THE WOMAN WAS   8a. kobjety spawy   THE WOMEN WERE
                     SLEEPING.   SLEEPING.
9. vuj pracuje   THE UNCLE IS WORKING.   9a. vujovje pracujõ THE UNCLES ARE
                                                                    WORKING.
10. ćotka pracuje   THE AUNT IS WORKING.   10a. ćotki pracujõ   THE AUNTS ARE
                                                                    WORKING.
11. xwopjec   THE BOY WAS WORKING.   11a. xwopcy   THE BOYS WERE
    pracovaw   pracovali   WORKING.
12. krova   THE COW WAS WORKING.   12a. krovy   THE COWS WERE
    pracovawa   pracovawy   WORKING.

3. Hungarian intransitive clauses

Edit and analyse the following Hungarian clause data and present a complete syntactic account of the edited results.

 1. e:n olvašok   I AM READING.
 2. te olvašol   YOU (SG) ARE READING.
 3. ö: olvaš   HE/SHE IS READING.
 4. mi olvašunk   WE ARE READING.
 5. ti olvaštok   YOU (PL) ARE READING.
 6. ö:k olvašnak   THEY ARE READING.
 7. e:n fo:zök   I AM COOKING.
 8. te vesel   YOU (SG) ARE BUYING.
 9. ö: ke:rdez   HE/SHE IS ASKING.
10. mi ke:rdezünk   WE ARE ASKING.
11. ti fö:stök   YOU (PL) ARE COOKING.
12. ö:k vesnek   THEY ARE BUYING.
13. e:n olvaštam   I WAS READING.
14. te olvašta:l   YOU (SG) WERE READING.
15. ɥo: olvašott   HE/SHE WAS READING.
16. mi olvaštunk   WE WERE READING.
17. ti olvaštatok   YOU (PL) WERE READING.
18. ö:k olvaštak   THEY WERE READING.
19. e:n vettem   I WAS BUYING.
20. te ke:rdeste:l   YOU (SG) WERE ASKING.
21. ö: fö:zött   HE/SHE WAS COOKING.
22. mi fö:stünk   WE WERE COOKING.
23. ti ke:rdestetek   YOU (PL) WERE ASKING.
24. ö:k vettek   THEY WERE BUYING.

4. Luiseño clauses

The following data from Luiseño, a Uto-Aztecan language of southern California, provides evidence for case determination. Edit the data (items 1–15) and provide a complete solution.

1.	hunwut yaʔaši toowq	THE BEAR SEES THE MAN.
2.	yaʔaš hunwuti ʔamooquṣ	THE MAN WAS HUNTING THE BEAR.
3.	ṣuŋaal hunwuti noonomiq	THE WOMAN IS FOLLOWING THE BEAR.
4.	hunwut yaʔaši noonomiq	THE BEAR IS FOLLOWING THE MAN.
5.	tukwut hunwuti toowquṣ	THE MOUNTAIN LION SAW THE BEAR.
6.	ʔawaal ṣuŋaali noonomiuṣ	THE DOG WAS FOLLOWING THE WOMAN.
7.	kaṣilla yaʔaši toowquṣ	THE LIZARD SAW THE MAN.
8.	yaʔaš kaṣillay ʔamooq	THE MAN IS HUNTING THE LIZARD.
9.	heŋeemal ʔawaali toowquṣ	THE BOY SAW THE DOG.
10.	ʔaṣwut tapašmali ʔamooquṣ	THE EAGLE WAS HUNTING THE MOUSE.
11.	heŋeemal tukwuti ʔamooq	THE BOY IS HUNTING THE MOUNTAIN LION.
12.	hunwut heŋeemali ʔamoon	THE BEAR WILL HUNT THE BOY.
13.	heŋeemal tukwuti toowan	THE BOY WILL SEE THE MOUNTAIN LION.
14.	yaʔaš heŋeemali noonimin	THE MAN WILL FOLLOW THE BOY.
15.	kaṣilla ʔaṣwuti toowan	THE LIZARD WILL SEE THE EAGLE.

Add the following data to the above set, and determine the changes necessary in the account produced for items 1–15. What major additional phenomenon is illustrated by the new data?

16.	hunwutum yaʔaši toowwun	THE BEARS SEE THE MAN.
17.	yaʔaš hunwutumi toowan	THE MAN WILL SEE THE BEARS.
18.	ʔaṣwutum kaṣillami ʔaamowun	THE EAGLES ARE HUNTING THE LIZARDS.
19.	kaṣillam ṣuŋaali toowan	THE LIZARDS WILL SEE THE WOMAN.
20.	yaʔašum hunwuti ʔaamoquṣ	THE MEN WERE HUNTING THE BEAR.
21.	ʔawaal kaṣillami noonomiquṣ	THE DOG IS FOLLOWING THE LIZARDS.
22.	ʔano tukwutumi toowquṣ	THE COYOTE SAW THE MOUNTAIN LIONS.
23.	tukwutum tapašmalumi ʔammowun	THE MOUNTAIN LIONS ARE HUNTING THE MICE.
24.	tapašmal ʔawaalumi noonomiquṣ	THE MOUSE WAS FOLLOWING THE DOGS.
25.	ṣuŋaalum ʔanomi toowan	THE WOMEN WILL SEE THE COYOTES.
26.	muutam tapašmali noonomiquṣ	THE OWLS WERE FOLLOWING THE MOUSE.
27.	heŋeemalum ʔanomi noonomin	THE BOYS WILL HUNT THE COYOTES.
28.	ʔawaalum heŋeemali maʔmaan	THE DOGS LIKE THE BOY.
29.	heŋeemal hunwutumi maʔmaan	THE BOY WILL LIKE THE BEARS.
30.	ʔamom tapašmalumi maʔmaquṣ	THE COYOTES LIKED THE MICE.

5. Transitive clauses in Russian

Edit the following Russian data (presented in a transliteration of the Cyrillic orthography) and prepare an account for the edited data.

1.	*Ivan vidit Mašu.*	IVAN SEES MASHA.
2.	*Maša vidit Ivana.*	MASHA SEES IVAN.
3.	*Maša pugaet Borisa.*	MASHA SCARES BORIS.
4.	*Boris pugaet Ol'gu.*	BORIS SCARES OLGA.
5.	*Miša udarjaet Veru.*	MIKE HITS VERA.
6.	*Sergej udarjaet Mišu.*	SERGEY HITS MIKE.
7.	*Pavel zaviduet Ol'ge.*	PAUL ENVIES OLGA.
8.	*Vera grozit Ivanu.*	VERA THREATENS IVAN.
9.	*Sergej grozit Vere.*	SERGEY THREATENS VERA.

10.	*Maša gorditsja Pavlom.*	MASHA IS PROUD OF PAUL.
11.	*Sergej gorditsja Ivanom.*	SERGEY IS PROUD OF IVAN.
12.	*Ol'ga interesuetsja Sergeem.*	OLGA IS INTERESTED IN SERGEY.
13.	*Miçsa interesuetsja Veroj.*	MIKE IS INTERESTED IN VERA.
14.	*Boris ljubuetsja Mišej.*	BORIS ADMIRES MIKE.
15.	*Vera ljubuetsja Mašej.*	VERA ADMIRES MASHA.

6. Hebrew transitive clauses

Account for the following transitive clause data from Modern Israeli Hebrew. You will particularly need to pay attention to concord and the use of the marker /ʔet/, which should be regarded as a preposition. You may wish to compare the noun phrase data seen earlier, in Chapter 4.

1.	dan roʔe para	DAN SEES A COW.
2.	rut roʔet talmid tov	RUTH SEES A GOOD PUPIL.
3.	hamore roʔe šaxen	THE TEACHER SEES A NEIGHBOR.
4.	moše roʔe ʔet hapara haxadaša	MOSHE SEES THE NEW COW.
5.	hapara hatova roʔet ʔet dan	THE GOOD COW SEES DAN.
6.	habaxura roʔet ʔet hamore	THE GIRL SEES THE TEACHER.
7.	raxel mocet talmid xadaš	RACHEL FINDS A NEW PUPIL.
8.	rut mocet ʔet raxel	RUTH FINDS RACHEL.
9.	para šomaʔat ʔet hatalmid	A COW HEARS THE PUPIL.
10.	hašaxen šomeaʔ kanar	THE NEIGHBOR HEARS A VIOLINIST.
11.	dan ʔohev ʔet rut	DAN LIKES RUTH.
12.	raxel ʔohevet ʔet moše	RACHEL LIKES MOSHE.
13.	hamore pogeš baxura	THE TEACHER MEETS A GIRL.
14.	habaxura pogešet more xadaš	THE GIRL FINDS A NEW TEACHER.
15.	habaxurot mocʔot ʔet raxel	THE GIRLS FIND DAN.
16.	hamorim ʔohavim ʔet hatalmidim	THE TEACHERS LIKE THE PUPILS.
17.	rut pogešet ʔet hašaxenim haxadašim	RUTH MEETS THE NEW NEIGHBORS.
18.	hakanar ʔohev baxurot katanot	THE VIOLINIST LIKES LITTLE GIRLS.
19.	habaxura hakatana ʔohevet parot	THE LITTLE GIRL LIKES COWS.
20.	hatalmidim šomʔim ʔet hamore	THE PUPILS HEAR THE TEACHER.

Terminology

CASE GOVERNMENT	DETERMINATION
DEFINITENESS GOVERNMENT	EXTENDED SUPERSCRIPTS

8

Identification and description of clitics

What is a clitic?

Table 8.1 shows some English grammatical data arranged so as to reflect a suggested morphological analysis that recognizes categories of definiteness and case. If this data came from an unfamiliar language, the given treatment might indeed seem reasonable to many. To any linguist who knows English, however, it is obviously incorrect. It is not legitimate, that is, to treat the indefinite and definite articles as prefixes rather than words, or to view /əv/, /tuw/~/tə/, /fər/, or /in/ as prefixes rather than prepositions. The data in the table is not, however, incorrect, but merely incomplete. It fails to show some of the other ways in which articles and prepositions can be used in English, and so it is misleading.

Table 8.2 shows some additional data which clarifies the point. With regard to the articles, it shows that they are not regularly prefixed to the noun, as seems to be the case from the preceding data, but are attached instead to an adjective such as *big*, *first*, or *tin*, when it precedes the noun. For the prepositions, it similarly shows them attached to an article or to one of the demonstrative adjectives *this*, *that*. If we were to insist that these elements are still prefixes, our treatment of them would have to be quite complex, requiring the noun to be inflected for case and definiteness in some instances, and the adjective to be inflected for those categories instead in other instances. The alternative solution to this kind of data involves treating these items not as affixes, but as unaccented words which just happen to attach to the

Table 8.1 A suggested morphological treatment of some English data

	A CAN	THE CAN	A BOX	THE BOX
DIRECT	əkǽn	ðəkǽn	əbáks	ðəbáks
GENITIVE	əvəkǽn	əvðəkǽn	əvəbáks	əvðəbáks
ALLATIVE	tuwəkǽn	təðəkǽn	tuwəbáks	təðəbáks
BENEFACTIVE	fərəkǽn	fərðəkǽn	fərəbáks	fərðəbáks
INESSIVE	inəkǽn	inðəkǽn	inəbáks	inðəbáks

	A HOUSE	THE HOUSE	A PIG	THE PIG
DIRECT	əháws	ðəháws	əpíg	ðəpíg
GENITIVE	əvəháws	əvðəháws	əvəpíg	əvðəpíg
ALLATIVE	tuwəháws	təðəháws	tuwəpíg	təðəpíg
BENEFACTIVE	fərəháws	fərðəháws	fərəpíg	fərðəpíg
INESSIVE	inəháws	inðəháws	inəpíg	inðəpíg

Table 8.2 English prepositions and articles in expanded noun phrases

əbíg háws	A BIG HOUSE	inðís háws	IN THIS HOUSE
ðəfə́rst píg	THE FIRST PIG	fərðǽt píg	FOR THAT PIG
fərətín kǽn	FOR A TIN CAN	təðís kǽn	TO THIS CAN
inəbíg báks	IN A BIG BOX	əvðǽt báks	OF THAT BOX

following accented word, whatever it is. The ancient Greeks had such words in their language, and they saw them as in effect "leaning forward" to the following accented word. Based on their morphemes for "leaning" and "forward", they termed them PROCLITICS. They had other unaccented words that attached to the preceding word, depending on it for accent, and they named them ENCLITICS, meaning words that "lean backward". Based on the root found in these two words, modern linguists have coined the more general term CLITICS for such unaccented words, whichever way they may "lean".

In general, a clitic may be defined as a grammatical item that behaves like a full word syntactically, but like an affix phonologically, in that it attaches to a preceding or following word. In general, we will want to classify an affix-like element as a clitic only if doing so will result in a more economical account of the grammatical facts than would result if we failed to do so. In the next several sections, particular criteria which usually make clitics easy to recognize will be presented and exemplified.

Identification by separability

The identification of the English prepositions and articles, as in Table 8.2, as separate words depends on the fact that they are not always linked phonologically to the same kind of word. Table 8.1 made it appear that they were prefixes because they always seemed to attach to the nouns, but the further data made it clear that they attach to whatever word follows, and have particular syntactic positions in the phrase. We can say that words in such instances are identifiable as clitics by the criterion of SEPARABILITY, meaning, of course, that they occur apart from any particular word (in this case the noun) rather than attached specifically to such a word the way an affix would be. Another example allowing similar identification of clitics is found in the Basque data of Table 8.3. In this material, the simple examples, such as items 1–8, 17–18, 21–22, 25, 27, 29, and 31 are analogous to the preliminary English data of Table 8.1, while the remaining examples are more like the English material in Table 8.2. They show that the articles, which indicate number and case in addition to definiteness, are separate words because they come at the end of the phrase, attaching to the previous word regardless of whether it is a noun or an adjectival Modifier. In this case, of course, we have enclitics rather than proclitics.

Another difference between the Basque clitics in this data set and the English clitics in the previous ones is that the Basque article is inflected for both number and case. Examples 1 through 16 in the table show inflection for number: *SINGULAR* or *PLURAL*. In the second column,

Table 8.3 Inflected Basque articles in simple and expanded noun phrases

1.	*gizona*	THE MAN	17.	*gizonari*	TO THE MAN
2.	*gizonak*	THE MEN	18.	*gizonei*	TO THE MEN
3.	*trena*	THE TRAIN	19.	*gizon zaharrari*	TO THE BIG MAN
4.	*trenak*	THE TRAINS	20.	*gizon zaharrei*	TO THE BIG MEN
5.	*etxea*	THE HOUSE	21.	*trenarekin*	WITH THE TRAIN
6.	*etxeak*	THE HOUSES	22.	*trenekin*	WITH THE TRAINS
7.	*denda*	THE SHOP	23.	*tren luzearekin*	WITH THE LONG TRAIN
8.	*dendak*	THE SHOPS	24.	*tren luzekin*	WITH THE LONG TRAINS
9.	*gizon handia*	THE BIG MAN	25.	*etxeari*	TO THE HOUSE
10.	*gizon handiak*	THE BIG MEN	26.	*etxe zaharrei*	TO THE OLD HOUSES
11.	*tren luzea*	THE LONG TRAIN	27.	*extearekin*	WITH THE HOUSE
12.	*tren luzeak*	THE LONG TRAINS	28.	*etxe zaharrarekin*	WITH THE OLD HOUSE
13.	*etxe zaharra*	THE OLD HOUSE	29.	*dendarei*	TO THE SHOP
14.	*etxe zaharrak*	THE OLD HOUSES	30.	*denda txikarei*	TO THE SMALL SHOP
15.	*denda txikia*	THE SMALL SHOP	31.	*dendaekin*	WITH THE SHOPS
16.	*denda txikiak*	THE SMALL SHOPS	32.	*denda txikiarekin*	WITH THE SMALL SHOP

Table 8.4 Editing of inflected Basque articles

	ABSOLUTIVE	*DATIVE*	*COMITATIVE*
SINGULAR	a	ari	arekin
PLURAL	ak	ei	ekin

we see examples of the *DATIVE* case ("to") and the *COMITATIVE* ("with"), and these contrast with the *ABSOLUTIVE* case forms elsewhere. The editing of these definite article forms is summarized in Table 8.4.

Identification by comembership

The Malagasy data of Table 8.5 shows evidence for a somewhat different way of identifying certain elements as clitics. Items 1–3 and 6–8, considered alone, seem to indicate that possession is expressed via suffixes to the noun: /-ku/ for MY and /-ni/ for HIS. When we look at the rest of the data, however, we observe that a noun expressing a possessor is placed after the noun expressing the thing possessed, but is not attached to it. It would be awkward to handle this material by saying we use inflectional suffixes for pronominal possessors and separate words for nominal possessors. The notion of clitics, however, allows us to treat all the elements indicating possession as words, but some of them are clitics, while the others are not. We can put all of them into the same syntactic class, identifiable by its position after the possessed noun and by the common meaning of "possessor". When clitics are identified in this manner, we can say that they are identified by **COMEMBERSHIP**, meaning that both clitic and non-clitic words are members of a single syntactic class.

Table 8.5 Malagasy clitics identifiable via comembership

1.	*ničánu*	THE HOUSE
2.	*ničánuku*	MY HOUSE
3.	*ničánuni*	HIS HOUSE
4.	*ničánu nilèilái*	THE MAN'S HOUSE
5.	*ničánu nivèivávi*	THE WOMAN'S HOUSE
6.	*nibúki*	THE BOOK
7.	*nibúkiku*	MY BOOK
8.	*nibúkini*	HIS BOOK
9.	*nibúki nilèilái*	THE MAN'S BOOK
10.	*nibúki nivèivávi*	THE WOMAN'S BOOK
11.	*nivèivávi nivèivávi*	THE WOMAN'S MAN
12.	*nivèivávi nivèivávi*	THE MAN'S WOMAN

Another example of clitics identifiable by comembership is seen in the Russian data of Table 8.6. Here the elements /u-/ BY and /da-/ AS FAR AS attach to following words, but /ókolo/ NEAR has its own accent and does not attach, though it occupies the same position. So the situation is quite parallel to that seen with the Malagasy, except that we have proclitics here instead of enclitics. In addition, however, we have evidence allowing the identification of /u-/ and /da-/ as clitics by separability, since they attach either to the noun or to an adjective modifying that noun, depending on what comes in the second position in their phrase. This shows that in some cases we can identify a clitic in more than one way. In fact, the same two criteria apply to many of the cases of English clitics already discussed. So the English articles are identifiable as clitics by separability, as seen in the material in Table 8.2. At the same time, however, we find that there are accented words that occupy the same position as the articles do, such as the demonstratives *this* and *that*. The existence of these permits us to identify the articles as clitics by comembership as well. The same is true of English prepositions: those shown earlier (*of*, *to*, *for* and *in*) are usually unaccented clitics, but others such as *before*, *behind*, *over*, and *under* are normally accented, allowing the identification of the unaccented ones as clitics by comembership as well as by separability.

Table 8.6 Russian prepositions identifiable as clitics by both comembership and separability

1. udóma	BY THE HOUSE
2. uvášiva dóma	BY YOUR HOUSE
3. umajivó dóma	BY MY HOUSE
4. dadóma	AS FAR AS THE HOUSE
5. davášiva dóma	AS FAR AS YOUR HOUSE
6. damajivó dóma	AS FAR AS MY HOUSE
7. ókala dóma	NEAR THE HOUSE
8. ókala vášiva dóma	NEAR YOUR HOUSE
9. ókala majivó dóma	NEAR MY HOUSE
10. ugórada	BY THE CITY
11. uvášiva górada	BY YOUR CITY
12. umajivó górada	BY MY CITY
13. dagórada	AS FAR AS THE CITY
14. davášiva górada	AS FAR AS YOUR CITY
15. damajivó górada	AS FAR AS MY CITY
16. ókala górada	NEAR THE CITY
17. ókala vášiva górada	NEAR YOUR CITY
18. ókala majivó górada	NEAR MY CITY
19. umósta	BY THE BRIDGE
20. uvášiva mósta	BY YOUR BRIDGE
21. umajivó mósta	BY MY BRIDGE
22. damósta	AS FAR AS THE BRIDGE
23. davášiva mósta	AS FAR AS YOUR BRIDGE
24. damajivó mósta	AS FAR AS MY BRIDGE
25. ókala mósta	NEAR THE BRIDGE
26. ókala vášiva mósta	NEAR YOUR BRIDGE
27. ókala majivó mósta	NEAR MY BRIDGE

Identification by differential linkage

In still other cases, clitics can be identified because they are phonologically attached to a different constituent from the one they belong with grammatically. A fascinating example of such a situation is found in Kwakwala, a Wakashan language formerly known as Kwakiutl. In this language, clause constituents appear to be marked by suffixes which pertain to the next constituent following, rather than to the preceding one to which they attach, as seen in the following examples:

(a) nəp'idida   gənanəmχa   guk^{w}sa   t'isam
    THROW-THE   CHILD-OBJ   HOUSE-OBL   ROCK
    THE CHILD HIT THE HOUSE WITH A ROCK BY THROWING.

(b) k^{w}iχz?dida   bag^{w}anəmaχa   q'asasis   t'alwagayu
    CLUBBED-THE   MAN-OBJ   OTTER-INS-HIS   CLUB
    THE MAN CLUBBED THE SEA-OTTER WITH HIS CLUB.

Without the notion of a clitic, the syntax of this language would appear to be radically out of line with its morphology. If, however, the final elements are simply recognized as enclitics rather than suffixes, we can properly associate them with the following word rather than the preceding one in the grammar, and treat their attachment to the preceding word as a matter of phonology. In approximate terms, the syntactic analysis of these examples would be as depicted in Table 8.7. A more complete data set would be needed, of course, to justify all aspects of this analysis.

The criterion allowing the recognition of clitics in such cases as this may be called **DIFFERENTIAL LINKAGE**, since the clitics involved are linked in one direction in the grammar but in the other direction in the phonology. Although the cases where this criterion is applicable are fairly rare in comparison with cases of separability and comembership, there appear to be a couple of examples of its applicability in English, involving the colloquial forms commonly written as *wanna* and *gonna*. The final /ə/ in each of these forms can be seen as an alternative reduced form of the element *to*, so that *I wanna go* can be seen as a colloquial form of *I want to go*, and similarly *I'm gonna do it* is a reduced form of *I am going to do it*. While the /ə/ is clearly linked to the preceding word as a clitic, the *to* goes grammatically with the following verb, and may even be pronounced as a proclitic /tə/, phonologically linked in a way that matches its grammatical linkage.

Table 8.7 Constituency of some Kwakwala examples

(a) THE CHILD HIT THE HOUSE WITH A ROCK BY THROWING

Clause						
PREDICATOR	SUBJECT		OBJECT		ADJUNCT	
Verb Phrase	Noun Phrase		Prepositional Phrase		Prepositional Phrase	
HEAD$_V$	DETERMINER	HEAD$_N$	RELATOR	AXIS	RELATOR	AXIS
Verb	Dem. Adj.	Noun	Prep.	Noun	Prep.	Noun
əp'idi	-da	gənanəm	-χa	guk^W	-sa	t'isəm
[nəp'idida]		[gənanəmχa]		[guk^{W}sa]		t'isəm

(b) THE MAN CLUBBED THE SEA-OTTER WITH HIS CLUB

Clause							
PREDICATOR	SUBJECT		OBJECT		INSTRUMENT		
Verb Phrase	Noun Phrase		Prepositional Phrase		Prepositional Phrase		
HEAD$_V$	DETER-MINER	HEAD$_N$	RELATOR	AXIS	RELATOR	AXIS	
						Noun Phrase	
						POSS'R	HEAD$_N$
Verb	Dem. Adj.	Noun	Prep.	Noun	Prep.	Poss. Adj.	Noun
k^{W}iχz?d	-ida	bag^{W}anəma	-χa	q'asa	-s	-is	t'alwagayu
[k^{W}iχz?dida]		[bag^{W}anəmaχa]		[q'asasis]			[t'alwagayu]

Consideration of differential linkage may also be relevant in the analysis of Japanese conjunctive phrases, as discussed in Chapter 5: it was pointed out that certain conjunctions seem to be linked phonologically to the preceding words. Contrary to this appearance, however, the more realistic analysis from the standpoint of production has them going with the following words syntactically. The concept of differential linkage suggests that we can recognize these as enclitics linked phonologically to the preceding, much as with the Kwakwala examples.

Classification of clitics

We have already seen evidence of the subclassification of clitics into proclitics and enclitics, according to whether they attach to the preceding accented word or the following one. Of the examples seen so far, the English articles and prepositions as well as the Russian prepositions are proclitics, while the Malagasy possessive pronouns, the Basque article forms, and the Kwakwala elements just seen, as well as the English /ə/ of *wanna* and *gonna* are enclitics. A special, and fairly frequent variety of enclitic is seen in the Bulgarian data presented in Table 8.8.

Table 8.8 Evidence for postinitial enclitic definite articles in Bulgarian

1. kniga	A BOOK	13. kəšta	A HOUSE
2. knigata	THE BOOK	14. kəštata	THE HOUSE
3. dobra kniga	A GOOD BOOK	15. dobra kəšta	A GOOD HOUSE
4. dobrata kniga	THE GOOD BOOK	16. dobrata kəšta	THE GOOD HOUSE
5. nova kniga	A NEW BOOK	17. nova kəšta	A NEW HOUSE
6. novata kniga	THE NEW BOOK	18. novata kəšta	THE NEW HOUSE
7. edna kniga	ONE BOOK	19. edna kəšta	ONE HOUSE
8. ednata kniga	THE ONE BOOK	20. ednata kəšta	THE ONE HOUSE
9. edna dobra kniga	ONE GOOD BOOK	21. edna dobra kəšta	ONE GOOD HOUSE
10. ednata dobra kniga	THE ONE GOOD BOOK	22. ednata dobra kəšta	THE ONE GOOD HOUSE
11. edna nova kniga	ONE NEW BOOK	23. edna nova kəšta	ONE NEW HOUSE
12. ednata nova kniga	THE ONE NEW BOOK	24. ednata nova kəšta	THE ONE NEW HOUSE

The clitic seen in this data is the definite article /ta/, which appears as an enclitic at the end of some words. The most peculiar thing about it, however, is its position of occurrence: it is always attached as an enclitic to the end of the first accented word of the phrase. As can be seen in the various examples, the preceding word may be the noun, a descriptive adjective, or a numeral. These other elements come in the order numeral, adjective, noun, with the first two of these being optional, but the article, when it occurs, always comes in the second position, attaching as an enclitic to whatever word is in the first position.

Such enclitics are not at all uncommon in various languages. Another example can be seen in the Amharic data of Table 8.9. Here again the clitic is a definite article, and it occurs following the first word of the phrase, which may be either a noun or an adjective. In this case, however, there is also evidence that the clitics take different shapes in different grammatical and phonological circumstances. The three shapes involved are /u/, /w/, and /wa/. The difference between the first two is based on phonological conditioning: the syllabic allomorph /u/ occurs after a consonant, while the non-syllabic /w/ comes after a vowel. The occurrence of one of these versus /wa/, however, is grammatically determined by the gender of the noun that serves as the head of the noun phrase. The words meaning HOUSE and STUDENT are masculine, while those meaning COW and HEN are feminine.

All of this suggests, then, that one dimension for classifying clitics involves their position. Essentially we distinguish proclitics and enclitics here, and within the category of enclitic we distinguish **ORDINARY** and **POSTINITIAL** subtypes. (Logically, we might ask whether there is a "prefinal proclitic" analogous to a postinitial enclitic, but the answer seems to be "no".)

Table 8.9 Evidence for postinitial enclitics in Amharic

1.	bet	A HOUSE
2.	tɨllɨk' bet	A BIG HOUSE
3.	t'ɨru bet	A GOOD HOUSE
4.	betu	THE HOUSE
5.	tɨllɨk'u bet	THE BIG HOUSE
6.	tɨruw bet	THE GOOD HOUSE
7.	təmari	A STUDENT
8.	tɨllɨk' təmari	A BIG STUDENT
9.	t'ɨru təmari	A GOOD STUDENT
10.	təmariw	THE STUDENT
11.	tɨllɨk'u təmari	THE BIG STUDENT
12.	t'ɨruw təmari	THE GOOD STUDENT
13.	lam	A COW
14.	tɨllɨk' lam	A BIG COW
15.	t'ɨru lam	A GOOD COW
16.	lamwa	THE COW
17.	tɨllɨk'wa lam	THE BIG COW
18.	t'ɨruwa lam	THE GOOD COW
19.	doro	A HEN
20.	tɨllɨk' doro	A BIG HEN
21.	t'ɨru doro	A GOOD HEN
22.	dorowa	THE HEN
23.	tɨllɨk'wa doro	THE BIG HEN
24.	t'ɨruwa doro	THE GOOD HEN

Table 8.10 Some examples of English variant clitics

	Full form	Clitic form	Phonemic shape of clitic
1.	*I **have** worked*	*I've worked*	/v/
2.	*you **have** worked*	*you've worked*	/v/
3.	*he **has** worked*	*he's worked*	/z/
4.	*it **has** worked*	*it's worked*	/s/
5.	*Buzz **has** worked*	*Buzz's worked*	/əz/
6.	*I **had** done it*	*I'd done it*	/d/
7.	*Red **had** done it*	*Red'd done it*	/əd/
8.	*I **am** here*	*I'm here*	/m/
9.	*you **are** there*	*you're there*	/r/
10.	*she **is** here*	*she's here*	/z/
11.	*it **is** there*	*it's there*	/s/
12.	*Buzz **is** tired*	*Buzz's tired*	/əz/
13.	*the men **are** here*	*the men're here*	/ər/
14.	*I **will** go*	*I'll go*	/l/
15.	*it **will** go*	*it'll go*	/əl/
16.	*you **would** go*	*you'd go*	/d/
17.	*I could **have** gone*	*I could've gone*	/əv/

Another dimension involved in the classification of clitics can be discussed in connection with the English data of Table 8.10. Here it can be seen that some clitics occur as variants, often stylistically conditioned, of fuller forms. In each example here, two different ways of saying essentially the same thing are given. In the full forms of the first column, no clitics are used, while the equivalents in the second column contain clitics. Clitics that occur in this fashion can be termed **VARIANT CLITICS**, meaning that they have alternative shapes that are not clitics. Any other clitic that has only a clitic shape (or alternative clitic shapes) can be termed a **CONSTANT CLITIC**.

In English, most of the clitics that occur are of the variant type. The most outstanding exception is illustrated by the data of Table 8.11. This shows the use of the element -'s, which is usually treated as a suffix in traditional grammars. In older stages of English, it was indeed a genitive case suffix that occurred only on nouns. In Old English, in fact, there were various patterns of inflection, only some of which involved the /s/. In modern English, however, the former suffix has evolved in such a way that it does not necessarily attach to a noun, but simply to the last element of the noun phrase, whatever that may be. Properly speaking, -'s is now an enclitic postposition, and since it does not have any full-word variants, it is a constant clitic. (Traditional grammarians who insist on treating this as a suffix would also tend to reject most of the examples in this table as unacceptable English.)

Table 8.11 Evidence for the enclitic status of the traditional English "genitive" marker

1. *Uncle John's mustache*
2. *Elizabeth the Second's heir*
3. *someone else's car*
4. *the King of Thailand's visit*
5. *an hour and a half's discussion*
6. *a week or so's sunshine*
7. *a man I know's car*
8. *the woman over there's coat*
9. *old man what-do-you-call-him's house*
10. *people who worry's indigestion*

The various categories of clitics discussed in this section are summarized in Table 8.12.

Table 8.12 Subtypes of clitics

	Proclitics	Enclitics	
		ORDINARY	**POSTINITIAL**
CONSTANT	X	X	X
VARIANT	X	X	X

Fitting clitics into syntactic description

In essence, clitics are simply grammatical words, so their syntactic description should simply treat them as such. Obviously, however, they have special phonological properties, so some special means is needed to, in effect, allow the phonology to know that it is dealing with a clitic rather than with an ordinary word. In the context of the syntactic notation presented in this book, this can be done by using special markings for clitics. For proclitics and ordinary enclitics, we can quite straightforwardly use hyphens to indicate the direction of phonological linkage for clitics. Some examples, based on material presented earlier, are provided in Figures 8.1 through 8.3. In the Malagasy solution of Figure 8.1, the enclitic possessive pronouns seen in the presentation of the data in Table 8.5 are identified as enclitics by the hyphen that precedes them. Analogously, the Russian solution in Figure 8.2 (based on the data originally seen in Table 8.6), identifies the proclitic prepositions /u-/ BY and /da-/ AS FAR AS as proclitics by the hyphen following them. The Basque data originally presented in Table 8.3 is solved in Figure 8.3. The additional complication presented by this material is that the enclitics are words inflected for case and number rather than uninflected particles. In such an instance, the preposed hyphen identifying the enclitic is placed on the word-box label rather than on the individual word elements, which are subject to the usual editing.

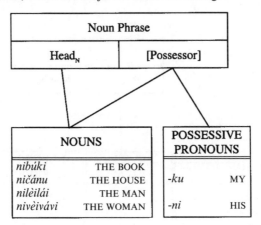

Figure 8.1 Solution to the Malagasy data of Table 8.5

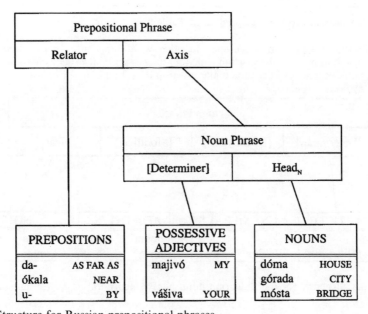

Figure 8.2 Structure for Russian prepositional phrases

Figure 8.4 shows the special considerations necessary in the case of postinitial enclitics, such as those seen in the Bulgarian data of Table 8.8. Here the enclitics are identified by a special symbol placed in front of them: ~. This occupies the same position at the beginning of the word, as the hyphen for an ordinary enclitic, but it is intended to indicate that the clitic will actually occur *after* the word that follows it in the construction. This is the most efficient way

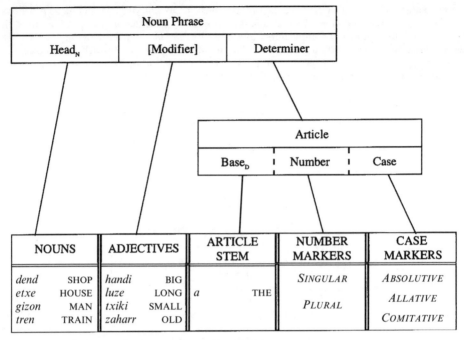

Figure 8.3 Solution to the Basque data of Table 8.3

to deal with such facts in this model. In other words, the postinitial enclitic is treated as abstractly initial because the word to which it attaches is not always of the same class, and the special notation tells us how to actually position it in the phrase or clause.

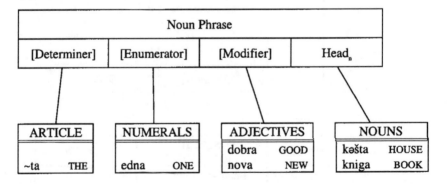

Figure 8.4 Structure for the Bulgarian noun phrase incorporating postinitial enclitic definite articles

Exercises

A. Interpretation problems

1. Prepositional and noun phrases in Polish

Examine the following account of the prepositional phrase and related noun phrase in Polish and answer the questions on page 178.

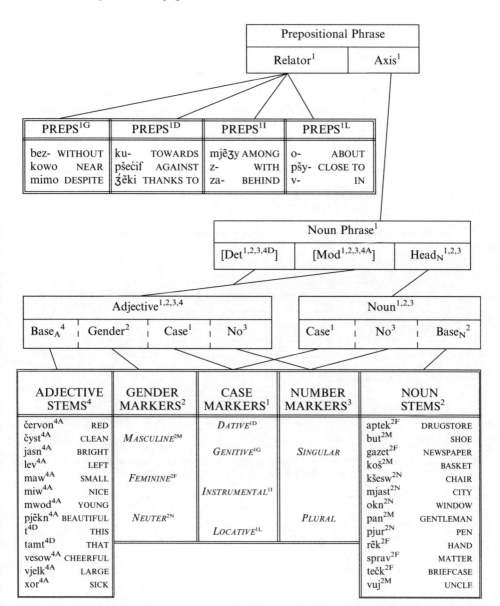

a.   Identify the clitics in the above account and explain by what criteria we can recognize each as a clitic.
b.   Show the grammatical representation of Polish phrases with the following meanings according to the above account. Show the full boxed form for item a. Note that there is no need to translate the English articles, since Polish has no articles.

1.   AGAINST THAT NICE GENTLEMAN

   _____

2.   ABOUT THESE BRIEFCASES

   _____

3.   WITHOUT THIS LARGE NOTEBOOK

   _____

4.   WITH SMALL NEWSPAPERS

   _____

5.   BEHIND THAT DRUGSTORE

   _____

6.   IN THE LEFT HAND

   _____

7.   NEAR THOSE CLEAN CITIES

   _____

8.   TOWARDS YELLOW BASKETS

   _____

c.   Construct three additional phrases of your own, giving their representations and English translations. Show the full boxed form for any one of these.

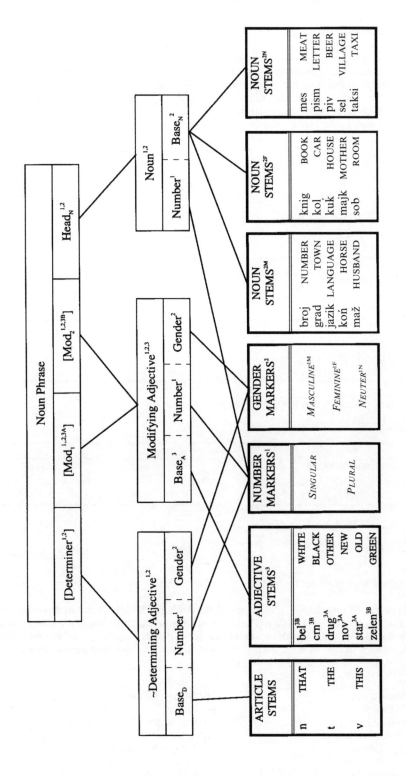

Noun phrase structure of Macedonian

2.   Macedonian noun phrase structure

The description on the preceding page formalizes a fragment of the noun phrase structure of Macedonian, a Slavic language with official status in the Republic of Macedonia (formerly a part of Yugoslavia). Use this to translate the following English phrases into Macedonian, on the understanding that the English indefinite article requires no translation. A number of these forms will involve a difference between the abstracted word-order shown in the analysis and the actual order seen in the data. In such a case, the translation should show the actual order.

1.   THIS OTHER NUMBER

_____

2.   THAT OLD WHITE HOUSE

_____

3.   THE NEW LETTER

_____

4.   A NEW RED CAR

_____

5.   THESE OTHER BLACK BOOKS

_____

6.   THOSE WHITE TAXIS

_____

B.   Analysis problems

1.   Affixes and clitics in Amharic

In the course of this chapter, the nature of the Amharic definite article as a postinitial enclitic was illustrated and established (Table 8.9). Assuming that much, consider further the following phrasal data, deciding whether each additional phonologically bound form should be seen as a clitic or an affix. Explain each such case in prose, and account for the properly analysed data, including the original set.

1.   tɨnnɨšu bet   THE SMALL HOUSE
2.   betočč   HOUSES
3.   betočču   THE HOUSES
4.   tɨllɨk'očču betočč   THE BIG HOUSES
5.   tɨgu təmari   A DILIGENT STUDENT

6. tɨguw təmari   THE DILIGENT STUDENT
7. tɨgočč təmaročč   DILIGENT STUDENTS
8. tɨgočč_u təmaročč   THE DILIGENT STUDENTS
9. ɨbetu   AT THE HOUSE
10. ləbetu   FOR THE HOUSE
11. kəbetu   FROM THE HOUSE
12. wədə betu   TO THE HOUSE
13. ɨtɨllɨk'u bet   AT THE BIG HOUSE
14. lətɨnnɨšu bet   FOR THE SMALL HOUSE
15. kək'onjo bet   FROM A PRETTY HOUSE
16. wədə t'ɨruw bet   TO/TOWARD THE GOOD HOUSE
17. ɨməkinaw   AT THE CAR
18. kətɨnnɨšu məkina   FROM THE SMALL CAR
19. lək'onjow məkina   FOR THE PRETTY CAR
20. wədə k'əyyɨw məkina   TO THE RED CAR
21. it'ɨročču betočč   AT THE GOOD HOUSES
22. ləbetočču   FOR THE HOUSES
23. kətɨnnɨšočču betočč   FROM THE SMALL HOUSES
24. wədə k'onjowočč betočč   TO PRETTY HOUSES
25. ləməkinaw   IN THE CAR
26. kəlamočču   FROM THE COWS
27. wədə t'ɨllɨk'wa lam   TO THE BIG COW
28. kətɨgočču təmaročč   FROM THE DILIGENT STUDENTS
29. ɨtɨnnɨšu məkina   AT THE SMALL CAR
30. kət'ɨllɨk' gəbəya   FROM A BIG MARKET

2. Noun phrases in Mokilese

Present an account of the following noun phrases in Mokilese, a Micronesian language spoken on the atoll of Mokil in the eastern Caroline Islands (Western Pacific). Pay especial attention to clitics, identifying each one explicitly and explaining the basis for treating it as a clitic rather than as an affix.

1. ceripeinwa   THE GIRL
2. ceripein siksikwa   THE LITTLE GIRL
3. ceripeino   YON GIRL
4. ceripein cepiriro   YON CLUMSY GIRL
5. pɛɛrokɛn   THAT FROG
6. pɛɛrok kɔlikɛn   THAT BIG FROG
7. kasɛ   THIS CAT
8. kas kɔlikɛ   THIS OLD CAT
9. kululɛn   THAT COCKROACH
10. kulul kɔlikɛn   THAT BLACK COCKROACH
11. wɔlɛ   THIS MAN
12. wɔl pɛrɛnɛ   THIS HAPPY MAN
13. wɔlmɛn   A MAN
14. wɔl cɔɔpicɛkmɛn   A BUSY MAN
15. lɔŋwa   THE FLY
16. lɔŋ sɔlwa   THE BLACK FLY
17. m^wum^{w}ɛ   THIS FISH
18. m^wum^w siksikɛ   THIS LITTLE FISH
19. maansaŋo   YON BIRD
20. maansaŋ rɔŋrɔŋo   YON YELLOW BIRD
21. kas solwa   THE BLACK CAT
22. maansaŋ pɛrɛnmɛn   A HAPPY BIRD

23. sɔsok siksikɛn	THAT LITTLE GECKO
24. wɔl kacam\(^w\)p\(^w\)alɛ	THIS IMPORTANT MAN
25. sinɛk kriino	YON GREEN SNAKE

Notes

1. This is based on material contained in the *Mokilese Reference Grammar* and the *Mokilese–English Dictionary* by Sheldon P. Harrison and Salich Y. Albert (Honolulu: University of Hawaii Press, 1976, 1977). The transcription system was devised by the present author.
2. Some phonological alternations of no syntactic importance have been abstracted out in the presentation of this data.
3. For the purpose of easy glossing, the archaic English YON has been used for THAT OVER THERE, while THAT is used for THAT (NEAR THE HEARER).

3. Phrases in Israeli Hebrew

Analyse and account for the structure of phrases in the following data from Modern Israeli Hebrew, paying special attention to clitics. For each clitic postulated, explain why it is better to view it as a clitic rather than an affix.

1. ʔim basar	WITH MEAT
2. bli basar tov	WITHOUT GOOD MEAT
3. ʔim para tova	WITH A GOOD COW
4. bli para	WITHOUT A COW
5. lepara	TO A COW
6. beʔad hapara hatova	FOR THE GOOD COW
7. ʔim talmid	WITH A PUPIL
8. bli talmid tov	WITHOUT A GOOD PUPIL
9. mitalmid	FROM A PUPIL
10. ʔecel hatalmid	AT THE PUPIL'S PLACE
11. beʔad talmid	FOR A PUPIL
12. letalmid	TO A PUPIL
13. beʔad hatalmid haxadaš	FOR THE NEW PUPIL
14. latalmid	TO THE PUPIL
15. bli hapara	WITHOUT THE COW
16. lapara hayišana	TO THE OLD COW
17. ʔim sefer yašan	WITH AN OLD BOOK
18. lesefer	TO A BOOK
19. bli hasefer haxadaš	WITHOUT THE GOOD BOOK
20. lasefer hayašan	TO THE OLD BOOK
21. misefer	FROM A BOOK
22. mehasefer	FROM THE BOOK
23. mehapara	FROM THE COW
24. mehatalmid hatov	FROM THE GOOD PUPIL
25. mehabasar hayašan	FROM THE OLD MEAT

4. Clauses in Mesa Grande Diegueño

The following data comes from the Mesa Grande dialect of Diegueño, a Yuman language spoken in the vicinity of San Diego, California. Account for this data paying especial attention to clitics. Include a brief narrative identifying each clitic and briefly explaining why it should be treated as such.

1. ʔəlʸmaamč ʔəšaš THE CHILD IS PRETTY.
2. xəčkuḻkč wənuw THE WOLF RUNS.
3. siñ pəyaač ʔəxpank əwuuw THIS WOMAN SEES THE WHALE.
4. xaṭəpaač ʔəpxar wəñay THE COYOTE IS HUNTING A RABBIT.
5. xəčkuḻk puuč wənuw YON WOLF RUNS.
6. ʔəxtaay pəyaač šawii šuuxuu THIS CROW STEALS THE ACORN MUSH.
7. ʔaašaa kʷaʔšaš ñipč ʔəxʷat THAT BEAUTIFUL BIRD IS RED.
8. ʔəxaṭ ñipč ʔəməkay kuñiḻʸ pəyaa yip THAT DOG HEARS THIS BLACK MOUSE.
9. siñ kʷaʔstik pəyaač ʔəxtaay ñip wəmiř THIS LITTLE WOMAN LIKES THAT CROW.
10. milʸaapanč siñ kʷaʔšaš puu wəmiř THE BAT LIKES YON PRETTY WOMAN.
11. ʔiikʷič ñipč ʔəlʸmaam əwuuw THAT MAN SEES THE CHILD.
12. ʔəlʸmaamč ʔiikʷič puu wətoo THE CHILD HITS YON MAN (WITH A STICK).
13. siñ pəyaač ʔəwaak wənuw THIS WOMAN RUNS FROM THE HOUSE.
14. ʔiikʷiič kʷaʔstik ñipč ḻəxup pəyaak wənuw THAT LITTLE MAN RUNS FROM THIS CAVE.
15. ʔəlmaam puuč ʔəwaa kwaʔiik puum wənuw YON CHILD RUNS TO YON BIG HOUSE.
16. kavaay kuñiḻʸ pəyaač ḻəxupm wamp THIS BLACK HORSE WALKS TO THE CAVE.
17. ʔəlʸmaam pəyaač ḻəxup kʷaʔstikm wamp THIS CHILD WALKS TO THE LITTLE CAVE.
18. ʔəxaṭ puuč ʔəwaaḻʸ wip YON DOG BARKS INSIDE THE HOUSE.
19. ʔəxaṭ pəyaač ḻəxup kʷaʔiikuuḻʸ wəxʷaḻ THIS DOG DIGS INSIDE THE BIG CAVE.
20. kavaayč ḻəxupḻʸ ñəwaayp THE HORSE LIVES INSIDE THE CAVE.

5. Clitics in Luiseño clauses

In Chapter 7, we considered an exercise from Luiseño, a Uto-Aztecan language of southern California. In fact, this language can be spoken in two styles. The one described as "more Indian" in textbook treatments includes clitic particles, as illustrated by the following examples, which correspond in meaning to the correspondingly-numbered examples in the other style. The clitics are shown in square brackets, indicating their omissibility. Modify your solution to the earlier problem as necessary to show these optional elements and their grammatical properties.

1. hunwut[up] yaʔaši toowq THE BEAR SEES THE MAN.
2. yaʔaš[upil] hunwuti ʔamooquṣ THE MAN WAS HUNTING THE BEAR.
3. ṣuʔaal[up] hunwuti noonomiq THE WOMAN IS FOLLOWING THE BEAR.
4. hunwut[up] yaʔaši noonomiq THE BEAR IS FOLLOWING THE MAN.
5. tukwut[upil] hunwuti toowquṣ THE MOUNTAIN LION SAW THE BEAR.
6. ʔawaal[upil] sʼụaali noonomiuṣ THE DOG WAS FOLLOWING THE WOMAN.
7. kaṣilla[upil] yaʔaši toowquṣ THE LIZARD SAW THE MAN.
8. yaʔaš[up] kaṣillay ʔamooq THE MAN IS HUNTING THE LIZARD.
9. heʔeemal[upil] ʔawaali toowquṣ THE BOY SAW THE DOG.
10. ʔaṣwut[upil] tapašmali ʔamooquṣ THE EAGLE WAS HUNTING THE MOUSE.
11. heʔeemal[up] tukwuti ʔamooq THE BOY IS HUNTING THE MOUNTAIN LION.
12. hunwut[po] heʔeemali ʔamoon THE BEAR WILL HUNT THE BOY.
13. heʔeemal[po] tukwuti toowan THE BOY WILL SEE THE MOUNTAIN LION.
14. yaʔaš[po] heʔeemali noonimin THE MAN WILL FOLLOW THE BOY.
15. kaṣilla[po] ʔaṣwuti toowan THE LIZARD WILL SEE THE EAGLE.
16. hunwutum[pum] yaʔaʼsi toowwun THE BEARS SEE THE MAN.
17. yaʔas[poʼ] hunwutumi toowan THE MAN WILL SEE THE BEARS.
18. ʔaṣwutum[pum] kaṣillami ʔaamowun THE EAGLES ARE HUNTING THE LIZARDS.
19. kasʼillam[mo] ṣuʔaali toowan THE LIZARDS WILL SEE THE WOMAN.
20. yaʔašum[mil] hunwuti ʔaamoquṣ THE MEN WERE HUNTING THE BEAR.
21. ʔawaal[up] kaṣillami noonomiquṣ THE DOG IS FOLLOWING THE LIZARDS.
22. ʔano[upil] tukwutumi toowquṣ THE COYOTE SAW THE MOUNTAIN LIONS.

23. tukwutum[pum] tapašmalumi ʔammowun — THE MOUNTAIN LIONS ARE HUNTING THE MICE.
24. tapašmal[upil] ʔawaalumi noonomiquṣ — THE MOUSE WAS FOLLOWING THE DOGS.
25. ṣuʔaalum[mo] ʔanomi toowan — THE WOMEN WILL SEE THE COYOTES.
26. muutam[mil] tapašmali noonomiquṣ — THE OWLS WERE FOLLOWING THE MOUSE.
27. heʔeemalum[mo] ʔanomi noonomin — THE BOYS WILL HUNT THE COYOTES.
28. ʔawaalum[pum] heʔeemali maʔmaan — THE DOGS LIKE THE BOY.
29. heʔeemal[po] hunwutumi maʔmaan — THE BOY WILL LIKE THE BEARS.
30. ʔamom[mil] tapašmalumi maʔmaquṣ — THE COYOTES LIKED THE MICE.

The next set of examples illustrates another property of the occurrence of these enclitics, when an adverb such as /pitoo/ NOW, TODAY accompanies various of these examples:

31. pitoo[up] hunwutyaʔaši toowq — THE BEAR SEES THE MAN TODAY.
32. pitoo[upiľ] yaʔashunwuti ʔamooquṣ — THE MAN WAS HUNTING THE BEAR TODAY.
33. pitoo[po] hunwut heʔeemali ʔamoon — THE BEAR WILL HUNT THE BOY TODAY.
34. pitoo[up] hunwut yaʔaši noonomiq — THE BEAR IS FOLLOWING THE MAN NOW.
35. pitoo[upil] tukwuthunwuti toowquṣ — THE MOUNTAIN LION SAW THE BEAR TODAY.
36. pitoo[mo] ṣuʔaalum ʔanomi toowan — THE WOMEN WILL SEE THE COYOTES TODAY.

Assuming that this possibility represents a variety of all of these sentences, modify the solution produced for items 1–30 to reflect it.

Terminology

CLITIC	COMEMBERSHIP
CONSTANT CLITIC	
ENCLITIC	DIFFERENTIAL LINKAGE
POSTINITIAL ENCLITIC	
PROCLITIC	SEPARABILITY
VARIANT CLITIC	

9

Negation in the clause

It can hardly be surprising that negation plays a grammatical role in all languages. It is an obvious language universal, presumably fulfilling a basic need to negate as well as to affirm statements in the course of human communication. In linguistic tradition, it should be noted, the opposite of "negative" is not "positive" (as would be used in physics), but **AFFIRMATIVE**. Not all linguists nowadays adhere to this, but it is followed here because of the potential confusion with the use of "positive" as a term in the comparison of adjunctive words such as adjectives and adverbs, alongside the contrasting terms "comparative", and "superlative". Since no tradition provides a serviceable alternative to "positive" in the latter meaning, it is best here to follow the tradition and avoid the use of "positive" as the opposite of negative.

Inflectional negation

One simple way of negating a clause is by means of inflection, providing verbs with both affirmative and negative forms. This is illustrated by the Central Alaskan Yup'ik Eskimo data seen in Table 9.1. It shows verbs in different tenses reflecting both affirmative and negative polarity. So in the present-tense forms (1a/b and 4a/b) the difference involves the presence of the suffix /nʁit/ in the negative and its absence in the affirmative. The past-tense forms (3a/b and 6a/b) differ similarly, with the suffix coming after the past-tense marker /ɬχu/. In the future tense, the affirmatives show /ciq/ while the negatives show /ŋait/. While a morphological analysis might subject these latter to a more detailed treatment, all the syntactic analyst needs to do is observe the inflectional differences and edit them as expressions of **POLARITY**, going along with the other inflectional dimensions of **TENSE**, **PERSON**, and **NUMBER** evident in this material. By itself, this kind of negation presents no particular problems at all for the treatment of syntax. The basic treatment of this data set (projecting some combinations of person and number not directly in evidence here) is seen in Figure 9.1.

Table 9.1 Inflectional negation in Central Alaskan Yup'ik Eskimo

1a. caliuq	HE IS WORKING.
1b. calinʁituq	HE IS NOT WORKING.
2a. caliciqutɨn	YOU WILL WORK.
2b. caliŋaitutɨn	YOU WILL NOT WORK.
3a. caliɬχuukut	WE WORKED.
3b. caliɬχunʁitukut	WE DID NOT WORK.
4a. uitaut	THEY ARE STAYING.
4b. uitanʁitut	THEY ARE NOT STAYING.
5a. uitaciqua	I WILL STAY.
5b. uitaŋaitua	I WILL NOT STAY.
6a. uitaɬχuuq	HE STAYED.
6b. uitaɬχunʁituq	HE DID NOT STAY.

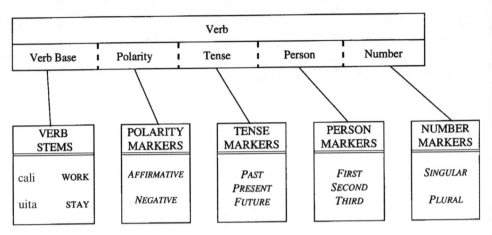

Figure 9.1 Solution to the Central Alaskan Yup'ik negation data

Negation by simple particles

Another very common way of negating a clause is seen in the Latin data of Table 9.2, in which the word *nōn* NOT is placed before the verb in each of the negative forms to distinguish it from the corresponding affirmative. This material likewise presents little problem, though it does involve a kind of syntax in the form of an optional position for a negator in the structure of the verb phrase.

The solution to this material is presented in Figure 9.2. It is more complex than the Yup'ik only in that it involves structures on the clause and phrase ranks as well as the word. This is not a genuine difference, however, since the Yup'ik data could certainly be expanded to include more clausal and phrasal options. The basic difference is that in Latin the negation is indicated by an optional phrasal constituent rather than by the use of inflectional distinctions indicating polarity as *AFFIRMATIVE* versus *NEGATIVE*, with the absence of the overt *NEGATIVE* marker *nōn* implying the *AFFIRMATIVE*.

A somewhat more complex situation involving simple particles is presented by the Hindi data seen in Table 9.3. As in Latin, the negative particle simply occurs optionally before the verb in a verb phrase, but it takes different forms according to the tense and mood of the verb involved. So in the Present and Past Continuous tenses (1 and 2), the word NOT takes the form /nahī·/, while in the Simple Past and Future (3 and 4) it may occur either in the same form or

Table 9.2 Simple particle negation in Classical Latin

1a.	*librum videō*	I SEE A BOOK.
1b.	*librum nōn videō*	I DON'T SEE A BOOK.
2a.	*librum habet*	HE HAS A BOOK.
2b.	*librum nōn habet*	HE DOESN'T HAVE A BOOK.
3a.	*leōnem timeō*	I AM AFRAID OF THE LION.
3b.	*leōnem nōn timeō*	I AM NOT AFRAID OF THE LION.
4a.	*leōnem vident*	THEY SEE THE LION.
4b.	*leōnem nōn vident*	THEY DON'T SEE THE LION.
5a.	*pecūniam habent*	THEY HAVE MONEY.
5b.	*pecūniam nōn habent*	THEY DON'T HAVE MONEY.
6a.	*equum timet*	HE IS AFRAID OF THE HORSE.
6b.	*equum nōn timet*	HE ISN'T AFRAID OF THE HORSE.

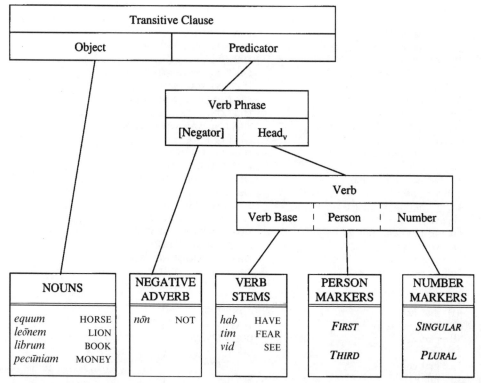

Figure 9.2 Solution to the Latin negation problem

as /na·/. The latter form occurs as the only possibility in the subjunctive (5) and the formal imperative (8), while the other imperatives use still another form /mat/. In treating this kind of case, we can postulate a single abstract negative element and specify different realizations for it in different environments. So our editing of the material could be seen as assigning a single shape NA for all forms of the negative particle, with the different manifestations we can observe being conditioned by the grammatical nature of its co-constituents in the verb phrase. Figure 9.3 shows a syntactic solution based on such assumptions, along with further editing of the inflected verbs. It would need to be supplemented by a realization statement such as the following:

NA || ____ {*FORMAL-IMP*; *SUBJUNCTIVE*} / na·

|| _____ {*PRESENT*; *PAST-CONTINS*} / nahĩ·

|| _____ *IMPERATIVE* / mat

|| _____ / na· ~ nahĩ·

Table 9.3 Data for negation in Hindi

1.	vo calta˙ hɛ	THAT ONE GOES.
1a.	ye nahĩ˙ calta˙ hɛ	THIS ONE DOES NOT GO.
1b.	ye rahta˙ hɛ	THIS ONE STAYS.
1c.	vo nahĩ˙ rahta˙ hɛ	THAT ONE DOES NOT STAY.
2.	ye calta˙ tʰa˙	THIS ONE WAS GOING.
2a.	vo nahĩ˙ calta˙ tʰa˙	THAT ONE WAS NOT GOING.
2b.	vo rahta˙ tʰa˙	THAT ONE WAS STAYING.
2c.	ye nahĩ˙ rahta˙ tʰa˙	THIS ONE WAS NOT STAYING.
3.	vo cala˙	THAT ONE WENT.
3a.	ye na˙/nahĩ˙ cala˙	THIS ONE DID NOT GO.
3b.	ye raha˙	THIS ONE STAYED.
3c.	vo na˙/nahĩ˙ raha˙	THAT ONE DID NOT STAY.
4.	vo calega˙	THIS ONE WILL GO.
4a.	ye na˙/nahĩ˙ calega˙	THAT ONE WILL NOT GO.
4b.	ye rahega˙	THAT ONE WILL STAY.
4c.	vo na˙/nahĩ˙ rahega˙	THIS ONE WILL NOT STAY.
5.	vo cale	THAT ONE MIGHT GO.
5a.	ye na˙ cale	THIS ONE MIGHT NOT GO.
5b.	ye rahe	THIS ONE MIGHT STAY.
5c.	vo na˙ rahe	THAT ONE MIGHT NOT STAY.
6.	cal	GO! ⎫
6a.	mat cal	DON'T GO! ⎪
6b.	rah	STAY! ⎬ *INFORMAL*
6c.	mat rah	DON'T STAY! ⎭
7.	calo	GO! ⎫
7a.	mat calo	DON'T GO! ⎪
7b.	raho	STAY! ⎬ *SEMIFORMAL*
7c.	mat raho	DON'T STAY! ⎭
8.	calle	GO! ⎫
8a.	na˙ calle	DON'T GO! ⎪
8b.	rahle	STAY! ⎬ *FORMAL*
8c.	na˙ rahle	DON'T STAY! ⎭

Discontinuous negation

A greater complication for negation occurs when it involves more than one negating word. Probably the best known language with this property is French, as displayed in the data of Table 9.4. Here the negation is indicated by the combination of the particle /nə/ before the verb and the particle /pa/ following it. As can be seen in the solution presented in Figure 9.4, this kind of situation complicates our syntactic description by requiring the postulation of two distinct verb phrase types, one for the affirmative and another for the negative.

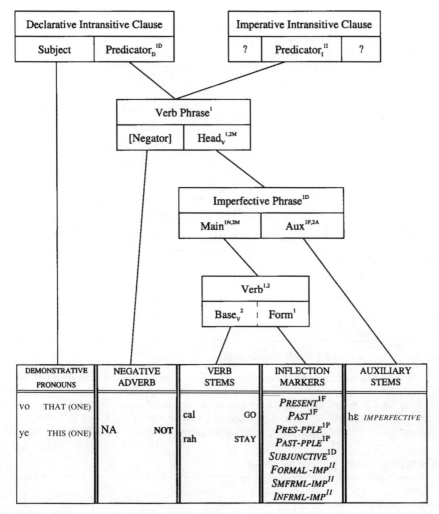

Figure 9.3 Solution to the Hindi negation data

Table 9.4 Data for negation in Modern Standard French

1a.	pyɛr naž	PIERRE IS SWIMMING.
1b.	pyɛr nə naž pa	PIERRE IS NOT SWIMMING .
2a.	mɔnik naž	MONIQUE IS SWIMMING.
2b.	mɔnik nə naž pa	MONIQUE IS NOT SWIMMING.
3a.	šarl sot	CHARLES IS JUMPING.
3b.	šarl nə sot pa	CHARLES IS NOT JUMPING .
4a.	mari marš	MARIE IS WALKING.
4b.	mari nə marš pa	MARIE IS NOT WALKING.
5a.	žak kur	JACQUES IS RUNNING.
5b.	žak nə kur pa	JACQUES IS NOT RUNNING.
6a.	žan marš	JEANNE IS WALKING.
6b.	žan nə marš pa	JEANNE IS NOT WALKING.

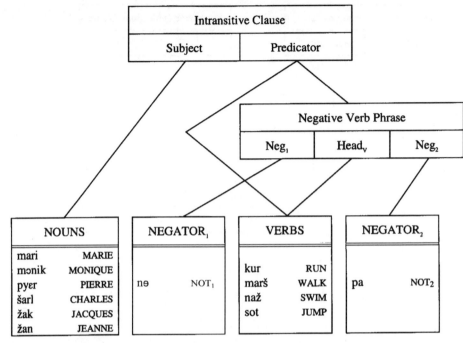

Figure 9.4 Solution to the French negation data

A somewhat different case of discontinuous negation is seen in the Afrikaans data of Table 9.5. Here there is always some kind of a verb in second position, and there will be a negation signaled by *nie*, after this. Then, in those cases where an additional word comes after this, the same *nie* is repeated at the end of the sentence. This material could be treated with four different kinds of predicate phrases: Present Affirmative, Present Negative, Non-Present Affirmative, and Non-

Table 9.5 Data for negation in Afrikaans

1.	*ek loop*	I WALK.
2.	*ek het geloop*	I WALKED.
3.	*ek sal loop*	I WILL WALK.
4.	*jy sal loop*	YOU WILL WALK.
5.	*hy loop*	HE WALKS.
6.	*sy het geloop*	SHE WALKED.
7.	*sy kom*	SHE COMES.
8.	*hy het gekom*	HE CAME.
9.	*sy sal staan*	SHE WILL STAND.
10.	*hy loop nie*	HE DOESN'T WALK.
11.	*ek kom nie*	I DON'T COME.
12.	*jy staan nie*	YOU DON'T STAND.
13.	*sy het nie geloop nie*	SHE DIDN'T WALK.
14.	*hy sal nie kom nie*	HE WON'T COME.
15.	*ek het nie gestaan nie*	I DIDN'T STAND.
16.	*sy sal nie staan nie*	SHE WON'T STAND.
17.	*jy het nie geloop nie*	YOU DIDN'T WALK.
18.	*hy sal nie loop nie*	HE WON'T WALK.

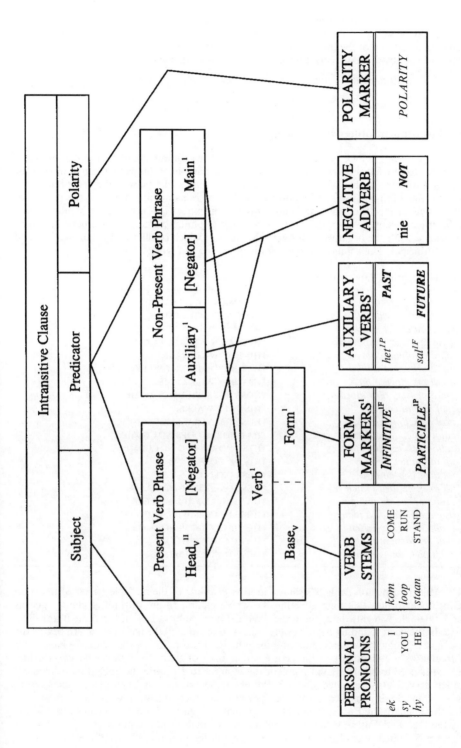

Figure 9.5 A solution to the Afrikaans negation data

Present Negative. The last-named would then be the one with two negative words, one after the first verb and the second at the end. A somewhat less complex treatment, as offered in Figure 9.5, is based on an editing of the final negation in relation to its absence. Each example is treated as ending with an abstract item called polarity. It is assumed that this will be realized as follows:

$$\text{POLARITY} \quad || \; \textit{nie} \; \text{Verb} \; \underline{\hspace{1cm}} \; / \; \textit{nie}$$
$$|| \; \underline{\hspace{3cm}} \; / \; \varnothing$$

Special constituent orders in the negative

In some languages, the presence of a negative marker requires a different order of clause constituents from what is found in the affirmative. An example of this can be seen in the Basque corpus of Table 9.6. In this material, there is a single clause structure with the order Subject + Predicator, but we need to posit two distinct verb phrases as manifestations of the predicator function, one for the affirmative, and another for the negative. This is needed to handle the fact that the order of constituents is different: the affirmative phrase contains a Principal followed by an Auxiliary, while the negative begins with the Negator which is followed by the Auxiliary and then the Principal. The solution to this data is presented in Figure 9.6.

Table 9.6 Negation data from Basque

1.	*gizon ori etoŕiko da*	THAT MAN WILL COME.
1a.	*gizon oiek etoŕiko dira*	THOSE MEN WILL COME.
1b.	*gizon au ez da etoŕiko*	THIS MAN WILL NOT COME.
1c.	*gizon auek ez dira etoŕiko*	THESE MEN WILL NOT COME.
2.	*mutil au ibiliko da*	THIS BOY WILL WALK.
2a.	*mutil ori ez da ibiliko*	THAT BOY WILL NOT WALK.
2b.	*mutil ori etoŕiko da*	THAT BOY WILL COME.
2c.	*mutil oiek ez dira etoŕiko*	THOSE BOYS WILL NOT COME.
3.	*txal au ibiltzen da*	THIS CALF WALKS.
3a.	*txal oiek ibiltzen dira*	THOSE CALVES WALK.
4.	*zaldi ori ez da etortzen*	THAT HORSE DOES NOT COME.
4a.	*zaldi auek ez dira etortzen*	THESE HORSES DO NOT COME.
5.	*idi au joaten da*	THIS OX GOES.
5a.	*idi auek joaten dira*	THESE OXEN GO.
5b.	*idi auek ez dira joaten*	THESE OXEN DO NOT GO.
6.	*osaba ori ez da joango*	THAT UNCLE WILL NOT GO.
6a.	*osaba oiek ez dira joango*	THOSE UNCLES WILL NOT GO.
6b.	*osaba au ez da joaten*	THIS UNCLE DOES NOT GO.
7.	*txal ori joango da*	THAT CALF WILL GO.
8.	*zaldi oiek joango dira*	THOSE HORSES WILL GO.

The Maori corpus of Table 9.7 shows another example of the possible effects of negation on constituent order, this time affecting the whole clause. In an affirmative clause such as items 1 through 5 in this data, the order Predicator + Subject is seen for these intransitive clauses. In the corresponding negatives (as in items 6 through 9) the negative adverb begins the clause, and is followed by the Subject and then the Predicator. So in such a case the Negator is best treated as a constituent of the clause rather than of the verb phrase, and two distinct clause types need to be postulated syntactically in order to deal with the obligatory differences of order. It will also be noted that the Present tense (glossed in English with the Present Progressive) is doubly marked, with a postposed /ana/ in combination with the preposed /e/, which alone signals the Future tense. The treatment in Figure 9.7 is based on an editing which treats the Past and Future tenses as involving a zero marker in the postverbal position. An alternative treatment would require the use of two different forms of verbal phrase.

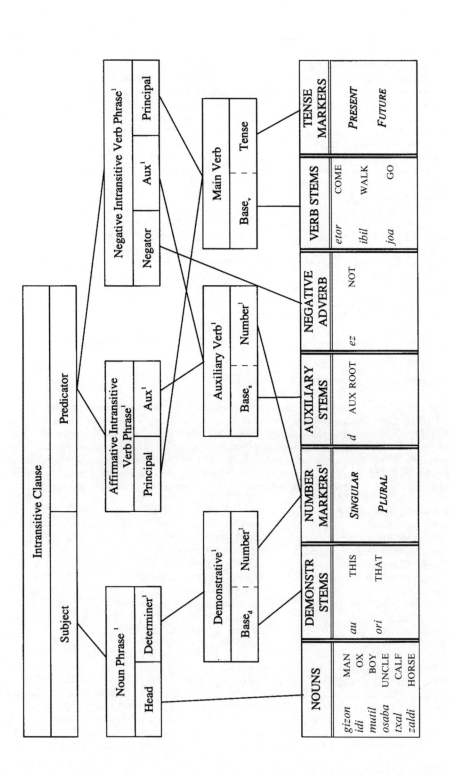

Figure 9.6 A solution to the Basque negatives

Table 9.7 Negation in Maori

1.	*e koorero ana te waahine*	THE WOMAN IS TALKING.
2.	*e koorero ana ngaa waahine*	THE WOMEN ARE TALKING.
3.	*e koorero ana he waahine*	A WOMAN/SOME WOMEN TALKED.
4.	*i koorero te waahine*	THE WOMAN TALKED.
5.	*e koorero ngaa waahine*	THE WOMEN WILL TALK.
6.	*kaahore ngaa waahine e koorero ana*	THE WOMEN ARE NOT TALKING.
7.	*kaahore te taane e koorero ana*	THE MAN IS NOT TALKING.
8.	*kiihai ngaa taane i koorero*	THE MEN WERE NOT TALKING.
9.	*e kore te waahine e koorero*	THE WOMAN WILL NOT TALK.
10.	*e haere ana he waahine*	A WOMAN/SOME WOMEN IS/ARE GOING.
11.	*kaahore te kootiro e haere ana*	THE GIRL IS NOT GOING.
12.	*i hinga te rangatira*	THE CHIEF FELL.
13.	*e kore ngaa rangatira e hinga*	THE CHIEFS WILL NOT FALL.
14.	*i noho he rangatira*	A CHIEF/SOME CHIEFS SAT.
15.	*kiihai ngaa kootiro i noho*	THE GIRLS DID NOT SIT.
16.	*e kore te taane e haere*	THE MAN WILL NOT GO.
17.	*kaahore te tohunga e kai ana*	THE PRIEST IS NOT EATING.
18.	*e oma ana he kurii*	A DOG/SOME DOGS IS/ARE RUNNING.
19.	*i kai ngaa kurii*	THE DOGS ATE.
20.	*kaahore te kiore e oma ana*	THE RAT IS NOT RUNNING.
21.	*kiihai te rangatira i kai*	THE CHIEF DID NOT EAT.
22.	*e kai ana he kiore*	A RAT/SOME RATS IS/ARE EATING.

Special relations of government in the negative

Another complication that sometimes arises in negative clauses concerns case government. One of the better known examples of this is seen in the Russian corpus of Table 9.8. The negation proper is similar to that seen earlier in the Latin corpus, with the negative adverb *ne* placed just before the verb. It will be noted, however, that the nouns serving as Objects have different case forms depending on whether they serve as Objects in a negative clause or an affirmative one. The solution, as presented in Figure 9.8, uses the traditional names for the Russian cases – *ACCUSATIVE* for the affirmative Object versus *GENITIVE* for the negative.

Table 9.8 Negation data from Russian

1.	*miša vidit tanju*	MIKE SEES TANYA.
1a.	*miša ne vidit tani*	MIKE DOESN'T SEE TANYA.
2.	*tanja vidit sašu*	TANYA SEES ALEX.
2a.	*tanja ne vidit saši*	TANYA DOESN'T SEE ALEX.
3.	*vanja znaet mišu*	JOHNNY KNOWS MIKE.
3a.	*vanja ne znaet miši*	JOHNNY DOESN'T KNOW MIKE.
4.	*maša znaet olju*	MASHA KNOWS OLYA.
4a.	*maša ne znaet oli*	MASHA DOESN'T KNOW OLYA.
5.	*saša vstrečaet vanju*	ALEX MEETS JOHNNY.
5a.	*saša ne vstrečaet vani*	ALEX DOESN'T MEET JOHNNY.
6.	*olja vstrečaet mašu*	OLYA MEETS MASHA.
6a.	*olja ne vstrečaet maši*	OLYA DOESN'T MEET MASHA.

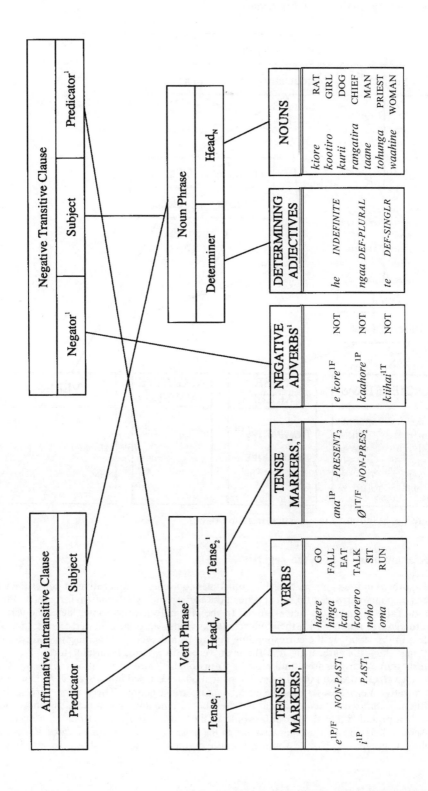

Figure 9.7 Solution to the Maori negation data

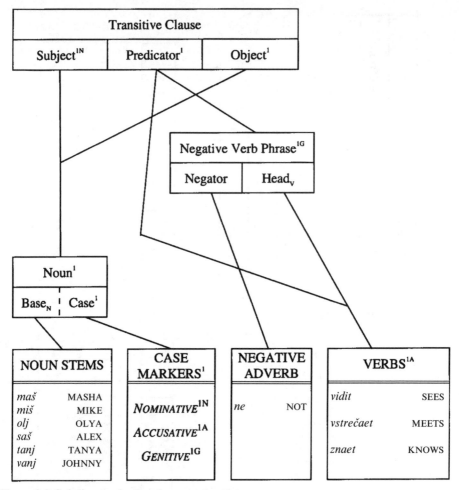

Figure 9.8 Solution to the Russian negation data

Special auxiliary uses in the negative

Still another kind of complication that sometimes comes up with negatives involves the use of special auxiliary verbs that do not appear in the corresponding affirmative forms. The Finnish data of Table 9.9 provides one example. In the affirmative forms shown here, the verbs are seen to agree in number with their subjects (there is also agreement in person, but that is not evident in this data). In the corresponding negatives, however, it is the negative words *ei* and *eivät* that show the agreement, and the main verb is in a third, invariable form. Traditional Finnish grammars refer to *ei* and *eivät* as forms of the "verb of negation". Here we simply term it a **NEGATIVE AUXILIARY**. Its use can be treated as sketched in Figure 9.9. As can be seen, the Negative Verb Phrase must be in a separate construction. There is no corresponding Affirmative Phrase for this particular data set, because no adjuncts to verbs are shown in the data. It is probable that further data would in the end justify such a structure, however.

Another language that uses an auxiliary in the negative, at least for most cases, is, of course, English. Consider the glosses for the Finnish examples – they all show the auxiliary DO.

Table 9.9 Data for negation in Finnish

1.	*räätali nauraa*	THE TAILOR LAUGHS.
1a.	*räätalit nauravat*	THE TAILORS LAUGH.
1b.	*räätali ei naura*	THE TAILOR DOES NOT LAUGH.
1c.	*räätalit eivät naura*	THE TAILORS DO NOT LAUGH.
2.	*ystävä kävelee*	THE FRIEND WALKS.
2a.	*ystävät kävelevät*	THE FRIENDS WALK.
2b.	*ystävä ei kävele*	THE FRIEND DOES NOT WALK.
2c.	*ystävät eivät kävele*	THE FRIENDS DO NOT WALK.
3.	*mestari puhuu*	THE MASTER SPEAKS.
3a.	*mestarit puhuvat*	THE MASTERS SPEAK.
3b.	*mestari ei puhu*	THE MASTER DOES NOT SPEAK.
3c.	*mestarit eivät puhu*	THE MASTERS DO NOT SPEAK.
4.	*opiskelija laulaa*	THE STUDENT SINGS.
4a.	*opiskelijat laulavat*	THE STUDENTS SING.
4b.	*opiskelija ei laula*	THE STUDENT DOES NOT SING.
4c.	*opiskelijat eivät laula*	THE STUDENTS DO NOT SING.
5.	*opettaja tulee*	THE TEACHER COMES.
5a.	*opettajat tulevat*	THE TEACHERS COME.
5b.	*opettaja ei tule*	THE TEACHER DOES NOT COME.
5c.	*opettajat eivät tule*	THE TEACHERS DO NOT COME.

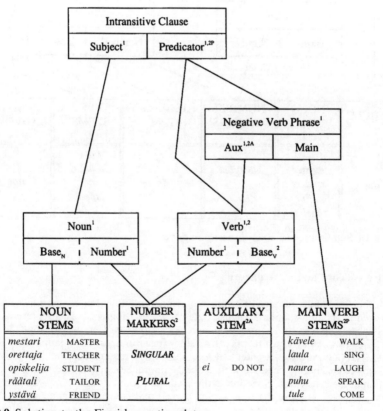

Figure 9.9 Solution to the Finnish negation data

In English, however, the word *not* (or its clitic variant written *-n't*) is what actually carries the negative meaning, and *do* can also occur as a main verb, as in such an example as *They always do the work well*. Also, *do* can further be used as an auxiliary in interrogative contexts, as in *Where do they live?* or in emphatic cases, as in *They do too speak Russian!* A solution based on these English glosses to the Finnish is presented in Figure 9.10. The parallel to the Finnish is considerable, as can be seen, but there are differences involved with the use of a separate negator in English and with the use of articles in English.

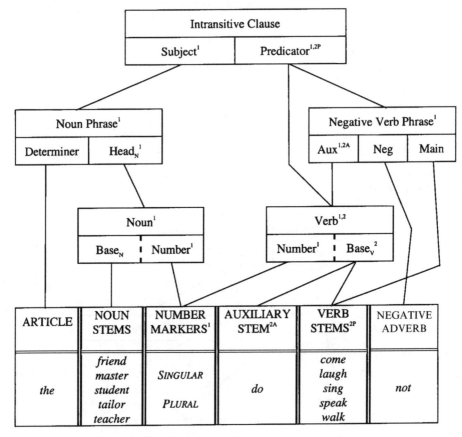

Figure 9.10 Solution to the English negation data

Negative concord and anti-concord

Still another special grammatical phenomenon sometimes found in connection with negation can be seen in the non-standard English data shown in Table 9.10. This represents a variety which is widely spoken, but strongly condemned by purists. Here we see that the verb and some of the other clausal constituents can all show forms of negation, creating what some have called **NEGATIVE CONCORD**. Essentially it has to do with a requirement that a negative Subject and/or Object, or another negative such as the Temporal *never* represented here, also requires a negation in the Predicator. Negation in the Predicator, on the other hand, can occur without negation anywhere else. So it is a less symmetrical matter than true concord, which would seem to suggest that if one constituent is negative, they would all have to be negative, and vice versa. Figure 9.11 presents a solution to this data, which involves showing a link between the

Predicator and the Subject and Object regarding polarity. Taken literally, this seems to incorrectly suggest that if any of these basic constituents is affirmative or negative, the rest must be of the same polarity. In actual fact, however, it means that the Predicator has to be negative if either the Subject, the Object (or both) is, but it is otherwise free to be either affirmative or negative. Also, the negativity of the Subject and Object is an independent matter, both *can* be negative, but one may be negative while the other is not. These facts are reflected in the solution by the way the superscripts appear in relation to the nominal words in the function of Subject or Object and the expressions used for the Predicator. While all manifestations of the latter function have superscripts to distinguish affirmative (^{1A}) from negative (^{1N}), only the explicitly negative nominals *nobody* and *nothing* (the latter not actually in the data set, but added to make the solution more complete, since it works the same way) are marked with ^{1N}. Since in selecting nominals one can always go to a box with no superscript, this takes care of the necessary facts, precluding an affirmative manifestation of Predicator with a negative Subject or Object while allowing a free choice in their absence, and allowing any one or both of the nominals to be negative without the incorrect stipulation that Subject and Object would have to agree in polarity. For the sake of simplicity, only Subject and Object are included in this data and its solution. But the same general principle applies to other functions such as Indirect Object and Instrument in this dialect, as in *Tom didn't give nobody nothing* TOM DIDN'T GIVE ANYBODY ANYTHING or *John didn't hit Tom with nothing* JOHN DIDN'T HIT TOM WITH ANYTHING.

Table 9.10 Data for negation in non-standard English

1. *John hit Tom.*	JOHN HIT TOM.
2. *John didn't hit Tom.*	JOHN DIDN'T HIT TOM.
3. *Nobody didn't hit Tom.*	NOBODY HIT TOM.
4. *John didn't hit nobody.*	JOHN HIT NOBODY.
	JOHN DIDN'T HIT ANYBODY.
5. *Nobody didn't hit nobody.*	NOBODY HIT ANYBODY.
6. *John didn't never hit Tom.*	JOHN NEVER HIT TOM.
	JOHN DIDN'T EVER HIT TOM.
7. *Nobody didn't never hit Tom.*	NOBODY EVER HIT TOM.
8. *John didn't never hit nobody.*	JOHN NEVER HIT ANYBODY.
	JOHN DIDN'T EVER HIT ANYBODY.
9. *Nobody didn't never hit nobody.*	NOBODY EVER HIT ANYBODY.

While this material comes from a non-standard variety of English, there are similar phenomena in many standard languages, such as Russian and Spanish, to name two of the better-known ones.

In standard English, as reflected in the glosses in Table 9.10, the governing principle is essentially that there can be only one explicit negative per main clause. After that potential negative is used up, so to speak, remaining elements of the clause which might be ordinary negatives in the non-standard dialect have to occur in alternative forms, usually using *any* instead of *no*, such as *anybody, anything* and *anywhere*. (There is also *ever* as an alternative to *never* for use in such circumstances.) If we assume an abstract element NONY realizable as either *no* or *any* according to circumstances, we can solve the standard forms as in Figure 9.12.

In contrast to the previous solution, this version specifies a tie only between Subject and Predicator, but uses the abstract NONY element to deal with the other matters. Essentially the selection of a negative as Subject requires the use of an affirmative (though it is superscripted as ^{1N}) for the Predicator. The element NONY is then realized as *any-* if there has been a previous occurrence of a negative in the clause (in this case either another NONY element or *didn't*) and otherwise as *no*. The alternation of *never* with *didn't ever* is handled here as a free

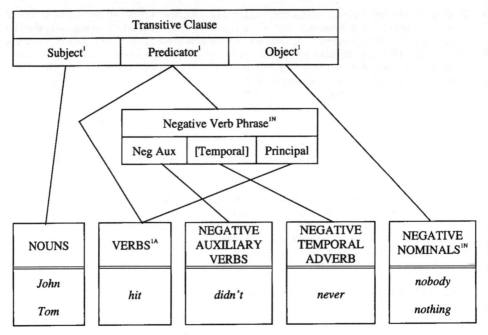

Figure 9.11 Solution to "negative concord" in non-standard English

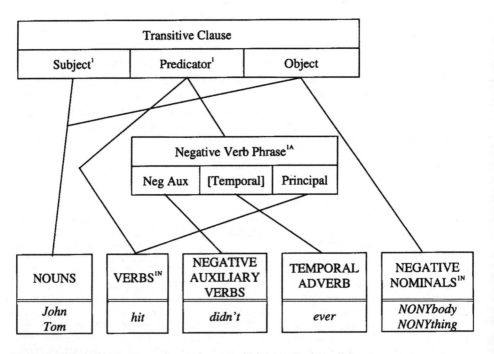

Figure 9.12 Solution to "negative anti-concord" in standard English

variation, allowing *never* as an alternate way of realizing the sequence *didn't ever*. Of course, since these last two solutions are based on very limited data, they would need to be refined if more details are to be taken into account. They should be sufficient, however, to illustrate the general idea of how these matters of negative concord and anti-concord can be handled.

In general, this chapter has illustrated the fact that, while negation may in some cases involve a simple inflection or optional constituent, it may at other times involve relatively complicated manifestations requiring separate constructions to handle multiple negation, special element orders, the occurrence of special negative auxiliaries, or other more complex situations.

Exercises

A.   Interpretation problems

1.   Spanish clausal negation

The following diagram illustrates the formation of affirmative and negative locative clauses in modern Spanish. Use this diagram to produce edited versions corresponding to the following English sentences.

1.   THE WOMAN WILL BE AT HOME.

---

2.   THE CHILD WAS NOT DOWNSTAIRS.

---

3.   THE GRANDMOTHERS WERE NOT THERE.

---

4.   THE CHILD WAS OUT BACK.

---

5.   THE MAN IS NOT HERE.

---

6.   THE WOMEN ARE NOT UPSTAIRS.

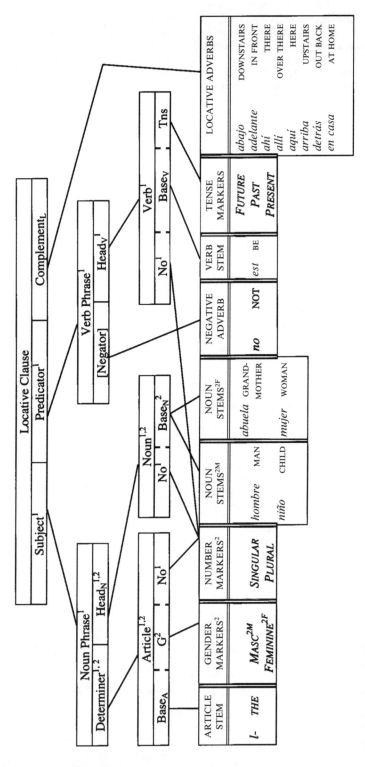

The formation of affirmative and negative locative clauses in modern Spanish

2. Negation in Hausa clauses

The following diagram illustrates the formation of affirmative and negative locative clauses in Hausa, a language of the Chadic group of the Afro-Asiatic family spoken primarily in northern Nigeria. Using this diagram, produce edited versions corresponding to the following English sentences, also reflecting the following principles of the manifestation of the abstract element BA:

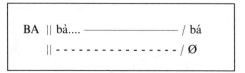

1. AUDU HAS COME.

_____

2. HE WILL NOT SEE THE HOUSE.

_____

3. HE WILL NOT COME.

_____

4. AUDU HAS NOT SEEN THE HOUSE.

_____

5. YOU WILL SEE THE HOUSE.

_____

6. YOU WILL NOT COME.

_____

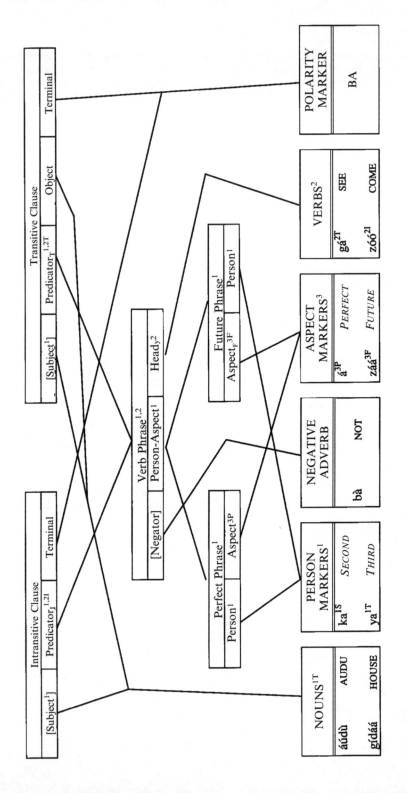

The formation of affirmative and negative locative clauses in Hansa

B.   Analysis problems

The following data sets illustrate the distinction between affirmative and negative clauses in various languages. Edit and account for each of these as economically as possible. In some cases separate constructions for the affirmative and negative will be needed, but this will not always be the case, so separation should be made only if it is required by the complexities seen in the data.

1. Japanese

1.	neko wa sakana o taberu	THE CAT EATS FISH.
1a.	neko wa sakana o tabeta	THE CAT ATE FISH.
1b.	neko wa sakana o tabenai	THE CAT DOESN'T EAT FISH.
1c.	neko wa sakana o tabenakatta	THE CAT DIDN'T EAT FISH.
2.	kodomo wa kimono o kiru	THE CHILD WEARS A KIMONO.
2a.	kodomo wa kimono o kita	THE CHILD WORE A KIMONO.
2b.	kodomo wa kimono o kinai	THE CHILD DOESN'T WEAR A KIMONO.
2c.	kodomo wa kimono o kinakatta	THE CHILD DIDN'T WEAR A KIMONO.
3.	neko wa miruku o nomu	THE CAT DRINKS MILK.
3a.	neko wa miruku o nonda	THE CAT DRANK MILK.
3b.	neko wa miruku o nomanai	THE CAT DOESN'T DRINK MILK.
3c.	neko wa miruku o nomanakatta	THE CAT DIDN'T DRINK MILK.
4.	gakusei wa biiru o nomu	THE STUDENT DRINKS BEER.
4a.	gakusei wa biiru o nonda	THE STUDENT DRANK BEER.
4b.	gakusei wa biiru o nomanai	THE STUDENT DOESN'T DRINK BEER.
4c.	gakusei wa biiru o nomanakatta	THE STUDENT DIDN'T DRINK BEER.
5.	inu wa neko o miru	THE DOG SEES A CAT.
5a.	inu wa neko o mita	THE DOG SAW A CAT.
5b.	inu wa neko o minai	THE DOG DOESN'T SEE A CAT.
5c.	inu wa neko o minakatta	THE DOG DIDN'T SEE A CAT.

2. Swahili

1.	alifika	HE ARRIVED.
1a.	hakufika	HE DID NOT ARRIVE.
2.	mgeni alifika	THE VISITOR ARRIVED.
2a.	mtu hakufika	THE PERSON DID NOT ARRIVE.
3.	walifika	THEY ARRIVED.
3a.	hawakufika	THEY DID NOT ARRIVE.
4.	watu walifika	THE PEOPLE ARRIVED.
4a.	wageni hawakufika	THE VISITORS DID NOT ARRIVE.
5.	atafika	HE WILL ARRIVE.
5a.	hatafika	HE WILL NOT ARRIVE.
6.	mtoto atafika	THE CHILD WILL ARRIVE.
6a.	mzee hatafika	THE ELDER WILL NOT ARRIVE.
7.	watafika	THEY WILL ARRIVE.
7a.	hawatafika	THEY WILL NOT ARRIVE.
8.	wazee watafika	THE ELDERS WILL ARRIVE.
8a.	watoto hawatafika	THE CHILDREN WILL NOT ARRIVE.
9.	mwalimu alitoka	THE TEACHER WENT OUT.
9a.	mwalimu hakutoka	THE TEACHER DID NOT GO OUT.
10.	wezi watarudi	THE THIEVES WILL RETURN.
10a.	wezi hawatarudi	THE THIEVES WILL NOT RETURN.

3. Tahitian

1a.	te taʔoto nei au	I AM SLEEPING.
1b.	ʔaita au te taʔoto nei	I AM NOT SLEEPING.
2a.	ʔe taʔoto au	I WILL SLEEP.
2b.	ʔeʔita au ʔe taʔoto	I WILL NOT SLEEP.
3a.	ʔe ʔāu ʔoe	YOU WILL SWIM.
3b.	ʔeʔita ʔoe ʔe ʔāu	YOU WILL NOT SWIM.
4a.	te tae nei ʔoia	HE IS ARRIVING.
4b.	ʔaita ʔoia te tae nei	HE IS NOT ARRIVING.
5a.	ʔi tae na ʔoe	YOU ARRIVED.
5b.	ʔaita ʔoe ʔi tae na	YOU DID NOT ARRIVE.
6a.	ʔi taʔoto na au	I SLEPT.
6b.	ʔaita au ʔi taʔoto na	I DID NOT SLEEP.
7a.	ʔi tae na æoia	HE ARRIVED.
7b.	ʔaita ʔoia ʔi tae na	HE DID NOT ARRIVE.

4. Estonian

1.	*mina tõusen*	I GET UP.	1a.	*mina ei tõuse*	I DO NOT GET UP.
2.	*sina tõused*	YOU GET UP.	2a.	*sina ei tõuse*	YOU DO NOT GET UP.
3.	*tema tõuseb*	HE/SHE GETS UP.	3a.	*tema ei tõuse*	HE/SHE DOES NOT GET UP.
4.	*mina tõusin*	I GOT UP.	4a.	*mina ei tõunud*	I DID NOT GET UP.
5.	*sina tõusid*	YOU GOT UP.	5a.	*sina ei tõunud*	YOU DID NOT GET UP.
6.	*tema tõusis*	HE/SHE GOT UP.	6a.	*tema ei tõunud*	HE/SHE DID NOT GET UP.
7.	*mina töötan*	I WORK.	7a.	*mina ei tööta*	I DO NOT WORK.
8.	*sina töötad*	YOU WORK.	8a.	*sina ei tööta*	YOU DO NOT WORK.
9.	*tema töötab*	HE/SHE WORKS.	9a.	*tema ei tööta*	HE/SHE DOES NOT WORK.
10.	*mina töötasin*	I WORKED.	10a.	*mina ei töötanud*	I DID NOT WORK.
11.	*sina töötasid*	YOU WORKED.	11a.	*sina ei töötanud*	YOU DID NOT WORK.
12.	*tema töötasis*	HE/SHE WORKED.	12a.	*tema ei töötanud*	HE/SHE DID NOT WORK.
13.	*mina kutsun arst*	I INVITE THE DOCTOR.	13a.	*mina ei kutsu arsti*	I DO NOT INVITE THE DOCTOR.
14.	*sina vaadad poiss*	YOU WATCH THE BOY.	14a.	*sina ei vaada poissi*	YOU DO NOT WATCH THE BOY.
15.	*tema armastab sõber*	HE/SHE LOVES THE FRIEND.	15a.	*tema ei armasta sõpra*	HE/SHE DOES NOT LOVE THE FRIEND.
16.	*mina armastasin sõber*	I LOVED THE FRIEND.	16a.	*mina ei armastanud poissi*	I DID NOT LOVE THE BOY.
17.	*sina kutsusin poiss*	YOU INVITED THE BOY.	17a.	*sina ei kutsunud sõpra*	YOU DID NOT INVITE THE FRIEND.
18.	*tema vaadasis arst*	HE/SHE WATCHED THE DOCTOR.	18a.	*tema ei vaadanud arsti*	HE/SHE DID NOT WATCH THE DOCTOR.

Terminology

AFFIRMATIVE	NEGATIVE AUXILIARY
NEGATIVE ANTI-CONCORD	NEGATIVE CONCORD

10

Varieties of clausal organization: accusative, ergative, and others

Accusative and ergative perspectives illustrated

In many languages of the world, case inflection is used to distinguish grammatical functions of at least some nominal words. The Russian data in Table 10.1 displays a pattern of such inflection that is typical of European languages, but also found widely in various parts of the world. In items 1 through 10, we see examples of transitive clauses with the order Subject + Predicator + Object. When we see the same noun sometimes as Subject and sometimes as Object, we observe that they have different suffixes according to their function. The group including *Ivan* has no suffix in the Subject function, but the suffix *-a* when occurring as Object. The other group, including *Maša*, has the suffix *-a* for the Subject and the suffix *-u* for the Object. The intransitive examples in items 11–15, furthermore, show the expected Subject forms for the only nouns that appear with them. Modern English has exactly the same pattern, but it is restricted in its occurrence: whereas most nominals in a language like Russian show different forms for these different functions, no actual nouns show it in English, but it does show up in personal pronoun forms such as *I, he, she, we, they* for Subjects as contrasted with *me, him, her, us, them* for Objects. So we find case differences in *I see her* versus *She sees me*, but not in *John sees Tom* versus *Tom sees John*. Traditional terminology, coming down to us from Latin grammar, refers to the Subject forms in such examples as being in the NOMINATIVE CASE, while the Object forms are in the ACCUSATIVE CASE. The term "nominative" is based on Latin *nōmen* NAME, and comes from the fact that this case is normally used in a language like Latin or Russian to simply name the object. The term "accusative" is less justified in reality, because it rests on an ancient mistranslation. Its functions have no particular relation at all to

Table 10.1 Nominative and accusative cases in Russian

1. *Ivan vidit Mašu.*	IVAN SEES MASHA.
2. *Maša vidit Ivana.*	MASHA SEES IVAN.
3. *Maša ljubit Sergeja.*	MASHA LOVES SERGEY.
4. *Sergej vidit Sašu.*	SERGEY SEES ALEX.
5. *Saša udarjaet Sergeja.*	ALEX HITS SERGEY.
6. *Ol'ga udarjaet Ivana.*	OLGA HITS IVAN.
7. *Ivan ljubit Ol'gu.*	IVAN LOVES OLGA.
8. *Saša vstrečaet Natašu.*	ALEX MEETS NATASHA.
9. *Nataša ljubit Sergeja.*	NATASHA LOVES SERGEY.
10. *Sergej vstrečaet Mašu.*	SERGEY MEETS MASHA.
11. *Maša begaet.*	MASHA IS RUNNING.
12. *Ivan plavaet.*	IVAN IS SWIMMING.
13. *Nataša begaet.*	NATASHA IS RUNNING.
14. *Saša plavaet.*	ALEX IS SWIMMING.
15. *Sergej begaet.*	SERGEY IS RUNNING.

making accusations, but it happens that the Greek term better translated as "objective" was similar to the Greek word for "accuse" and an ancient Roman translator got it wrong. Its use has now become so commonplace in grammatical discussion, however, that it would probably be impossible to eradicate it. The solution to this data requires editing to extract the cases, but is otherwise quite straightforward, as depicted in Figure 10.1.

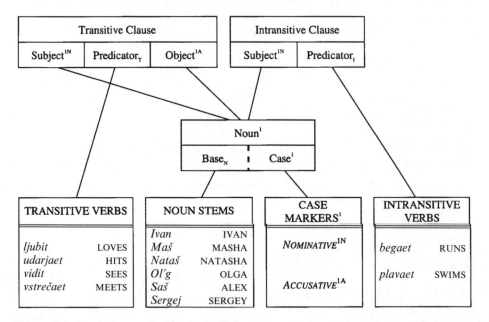

Figure 10.1 A solution to the Russian data

In Table 10.2 we see some roughly analogous data from Central Alaskan Yup'ik Eskimo. Here again the first ten examples show transitive clauses, this time with the order Subject + Object + Predicator. If we examine these first ten examples alone, it seems that there are two cases just as in Russian, with the Subject case ending in /-m/. When we go on to compare these with the intransitive examples in items 11–15, however, we may be surprised to observe that the Subjects in these examples do not have the same case forms as the Subjects of transitives, but rather show up in the same form as the Objects. In fact, this Yup'ik data illustrates a different pattern which is found in a number of languages in different parts of the world. According to this pattern, the intransitive Subjects and the transitive Objects occur in one case, while the transitive Subjects alone appear in another case. Here the special case used for the transitive Subject is termed the ERGATIVE, while the case used for the other two roles is called the ABSOLUTIVE. Following the names for the most distinctive cases in each of the systems involved, we may say that Russian and English, among other languages, have an ACCUSATIVE SYSTEM, while Yup'ik has an ERGATIVE SYSTEM.

One way to try to understand this situation involves seeing the accusative system as asking a different set of questions about the major participants in an event or state than the ergative. In the former one asks first "who or what is doing the action or in the state?" and puts the noun for it in the nominative case. Then if there is another major participant that is having something done to it, the noun for this is in the accusative case. For the ergative system the first question to ask is "who or what is affected by the action or state?", putting the noun for it in the absolutive. In the intransitive examples, this can only be the Subject, while for the transitive it will be the Object. Then if there is another major participant which causes the event to happen, its noun or pronoun will be in the ergative. A solution to this data set is presented in Figure 10.2.

Table 10.2 Ergativity in Central Alaskan Yup'ik Eskimo

1. aʁnam aŋun taŋχaa	THE WOMAN SEES THE MAN.
2. aŋutɨm aʁnaq taŋχaa	THE MAN SEES THE WOMAN.
3. mikɨłŋuum aana kɨnkaa	THE CHILD LOVES THE MOTHER.
4. aanam mikɨłŋuq kɨnkaa	THE MOTHER LOVES THE CHILD.
5. aʁnam mikɨłŋuq nunuʁaa	THE WOMAN SCOLDS THE CHILD.
6. aatam aŋun nunuʁaa	THE FATHER SCOLDS THE MAN.
7. aŋutɨm tuntuvak alikaa	THE MAN IS AFRAID OF THE MOOSE.
8. tuntuviim taqukaq alikaa	THE MOOSE IS AFRAID OF THE BEAR.
9. qimuxtɨm aʁnaq niitaa	THE DOG HEARS THE WOMAN.
10. aʁnam qimuxta niitaa	THE WOMAN HEARS THE DOG.
11. qimuxta ayaxtuq	THE DOG IS LEAVING.
12. mikɨłŋuq miʁnuχtuq	THE CHILD IS TIRED.
13. aata taʁiŋuq	THE FATHER UNDERSTANDS.
14. aŋun ayaxtuq	THE MAN IS LEAVING.
15. aʁnaq taʁiŋuq	THE WOMAN UNDERSTANDS.

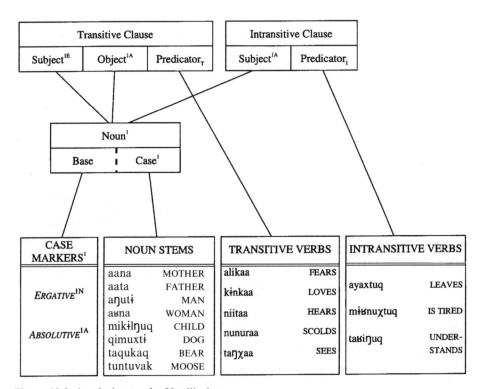

Figure 10.2 A solution to the Yup'ik data

In both of these examples, the difference between the types is recognizable in terms of morphological case, either affecting nominals in general, as in Russian and Yup'ik, or affecting a subset of them, as in English. It is also possible, however, to apply the terms "accusative" or "ergative" in situations where a language is lacking morphological case inflection, but expresses the distinction in a more purely syntactic fashion. One of the more obvious ways involved is the expression of roles by adpositions instead of inflections. In

Chapter 7 we saw the use of postpositions in Japanese for just such a purpose, specifically in Table 7.9 (solved in Figure 7.11), which shows an accusative system in the use of the postposition /o/ to mark Object function and /wa/ for the Subject. Table 10.3 shows some data from Tongan, a Polynesian language, which uses prepositions in an ergative system. /ʔa/ is used to mark the following nominal word as absolutive, and /ʔe/ marks it as ergative. The solution to this data is presented in Figure 10.3.

Table 10.3 Prepositional expression of ergativity in Tongan

1.	naʔe mohe ʔa pita	PETER SLEPT.
2.	ʔe ʔalu ʔa pita	PETER WILL GO.
3.	ʔe mohe ʔa mele	MARY WILL SLEEP.
4.	naʔe ʔalu ʔa siō	JOE WENT.
5.	ʔe mone ʔa sione	JOHN WILL SLEEP.
6.	naʔe ʔalu ʔa mele	MARY WENT.
7.	naʔe ʔomi ʔe siō ʔa mele	JOE BROUGHT MARY.
8.	naʔe ʔilo ʔe mele ʔa siō	MARY KNEW JOE.
9.	ʔe kumi ʔe mele ʔa pita	MARY WILL LOOK FOR PETER.
10.	ʔe ʔomi ʔe pita ʔa sione	PETER WILL BRING JOHN.
11.	ʔe ʔilo ʔe sione ʔa pita	JOHN WILL KNOW PETER.
12.	naʔe kumi ʔe siō ʔa mele	JOE LOOKED FOR MARY.

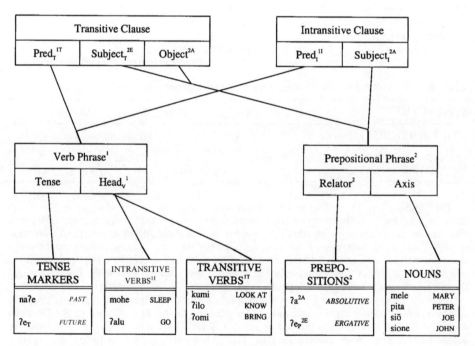

Figure 10.3 Solution to prepositional ergativity in Tongan

Split ergativity

Some languages show a seeming mixture of accusative and ergative characteristics in a phenomenon usually called **SPLIT ERGATIVITY**. One variety of this is seen in the data of Table

10.4, which comes from Pitjantjatjara, a language of Western Australia. Here we see that the forms of nouns, such as those meaning MAN, CHILD, and KANGAROO, clearly show an ergative pattern, but those of the first- and second-person pronouns seem to show an accusative pattern. The most reasonable way to analyse this phenomenon, which is reported for quite a few Australian languages, is to posit a distinct syntactic case for each of the functions as shown in the treatment presented in Figure 10.4. Table 10.5 then shows how the three syntactic cases relate to morphological cases: *NOMINATIVE* versus *ACCUSATIVE* in the pronoun system, but *ABSOLUTIVE* versus *ERGATIVE* in the nouns.

Table 10.4 Split ergativity in Pitjantjatjara

1. watiŋku kuḷpirpa kuḷṯuṉu	THE MAN SPEARED THE KANGAROO.
2. kuḷpirtu wati pirinu	THE KANGAROO SCRATCHED THE MAN.
3. t,it,iŋku wati pirinu	THE CHILD SCRATCHED THE MAN.
4. ŋayulu t,it,i kulinu	I HEARD THE CHILD.
5. kuḷpirtu ŋayuña ñaŋu	THE KANGAROO SAW ME.
6. ñura ŋayuña ñaŋu	YOU SAW ME.
7. ñura t,it,i kuḷṯuṉu	YOU SPEARED THE CHILD.
8. watiŋku ñuraña ñaŋu	THE MAN SAW YOU.
9. t,it,i pakaṉu	THE CHILD GOT UP.
10. wati mapiṯaŋu	THE MAN WENT AWAY.
11. kuḷpirpa iluriŋu	THE KANGAROO DIED.
12. ñura ŋalapit,aŋu	YOU CAME.
13. ŋayulu mapiṯaŋu	I WENT AWAY.
14. ñura pakaṉu	YOU GOT UP.
15. wati iluriŋu	THE MAN DIED.

Table 10.5 Syntactic and morphological case in Pitjantjatjara

SYNTACTIC →	*AGENTIVE*	*SUBJECTIVE*	*OBJECTIVE*
MORPHOLOGICAL ↓			
NOUNS	*ERGATIVE*	*ABSOLUTIVE*	
PRONOUNS	*NOMINATIVE*		*ACCUSATIVE*

This approach to the matter is superior, it can be argued, to any alternative that would insist on working with the morphological cases alone, because that would require splitting up the constructions depending on whether a noun or a pronoun is found in a particular function, so there would be subtypes of the transitive with *ERGATIVE + ABSOLUTIVE*, *ERGATIVE + ACCUSATIVE*, *NOMINATIVE + ABSOLUTIVE*, and *NOMINATIVE + ACCUSATIVE*. This would be unnecessarily complex and would miss the essential unity that is seen when the system with three distinct syntactic cases is adopted.

Another variety of split ergativity which is often found involves tense, or more properly, combinations of tense, aspect, and mood. An example of this may be seen in the Georgian data of Table 10.6. The items glossed as Present Tense (1–6) seem to display a nominative-accusative pattern; those glossed as Past Tense, however, appear to follow an ergative-absolutive pattern. Actually the "nominative" and "absolutive" cases are identical, so there are three cases, but their occurrence depends on the factor of tense as well as on syntactic roles. If we look further in Georgian grammars, we find that the other tenses that follow the pattern of the *PRESENT* with an accusative system are the *FUTURE, IMPERFECT, CONDITIONAL* and both the *IMPERFECTIVE* and *PERFECTIVE* forms of the *CONJUNCTIVE* mood. The past tense forms in items 7–12 represent a tense called the *AORIST*, and the other form that follows the same pattern is the *OPTATIVE* mood.

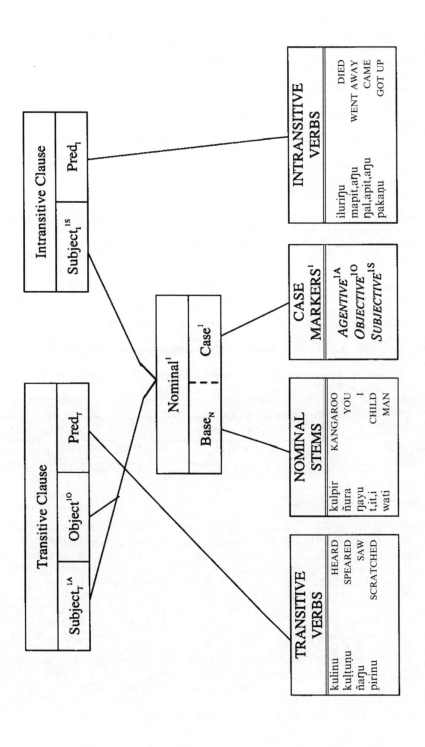

Figure 10.4 Solution to split ergativity in Pitjantjatjara

Table 10.6 Tense-based split ergativity in Georgian

1.	mama gogos ismens	THE FATHER LISTENS TO THE GIRL.
2.	gogo k'acs aʁc'ers	THE GIRL DESCRIBES THE MAN.
3.	k'aci mepes xetavs	THE MAN SEES THE KING.
4.	gogo midis	THE GIRL GOES.
5.	mepe modis	THE KING COMES.
6.	k'aci šedis	THE MAN ENTERS.
7.	mamam gogo moismena	THE FATHER LISTENED TO THE GIRL.
8.	gogom k'aci aʁc'era	THE GIRL DESCRIBED THE MAN.
9.	k'acma mepe naxa	THE MAN SAW THE KING.
10.	gogo cavida	THE GIRL WENT.
11.	mepe movida	THE KING CAME.
12.	k'aci ševida	THE MAN ENTERED.

In analysing these forms, we could again resort to a multiplication of constructions according to these matters of tense, but it would be better to have a more unified treatment of the transitive and intransitive clauses. This can be achieved if we treat the morphological cases in terms of two distinct dimensions of syntactic category. One of these is termed CASE, with terms *SUBJECTIVE* and *OBJECTIVE*, and the second is termed SERIES, with terms *SERIES A* and *SERIES B*. Each of the three morphological cases visible in this data set can then be seen as a manifestation of a syntactic case in combination with a series, as summarized in Table 10.7. The solution to the data set based on this analysis is then presented in Figure 10.5. It should be noted that intransitive Subjects are inherently specified as belonging to *SERIES A*.

Table 10.7 Morphological manifestations of syntactic cases in combination with series in Georgian

SERIES →	*SERIES A*	*SERIES B*
SYNTACTIC CASE ↓		
SUBJECTIVE	*ABSOLUTIVE*	*ERGATIVE*
OBJECTIVE	*ACCUSATIVE*	*ABSOLUTIVE*

Further varieties of organization

In addition to the ergative and accusative systems surveyed above and the various types of split ergativity, several other kinds of clausal organization are attested. The simplest of these is one in which there are no case distinctions at all for the various functions under consideration. English, in fact, comes close to being a language of this sort, since it does not distinguish cases in its nouns, but only in half a dozen personal pronouns (and optionally in the interrogative/ relative pronoun *who*). A language which does not even have this, however, is Chinese, as shown in the data of Table 10.8. In such a language as this, the order of clause elements alone serves to distinguish Subjects from Objects in the transitive clause, just as is the case in English examples with nouns or uninflected pronouns like *you* and *it*. The solution to this data set is presented in Figure 10.6. Such a system as this is called UNIPARTITE to indicate that it uses only one set of forms for the Subject and Object roles. In this sense it is to be distinguished from the accusative and ergative systems, which are BIPARTITE. A unipartite type does not necessarily indicate the complete absence of case in the language, since there could be other cases for other functions. This is not what we find in Chinese, but when we do find this situation we can use the term *DIRECT* for the single case used here in these functions.

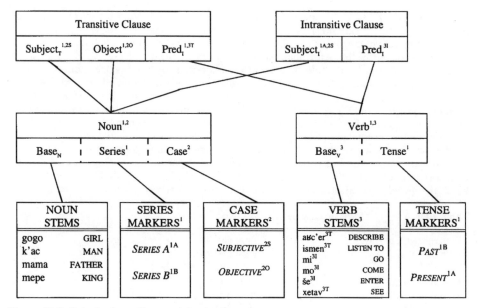

Figure 10.5 Solution to split ergativity in Georgian

Table 10.8 A caseless unipartite system in Mandarin Chinese

1. wǒ zuò	I SIT.
2. tā zuò	HE/SHE SITS.
3. nǐ qù	YOU GO.
4. tā qù	HE/SHE GOES.
5. nǐ jiàndào tā	YOU MET HIM/HER.
6. tā jiàndào wǒ	HE/SHE MET ME.
7. wǒ rènshi nǐ	I RECOGNIZE YOU.
8. nǐ rènshi wǒ	YOU RECOGNIZE ME.
9. tā kàn nǐ	HE/SHE LOOKS AT YOU.
10. wǒ kàn tā	I LOOK AT HIM/HER.

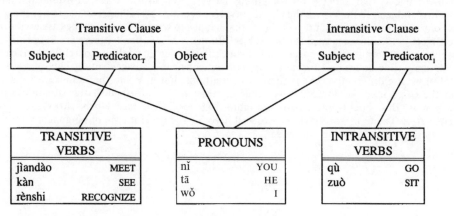

Figure 10.6 Solution to the Mandarin Chinese data set

Another possibility is a system in which a different case is used for each of the three functions, therefore a **TRIPARTITE** system. While they are not common, such systems are found in some Australian languages, as illustrated by the data in Table 10.9 from the Diyari language, spoken in the Australian state of South Australia. Here we distinguish the intransitive Subjects from both of the roles associated with transitive clauses. Though grammars of such languages vary as to the terms used, the ones adopted here are *AGENTIVE* and *OBJECTIVE* for the roles associated with the transitive clause, and *SUBJECTIVE* for the one found in the intransitive. The solution to this data set is presented in Figure 10.7. It should be noted, however, that the treatment of the kind of split ergativity seen in the Pitjantjatjara data of Table 10.4, as presented in Figure 10.4, is syntactically the same as what would be required for Diyari. Syntactically, that is, both of these languages have a tripartite system, but in Pitjantjatjara the nouns and pronouns have different bipartite morphological case systems, with correlation to syntactic cases as summarized above in Table 10.5. In Diyari, on the other hand, the morphological case system is tripartite, just like the syntactic case system.

Table 10.9 A tripartite basic case system in Diyari

1. ṉaṉi wapayi	I AM GOING.
2. ṉaṉi kiḻiyi	I AM DANCING.
3. yini kiḻiyi	YOU ARE DANCING.
4. yini wapaya	YOU WENT.
5. ṉawu wapayi	HE IS GOING.
6. ṉani wapaya	SHE WENT.
7. ṉaṯu yinaṉa ṉayiya	I SAW YOU.
8. yundu ṉaṉa ṉayiyi	YOU SEE ME.
9. yundu ṉaṉa ṉayiya	YOU SAW HER.
10. ṉandu ṉina yaṯaya	SHE SCOLDED HIM.
11. ṉulu yinaṉa yaṯayi	HE IS SCOLDING YOU.
12. ṉaṯu ṉaṉa yaṯayi	I AM SCOLDING HER.

Source: Peter Austin. *A Grammar of Diyari (South Australia)*. Cambridge: Cambridge University Press, 1981.

Finally, one other type of bipartite system is attested, as illustrated by some data from Eastern Pomo, as shown in Table 10.10. In this type, one of the cases distinguished in the transitive clauses is used for some intransitive Subjects, while the other is used for others, essentially according to the meaning involved. In examples 1 through 4, the intransitives involve Subjects that actually do something actively, and so are in the case used for the transitive Subject. In items 5–8, the clauses involve sneezing and falling, which are not things that one voluntarily does, but rather things that **happen to** someone. So here the case used for the Object in transitives is used for the Subject. In items 13–16, finally, there are happenings that can be either voluntary or accidental. So a child (or even an adult in a playful mood) can deliberately slide on ice as a form of play, but someone can also accidentally slip on ice. In English we use different verbs for these two situations, but in Pomo the same verb is used and the cases used for the Subjects occur contrastively to distinguish the situations. A solution to this data is presented in Figure 10.8, using the case-labels *AGENTIVE* and *PATIENTIVE*. The term **AGENTIVE** is also used here for the general type of language, though some authors call it "active" instead.

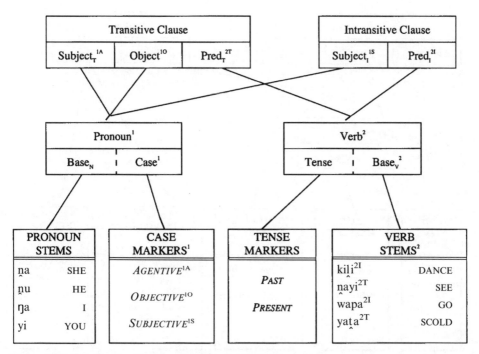

Figure 10.7 Solution to the tripartite system of Diyari

Table 10.10 Agentive clause organization in Eastern Pomo

1. háˑ káluhuya	I WENT HOME.
2. má wáˑduˑkiya	YOU WENT.
3. míˑp' wáˑduˑkiya	HE WENT.
4. míˑt' káluhuya	SHE WENT HOME.
5. wí ʔečkiya	I SNEEZED.
6. mí baˑkúˑma	YOU FELL.
7. míˑp'al ʔečkiya	HE SNEEZED.
8. míˑral baˑkúˑma	SHE FELL.
9. háˑ mí dɪˑkʰóya	I HIT YOU.
10. máˑ míˑral šáˑk'a	YOU KILLED HER.
11. míˑp' wí dɪˑkʰóya	HE HIT ME.
12. míˑt' míˑp'al šáˑk'a	SHE KILLED HIM.
13. háˑ c'eˑxélka	I SLID.
14. wí c'eˑxélka	I SLIPPED.
15. míˑp' baˑtéc'kiˑ	HE (PURPOSELY) WAS BUMPED.
16. míˑp'al baˑtéc'kiˑ	HE (ACCIDENTALLY) GOT BUMPED.

Source: Sally McLendon. Ergativity, Case, and Transitivity in Eastern Pomo. *International Journal of American Linguistics* 44.1–9 (1978).

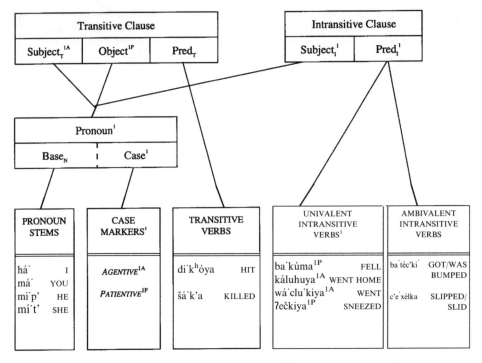

Figure 10.8 Solution to the agentive system of Eastern Pomo

Summary

Table 10.11 summarizes the various types of clause organization using real and pseudo-dialects of English for the examples. It is arranged, first of all according to the number of cases recognized, with two tripartite, three bipartite and one unipartite type. The tense-based variety of split ergativity exemplified by Georgian is treated as tripartite according to the number of morphological cases recognized. Of the English examples used, only the accusative type, of course, is real English. The others represent imaginable, though unattested dialects, with the form *hig* used for the third form in the tripartite types. Case labelings follow those introduced in the discussion above. It should be emphasized that traditional grammars of these various languages often use at least partly different terms for the cases. Grammars of Eskimo languages like Yup'ik, for instance, regularly use the term "absolutive", which was first introduced to linguists in general by Eskimo specialists, but they use "relative" instead of "ergative". Within the context of these languages, the alternative term makes quite good sense, because this case also has the function of indicating possession, so rather than "ergative" which suggests one main function or "genitive" which suggests the other (or a compound term like "ergative-genitive" which seems unnecessarily cumbersome), the term "relative" appears to be a reasonable choice. For many ergative (or split-ergative) languages of both the Caucasus and Australia, the term "nominative" has long been used instead of "absolutive". The latter term is adopted here, however, in line with most recent usages among linguists, because it helps to make the fundamental distinction between accusative and ergative types clearer.

Table 10.11 Summary of the types of clause organization

Type	Cases distinguished	
TRIPARTITE		
He hits him.	AGENTIVE	*he*
He hit him.	OBJECTIVE	*him*
Hig runs.	SUBJECTIVE	*hig*
Hig sleeps.		
SPLIT ERGATIVE		
He hits him.	ABSOLUTIVE	*he*
Hig hit he.	ACCUSATIVE	*him*
He runs.	ERGATIVE	*hig*
He sleeps.		
ACCUSATIVE		
He hits him.	NOMINATIVE	*he*
He hit him.	ACCUSATIVE	*him*
He runs.		
He sleeps.		
ERGATIVE		
He hits him.	ABSOLUTIVE	*him*
He hit him.	ERGATIVE	*he*
Him runs.		
Him sleeps.		
AGENTIVE		
He hits him.	AGENTIVE	*he*
He hit him.	PATIENTIVE	*him*
He runs.		
Him sleeps.		
UNIPARTITE		
He hits he.	None, or DIRECT *he*	
He hit he.		
He runs.		
He sleeps.		

Exercises

A. Interpretation problems

1. Dyirbal clauses

The description on the following page deals with some clauses in Dyirbal, an Australian language of northern Queensland. Using the description, show the structures for the Dyirbal clauses with the following meanings:

1. THIS WOMAN WILL LAUGH.

_____

2. THAT (VISIBLE) MAN WILL IGNORE THIS SMALL YAM.

_____

3. THAT (INVISIBLE) WOMAN HIT THAT (VISIBLE) SLEEPING MAN.

_____

4. THIS FAT FISH WAS GOING.

_____

5. THAT (VISIBLE) WOMAN WILL SING TO THAT HUNGRY MAN.

_____

6. THIS NEW MAN HID THAT (INVISIBLE) STONE.

_____

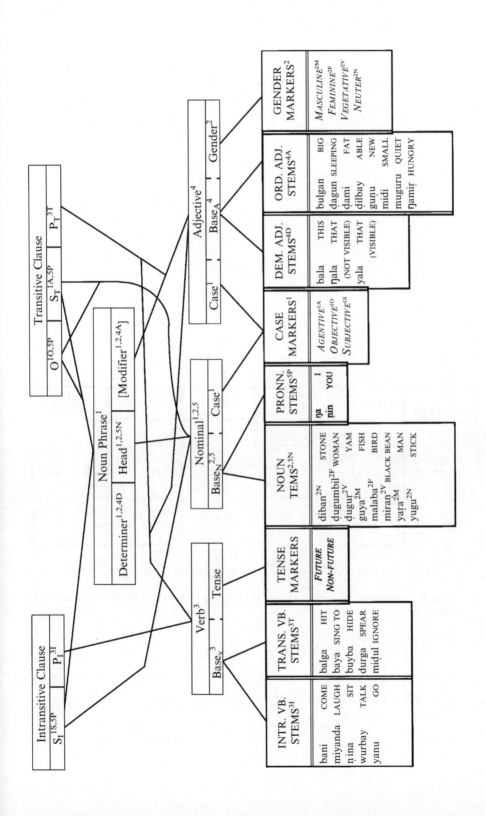

2. Samoan clauses

Use the description given below to answer the questions which follow.

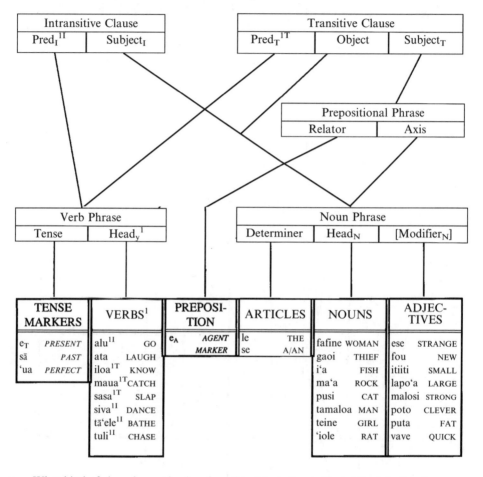

a.   What kind of clausal organization does this description indicate? Explain it as far as you can.

b.   Show the Samoan translation of each of the following English sentences according to this description.

1.   A FAT WOMAN LAUGHS.

_____

2.   THE STRONG MAN CHASED THE THIEF.

_____

3. THE SMALL WOMAN SLAPPED A LARGE THIEF.

_____

4. THE NEW FISH HAS GONE.

_____

5. THE CLEVER GIRL KNOWS THE WOMAN.

_____

6. THE FAT CAT HAS CAUGHT A RAT.

_____

B. Analysis problems

1. Basque clause structure

Edit the data and prepare a complete solution for this data set.

1. *Emakume honek mutil hori ikusten du.*   THIS WOMAN SEES THAT BOY.
2. *Mutil horrek ardi hau ikusten du.*   THAT BOY SEES THIS SHEEP.
3. *Ardi horrek emakume hau ikusten du.*   THAT SHEEP SEES THIS WOMAN.
4. *Mutil honek katu hori ikusko du.*   THIS BOY WILL SEE THAT CAT.
5. *Gizon horrek zaldi hau ikusko du.*   THAT MAN WILL SEE THIS HORSE.
6. *Emakume horrek gizon hau ikusko du.*   THAT WOMAN WILL SEE THIS MAN.
7. *Emakume hau joango da.*   THIS WOMAN WILL GO.
8. *Gizon hori joaten da.*   THAT MAN GOES.
9. *Ardi hori ibiltzen da.*   THAT SHEEP WALKS.
10. *Katu hau ibiliko da.*   THIS CAT WILL WALK.
11. *Mutil hau joaten da.*   THIS BOY GOES.
12. *Zaldi hori ibilitzen da.*   THAT HORSE WALKS.
13. *Zaldi horiek joango dira.*   THOSE HORSES WILL GO.
14. *Gizon hauek ikasiko dira.*   THESE MEN WILL WALK.
15. *Mutil horiek ibilitzen dira.*   THOSE BOYS WALK.
16. *Katu hauek joaten dira.*   THESE CATS GO.
17. *Ardi horiek ibiliko dira.*   THOSE SHEEP WILL WALK.
18. *Emakume hauek ikasten dira.*   THESE WOMEN STUDY.
19. *Emakume honek ardi horiek ikusten ditu.*   THIS WOMAN SEES THOSE SHEEP.
20. *Zaldi horrek gizon hauek ikusko.*   THAT HORSE WILL SEE THESE MEN.
21. *Gizon honek zaldi hauek salduko ditu.*   THIS MAN WILL SELL THESE HORSES.
22. *Mutil horrek katu horiek saltzen ditu.*   THAT BOY SELLS THOSE CATS.
23. *Mutil hauek zaldi hori salduko dute.*   THESE BOYS WILL SELL THAT HORSE.
24. *Ardi horiek emakume hau ikusko dute.*   THOSE SHEEP WILL SEE THIS WOMAN.
25. *Gizon horiek liburu hau saltzen dute.*   THOSE MEN SELL THIS BOOK.
26. *Zaldi hauek mutil hori ikusten dute.*   THESE HORSES SEE THAT BOY.
27. *Gizon hauek ardi horiek saltzen dituzte.*   THESE MEN SELL THOSE SHEEP.

28. *Emakume horiek zaldi hauek salduko dituzte.*   THOSE WOMEN WILL SELL THESE HORSES.
29. *Zaldi horiek katu horiek ikusko dituzte.*   THOSE HORSES WILL SEE THOSE CATS.
30. *Katu hauek liburu hauek ikusten dituzte.*   THESE CATS SEE THESE BOOKS.

2. Hindi transitive and intransitive clauses

Examine the following data carefully, noting the expression of the Subject and Object under different circumstances. Note that /ne/ is a postposition governing the *OBLIQUE CASE*, while the other nouns in the data set are in the contrasting *DIRECT CASE*. First explain the situation in prose as completely and concisely as you can, comparing and contrasting the situation with the examples discussed in this chapter. Then edit the data and prepare a complete account of the observable patterns.

1a. laṛka· bolta· hɛ   THE BOY SPEAKS.
1b. laṛke bolte hɛ̃   THE BOYS SPEAK.
1c. laṛka· bola·   THE BOY SPOKE.
1d. laṛke bole   THE BOYS SPOKE.
2a. beṭi· bolti· hɛ   THE DAUGHTER SPEAKS.
2b. beṭiyã· bolti· hɛ̃   THE DAUGHTERS SPEAK.
2c. beṭi· boli·   THE DAUGHTER SPOKE.
2d. beṭiyã· bolĩ·   THE DAUGHTERS SPOKE.
3a. dʰobi· calta· hɛ   THE WASHERMAN GOES.
3b. dʰobi· calte hɛ̃   THE WASHERMEN GO.
3c. dʰobi· cala·   THE WASHERMAN WENT.
3d. dʰobi· cale   THE WASHERMEN WENT.
4a. mahila· calti· hɛ   THE LADY GOES.
4b. mahila·ẽ calti· hɛ̃   THE LADIES GO.
4c. mahila· cali   THE LADY WENT.
4d. mahila·ẽ calĩ·   THE LADIES WENT.
5a. laṛka· kela· dekʰta· hɛ   THE BOY SEES A BANANA.
5b. laṛke kela· dekʰte hɛ̃   THE BOYS SEE A BANANA.
5c. laṛka· kela·ẽ dekʰta· hɛ   THE BOY SEES BANANAS.
5d. laṛke kela·ẽ dekʰte hɛ̃   THE BOYS SEE BANANAS.
6a. patni· santara· dekʰti· hɛ   THE WIFE SEES AN ORANGE.
6b. patniyã· santara· dekʰti· hɛ̃   THE WIVES SEE AN ORANGE.
6c. patni· santare dekʰti· hɛ   THE WIFE SEES ORANGES.
6d. patniyã· santare dekʰti· hɛ̃   THE WIVES SEE ORANGES.
7a. admi· pustak likʰta· hɛ   THE MAN WRITES A BOOK.
7b. admi· pustak likʰte hɛ̃   THE MEN WRITE A BOOK.
7c. admi· pustkẽ likʰta· hɛ   THE MAN WRITES BOOKS.
7d. admi· pustkẽ likʰte hɛ̃   THE MEN WRITE BOOKS.
8a. beṭi· lekʰ likʰti· hɛ   THE DAUGHTER WRITES AN ARTICLE/ARTICLES.
8b. beṭiyõ lekʰ likʰti· hɛ̃   THE DAUGHTERS WRITE AN ARTICLE/ARTICLES.
9a. laṛke ne pustak dekʰi·   THE BOY SAW A BOOK.
9b. laṛkõ ne pustak dekʰi·   THE BOYS SAW A BOOK.
9c. laṛke ne pustkẽ dekʰĩ·   THE BOY SAW BOOKS.
9d. laṛkõ ne pustkẽ dekʰĩ·   THE BOYS SAW BOOKS.
10a. mahila· ne santara· beca·   THE LADY SOLD AN ORANGE.
10b. mahila·õ ne santara· beca·   THE LADIES SOLD AN ORANGE.
10c. mahila· ne santare bece   THE LADY SOLD ORANGES.
10d. mahila·õ ne santare bece   THE LADIES SOLD ORANGES.
11a. admi· ne santara· kʰa·ya·   THE MAN ATE AN ORANGE.
11b. admiyõ ne kela· kʰa·i·   THE MEN ATE A BANANA.
11c. admi· ne kela·ẽ kʰa·ĩ·   THE MAN ATE BANANAS.

11d. admiyõ ne santare kʰaˑe	THE MEN ATE ORANGES.
12a. laṛke ne lekʰ likʰaˑ	THE BOY WROTE AN ARTICLE.
12b. patniˑ ne lekʰ likʰe	THE WIFE WROTE ARTICLES.
12c. laṛkõ ne lekʰ likʰaˑ	THE BOY WROTE AN ARTICLE.
12d. mahilaˑõ ne lekʰ likʰe	THE LADIES WROTE ARTICLES.

The following additional examples show further variations on the past tense forms, occurring when the object is specific rather than general. (The English translation may often involve a definite article associated with the object, but the special construction also occurs in other kinds of examples, such as personal names, in the Object function, as shown in 17a–d, where RAM and RADHA are male and female names, respectively.) Explain how these differ from the earlier examples and show how the solution will need to be modified.

13a. laṛke ne pustak ko dekʰaˑ	THE BOY SAW THE BOOK.
13b. laṛkõ ne pustak ko dekʰaˑ	THE BOYS SAW THE BOOK.
13c. laṛke ne pustkõ ko dekʰaˑ	THE BOY SAW THE BOOKS.
13d. laṛkõ ne pustkõ ko dekʰaˑ	THE BOYS SAW THE BOOKS.
14a. mahilaˑ ne santare ko becaˑ	THE LADY SOLD THE ORANGE.
14b. mahilaˑõ ne santare ko becaˑ	THE LADIES SOLD THE ORANGE.
14c. mahilaˑ ne santarõ ko becaˑ	THE LADY SOLD THE ORANGES.
14d. mahilaˑõ ne santarõ ko becaˑ	THE LADIES SOLD THE ORANGES.
15a. admi ne santare ko kʰaˑyaˑ	THE MAN ATE THE ORANGE.
15b. admiyõ ne kelaˑ ko kʰaˑyaˑ	THE MEN ATE THE BANANA.
15c. admi ne kelaˑõ ko kʰaˑyaˑ	THE MAN ATE THE BANANAS.
15d. admiyõ ne santarõ ko kʰaˑyaˑ	THE MEN ATE THE ORANGES.
16a. laṛke ne lekʰ ko likʰaˑ	THE BOY WROTE THE ARTICLE.
16b. patniˑ ne lekʰõ ko likʰaˑ	THE WIFE WROTE THE ARTICLES.
16c. laṛkõ ne lekʰ ko likʰaˑ	THE BOYS WROTE THE ARTICLE.
16d. mahilaˑõ ne lekʰõ ko likʰaˑ	THE LADIES WROTE THE ARTICLES.
17a. raˑm ne raˑdʰaˑ ko dekaˑ	RAM SAW RADHA.
17b. raˑdʰaˑ ne raˑm ko dekaˑ	RADHA SAW RAM.
17c. admiyõ ne raˑdʰaˑ ko dekaˑ	THE MEN SAW RADHA.
17d. mahilaˑõ ne raˑm ko dekaˑ	THE LADIES SAW RAM.

Terminology

AGENTIVE SYSTEM	SPLIT ERGATIVITY
AGENTIVE CASE	TENSE-BASED SYSTEM
PATIENTIVE CASE	NOMINAL-TYPE-BASED SYSTEM
ACCUSATIVE SYSTEM	TRIPARTITE SYSTEM
ACCUSATIVE CASE	OBJECTIVE CASE
NOMINATIVE CASE	SUBJECTIVE CASE
ERGATIVE SYSTEM	UNIPARTITE SYSTEM
ERGATIVE CASE	
ABSOLUTIVE CASE	

11

Voice and other forms of highlighting in the clause

Active and passive voices

In English and many, but not all, languages, there is a distinction between two (or sometimes more) ways of expressing some ideas which involves a grammatical category traditionally known as **VOICE**. Some simple examples of this distinction in English are shown in Table 11.1. In each set of examples, it can fairly be said that the second example, designated by the suffix "a" in its number, expresses the same essential idea as the one before it with the unsuffixed number. The example with the "b" suffix, on the other hand, differs from the other two in that it includes no indication of the doer of the action. An essential question that arises in regard to these examples is the extent to which the first and second members of each set of examples are "synonymous". It has already been suggested above that they communicate "the same essential idea". This means more specifically that the action, the relative time it was performed, the person performing it, and the other person on whom it was performed are all the same. For examples 1 and 1a, the action is slapping in the past, the performer is Susan and it is done to Tom. Still there is a meaning difference, because the active version in 1 is primarily about Susan and something she did, and the passive version in 1a (like the agentless passive in 1b) is primarily about Tom and something that happened to him. For a linguist, such a difference ought to be considered a real one. In the tradition of philosophers and logicians, however, such differences are considered less essential and relegated to "pragmatics" as opposed to a "semantics" dealing only with more essential distinctions. In this book, the study of linguistic meaning is seen as the subject of semology, and the semantic/pragmatic distinction is not considered important for the linguist, however important it may be for the logician or philosopher.

Following the general model used elsewhere in this book, the data in this table would be analysed in terms of two constructions, an Active Transitive Clause and a Passive Transitive Clause as displayed in Figure 11.1. According to a widespread tradition, however, it is claimed

Table 11.1 Active and passive transitive clauses in English

1.	*Susan slapped Tom.*
1a.	*Tom was slapped by Susan.*
1b.	*Tom was slapped.*
2.	*Bill saw Fido.*
2a.	*Fido was seen by Bill.*
2b.	*Fido was seen.*
3.	*Marian convinced Chester.*
3a.	*Chester was convinced by Marian.*
3b.	*Chester was convinced.*
4.	*Fido liked Susan.*
4a.	*Susan was liked by Fido.*
4b.	*Susan was liked.*

Table 11.2   Semological functions for a transitive clause

Event	Actor	Undergoer
TIME: Past		[Focus]
slap	Susan	Tom

that an approach such as this improperly puts these two constructions on a par. Rather, this tradition insists, we should somehow "derive" the passive from the corresponding active to indicate that actives are more basic than passives. It is true that actives are indeed more fundamental than passives, but it does not necessarily follow that such a "derivational" model is the only way to capture this idea of basicness. In order to explicate this point more thoroughly, we need to look more fully at the semology of actives and passives, beginning with what a corresponding active and passive have in common.

We can begin this consideration by looking at the first pair of examples in the table: 1. *Susan slapped Tom,* and 1a. *Tom was slapped by Susan.* In the grammar, the pertinent notions involve Subject, Predicator, and (Direct) Object for the active, and Subject, (a formally different) Predicator, and Agent in the passive. What they have in common is better viewed in terms of semology, where *Susan* indicates the one doing the slapping, which can be termed the ACTOR. Then *slap* indicates what happened, the EVENT, and *Tom* indicates the person that was slapped, the UNDERGOER. These facts, plus the RELATIVE TIME of the action – *PAST* – make up the common core of this active-passive pair, and the remaining examples in the table can be treated similarly. The difference between them, on the other hand, involves a special "emphasis" on the undergoer in the passive which is absent in the active. In diagrammatic form, this can be represented as in Table 11.2.

According to the view adopted in this book, then, the active and passive are related not because one is "derived" from the other, but because they share a common semological structure relating to the actor and undergoer associated with an event, but differ in that the passive has an extra specification to the effect that the undergoer carries "focus". The grammatical manifestation of this focus causes the expression of the undergoer, rather than the actor, to be the grammatical Subject, and it requires the Predicator to be manifested by a special passive form to signal this. The actor may be left unexpressed, or expressed in a prepositional phrase with *by* as its Relator.

In English, the passive variety of the Predicator involves a phrase using an appropriate tense of the verb *to be* together with the past participle of the main verb. In other languages, such as the Latin seen in Table 11.3, the difference between active and passive Predicators may be purely morphological. Other significant differences between the Latin and English structures involve the order of clause elements, with Predicator final in the Latin but medial in English, and the use of three different cases in Latin. The Subject function determines the nominative case (as in the forms *vir, vestis, fēmina, incola, pirāta, puer,* and *mūsica*). For the present data, the Object function in the clause could be said to determine the accusative case (always ending in *-m* for these nouns), and the Axis function in a prepositional phrase could be said to determine the third case, called the *ABLATIVE* in traditional Latin grammar, and here always ending in a long vowel. (In a broader context, the latter two cases could be shown to involve government, since some verbs and prepositions in otherwise similar structures govern different cases, as was shown for Latin in Chapter 7.) The solution to the Latin data is shown in Figure 11.2.

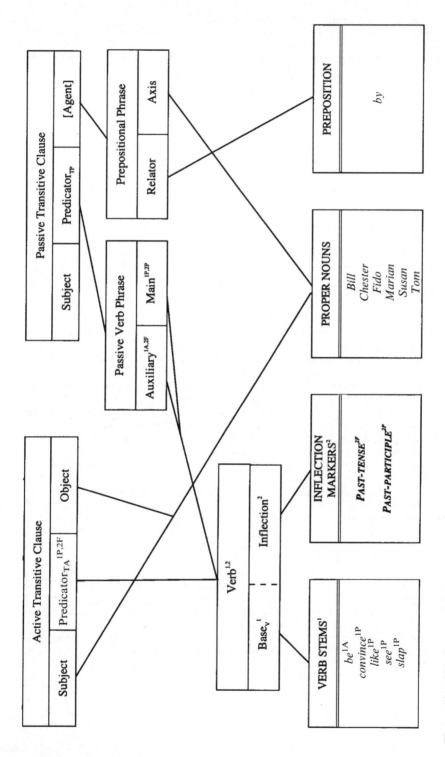

Figure 11.1 Solution to English active and passive transitive clauses

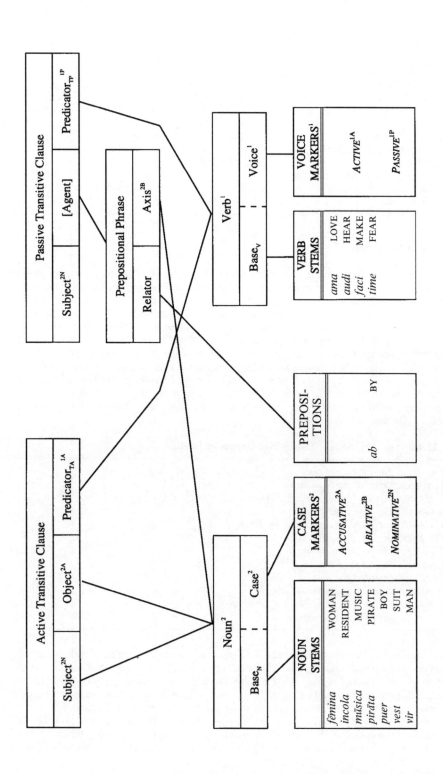

Figure 11.2 Solution to the Latin data of Table 11.3

Table 11.3 Active and passive transitive clauses in Classical Latin

1.	*vir vestem facit*	THE MAN MAKES THE SUIT.
1a.	*vestis ā virō facitur*	THE SUIT IS MADE BY THE MAN.
1b.	*vestis facitur*	THE SUIT IS MADE.
2.	*fēmina virum amat*	THE WOMAN LOVES THE MAN.
2a.	*vir ā fēminā amātur*	THE MAN IS LOVED BY THE WOMAN.
2b.	*vir amātur*	THE MAN IS LOVED.
3.	*incola pirātam timet*	THE RESIDENT FEARS A PIRATE.
3a.	*pirāta ab incolā timētur*	THE PIRATE IS FEARED BY THE RESIDENT.
3b.	*pirāta timētur*	THE PIRATE IS FEARED.
4.	*puer mūsicam audit*	THE BOY HEARS THE MUSIC.
4a.	*mūsica ā puerō audītur*	THE MUSIC IS HEARD BY THE BOY.
4b.	*mūsica audītur*	THE MUSIC IS HEARD.

Varieties of the passive

The English and Latin passives examined so far both involve the undergoer as Subject. Understood more generally, however, a passive may involve anything but the actor as Subject. This generalization, however, is restricted in ways which may vary from language to language. In English, specifically, we see two alternative passives in bitransitives, as illustrated by the data of Table 11.4. Bitransitives, of course, involve two Objects, one Direct and one Indirect. Semologically, the role corresponding to the Indirect Object in an active form can be termed the RECIPIENT, and the b and c examples in this table show the focus on the recipient, while the d and e examples show the focus on the undergoer instead. There are also two different orders in the active, with corresponding differences in whether the Indirect Object is expressed by the first Object after the Predicator or by the Axis in a prepositional phrase with *to* as Relator. Both passives, however, express the Predicator in the same way. Figure 11.3 presents the solution to this data set.

Table 11.4 Active and passive bitransitive clauses in English

1.	*Elvis gave Samantha the book.*
1a.	*Elvis gave the book to Samantha.*
1b.	*Samantha was given the book by Elvis.*
1c.	*Samantha was given the book.*
1d.	*The book was given to Samantha by Elvis.*
1e.	*The book was given to Samantha.*
2.	*Jennifer awarded Drew the prize.*
2a.	*Jennifer awarded the prize to Drew.*
2b.	*Drew was awarded the prize by Jennifer.*
2c.	*Drew was awarded the prize.*
2d.	*The prize was awarded to Drew by Jennifer.*
2e.	*The prize was awarded to Drew.*

Most languages of continental Europe have passives, but unlike English they have only one passive for a bitransitive, that involving the undergoer as Subject. So it is possible to translate undergoer-passive examples like 1/2 d/e quite literally into a language such as French or Russian, but literal translations of recipient-passives will not be acceptable in such languages. These languages, then, have restrictions on passives that are lacking in English.

A somewhat different situation can be seen if we examine the Swahili data of Table 11.5, which shows transitives, and Table 11.6, which shows bitransitives. This language has a morphologically expressed passive, as in Latin. Here there is only one possible Subject in the

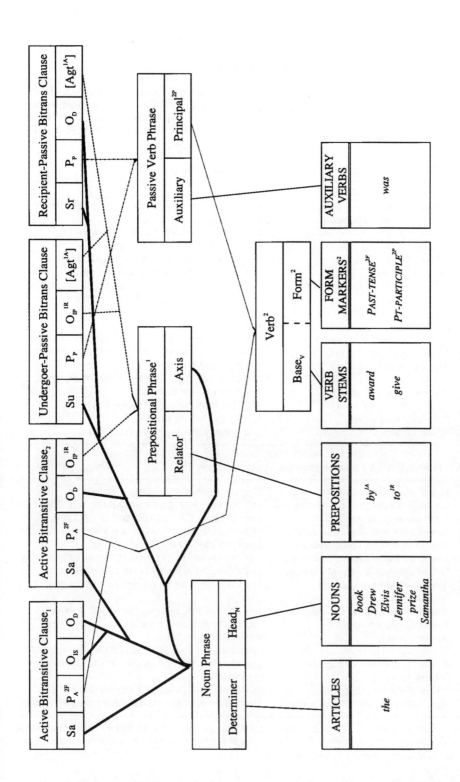

Figure 11.3 Solution to the English bitransitive clause data of Table 11.4

bitransitives, but instead of its being of the undergoer type, as is typical in Continental European languages, it is of the recipient type. So in Swahili one can translate *Samantha was given the gift* fairly literally, but not *The gift was given to Samantha*. It should also be noted that the Object corresponding to the passive Subject is always in the first position after the Predicator. The second (Direct) Object remains in the passive forms. As in English, the Actor can be optionally expressed using a prepositional phrase. In these and subsequent examples, optional expressions are given in square brackets to save space. The "a" examples therefore represent two different sentences. The solutions to these two sets of Swahili data are presented in Figures 11.4 and 11.5.

Table 11.5 Active and passive transitive clauses in Swahili

1.	*Mgeni anampiga mbwa.*	THE STRANGER IS BEATING THE DOG.
1a.	*Mbwa anapigwa [na mgeni].*	THE DOG IS BEING BEATEN [BY THE STRANGER].
2.	*Mwanamke alimpiga mtoto.*	THE WOMAN BEAT THE CHILD.
2a.	*Mtoto alipigwa [na mwanamke].*	THE CHILD WAS BEATEN [BY THE WOMAN].
3.	*Watoto walimpiga mbwa.*	THE CHILDREN BEAT THE DOG.
3a.	*Mbwa alipigwa [na watoto].*	THE DOG WAS BEATEN [BY THE CHILDREN].
4.	*Mtoto alimwamkia mgeni.*	THE CHILD GREETED THE STRANGER.
4a.	*Mgeni aliamkiwa [na mtoto].*	THE STRANGER WAS GREETED [BY THE CHILD].
5.	*Watu wanawaamkia wageni.*	THE PEOPLE ARE GREETING THE STRANGER.
5a.	*Wageni wanaamkiwa [na watu].*	THE STRANGERS ARE BEING GREETED [BY THE PEOPLE].
6.	*Walimu wanamwamkia mtoto.*	THE TEACHERS ARE GREETING THE CHILD.
6a.	*Mtoto anaamkia [na walimu].*	THE CHILD IS BEING GREETED [BY THE TEACHERS].
7.	*Watoto walimwona simba.*	THE CHILDREN SAW THE LION.
7a.	*Simba alionwa [na watoto].*	THE LION WAS SEEN [BY THE CHILDREN].
8.	*Watu walimwona paka.*	THE PEOPLE SAW THE CAT.
8a.	*Paka alionwa [na watu].*	THE CAT WAS SEEN [BY THE PEOPLE].
9.	*Paka aliwaona mbwa.*	THE CAT SAW THE DOGS.
9a.	*Mbwa walionwa [na paka].*	THE DOGS WERE SEEN [BY THE CAT].

Table 11.6 Active and passive bitransitive clauses in Swahili

1.	*Mpishi alimpa mtu mkate.*	THE COOK GAVE THE PERSON BREAD.
1a.	*Mtu alipewa mkate [na mpishi].*	THE PERSON WAS GIVEN BREAD [BY THE COOK].
2.	*Mzee anampa mtoto kitabu.*	THE ELDER IS GIVING THE CHILD A BOOK.
2a.	*Mtoto anapewa kitabu [na mzee].*	THE CHILD IS BEING GIVEN A BOOK [BY THE ELDER].
3.	*Watoto waliwapa simba nyama.*	THE CHILDREN GAVE THE LIONS MEAT.
3a.	*Simba walipewa nyama [na watoto].*	THE LIONS WERE GIVEN MEAT [BY THE CHILDREN].
4.	*Mpishi aliwapikia watoto chakula.*	THE COOK COOKED THE CHILDREN FOOD.
4a.	*Watoto walipikiwa chakula [na mpishi].*	THE CHILDREN WERE COOKED FOOD [BY THE COOK].
5.	*Mwalimu anamnunulia mpishi sukari.*	THE TEACHER IS BUYING THE COOK SUGAR.
5a.	*Mpishi ananunuliwa sukari [na mwalimu].*	THE COOK IS BEING BOUGHT SUGAR [BY THE TEACHER].
6.	*Mtu aliwasomea watoto kitabu.*	THE PERSON READ THE CHILDREN A BOOK.
6a.	*Watoto walisomewa kitabu [na mtu].*	THE CHILDREN WERE READ A BOOK [BY THE PERSON].
7.	*Mtoto alimletea mzee zawadi.*	THE CHILD BROUGHT THE ELDER A GIFT.
7a.	*Mzee aliletewa zawadi [na mtoto].*	THE ELDER WAS BROUGHT A GIFT [BY THE CHILD].

Note: Some of the translations in the above data set may sound stilted in English. They are set up so as to render the Swahili as literally as possible rather than to show the best English style a translator might use.

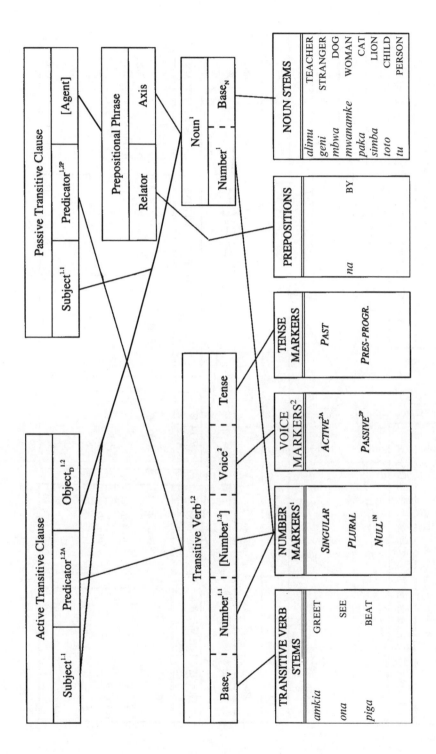

Figure 11.4 Solution to Swahili active and passive transitive clauses

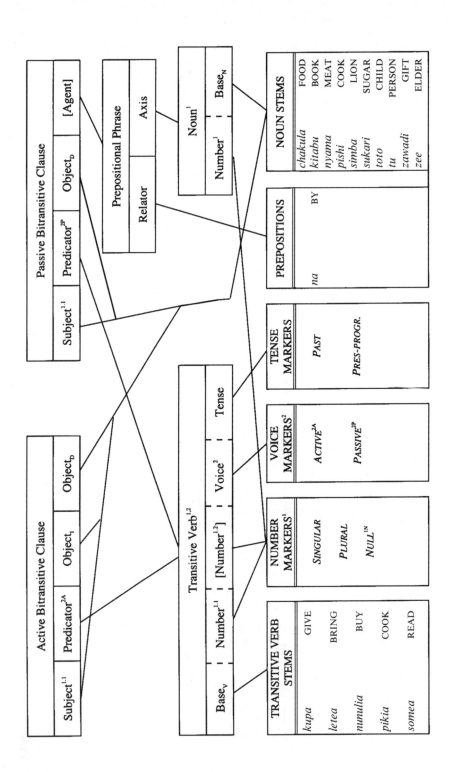

Figure 11.5 Solution to Swahili active and passive bitransitive clauses

We have so far seen two contrasting varieties of the passive voice with some verbs in English: the undergoer-passive and the recipient-passive, with the contrast possible in the passive forms of bitransitive clauses. In the typical language of continental Europe, bitransitives allow only the undergoer type of passive, while in Swahili, on the other hand, only the recipient type is allowed from a bitransitive, though from simple transitives the passive involves the undergoer. There are also languages that simply do not have passives at all, but more interesting is the case where we can get even more types of passive than are allowable in English. In Tagalog, the most important language of the Philippines, there are five different voices, all marked by differences of verb inflection as well as syntactic differences. One of them is an active, and the rest are passive, involving not only undergoer and recipient (sometimes better viewed as a beneficiary) as Subject, but also location and instrument. Examples are shown in Table 11.7. The location-passive and instrument-passive are particularly difficult to translate with an English passive. The glosses given are intended to emphasize the passive nature of the Tagalog examples, but in practical translations devices other than the English passive would normally be used.

Table 11.7 Multiple passive types in Tagalog

ACTIVE VOICE

1. *Bumili ang bata' ng saging sa tindahan para sa guro'.* — THE CHILD BOUGHT BANANAS AT THE STORE FOR THE TEACHER.
2. *Bibili ang guro' ng lapis sa tindahan para sa bata'.* — THE TEACHER WILL BUY A PENCIL AT THE STORE FOR THE CHILD.

UNDERGOER-PASSIVE VOICE

3. *Binili ng bata' ang saging sa tindahan para sa guro'.* — THE BANANAS WERE BOUGHT BY THE CHILD AT THE STORE FOR THE TEACHER.
4. *ng guro' ang lapis sa tindahan para sa bata'.* — THE PENCIL WILL BE BOUGHT BY THE TEACHER AT THE STORE FOR THE CHILD.

RECIPIENT-PASSIVE VOICE

5. *Ibinili ng bata' ang guro' ng saging sa tindahan.* — THE TEACHER WAS BOUGHT BANANAS AT THE STORE BY THE CHILD.
6. *Ipaglata ng guro' ang nanay ng damit.* — MOTHER HAD CLOTHES WASHED FOR HER BY THE TEACHER.

LOCATION-PASSIVE VOICE

7. *Binilhan ng bata' ng saging ang tindahan para sa guro'.* — THE STORE WAS BOUGHT BANANAS FROM BY THE CHILD FOR THE TEACHER.
8. *Bibilhan ng guro' ng lapis ang tindahan para sa bata'.* — THE STORE WILL BE BOUGHT A PENCIL FROM BY THE TEACHER FOR THE CHILD.

INSTRUMENT-PASSIVE VOICE

9. *Ipinambili ng bata ng saging ang pera niya.* — HIS OWN MONEY WAS USED BY THE CHILD TO BUY BANANAS.
10. *Ipambibili ng guro' ng lapis ang pera niya.* — HIS OWN MONEY WILL BE USED BY THE TEACHER TO BUY A PENCIL.

Looking at this material semologically, we can say that while a marked focus in English can come only on the undergoer or the bitransitive recipient, Tagalog allows the further option of putting focus on the location or the instrument, resulting in these additional types of passive clauses.

Though the details naturally differ from language to language, most other Philippine languages are like Tagalog in having at least some of these additional voice distinctions. They are also found in some other languages of the Austronesian family, such as Malagasy, the national language of Madagascar. Grammars of Philippine languages differ in the precise way they describe this matter. Some speak of different VOICES, and others speak of FOCUS on various elements of the clause. The approach used here actually combines the two, using the term focus in the semological treatment and speaking of voice in the syntactic discussion. This particular use of the term focus in fact originated from some traditional usages in Philippine-language grammars and differs from some other uses of the same term in the linguistic literature, where other traditions have used the term rather differently.

The antipassive

All the examples of voice distinctions seen so far have come from languages with accusative systems. One might wonder whether there can also be voice distinctions in ergative languages, and the answer appears to be yes, at least for some of them. Some ergative languages, such as Basque, seem not to have distinctions of voice, but others, such as Australian and Eskimo languages, do show what are interpreted as voice distinctions. An example is shown in the Central Alaskan Yup'ik data in Table 11.8. The solution is presented in Figure 11.6. Since the ordinary transitive clauses in such a language have a passive-like structure anyway, the special voice construction involved in such a language is called not the passive, but the ANTIPASSIVE. Just as the active/passive distinction typically is reflected both in the form of the Predicator and in the marking of the different participants, the difference here, termed *DIRECT* vs *ANTIPASSIVE*, shows up in the form of the verb as well as in the cases used for the various nouns. While the typical ergative structure has the same case for intransitive Subjects and transitive Objects, the antipassive has the same case for its Subject as the intransitive, just like the active voice in an accusative language. As already mentioned, the verb inflection for the antipassive examples (1a–6a) is distinct from what is found in the corresponding direct examples (1–6). Outside any further context, it might be thought that this is simply an inflection for voice, like that seen in Latin or Swahili, but this is not correct. In fact, this language has rather distinct transitive and intransitive forms of inflection, and most verbs are capable of taking either one. The transitive inflection reflects agreement in both person and number with the Subject and the Object, while the intransitive agrees only with the Subject. The forms shown here are all third-person Subject with third-person Object for the transitives used in the direct forms (1–6), and third-person Subject for the intransitives used for the antipassives. Based on this data alone, it would not be clear how to label the cases used, but the solution uses labels based on further consideration of the grammar of the language. The "ergative" form used for the transitive Subject is termed the *RELATIVE*. As mentioned in Chapter 10, this term is intended to reflect the fact that it also has a possessive use, like the genitive in some other languages. The term absolutive, already introduced, is used for the case of the intransitive Subject and transitive Object. The antipassive "object", whose expression is optional, as indicated, is in the *ABLATIVE* case, named for one of its other prominent functions. The antipassive forms, then, are somewhat like passives in that (1) there is a different form of Predicator; (2) the absolutive case is used for a different participant (the actor) in a way

Table 11.8 Antipassive in Central Alaskan Yup'ik Eskimo

1.	aʁnam niqa niʁiɫχua	A/THE WOMAN ATE THE FISH.
1a.	aʁnaq [niqmɨk] niʁiɫχuuq	A/THE WOMAN ATE [A FISH].
2.	pistɨm niqa kiniʁaa	A/THE SERVANT IS COOKING THE FISH.
2a.	pista [niqmɨk] kinɨχtuq	A/THE SERVANT IS COOKING [A FISH].
3.	aŋutɨm qimuxta taŋiɫχua	A/THE MAN SAW THE DOG.
3a.	aŋun [qimuxtɨmik] taŋiɫχuuq	A/THE MAN SAW [A DOG].
4.	aʁnam aŋun nunuʁaa	A/THE WOMAN IS SCOLDING THE MAN.
4a.	aʁnaq [aŋutɨmɨk] nunuχtuq	A/THE WOMAN IS SCOLDING [A MAN].
5.	qimuxtɨm tuntuvak qiluɫχua	A/THE DOG BARKED AT THE MOOSE.
5a.	qimuxta [tuntuvaγmɨk] qiluɫχuuq	A/THE DOG BARKED [AT A MOOSE].
6.	aŋutɨm kɨmɨk niʁaa	A/THE MAN IS EATING THE MEAT.
6a.	aŋun [kɨmɨγmɨk] niʁʁuq	A/THE MAN IS EATING [SOME MEAT].

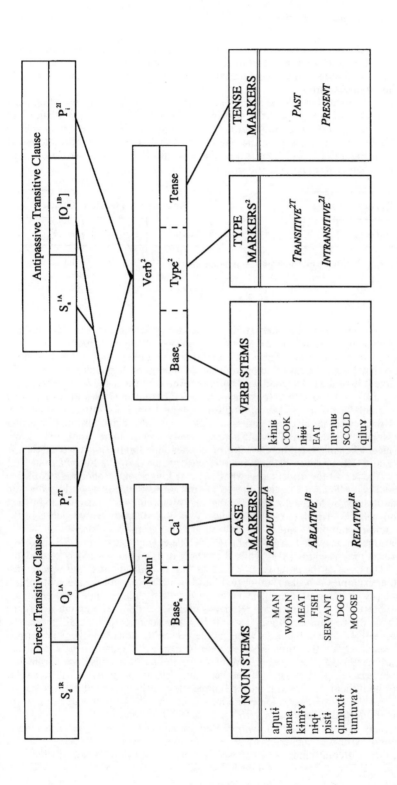

Figure 11.6 Solution to direct and antipassive transitive clauses in Yup'ik Eskimo

parallel to the use of the nominative for the undergoer in a passive clause from an accusative language; and (3) the expression of the remaining major participant (the undergoer) is optional, and has a different formal marking (the ablative case form) from what would be used in the corresponding direct forms.

In truth, this whole discussion has begged an important question about the use of the term "Subject" in an ergative language in the first place. The solution presented in Figure 11.6 follows a fairly traditional notion of subjecthood, but a case can alternatively be made for identifying the Subject with expression in the absolutive in such a language. This alternative labeling is shown in Figure 11.7, which gives only the boxes for the clause constructions, and would connect to an otherwise identical solution.

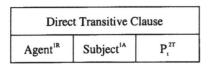
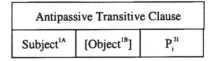

Figure 11.7 Alternative labelings for ergative participants

Highlighting in general

As it happens, voice is just the most widely studied of several phenomena in English grammar that involve placing some special kind of "emphasis" on one of the participants (or related circumstantials) involved in an event. Table 11.9 provides some examples of this based on the past-time event of catching by a cat as actor, to a rat as undergoer, happening in a barn the day before the time it is spoken. The matter of voice is covered by the distinction between the examples in 1 (active) and those in 2 (passive). But the different examples illustrate other devices that are available to a speaker of English wishing to convey different shades of meaning. One of the devices involves the contrastive placement of the main intonation center when the clause is spoken, indicated in writing here by **bold** type in the items numbered 1.1 and 2.1. The semological label suggested here for this phenomenon is EMPHASIS. A second device, illustrated in 1.2 and 2.2, involves placing some element other than the Subject first. This generally ties it to the rest of the discourse as what one is talking about. Following a tradition extending to the Prague School linguists in the period between the two world wars and followed in modern times by Michael A. K. Halliday and his disciples in Systemic Linguistics, this phenomenon will be termed THEME. (Technically, it is a MARKED THEME, since in the unmarked situation in examples 1 and 2, the Subject is in the theme position.)

Further variations are provided in 1.3–4 and 2.3–4. The examples used in 1/2.3 involve a construction termed the "pseudo-cleft", while the others in 1/2.4 show what is termed the "cleft sentence". The basis of the latter term is the fact that the information expressed in just one clause in other examples is broken or "clefted" into two clauses, with the element subject to special "emphasis" serving as Complement in an equative clause, while the remaining information is expressed in a subordinated relative clause. Since this construction leaves the special element near the beginning, although set off by a preceding phrase "it BE", it can be seen as involving THEME in combination with another element, which will here be termed TOPIC. In the "pseudo-cleft", the emphasized element is placed at the end of the expression, with a corresponding relative-interrogative word at the beginning. Since this does not involve placing the emphasized element as such at the beginning, it can be analysed via the topic element alone, without theme. There is, it must be emphasized, little agreement in the linguistic literature about the use of these semological terms, so one has to be prepared both to see different ones used and to see these same terms used in different senses.

Clauses that carry the same essential meaning but vary in these ways have been termed AGNATE. This useful term was suggested by H. A. Gleason, Jr. during the 1960s. A useful generic term for these different kinds of "emphasis" in general is HIGHLIGHTING, which can be defined as the use of different grammatical devices to indicate special kinds of "emphasis" on

Table 11.9 Some data illustrating highlighting in English

1.	*The cat caught the rat in the barn yesterday.*
1.1.1	*The **cat** caught the rat in the barn yesterday.*
1.1.2	*The cat **caught** the rat in the barn yesterday.*
1.1.3	*The cat caught the **rat** in the barn yesterday.*
1.1.4	*The cat caught the rat in the **barn** yesterday.*
1.1.5	*The cat caught the rat in the barn **yesterday**.*
1.2.1	*The rat, the cat caught in the barn yesterday.*
1.2.2	*In the barn, the cat caught the rat yesterday.*
1.2.3	*Yesterday, the cat caught the rat in the barn.*
1.3.1	*What caught the rat in the barn yesterday was the cat.*
1.3.2	*What the cat caught in the barn yesterday was the rat.*
1.3.3	*Where the cat caught the rat yesterday was in the barn.*
1.3.4	*When the cat caught the rat in the barn was yesterday.*
1.3.5	*What the cat did to the rat yesterday in the barn was to catch it.*
1.4.1	*It was the cat that caught the rat in the barn yesterday.*
1.4.2	*It was the rat that the cat caught in the barn yesterday.*
1.4.3	*It was in the barn that the cat caught the rat yesterday.*
1.4.4	*It was yesterday that the cat caught the rat in the barn.*
2.	*The rat was caught by the cat in the barn yesterday.*
2.1.1	*The **rat** was caught by the cat in the barn yesterday.*
2.1.2	*The rat was **caught** by the cat in the barn yesterday.*
2.1.3	*The rat was caught by the **cat** in the barn yesterday.*
2.1.4	*The rat was caught by the cat in the **barn** yesterday.*
2.1.5	*The rat was caught by the cat in the barn **yesterday**.*
2.2.1	*By the cat, the rat was caught in the barn yesterday.*
2.2.2	*In the barn, the rat was caught by the cat yesterday.*
2.2.3	*Yesterday, the rat was caught by the cat in the barn.*
2.3.1	*What was caught in the barn yesterday by the cat was the rat.*
2.3.2	*By what the rat was caught in the barn yesterday was the cat.*
2.3.3	*Where the rat was caught by the cat yesterday was in the barn.*
2.3.4	*When the rat was caught by the cat in the barn was yesterday.*
2.3.5	*What was done to the rat by the cat yesterday was to be caught.*
2.4.1	*It was the rat that was caught by the cat in the barn yesterday.*
2.4.2	*It was by the cat that the rat was caught in the barn yesterday.*
2.4.3	*It was in the barn that the rat was caught by the cat yesterday.*
2.4.4	*It was yesterday that the rat was caught by the cat in the barn.*

various elements of the situation described. Table 11.10 summarizes the usages discussed here. The different circumstances under which one or the other form of highlighting is appropriate depend heavily on the context of discourse. Interesting though they may be, their treatment is beyond the scope of this textbook, as are further details of how the different phenomena co-occur.

One more example of the use of marked theme is shown in the German data in Table 11.11. In this language, the finite verb normally occupies the second position in the clause (here the Predicator). The Subject precedes in the most neutral (unmarked) examples (numbers 1, 2, 3, 4). In the other examples, which have marked theme, some other element precedes the verb, and the Subject then comes in a position right after the Predicator. A full treatment of this material is presented in Figure 11.8, which recognizes four different constructions to account for the different types of theme that are found. This four-construction approach accounts for the data, but it admittedly leaves some fairly obvious generalizations unstated, including:

Table 11.10 Summary of highlighting phenomena in English

Semological phenomenon	Grammatical realization
FOCUS	Passive Voice with Focused item realized as Subject
EMPHASIS	Intonation Center (including strongest Accent) on Emphasized item
THEME	Clause-initial placement of Thematic item
TOPIC	Topical item identified via the "pseudo-cleft" construction (begins with Relative, ends with identified item)
THEMATIC TOPIC	Thematic-Topical item identified via "cleft" construction (beginning with *It BE that*)

1. The fact that every example contains a Theme, and the element before the Predicator, whatever its clause function, is the Theme;
2. The fact that the Subject comes right after the Predicator in those cases when it is not Theme;
3. The fact that there is one basic order of elements after the Subject and Predicator: Object + Temporal + Locational.

Figure 11.8 presents a schema incorporating these observations. Its use would be premised on the control of the syntax from a semological level. Without such control, the schema would not be workable by itself, because it would seem to suggest that any kind of Theme alone, followed by a Predicator, would constitute a Transitive Clause, and because it fails to indicate that a function picked for Theme cannot be repeated later. These things are taken care of in the more complex account seen in Figure 11.9. The simpler schema here could be used, however, in conjunction with a semology that indicates which participants and circumstantials (normally optional functions such as the Temporal and Locational) occur obligatorily and optionally with particular events. The semology would also show that some participant or circumstantial would have to occur as Theme, the default being the focused participant, here the Subject. In actuality, of course, the Temporal and Locational elements are optional in any case, and would have to be indicated as such in a fuller grammar of the language.

Transitive Clause					
Theme	Predicator	[Subject]	[Object]	[Temporal]	[Locational]

Figure 11.8 General schema for Theme in German transitive clauses

Table 11.11 Examples illustrating contrasts of theme in German

1.	*Der Arzt sah den Richter gestern in Berlin.*	THE DOCTOR SAW THE JUDGE YESTERDAY IN BERLIN.
1a.	*Gestern sah der Arzt den Richter in Berlin.*	YESTERDAY THE DOCTOR SAW THE JUDGE IN BERLIN.
1b.	*In Berlin sah der Arzt den Richter gestern.*	IN BERLIN THE DOCTOR SAW THE JUDGE YESTERDAY.
1c.	*Den Richter sah der Arzt gestern in Berlin.*	THE JUDGE, THE DOCTOR SAW YESTERDAY IN BERLIN.
2.	*Der Richter sah den Priester heute in Frankfurt.*	THE JUDGE SAW THE PRIEST TODAY IN FRANKFURT.
2a.	*Heute sah der Richter den Priester in Frankfurt.*	TODAY THE JUDGE SAW THE PRIEST IN FRANKFURT.
2b.	*In Frankfurt sah der Richter den Priester heute.*	IN FRANKFURT THE JUDGE SAW THE PRIEST TODAY.
2c.	*Den Priester sah der Richter heute in Frankfurt.*	THE PRIEST, THE JUDGE SAW TODAY IN FRANKFURT.
3.	*Der Priester traf den Bischof gestern in München.*	THE PRIEST MET THE BISHOP YESTERDAY IN MUNICH.
3a.	*Gestern traf der Priester den Bischof in München.*	YESTERDAY THE PRIEST MET THE BISHOP IN MUNICH.
3b.	*In München traf der Priester den Bischof gestern.*	IN MUNICH THE PRIEST MET THE BISHOP YESTERDAY.
3c.	*Den Bischof traf der Priester gestern in München.*	THE BISHOP, THE PRIEST MET IN MUNICH YESTERDAY.
4.	*Der Bischof traf den Lehrer heute in Hamburg.*	THE BISHOP MET THE TEACHER TODAY IN HAMBURG.
4a.	*Heute traf der Bischof den Lehrer in Hamburg.*	TODAY THE BISHOP MET THE TEACHER IN HAMBURG.
4b.	*In Hamburg traf der Bischof den Lehrer heute.*	IN HAMBURG THE BISHOP MET THE TEACHER TODAY.
4c.	*Den Lehrer traf der Bischof heute in Hamburg.*	THE TEACHER, THE BISHOP MET TODAY IN HAMBURG.

Space does not permit a fuller treatment of the various devices apart from voice that are used for highlighting in various languages. In general, one can expect every language to have at least a few highlighting devices, even if voice is not among them. (And even if voice is included, it may not be the most common.) One of the common devices that does not have a direct parallel in English is the use of a special topical particle before or after the highlighted element. It may express ideas similar to what is found in the English cleft or pseudo-cleft with a different grammatical device.

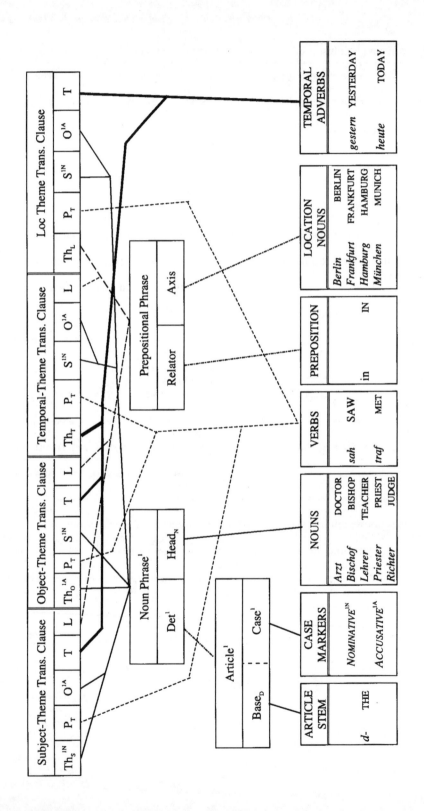

Figure 11.9 Solution to the contrasts of Theme in German

Exercises

A.   Interpretation problems

1. Voice in Modern Greek

The following two pages contain an account of the structure of some active and passive transitive clauses in Modern Greek. Use this account to show the edited structures for clauses with the following meanings.

Note that the Past Incompletive (usually called the "Imperfect" in Greek grammars) can be said to focus on the continuation or repetition of a past action, often translatable via the English progressive or the *used to* construction. The contrasting Past Completive (traditionally called the "Aorist") is translated into English by the simple past and indicates a single completed action in the past.

Note also that a possessive expression can occur with either a definite or an indefinite article in Greek to express a distinction such as MY DOG *(DEFINITE)* versus A DOG OF MINE *(INDEFINITE)*.

1.   THE FATHER HIT HER CAT.

2.   THE GOAT WAS LOVED BY MY DAUGHTER.

3.   THE MOTHER WAS KISSING A SOLDIER.

4.   THE FATHER'S BROTHERS ARE SEEN.

5.   YOUR DOG WAS UNTIED BY THE SOLDIERS.

6.   MY DAUGHTERS WERE SELLING MY DUCKS.

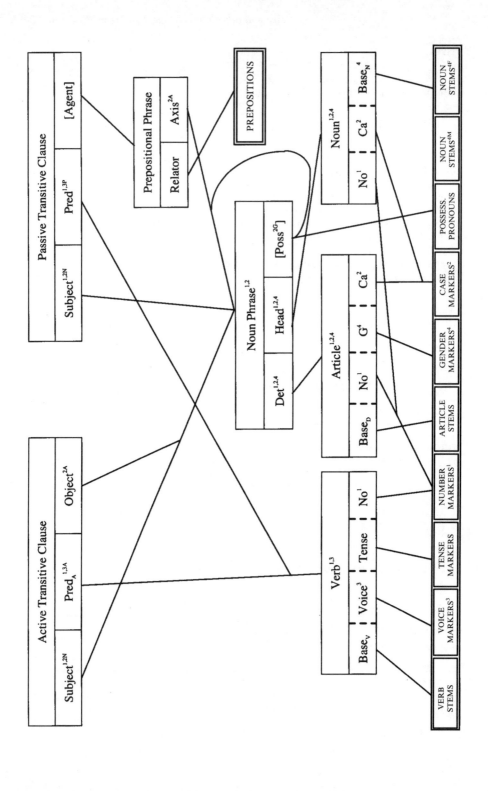

VOCABULARY

NUMBER MARKERS

Singular
Plural

TENSE MARKERS

Present
Past Completive
Past Incompletive

VOICE MARKERS[3]

Active[3A]
Passive[3P]

VERB STEMS

aɣap	LOVE
fil	KISS
ktip	HIT
lin	UNTIE
pol	SELL
vlep	SEE

POSSESSIVE PRONOUNS

-mu	MY
-su	YOUR
-tis	HER
-tu	HIS

CASE MARKERS[2]

Accusative[2A]
Genitive[2G]
Nominative[2N]

GENDER MARKERS[4]

Masculine[4M]
Feminine[4F]

ARTICLE STEMS

enak	A/SOME
t	THE

PREPOSITIONS

apo	BY (AGENT)

NOUN STEMS[4F]

aɣelað	COW
katsik	GOAT
kori	DAUGHTER
miter	MOTHER
papi	DUCK

NOUN STEMS[4M]

aðelf	BROTHER
ɣat	CAT
piter	FATHER
skil	DOG
stratioti	SOLDIER

2. *Voice in Kalagan*

Kalagan is a Philippine language with multiple passives. Use the description on the opposite page to show the edited translations of the following sentences. Note that editing categories will be involved only for the verbs. The highlighted clause element in the English is intended to guide the selection of Subject in Kalagan, since it is virtually impossible to translate Instrument-Passives and Location-Passives literally.

1. THE GUN WAS CARRIED BY THE BOY IN THE HOUSE.

   _____

2. IT WAS IN THE HOUSE THAT THE PIG SAW THE BOY.

   _____

3. IT IS WITH A GUN THAT THE MAN HUNTS THE PIG.

   _____

4. THE BOY SEES THE GUN IN THE HOUSE.

   _____

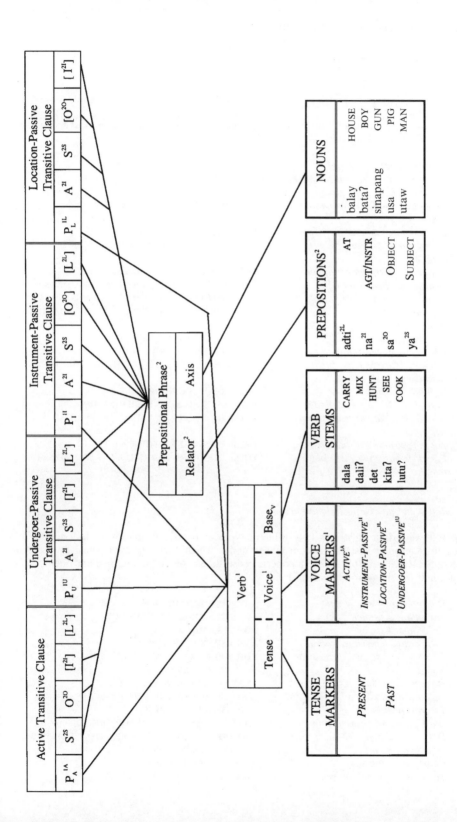

B.   Analysis problems

1.   *Gothic actives and passives*

Prepare an account of the following simple clauses in Gothic, the oldest and most archaic well-atttested Germanic language.

1. *sō mawi nimiþ þana fugl* — THIS MAIDEN TAKES THIS BIRD.
2. *sa fugls nimida fram þizái máujái* — THIS BIRD IS TAKEN BY THIS MAIDEN.
3. *sa skula sōkeiþ þana sunáu* — THIS DEBTOR SEEKS THIS SON.
4. *sa sunus sōkjada fram þamma skulin* — THIS SON IS SOUGHT BY THIS DEBTOR.
5. *þái mannans nimand þō máuja* — THESE MEN TAKE THIS MAIDEN.
6. *sō mawi nimida fram þáim mannam* — THIS MAIDEN IS TAKEN BY THESE MEN.
7. *þōs máujōs nasjand þō áiþein* — THESE MAIDENS TAKE THIS MOTHER.
8. *sō áiþei nasjada fram þáim máujōm* — THIS MOTHER IS TAKEN BY THESE MAIDENS.
9. *sō áiþei skalkinōþ þōs máujōs* — THIS MOTHER SERVES THESE MAIDENS.
10. *þōs máujōs skalkinōnda fram þizái áiþein* — THESE MAIDENS ARE SERVED BY THIS MOTHER.
11. *þōs máujōs skalkinōnda* — THESE MAIDENS ARE SERVED.
12. *þōs frijōndjōs baírand þana hláif* — THESE FRIENDS CARRY THIS BREAD.
13. *sa hláifs baírada fram þizái frijōndjōm* — THIS BREAD IS CARRIED BY THESE FRIENDS.
14. *sa hláifs baírada* — THIS BREAD IS CARRIED.
15. *sō frijōndi fōdeiþ þans niþjans* — THIS FRIEND FEEDS THESE KINSMEN.
16. *þái niþjōs fōdjanda fram þamma frijōndjái* — THESE KINSMEN ARE FED BY THIS FRIEND.
17. *þái magjus baírand þōs gibōs* — THESE BOYS CARRY THESE GIFTS.
18. *þōs gibōs baíranda fram þáim magum* — THESE GIFTS ARE CARRIED BY THESE BOYS.

2.   *Active and passive in Indonesian*

The following data illustrates two different types of passive formation in Indonesian. You need to determine first the circumstances under which they are used, since they are not generally interchangeable. Make a concise prose statement explaining this, and then proceed to account for the properly edited data.

1. *Dokter memeriksa saya.* — A DOCTOR EXAMINED ME.
2. *Saya diperiksa oleh dokter.* — I WAS EXAMINED BY A DOCTOR.
3. *Saya diperiksa.* — I WAS EXAMINED.
4. *Jururawat memeriksa kamu.* — A NURSE EXAMINED YOU.
5. *Kamu diperiksa oleh jururawat.* — YOU WERE EXAMINED BY A NURSE.
6. *Kamu diperiksa.* — YOU WERE EXAMINED.
7. *Dokter itu melihat jururawat.* — THAT DOCTOR SAW A NURSE.
8. *Jururawat dilihat oleh dokter itu.* — A NURSE WAS EXAMINED BY THAT DOCTOR.
9. *Jururawat dilihat.* — A NURSE WAS EXAMINED.
10. *Guru itu memuji dokter ini.* — THAT TEACHER PRAISED THIS DOCTOR.
11. *Dokter ini dipuji oleh guru itu.* — THIS DOCTOR WAS PRAISED BY THAT TEACHER.
12. *Dokter ini dipuji.* — THIS DOCTOR WAS PRAISED.
13. *Polisi menolong saya.* — A POLICEMAN HELPED ME.
14. *Saya ditolong oleh polisi.* — I WAS HELPED BY A POLICEMAN.

15. *Saya ditolong.*	I WAS HELPED.
16. *Saya melihat guru itu.*	I SAW THAT TEACHER.
17. *Guru itu saya lihat.*	THAT TEACHER WAS SEEN BY ME.
18. *Kamu memuji murid ini.*	YOU PRAISED THIS PUPIL.
19. *Murid ini kamu muji.*	THIS PUPIL WAS PRAISED BY YOU.
20. *Kami memeriksa anak.*	WE (EXCLUSIVE) EXAMINED A CHILD.
21. *Anak kami periksa.*	A CHILD WAS EXAMINED BY US.
22. *Kita menolong polisi.*	WE (INCLUSIVE) HELPED A POLICEMAN.
23. *Polisi kita tolong.*	A POLICEMAN WAS HELPED BY US.

3. Actives and passives in Welsh

Examine the following corpus of Welsh data and answer the questions which follow it.

1. *Gwêl y dyn y ferch.*	THE MAN SEES THE GIRL.
2. *Gwelodd y dyn y ferch.*	THE MAN SAW THE GIRL.
3. *Gwelasai y dyn y ferch.*	THE MAN HAD SEEN THE GIRL.
4. *Eistedd y dyn.*	THE MAN SITS (IS SITTING).
5. *Eisteddod y dyn.*	THE MAN SAT.
6. *Eisteddasai y dyn.*	THE MAN HAD SAT.
7. *Gwêl y ferch y dyn.*	THE GIRL SEES THE MAN.
8. *Gwel odd y ferch y dyn.*	THE GIRL SAW THE MAN.
9. *Gwel asai y ferch y dyn.*	THE GIRL HAD SEEN THE MAN.
10. *Eistedd y ferch.*	THE GIRL SITS (IS SITTING).
11. *Eisteddod y ferch.*	THE GIRL SAT.
12. *Eisteddasai y ferch.*	THE GIRL HAD SAT.
13. *Gwelir y ferch gan y dyn.*	THE GIRL IS SEEN BY THE MAN.
14. *Gwelir y ferch.*	THE GIRL IS SEEN.
15. *Gwelwyd y ferch gan y dyn.*	THE GIRL WAS SEEN BY THE MAN.
16. *Gwelwyd y ferch.*	THE GIRL WAS SEEN.
17. *Gwelasid y ferch gan y dyn.*	THE GIRL HAD BEEN SEEN BY THE MAN.
18. *Gwelasid y ferch.*	THE GIRL HAD BEEN SEEN.
19. *Eisteddir gan y dyn.*	THERE IS SITTING BY THE MAN.
20. *Eisteddir.*	THERE IS SITTING.
21. *Eisteddwyd gan y dyn.*	THERE WAS SITTING BY THE MAN.
22. *Eisteddwyd.*	THERE WAS SITTING.
23. *Eisteddasid gan y dyn.*	THERE HAD BEEN SITTING BY THE MAN.
24. *Eisteddasid.*	THERE HAD BEEN SITTING.
25. *Gwelir y dyn gan y ferch.*	THE MAN IS SEEN BY THE GIRL.
26. *Gwelir y dyn.*	THE MAN IS SEEN.
27. *Gwelwyd y dyn gan y ferch.*	THE MAN WAS SEEN BY THE GIRL.
28. *Gwelwyd y dyn.*	THE MAN WAS SEEN.
29. *Gwelasid y dyn gan y ferch.*	THE MAN HAD BEEN SEEN BY THE GIRL.
30. *Gwelasid y dyn.*	THE MAN HAD BEEN SEEN.
31. *Eisteddir gan y ferch.*	THERE IS SITTING BY THE GIRL.
32. *Eisteddwyd gan y ferch.*	THERE WAS SITTING BY THE GIRL.
33. *Eisteddasid gan y ferch.*	THERE HAD BEEN SITTING BY THE GIRL.

A. The functional elements involved in these clauses include Subject, Object, Predicator, and Agent. Which of these comes first in these examples?
B. What element occurs in second position in examples 1–12?
C. What is the third element in examples 1–3 and 7–9?
D. Characterize the relationship between examples 1–3 and 13–18 in general grammatical terms.

E.   What formal differences do we see between 1 and 13, 2 and 15, and 3 and 17 reflecting the grammatical distinction described in the answer to D?
F.   Given the conclusions to D and E, what is the most reasonable way to characterize the relation between 4–6 and 19–24?
G.   We have described English passives as having focus associated with the undergoer or the recipient. Will a parallel analysis work for this Welsh data? Why or why not, and if not, what alternative placement of focus might be considered?
H.   Give a syntactic analysis accounting for a properly edited version of this data.

4.   Topicalized clauses in Yapese

The following data set shows topicalized constructions (glossed via IT IS … THAT) in Yapese. Account for these and the corresponding non-topical forms.

1.	rō yān tɔmɒg	TAMAG WILL GO.
2.	rō yān tɔmɒg gɒbūl	TAMAG WILL GO TOMORROW.
3.	kɛ yān tinɒg	TINAG WENT/HAS GONE.
4.	kɛ yān tinɒg dɒbɒʔ	TINAG WENT/HAS GONE TODAY.
5.	tɔmɒg ɛ rō yān	IT IS TAMAG THAT WILL GO.
6.	gɒbūl ɛ rō yān tɔmɒg	IT IS TOMORROW THAT TAMAG WILL GO.
7.	tɔmɒg ɛ rō yān gɒbūl	IT IS TAMAG THAT WILL GO TOMORROW.
8.	tinɒg ɛ kɛ yān	IT IS TINAG THAT WENT.
9.	dɒbɒʔ ɛ kɛ yān tinɒg	IT IS TODAY THAT TINAG WENT.
10.	tinɒg ɛ kɛ yān dɒbɒʔ	IT IS TINAG THAT WENT TODAY.
11.	rō guy tɔmɒg tinɒg	TAMAG WILL SEE TINAG.
12.	rō guy tinɒg tɔmɒg	TINAG WILL SEE TAMAG.
13.	tɔmɒg ɛ rō guy tinɒg	IT IS TAMAG THAT WILL SEE TINAG or
		IT IS TAMAG THAT TINAG WILL SEE.
14.	tinɒg ɛ rō guy tɔmɒg	IT IS TINAG THAT WILL SEE TAMAG or
		IT IS TINAG THAT TAMAG WILL SEE.
15.	kɛ guy tinɒg tɔmɒg dɒbɒʔ	TINAG HAS SEEN TAMAG TODAY.
16.	tinɒg ɛ kɛ guy tɔmɒg dɒbɒʔ	IT IS TINAG THAT TAMAG SAW TODAY or
		IT IS TINAG THAT SAW TAMAG TODAY.
17.	tɔmɒg ɛ kɛ guy tinɒg dɒbɒʔ	IT IS TAMAG THAT TINAG SAW TODAY or
		IT IS TAMAG THAT SAW TINAG TODAY.
18.	dɒbɒʔ ɛ kɛ guy tinɒg tɔmɒg	IT IS TODAY THAT TINAG SAW TAMAG.
19.	dɒbɒʔ ɛ kɛ guy tɔmɒg tinɒg	IT IS TODAY THAT TAMAG SAW TINAG.
20.	gɒbūl ɛ rō guy tinɒg tɔmɒg	IT IS TOMORROW THAT TINAG WILL SEE TAMAG.

1.   Yapese is the native language of the Micronesian island of Yap, located in the Western Pacific east of the Philippines. The island is well-known for its ancient stone money carved from large rocks.
2.   These examples are based on the data in John Thayer Jensen's *Yapese Reference Grammar* (Honolulu: University Press of Hawai'i, 1977). The system of transcription used is an adaptation by the present author.
3.   It should be noted that "Tamag" and "Tinag" are male and female given names, respectively, in Yapese.

Terminology

ACTIVE VOICE	HIGHLIGHTING
ACTOR	PASSIVE VOICE
AGENT	INSTRUMENT-PASSIVE
AGNATE	LOCATION-PASSIVE
ANTIPASSIVE VOICE	RECIPIENT-PASSIVE
THEME	UNDERGOER-PASSIVE
DIRECT TRANSITIVE CLAUSE	TOPIC
EMPHASIS	THEMATIC TOPIC
EVENT	UNDERGOER
FOCUS	

12

Sentence constructions

The rank hierarchy

Up to this point, the chapters of this book have concentrated on the structure of phrases and clauses, with due attention to those aspects of word structure which are syntactically relevant. These structures are typically arranged in a definite hierarchy of size, such that clauses can be seen as containing phrases, and phrases as containing words. It can further be said that there is one more level in this hierarchy higher than the clause, namely the SENTENCE. An English example illustrating this point quite well is *The women quickly went to the dining room, and the men stayed in the smoky study*. The division of this material into units at these various levels, conveniently termed RANKS, is shown in Figure 12.1. The four ranks just mentioned are indicated in the portion of the diagram included inside the heavy borders. Below this portion, there is a further indication of "elements" (designated by E) – these are the various inflectable stems, uninflectable words, and categorial terms, such as would be listed in the vocabulary boxes following the kind of descriptive model used here. Although on the whole this representation allows us to see how the sentence is broken down on the various ranks, it nevertheless contains some deviations from a perfect and simple breakdown. This shows up, for one thing, in the phrase examples labeled 3A and 6A, which are not directly inside clauses, but are rather parts of other phrases. Specifically they are noun phrases that occur as Axes within prepositional phrases, in general accordance with the points developed concerning such phrases in Chapter 3. The extra level where these subordinated phrases are indicated is shaded in gray where there is no such phrase. The status of the conjunction *and* in the sentence structure is also problematic when it comes to phrases. In effect, the word goes directly into the clause here without forming any part of a phrase, hence the use of gray shading in this portion of the main phrase rank as well. Though no example is found in this sentence, it is also possible for a clause to fulfill a function inside another clause, or even in a phrase. For example, in the sentence *He visits us when he can find the time* the function of Temporal in the main clause is manifested by a subordinate clause beginning with *when*, and in the sentence *We know the man that you are talking about*, a subordinate clause beginning with *that* is used as a Qualifier in a noun phrase headed by the noun *man*.

Actually, the labeling of phrases here has been pursued in a more conservative fashion than what was suggested in earlier chapters, in that all but one of the labeled phrases consist of more than one word. The only exception is Phrase 5, the verb phrase in the second clause, consisting only of the word *stayed*. If the policy behind its labeling had been followed more consistently, the words *quickly* and *smoky* would have been treated as phrases also, in view of the fact that they may be expanded, as in *very quickly* or *quite smoky*. Considerations of expandability taken together mean that in some cases a word may be a phrase, as in these examples, but also such a one-word phrase may sometimes also be a clause and a sentence. In English, the clearest examples of such a phenomenon is an imperative like *Run!* or *Enter!* In languages where Subjects and Objects are regularly optional, such a phenomenon is much more common. So in Central Alaskan Yup'ik Eskimo we very often get one-word sentences like /qayauɣuq/ IT IS A KAYAK or /taʁiŋaqa/ I UNDERSTAND HIM. The latter example can be expanded to /taʁiŋaqa taʁiŋaaŋa-ɬu/ I UNDERSTAND HIM AND HE UNDERSTANDS ME, where either of the verbs could be a sentence by itself. As a one-clause sentence it could be expanded by the addition of an explicit Object, as in

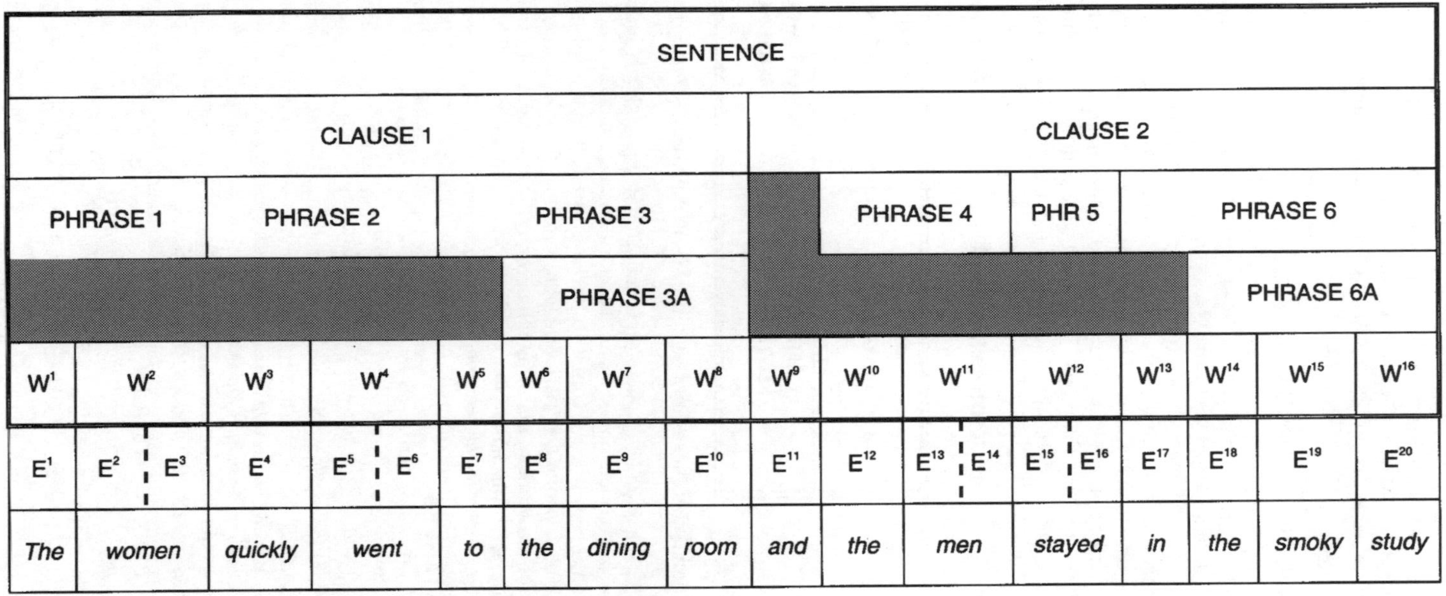

SENTENCE
CLAUSE 1
CLAUSE 2
PHRASE 1
PHRASE 2
PHRASE 3
PHRASE 4
PHR 5
PHRASE 6
PHRASE 3A
PHRASE 6A
W1 W2 W3 W4 W5 W6 W7 W8 W9 W10 W11 W12 W13 W14 W15 W16
E1 E2 E3 E4 E5 E6 E7 E8 E9 E10 E11 E12 E13 E14 E15 E16 E17 E18 E19 E20
The women quickly went to the dining room and the men stayed in the smoky study

Figure 12.1 Basic ranks in a sample English sentence

/kassaq taʁiŋaqa/ I UNDERSTAND THE WHITE MAN. Though many English adverbs are translated into Yup'ik with verbal suffixes, some involve separate uninflected words, so we could treat /akka taʁiŋaqa/ I ALREADY UNDERSTAND HIM as evidence of the expansion of the verb into a verb phrase, which is simultaneously a clause and a sentence.

A traditional classification

In the traditional English grammar presented in American elementary schools, students are taught a four-way classification of sentences which may be summarized in Figure 12.2, with appropriate examples in Table 12.1. As the figure shows, the suggested classification is two-dimensional. The COMPOUND/NON-COMPOUND distinction is based on the number of independent clauses in a sentence, with the non-compound type having just one, and the compound having at least two. It must be emphasized that a compound sentence, at least according to this traditional definition, has to contain at least two sequences that could be independent sentences by themselves. It is not sufficient for it to have one, or even more, compound parts, such as Subjects, Predicators, or

	Non-compound	**Compound**
Non-complex	SIMPLE SENTENCE	COMPOUND SENTENCE
Complex	COMPLEX SENTENCE	COMPOUND-COMPLEX SENTENCE

Figure 12.2 A traditional classification of sentences from American school grammar

Table 12.1 Illustrations of English sentences in the compound/complex classification

SIMPLE SENTENCES
1. *The children and their pets might disturb their parents.*
2. *Can you finish the job by the tenth of next month?*
3. *Why have you changed your hairstyle so often?*
4. *Take your work with you to the beach or the mountains!*

COMPOUND SENTENCES
5. *I can mow the lawn and my brother can trim the shrubs.*
6. *Do you have the money, or should I ask Dad?*
7. *Where are your friends, and when will they be visiting?*
8. *Do your work, and then bring it up to me!*

COMPLEX SENTENCES
9. *The children you see are our neighbors'.*
10. *Do you know whether we can stay there?*
11. *When can you work on the plan that we discussed?*
12. *Do the work when you get the time!*

COMPOUND-COMPLEX SENTENCES
13. *The woman you met is my aunt, and she is quite wealthy.*
14. *Can you see it, or should we ask the people that live closer?*
15. *When did you know you were in danger, and what were the signs?*
16. *As you go in, turn on the light, and as you leave, lock the door!*

Objects. The **COMPLEX/NON-COMPLEX** difference is based on whether there are any subordinate clauses, with the non-complex lacking such clauses and the complex containing at least one.

The general usefulness of this traditional classification cannot be denied, and it is not too difficult to teach children of normal intelligence to apply it to examples. It is one thing to say this, however, and quite another to say that it is a basic and essential classification for sentence types. In discussions of phrase and clause types in previous chapters, it was suggested that examples which differ only in the presence or absence of a particular constituent, or in the choice of a manifestation for a particular function and that alone were not to be treated as separate. In line with this, we might ask whether the compound/non-compound and the complex/non-complex distinctions define what we would reasonably want to treat as distinct constructions or not. For English, at least, the answer seems to be that they are not particularly essential, because they can be generally characterized as involving simple matters of optional constituents or choices in how to manifest a particular function. So the difference between a simple and a compound sentence essentially involves a choice of whether to end one's sentence after one independent clause, or to exercise the option to continue it, as for example by a second clause preceded by a conjunction such as *and*. The difference between a simple and complex type similarly involves a minor option, which generally concerns how to manifest certain functions in the clause or the phrase. Take, for example, the simple sentence *The people here are very friendly* and the similar (and nearly synonymous) complex sentence *The people who live here are very friendly*. The difference between these two in terms of syntactic structures involves a choice of how to manifest the function of Qualifier in the noun phrase that serves as the Subject. In the case of the simple sentence, a simple locative adverb has been chosen, while in the other case the choice of a relative clause instead gives us a complex sentence. In general, complex sentences differ from simple ones in just this kind of way. So, whatever the practical usefulness of this traditional classification, it does not give us distinct sentence constructions according to the approach to syntax presented here.

An alternative traditional classification

On the other hand, the classification just discussed is not the only kind of classification to be found in traditional grammar books. Another cross-cutting classification for sentences involves the difference between **DECLARATIVE**, **INTERROGATIVE**, and **IMPERATIVE** sentences. Examples of these types have, in fact, already been provided in Table 12.1, where they can be identified by their punctuation, ending with a period, question mark, and exclamation point, respectively. (The use of exclamation points for imperatives is far from standard in modern English usage, but it is followed here to help in the ready identification of imperatives.)

In English, at least, this distinction seems to be far more fundamental than the other traditional one. Corresponding declarative, interrogative, and imperative examples generally differ in more intricate ways than the simple/compound/complex examples do. So, for instance, we could cite the declarative *He washed it* alongside the interrogative *Did he wash it?* and the imperative *Wash it!* The differences of punctuation imply intonational differences, which surely do exist. But in addition to this, the interrogative differs from the declarative in the use of *do*, which also carries the tense inflection. The imperative differs first in the optionality of the Subject (and its restriction to second person), as well as in the fact that neither tense nor various modal auxiliaries are usable in the imperative. (So *Will wash it* and *Might wash it* are not possible English imperatives, although instead of *Can wash it!* we have *Be able to wash it!*) In most languages, it is fair to say, such types will constitute separate constructions. (Details of interrogatives and their further classification are provided in the next chapter.)

As suggested in prior discussion, the difference between simple and compound sentences involves a choice of taking an option that allows for more than one independent clause. Figure 12.3 shows an account designed to capture the essence of the structure of a declarative

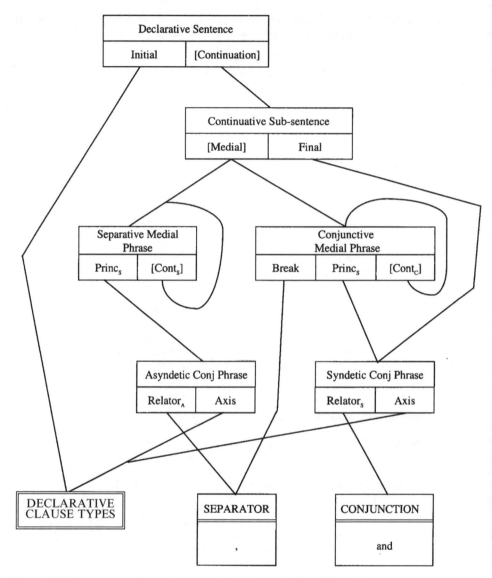

Figure 12.3 Structure of the basic declarative sentence in English

sentence in English. It formalizes the idea that a declarative sentence consists of two functional parts, an obligatory Initial and an optional Continuation. Opting to omit the Continuation, one gets a simple sentence, and opting to take it, one gets a compound sentence. The Continuation is then manifested by a continuative sub-sentence, which consists of an optional Medial followed by an obligatory Final. Omitting the Medial, one gets a minimal compound sentence consisting of just two independent clauses joined by *and*. If one opts to take the Medial, however, there will be at least three independent clauses, and there is no upper limit of how many could theoretically be taken. When one takes the Medial, furthermore, there is a further option to select one of two further structures. When one takes the conjunctive medial phrase, the result is the phenomenon termed **POLYSYNDETON** in Chapter 5: each of the clauses

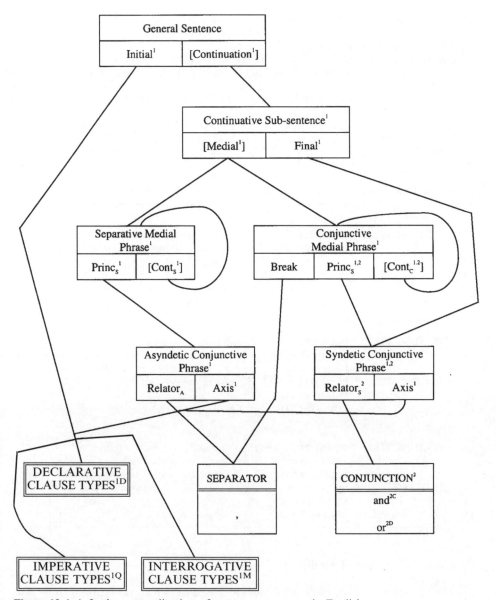

Figure 12.4 A further generalization of sentence structures in English

in the Continuation will be preceded by the conjunction *and*. The other option, termed the separative medial phrase, results in the alternative phenomenon, MONOSYNDETON, with intonation breaks (as symbolized by commas) rather than explicit conjunctions within the Medial. The box labeled declarative clause types indicates that any kind of declarative clause may be selected within a declarative sentence.

If we wanted to represent the structure of the imperative or interrogative sentence, we could simply replace the sentence label and the label in the clause box, as appropriate, but a much more general way to accomplish the task would be to adopt the structure in Figure 12.4. The basic configuration of this account is the same as the one seen in Figure 12.3, but a choice of three special boxes for clause types has been provided at the bottom. Superscripts have also been added, because all of the independent clauses included in a single compound sentence must be of the same basic type, as we have seen.

Another use of concording superscripts in this structure allows us to cover both the conjunctive type of coordination with *and* and the disjunctive type, using *or*. If we had to deal only with monosyndetic examples, no special restriction would be necessary, but with polysyndetic cases we need to guarantee that all of the coordinated examples have either *and* or *or*, not an arbitrary mixture of the two.

Table 12.2 provides some examples of the compound sentence varieties allowed by this revised account. The examples are necessarily brief so they can be represented on a single page, but they illustrate conjunctive and disjunctive monosyndetic and polysyndetic varieties of declarative, interrogative, and imperative sentences.

Table 12.2 Conjunctive and disjunctive types of compound sentences

DECLARATIVE

1.	**CONJUNCTIVE:**	BIPARTITE	*John worked and Peter played.*
2.		MONOSYNDETIC	*Tim ate, Al read, and Susan slept.*
3.		POLYSYNDETIC	*Dogs ran, and cats jumped, and we fled.*
4.	**DISJUNCTIVE:**	BIPARTITE	*She left or they all disappeared.*
5.		MONOSYNDETIC	*He read, she wrote, or they both talked.*
6.		POLYSYNDETIC	*Tom borrowed it, or Mel stole it, or they had it.*

INTERROGATIVE

7.	**CONJUNCTIVE:**	BIPARTITE	*Are they there, and will they stay?*
8.		MONOSYNDETIC	*When was it, why did it happen, and how do we know?*
9.		POLYSYNDETIC	*How are you, and how is Jan, and are you coming?*
10.	**DISJUNCTIVE:**	BIPARTITE	*Should I come there, or should we meet?*
11.		MONOSYNDETIC	*Are they coming, are they leaving, or what?*
12.		POLYSYNDETIC	*Is it here, or is it there, or did you lose it?*

IMPERATIVE

13.	**CONJUNCTIVE:**	BIPARTITE	*Hurry up and don't make excuses!*
14.		MONOSYNDETIC	*Come early, bring your suit, and have fun!*
15.		POLYSYNDETIC	*Take your time, and go slowly, and enjoy it all!*
16.	**DISJUNCTIVE:**	BIPARTITE	*Finish the work, or abandon the project!*
17.		MONOSYNDETIC	*Rest, take a walk, or go swimming!*
18.		POLYSYNDETIC	*Do it, or have them do it, or find a substitute!*

Special sentence types of English

In addition to the rather straightforward kinds of compound sentences illustrated by the data just considered, there are several other patterns of clause combination that are somewhat more special. One of these is the ADVERSATIVE SENTENCE, as illustrated by the examples in Table 12.3. In all of these, the conjunction *but* is used to introduce a statement, question, or command with an implication that it is to some degree in contrast with a preceding statement, if not unexpected in view of it. The declarative, interrogative, or imperative type of the whole sentence is implied by the contrastive part, after *but*, so examples 1 and 4 are declarative, 2 and 5 are interrogative, and 3 and 6 are imperative. The preceding part is more restricted, in that it can never be interrogative. This is different from the simple conjunctive or disjunctive compounds seen above, where all coordinated clauses must be of the same type. It can also be seen from examples 1, 5, and 6 that either of the positions before or after *but* can be filled by what is already a compound sentence. So, in some sense this is a kind of SUPERSENTENCE.

Table 12.3 Examples of adversative sentences in English

1. *John lives here, and Tom lives nearby, but Suzy has settled in California.*	Th$_{DEC}$-Ant$_{DEC}$
2. *I know that you like to travel, but why do you go so far away every time?*	Th$_{DEC}$-Ant$_{INT}$
3. *He won't recognize you, but visit him anyway!*	Th$_{DEC}$-Ant$_{IMP}$
4. *Try the door, but I'm sure no one is home.*	Th$_{IMP}$-Ant$_{DEC}$
5. *Go up and ask him your question, but are you sure you really want to bother him with it?*	Th$_{IMP}$-Ant$_{INT}$
6. *Sit down over there, but be quiet and don't bother us!*	Th$_{IMP}$-Ant$_{IMP}$

In analysing such examples, we may call the part before *but* the THESIS, and the contrastive part introduced by *but* the ANTITHESIS. A suggested schema for this structure is given in Figure 12.5. In line with the observations already made, this indicates that the Thesis is manifested by any declarative or imperative sentence, while the Axis in the Antithesis may be manifested by any of the basic sentence types. The analysis of each of the sample sentences in Table 12.3 is given in the final column of that table, which indicates which type of Thesis (declarative or imperative) and Antithesis (declarative, imperative, or interrogative) is involved.

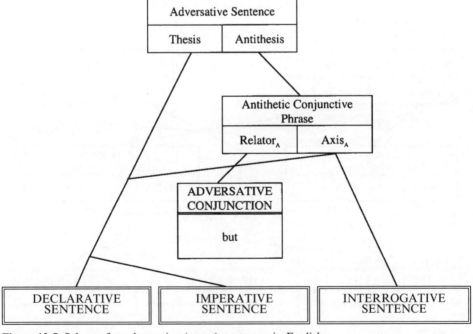

Figure 12.5 Schema for adversative (super) sentences in English

Special sentence types of another variety are illustrated in the data of Tables 12.4 and 12.5, which show two basic varieties of CONDITIONAL SENTENCES. All of these have one part which specifies a condition, usually introduced by the word *if*, and a second part which involves a statement, question, or command whose effect depends on the condition. The latter part is sometimes introduced by *then*. In much traditional grammar, these parts are referred to as the *if*-clause and the *then*-clause. In the tradition of Greek rhetoric, these are called, respectively, the **PROTASIS** and the **APODOSIS**. Since these latter terms refer to functions rather than forms, they will be used here. Etymologically "protasis" means "what is extended before" and "apodosis" means "what is given afterward". This can be seen as applying to logical relations, and not necessarily to physical position, since in some cases a Protasis may follow an Apodosis. Table 12.4 exemplifies the simpler variety of conditional sentence, called **REAL CONDITIONAL**. In these, the protasis contains a declarative sentence, while the apodosis may be declarative, interrogative, or imperative. The latter may be in any appropriate tense, while the former may be in the past or present, but not the future. The two syntactic varieties of this type of sentence are shown in the schemas given in Figure 12.6. The first variety shown, labeled with the subscript $_1$, has the logical order of protasis and apodosis, while the other has the inverse sequence. The postposed variety of apodosis may either be manifested by an apodotic conjunctive phrase with *then*, or it may be manifested directly by a sentence. For the preposed apodosis, on the other hand, only the direct sentence manifestation is possible.

Table 12.4 Examples of real conditional sentences in English

1. *If I get the money, then I'll buy the car and go to the West Coast for a month.*	Pro-Ap$_{\text{DEC}}$
2. *She can afford the trip to Europe if her inheritance is cleared up.*	Ap$_{\text{DEC}}$-Pro
3. *If you hear that she's going to be in town, will you welcome her or try to avoid her?*	Pro-Ap$_{\text{INT}}$
4. *Where will you go if danger threatens?*	Ap$_{\text{INT}}$-Pro
5. *If you get the letter, then be sure to answer it as soon as possible!*	Pro-Ap$_{\text{IMP}}$
6. *Be sure to visit Aunt Sarah if you hear she's in the hospital again!*	Ap$_{\text{IMP}}$-Pro

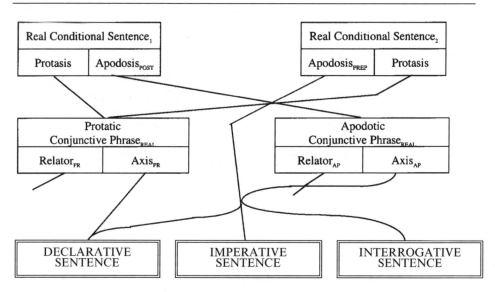

Figure 12.6 Schemas for two varieties of real conditionals

The examples in Table 12.5 illustrate a second basic type of conditional sentence, which has a fairly similar overall structure (Figure 12.7), but has much more specific restrictions on the verb forms that can be used. Since it deals with conditions which the speaker believes to be unreal, it is termed the **HYPOTHETICAL CONDITIONAL**. The basic notion of prothesis and apodosis in either order, with the marked *then* possible with the postposed apodosis only, applies to this variety just as it does to the real conditional. The protasis, however, must contain a sentence in the past subjunctive, and the apodosis will contain a sentence in the conditional mood, signaled in English with *would* (and in some varieties and contexts by *should*). Furthermore, there is an alternative way of expressing the protasis which uses word order in place of the overt conjunction *if,* as exemplified in items 2, 4, 6, and 8. This is a formal variant, so it is rather uncommon in colloquial speech, but it expresses the conditional meaning of IF with a construction using the past subjunctive together with a selection of sequence which places the finite verb before the Subject, rather like a question. (In modern English, the difference between the past subjunctive and the regular past, it should be noted, shows up only with the verb *to be,* where *were* is used for all persons and numbers in the subjunctive, whereas the ordinary past uses *was* instead for the first and third persons singular [*If I was*]. Even this usage has disappeared in many colloquial styles, which therefore entirely lack the indicative/subjunctive distinction in their morphology.) Another difference between the real and hypothetical conditional sentence affects the mode selection in the apodosis, and therefore of the sentence as a whole: there is no possibility of using the imperative in a sentence of the hypothetical conditional type.

Table 12.5 Examples of hypothetical conditional sentences in English

1. *If she had been home, then we would have seen a light.*	Pro_{HC}-$Ap_{H/DEC}$
2. *Had I been able to finish the work, I would be free now.*	Pro_{HI}-$Ap_{H/DEC}$
3. *They would have phoned you if they hadn't been so busy.*	$Ap_{H/DEC}$-Pro_{HC}
4. *Everyone would have seen him had he arrived yesterday.*	$Ap_{H/DEC}$-Pro_{HI}
5. *If there were a larger population in this town, would you still prefer to live here?*	Pro_{HC}-$Ap_{H/INT}$
6. *Were I to come tomorrow, would I find him at home?*	Pro_{HI}-$Ap_{H/INT}$
7. *What would you have done if the monster had attacked in broad daylight?*	$Ap_{H/INT}$-Pro_{HC}
8. *Where would you have gone had there been a flood?*	$Ap_{IH/NT}$-Pro_{HI}

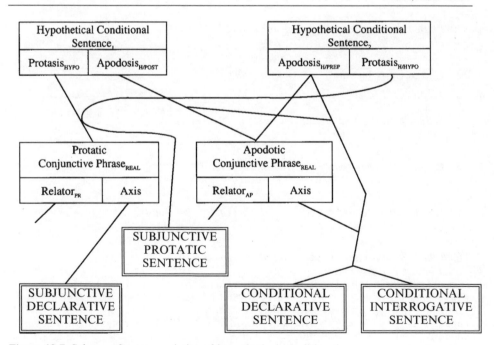

Figure 12.7 Schemas for two varieties of hypothetical conditionals

Summary of sentence structures

Data for clause and phrase structures in various languages is much easier to find than data for sentence structures as such. For that reason, this chapter has concentrated on examples from English. In the traditional terminologies used in some European countries, it is even difficult to make the kind of clear distinction between a clause and a sentence that English speakers are accustomed to. The German word *Satz*, for instance, is commonly used for both, as is Russian *predloženie*, the latter a calque of the Latin logical term *propositiō* PROPOSITION. (In Russian, furthermore, the phrase *složnoe predloženie* refers to both compound and complex sentences in the traditional classification.)

   In the next two chapters, however, some of the matters mentioned in this chapter are treated in greater detail. So in Chapter 13 interrogatives are examined cross-linguistically, and although the emphasis is on the clause, it allows one to examine in greater detail the kinds of interrogative clauses that manifest sentence-rank functions. Then Chapter 14 includes treatments of subordinate clauses, whose presence is needed in the traditional complex sentence types.

Exercises

1.   English sentence classification: traditional categories

Classify the following English sentences according to the traditional distinctions simple, compound, complex, and compound-complex. Recall that a genuine compound sentence in this view must contain two or more potentially independent clauses. A compound Subject, Predicator, or other clause constituent does not make the sentence compound. Answers may be indicated by using the letters **S**, **Cd**, **Cx**, and **Cd-Cx**.

1.   *I have been negotiating with both John and Timothy.*

   _____

2.   *Have you ever met the man he was describing?*

   _____

3.   *Sally mowed the lawn and Ellie watered the flowers.*

   _____

4.   *People from many countries attend this university.*

   _____

5.   *Why have you refused to see the truth about this whole matter?*

   _____

6.   *I think he was simply mistaken, but they are sure he was deliberately lying.*

   _____

7.   *They all claimed that the report had been mailed last week.*

   _____

8. *That they will be tired is not at all certain.*

    _____

9. *The queen was pleased to receive the ambassador who had been recently assigned.*

    _____

10. *I'll read the reports, Mary will prepare the response, and then we will submit it for approval by the people who requested it.*

    _____

2. English compound sentences: basic and special types

The following are all kinds of compound sentences which need to be classified along two dimensions. First, classify each sentence as a whole by its BASIC TYPE as **Declarative**, **Interrogative**, or **Imperative** (**Dc**, **In**, **Im**). Next, classify it by its SPECIAL TYPE as **Adversitive** (**Ad**), **Real Conditional** (**RC**) or **Hypothetical Conditional** (**HC**).

	BASIC TYPE	SPECIAL TYPE
1. *I wanted to go there, but we didn't have the time.*		
2. *Could you help us tomorrow if I phone you?*		
3. *Had they asked, I would have given them all the information they needed.*		
4. *Why does she keep trying to make friends with them if they are always so hostile?*		
5. *I am doubtful about your success on that, but see what you can do about it.*		
6. *If my friend had stopped when we were away, he surely would have left a note for us.*		
7. *Be sure to let us know if you need any help in getting the job done on time.*		
8. *I know how much you love to go skating on the lake, but do you really think the ice is safe this time of year?*		
9. *If they are ready for the test, they will do well on it.*		
10. *If they had prolonged their search, do you think they would have found the missing item?*		

3.   English compound sentences: coordination patterns

In English and many other languages, the patterns of coordination for clauses in compound sentences are very similar to those found in the coordination of words and phrases, as discussed in Chapter 5. The following types are common in English. The main thing to note is the absence of conjunctive (*both ... and*) and negative (*neither ... nor*) correlatives with whole clauses. For each of the six types, devise two examples of your own. Make one of each pair either imperative or interrogative.

1.   *He won't go there, I can't imagine it!*

   CONJUNCTIVE: ASYNDETIC

2.   *Marion folded the laundry and Sam repainted the porch.*

   CONJUNCTIVE: MONOSYNDETIC*

3.   *Marv works at a grocery store, and Carl writes computer software, and Emma is in law school.*

   CONJUNCTIVE: POLYSYNDETIC

4.   *I will leave the tickets for you tomorrow morning, or you can stop by to get them.*

   DISJUNCTIVE: MONOSYNDETIC*

5.   *You could come here, or I could go there, or we could meet somewhere in between.*

   DISJUNCTIVE: POLYSYNDETIC

6.   *Either Irving will be killed off or that soap opera will go off the air.*

   DISJUNCTIVE: CORRELATIVE

*   These monosyndetic examples have just two correlated clauses, but examples with three or more are possible as long as just one overt conjunction is used.

4.   Clause coordination in Hebrew

Account for the patterns of clause coordination shown, relating them to conjunctions, the intonation break and the clause types. It is not, however, necessary to specify the details of the clause types in this write-up.

1.	dan ʔohev ʔet rut veraxel ʔohevet ʔet moše	DAN LIKES RUTH AND RACHEL LIKES MOSHE.
2.	rut roʔa talmid tov vehamore roʔe šaxen	RUTH SEES A GOOD PUPIL AND THE TEACHER SEES A NEIGHBOR.
3.	hamore pogeš baxura verut pogešet ʔet hašxenim haxadašim	THE TEACHER MEETS A GIRL AND RUTH MEETS THE NEW NEIGHBORS.
4.	habayit haxadaš yafe meʔod	THE NEW HOUSE IS VERY NICE.
5.	haʔir gdola	THE CITY IS LARGE.
6.	habayit haxadaš yafe meʔod vehaʔir gdola	THE NEW HOUSE IS VERY NICE AND THE CITY IS LARGE.
7.	rut ktana	RUTH IS SMALL.
8.	moše gadol	MOSHE IS BIG.
9.	rut ktana vemoše gadol	RUTH IS SMALL AND MOSHE IS BIG.
10.	dan katan	DAN IS SMALL.
11.	raxel gdola	RACHEL IS BIG.

12. dan katan veraxel gdola	DAN IS SMALL AND RACHEL IS BIG.
13. haxalav zol	THE MILK IS CHEAP.
14. haglida yekara	THE ICE CREAM IS EXPENSIVE.
15. haxalav zol vehaglida yekara	THE MILK IS CHEAP AND THE ICE CREAM IS EXPENSIVE.
16. hasefer ʔadom	THE BOOK IS RED.
17. hašulxan xum	THE TABLE IS BROWN.
18. hasefer ʔadom vehašulxan xum	THE BOOK IS RED AND THE TABLE IS BROWN.
19. dan more	DAN IS A TEACHER.
20. rut talmida	RUTH IS A PUPIL.
21. dan more verut talmida	DAN IS A TEACHER AND RUTH IS A PUPIL.
22. moše baxur, david more, veraxel mora	MOSHE IS A BOY, DAVID IS A TEACHER, AND RACHEL IS A TEACHER.
23. rut mora, vedan kanar, veyosef student	RUTH IS A TEACHER, AND DAN IS A VIOLINIST AND JOSEPH IS A STUDENT.

Terminology

ADVERSATIVE SENTENCE	HYPOTHETICAL CONDITIONAL SENTENCE
ANTITHESIS	IMPERATIVE SENTENCE
APODOSIS	INTERROGATIVE SENTENCE
COMPLEX SENTENCE	PROTASIS
COMPOUND SENTENCE	RANK
COMPOUND-COMPLEX SENTENCE	REAL CONDITIONAL SENTENCE
CONJUNCTIVE SENTENCE	SENTENCE
DECLARATIVE SENTENCE	SUPERSENTENCE
DISJUNCTIVE SENTENCE	THESIS

13

Interrogation in clause and sentence structures

Basic classification of interrogatives

It is certainly understandable that the syntactic structure of every language includes ways of asking questions, because questions and answers form a vital part of the human interaction which language serves to facilitate. Furthermore, every language appears to distinguish two fundamental kinds of questions. One of these, usually the simpler, just asks the listener to affirm or deny the truth of some statement. Based on their possible answers, these kinds of questions are often called "yes-no questions". A more scientific-sounding term for them is POLARITY QUESTIONS, based on the fact that they inquire about the affirmative or negative polarity of a statement. Some examples of such questions in English would be *Does he speak French?* and *Isn't she there?* These examples also illustrate the fact that such questions may be phrased either affirmatively or negatively. The affirmative phrasing in such a case indicates no particular expectation on the part of the questioner. The negative phrasing, however, suggests that the questioner has the expectation that the state of affairs asked about is true, and would be at least mildly surprised if it were not.

The second fundamental type of question is illustrated by such English examples as *Where are you?*, *Why did she leave so early?*, *When will they be arriving?*, and *What did you see there?* These have sometimes been called "question-word questions" or "information questions", but perhaps the most useful general term for them is SUPPLEMENT QUESTIONS. This term was used by the leading American linguist of the first half of the twentieth century, Leonard Bloomfield. It suggests that the questioner is asking for some specific bit of supplementary information about the situation under discussion. While a simple *yes* or *no* would constitute a sufficient answer to a typical polarity question, a supplement question requires something more specific in a responsive answer, and often the number of possible responsive answers to such a question is indefinitely large. Unfortunately, the most popular term for these questions comes from their form in written English: "Wh-questions". In a purely English-grammar context, this term is acceptable. It should not be considered appropriate, however, to extend this term to other languages, where it does not in any way correspond to the form of their interrogative words.

Expression of polarity questions

The difference between a statement and the corresponding polarity question in a language may be indicated by any of four different grammatical devices, either singly or in combination, and languages differ both in which ones they use and how they use them. One of these devices is intonation: it is very common to signal the difference between a statement and a corresponding polarity question simply by applying different intonation contours to them. In such cases, a rising intonation is the one virtually always used for the question, contrasting with a falling intonation for the corresponding statement. In modern spoken Russian, this is the most common way to differentiate statements and polarity questions, as illustrated by the data in Table 13.1. The examples here are given in a transliteration of the Cyrillic orthography, but in place of punctuation at the end, the symbols /↓/ and /↑/ are used to indicate the falling and rising intonation patterns, respectively.

Table 13.1 Statements and polarity questions in spoken Russian

1. *on čitaet knigu*↓	HE IS READING A BOOK.
2. *on čitaet knigu*↑	IS HE READING A BOOK?
3. *ona pišet knigu*↓	SHE IS WRITING A BOOK.
4. *ona pišet knigu*↑	IS SHE WRITING A BOOK?
5. *ona čitaet gazetu*↓	SHE IS READING A NEWSPAPER.
6. *ona čitaet gazetu*↑	IS SHE READING A NEWSPAPER?
7. *on pišet doklad*↓	HE IS WRITING A REPORT.
8. *on pišet doklad*↑	IS HE WRITING A REPORT?
9. *ona rabotaet*↓	SHE IS WORKING.
10. *on rabotaet*↑	IS HE WORKING?

A second way in which polarity questions are indicated in some languages involves verbal inflection. Such languages distinguish declarative and interrogative modes in their verbal system. One language with this characteristic is Central Siberian Yup'ik, an Eskimo language spoken on St. Lawrence Island, Alaska, as exemplified in Table 13.2. This data shows verbs inflected for both person and declarative vs. interrogative mode, and these factors would be extracted in the morphological editing of the data.

Table 13.2 Inflectional interrogation in Central Siberian Yup'ik Eskimo

1. taɣiitɨn	YOU CAME.
2. taɣiiq	HE CAME.
3. taɣizin	DID YOU COME?
4. aʙnaʙaq taɣii	DID THE GIRL COME?
5. qiyaatɨn	YOU CRIED.
6. apa qiyaaq	GRANDFATHER CRIED.
7. qiyazin	DID YOU CRY?
8. qiyaa	DID HE CRY?
9. aanutɨn	YOU WENT OUT.
10. panik aanuq	THE DAUGHTER WENT OUT.
11. aanzin	DID YOU GO OUT?
12. apa aana	DID GRANDFATHER GO OUT?

Another device for indicating questions, which is much more common than inflection, involves, in effect, pure syntax – the use of different arrangements of clause elements to signal a polarity question. This is found to some degree in modern English, and was much more widely usable at the time of Shakespeare and earlier. Here it can be seen in the Dutch data of Table 13.3. Some linguists habitually describe the difference between the statements in relation to the corresponding questions as a matter of "inversion" of the Subject and Predicator, but this is not a scientifically defensible way of stating the matter. Objectively, we must state that the order of constituents in statements and corresponding questions differs, such that it involves Subject + Predicator in the statement and the opposite in a polarity question.

Still another very common way of structuring polarity questions involves the use of special vocabulary. Most typically, a special grammatical particle is put in a characteristically prominent position in the clause to signal a question. In Polish, for instance, questions may be indicated by the use of the particle /čy/ positioned before what would otherwise be a declaration, as shown in the data of Table 13.4.

Other languages work similarly, except that the interrogative particle is placed at the end of the clause instead of at the beginning. Mandarin Chinese, as exemplified in Table 13.5, provides a good example of this kind of structure. Still another variety involving interrogative particles is found in Tahitian. The second portion of Table 13.6 provides the polarity-

Table 13.3 Positional interrogatives in Dutch

1. *Hij woont heer.*	HE LIVES HERE.
2. *Wonen zij heer?*	DO THEY LIVE HERE?
3. *Zij wonen daar.*	THEY LIVE THERE.
4. *Woont hij daar?*	DOES HE LIVE THERE?
5. *Hij komt uit Nederland.*	HE COMES FROM THE NETHERLANDS.
6. *Komt hij uit Londen?*	DOES HE COME FROM LONDON?
7. *Zij komen uit Engeland.*	THEY COME FROM ENGLAND.
8. *Komen zij uit Amsterdam?*	DO THEY COME FROM AMSTERDAM?
9. *Hij spreekt Nederlands.*	HE SPEAKS DUTCH.
10. *Spreken zij Engels?*	DO THEY SPEAK ENGLISH?
11. *Zij spreken Duits.*	THEY SPEAK GERMAN.
12. *Spreekt hij Frans?*	DOES HE SPEAK FRENCH?

Table 13.4 Polarity questions in Polish

1. jan ma kśõške	JAN HAS A BOOK.
2. čy jan ma kśõške	DOES JAN HAVE A BOOK?
3. vanda ma pwašč	WANDA HAS A COAT.
4. čy vanda ma gazete	DOES WANDA HAVE A NEWSPAPER?
5. jan viʒi gazete	JAN SEES A NEWSPAPER.
6. čy tadeuš viʒi pwašč	DOES THADDEUS SEE A COAT?
7. olga kupi lusterko	OLGA BUYS A MIRROR.
8. čy zośa kupi lusterko	DOES SOPHIE BUY A MIRROR?
9. tadeuš kupi zešyt	THADDEUS BUYS A NOTEBOOK.
10. čy olga ma zešyt	DOES OLGA HAVE A NOTEBOOK?
11. ježy viʒi pjuro	GEORGE SEES A PEN.
12. čy olga kupi pjuro	DOES OLGA BUY A PEN?

Table 13.5 Polarity questions in Mandarin Chinese

1. tā kàn shū	HE IS READING A BOOK.
2. tā kàn shū ma	IS HE READING A BOOK?
3. tāmen mǎi bào	THEY ARE BUYING A NEWSPAPER.
4. tāmen mǎi shū ma	ARE THEY BUYING A BOOK?
5. wǒ mǎi bǐ	I AM BUYING A PEN.
6. wǒmen mǎi bǐ ma	ARE WE BUYING A PEN?
7. wǒ bu kàn bào	I AM NOT READING A NEWSPAPER.
8. tā bu kàn bào ma	ISN'T HE READING A NEWSPAPER?
9. wǒmen bu mǎi zhōng	WE ARE NOT BUYING A CLOCK.
10. tāmen bu mǎi zhōng ma	AREN'T THEY BUYING A CLOCK?
11. wǒmen bu mǎi zhuōzi	WE AREN'T BUYING A TABLE.
12. wǒ bu mǎi fàn ma	AM I NOT BUYING FOOD?

interrogative counterparts for each of the Tahitian examples seen in the first part. A comparison of these interrogatives with the corresponding declaratives will show that the particle marking polarity questions here is /anei/, and it is placed after the first major constituent of the clause. In the affirmative clauses, this is the verb phrase serving as Predicator, but in the negatives (which have a different basic order for their constituents, similar to what we saw for Maori in Chapter 9) this is the Negator. In effect, then, the interrogation marker can be seen as an additional, optional constituent of the clause structure here, just as it can in the previous examples from Polish and Mandarin Chinese.

Sometimes a polarity question may be indicated by something more than a simple particle.

Table 13.6 Declarative and interrogative clauses in Tahitian

1a.	te ta?oto nei au	I AM SLEEPING.	1c. te ta?oto nei anei au	AM I SLEEPING?
1b.	?aita au te ta?oto nei	I AM NOT SLEEPING.	1d. ?aita anei au te ta?oto nei	AM I NOT SLEEPING?
2a.	?e ta?oto au	I WILL SLEEP.	2c. ?e ta?oto anei au	WILL I SLEEP?
2b.	?e au ?e ta?oto	I WILL NOT SLEEP.	2d. ?e anei au ?e ta?oto	WON'T I SLEEP?
3a.	?e ?āu ?oe	YOU WILL SWIM.	3c. ?e ?āu anei ?oe	WILL YOU SWIM?
3b.	?e?ita ?oe ?e ?āu	YOU WILL NOT SWIM.	3d. ?e anei ?ita ?oe ?e ?āu	WON'T YOU SWIM?
4a.	te tae nei ?oia	HE IS ARRIVING.	4c. te tae nei anei ?oia	IS HE ARRIVING?
4b.	?aita ?oia te tae nei	HE IS NOT ARRIVING.	4d. ?aita anei ?oia te tae nei	ISN'T HE ARRIVING?
5a.	?i tae na ?oe	YOU ARRIVED.	5c. ?i tae na anei ?oe	DID YOU ARRIVE?
5b.	?aita ?oe ?i tae na	YOU DID NOT ARRIVE.	5d. ?aita anei ?oe ?i tae na	DIDN'T YOU ARRIVE?
6a.	?i ta?oto na au	I SLEPT.	6c. ?i ta?oto na anei au	DID I SLEEP?
6b.	?aita au ?i ta?oto na	I DID NOT SLEEP.	6d. ?aita anei au ?i ta?oto na	DIDN'T I SLEEP?
7a.	?i tae na ?oia	HE ARRIVED.	7c. ?i tae na anei ?oia	DID HE ARRIVE?
7b.	?aita ?oia ?i tae na	HE DID NOT ARRIVE.	7d. ?aita anei ?oia ?i tae na	DIDN'T HE ARRIVE?

An example of this is provided by the data in Table 13.7, which shows an alternative way of asking a polarity question in Mandarin. Examples 1–6 show alternatives to the affirmative questions already seen in Table 13.5 above, while items 7–12 present some declarative and interrogative clauses using stative verbs. In effect, such a question is like asking "Is he reading a book or not?" or "Is she busy or not?" in English, though the Chinese forms are reportedly much more common than these rather literal English translations. While experts in Chinese grammar can point out circumstances where only the /ma/-question or only the disjunctive question would be usable, they are for most examples interchangeable. Since they already use the negator /bu/, however, it is understandable that there is no counterpart of the distinction between affirmative and negative /ma/-questions in the disjunctive type.

Table 13.7 Disjunctive polarity questions in Mandarin Chinese

1.	tā kàn bu kàn shū	IS HE READING A BOOK?
2.	tāmen mǎi bu mǎi shū	ARE THEY BUYING A BOOK?
3.	wǒmen mǎi bu mǎi bǐ	ARE WE BUYING A PEN?
4.	wǒ kàn bu kàn bào	AM I READING A NEWSPAPER?
5.	tāmen mǎi bu mǎi zhōng	ARE THEY BUYING A CLOCK?
6.	wǒ mǎi bu mǎi fàn	AM I BUYING FOOD?
7.	tā máng	HE IS BUSY.
8.	tāmen máng bu máng	ARE THEY BUSY?
9.	wǒ lèi	I AM TIRED.
10.	nǐ lèi bu lèi	ARE YOU TIRED?
11.	wǒmen hǎo	WE ARE WELL.
12.	tā hǎo bu hǎo	IS HE WELL?

Solutions to the data presented so far mostly involve using the same descriptive devices seen earlier. The Siberian Yup'ik data in Table 13.2, for example, we may solve as in Figure 13.1, differentiating the declarative and interrogative types purely by inflectional choices at the word rank. For Dutch (Table 13.3), however, separate constructions for declarative and interrogative are required to handle the different orders of elements involved. Since the Dutch data presents declarative and interrogative varieties of three different basic clause types, a total of six constructions are required. In the solution presented in Figure 13.2, only two of these are shown, but the other pairs would work similarly. A single construction can again be used, on the other hand, to handle the occurrence of interrogative particles at the beginning, as in Polish, or those at the end, as in Mandarin. The solution to the latter is shown in Figure 13.3.

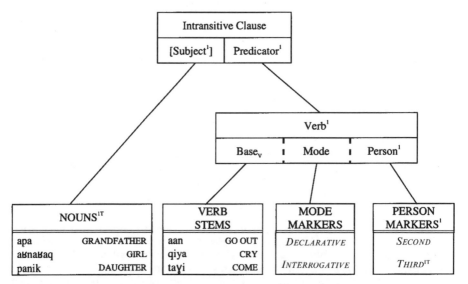

Figure 13.1 An account of inflectional interrogation in Central Siberian Yup'ik Eskimo

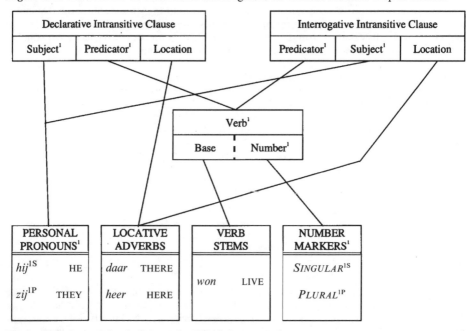

Figure 13.2 A partial solution to the Dutch interrogatives

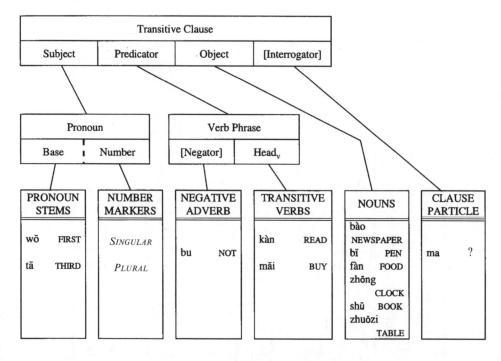

Figure 13.3 Solution to the Mandarin declarative/interrogative data

No separate solution to the Polish interrogative data of Table 13.4 will be given, because this would work exactly like that given for Mandarin in Figure 13.3, in simply requiring an optional particle to distinguish interrogatives from the corresponding declaratives. The only difference will be its position – at the beginning of the clause instead of at the end. For the Tahitian data of Table 13.6, the one additional complication is the one we already saw when Tahitian negation was considered in Chapter 9: the negatives and affirmatives require separate structures. Given this, however, we simply require an optional interrogator after the first clause element to provide for polarity interrogatives. The solution to this is presented in Figure 13.4.

Figure 13.5 then presents the solution for the disjunctive form of interrogation seen in the Mandarin data of Table 13.7. Here the phrase beginning with /bu/ NOT is treated as the optional interrogator. The verb selected after this word, however, must be the same as the one preceding it. This fact is shown by the use of concording superscripts.

The one general type of polarity question not yet illustrated in the solutions presented is the intonational type exemplified by the Russian data in Table 13.1. A solution to this is presented in Figure 13.6. The major innovation necessary to deal with this material is the provision for handling intonation contours as syntactic constituents. Some discussion of intonation suggests that it is a purely "phonological" matter, but this is a misunderstanding. It has its phonological aspects, of course, but so do ordinary words. This does not negate the morphological and syntactic aspects of ordinary words, and it should not be seen as negating the fact that intonational matters are often syntactically relevant. So here a construction tentatively labeled the "macro-clause" is taken to consist of a Core simultaneous with a "Modulation", the latter being manifested by an intonational contour distinguishing declarative and interrogative forms. It should be noted also that the Core function in this structure can be manifested by more than one clause type, so the same overarching structure is used for both transitive and intransitive examples here.

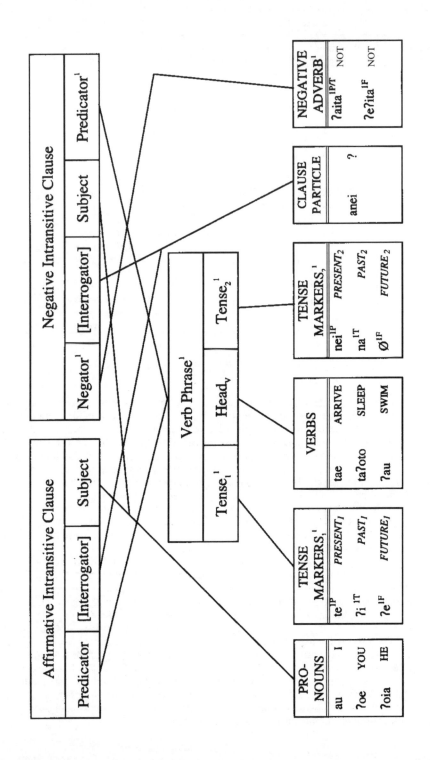

Figure 13.4 Solution to the Tahitian interrogatives of Table 13.6

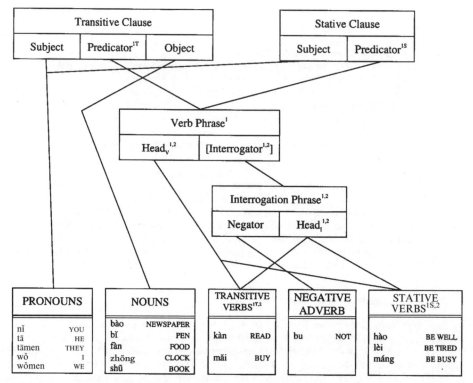

Figure 13.5 Solution to disjunctive polarity questions in Mandarin Chinese

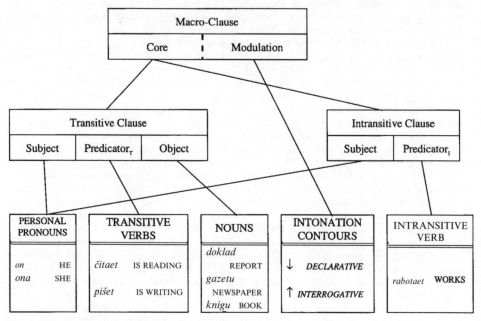

Figure 13.6 Solution to the Russian declaratives and interrogatives

In summary, then, we have seen four fundamental ways of signaling the difference between a statement and a polarity question:

1.   By intonational differences, as in Russian.
2.   By differences of inflectional morphology, as in Central Siberian Yup'ik Eskimo.
3.   By differences in constituent order in the clause, as in Dutch.
4.   By the use of special lexical material, either dedicated specifically to interrogation, like the /ma/ particle in Mandarin and the /čy/ of Polish, or with special constructions such as the one used for disjunctive interrogatives in Mandarin or the English interrogatives with *do*.

Those of type 3 are the ones that require the most extra machinery for their description in a syntactic system.

It should further be noted that more than one of these types will often coexist in the same language, and the coexistence can involve both alternatives and combinations. We have seen two varieties of polarity question in Mandarin already, and we know that English uses constituent order in cases involving *to be* and various auxiliaries. Also intonational differences do not always function alone, but often combine with one or more of the other devices to help signal a question. In such an English example as *He went there* in comparison with the corresponding polarity question *Did he go there?*, for instance, we find a combination of intonation, order, and extra lexical material (the form of *do*) in the interrogative form.

Varieties of supplement questions

By their very nature, supplement questions are more varied than polarity questions, because the variety of specific details about a given situation that can be asked about is considerable. Some of the major kinds of English supplement questions are shown in Table 13.8, which is classified according to the basic part of speech of the interrogative word, and then according to the area of meaning they inquire about. This chart makes no claims of being exhaustive, but it sets forth 14 distinct types each generally characterized by its own interrogative word (or phrase). Each of these words (or phrases) can be seen as having a dual function, namely that of indicating a supplement question in the first place, and then of indicating the specific nature of what is being asked about (such as subject, location, or reason).

In English, it is characteristic of the interrogative words used for supplement questions that they normally occur clause-initially, regardless of the position of the corresponding element in a statement. So one says *You saw the book* but one asks *What did you see?* In some other languages such as Mandarin Chinese, however, the situation is quite otherwise. There are many languages in the world where the interrogative words used in supplement questions occupy the same positions that are occupied by non-interrogative words of similar function. An example of this from Mandarin is seen in the data of Table 13.9. Supplement interrogatives of this variety are generally easy to fit into descriptions, because one can simply list the interrogative words as alternatives to the non-interrogative expressions that appear in the same positions. Figure 13.7 shows how this would work for the Mandarin data.

For the English translations of these various Mandarin interrogatives, on the other hand, we would seemingly need to have a separate interrogative construction for each type of interrogation, as summarized in Table 13.10. This summary suggests that we would need four separate constructions here, and it only includes a limited sample of the kinds of supplement questions that would be possible. Then still further varieties would occur if we consider other basic clause types, such as intransitive and bitransitive. Yet when we examine the material more carefully, these varieties have a lot in common. The formulas given for each differ in two ways: (1) in the role of the interrogative in initial position; and (2) in the fact that that clause role then fails to occur, even optionally, later in the clause. Obviously, then, there is a generalization that is missed in this approach, and an alternative that does not miss it would seem to be superior. For more than forty years, many linguists, often a majority, have concluded that data such as this – and what is shown here is only a small sample – justifies a

Table 13.8 Classification of supplement questions according to what is being asked about

TYPES USING PRONOUNS

SUBJECT	INDIRECT OBJECT
Who arrived?	*To whom did he give the present?* ~
What happened?	*Who'd he give the present to?*
DIRECT OBJECT	COMPLEMENT
Who(m) did you see?	*Who is he?*

TYPES USING ADJECTIVES

POSSESSIVE	CLASSIFICATORY
Whose books are those?	*What kind of a car is that?*
SPECIFICATORY	
Which furniture do you mean?	

TYPES USING ADVERBS

LOCATIONAL	TEMPORAL
Where are they?	*When will they arrive?*
DESTINATIVE	MANNER
Where are you going? ~	*How can you help them?*
[Whither are you going?]	
SOURCE	REASON
Where did they come from? ~	*Why did you buy that?* ~
From where did they come? ~	*[Wherefore did you buy that?]*
[Whence did they come?]	

Note: Bracketed examples use obsolete interrogative words which would now be found only in older literature.

Table 13.9 Declaratives and supplement interrogatives in Mandarin Chinese

1. nǐ mǎi shū	YOU ARE BUYING A BOOK.
2. shéi mǎi shū	WHO IS BUYING A BOOK?
3. nǐ mǎi shénme	WHAT ARE YOU BUYING?
4. tā xiànzài mǎi bào	HE IS BUYING A NEWSPAPER NOW.
5. shéi xiànzài mǎi bào	WHO IS BUYING A NEWSPAPER NOW?
6. tā shénme shíhou mǎi bào	WHEN IS HE BUYING A NEWSPAPER?
7. tā xiànzài mǎi shénme	WHAT IS HE BUYING NOW?
8. wǒ zài zhèr kàn bào	I AM READING A NEWSPAPER HERE.
9. shéi zài zhèr kàn bào	WHO IS READING A NEWSPAPER HERE?
10. wǒ zài nàr kàn bào	WHERE AM I READING A NEWSPAPER?
11. wǒ zài nàr kàn shénme	WHAT AM I READING THERE?
12. tā jīntiān zài nàr kàn shū	HE IS READING A BOOK THERE TODAY.
13. shéi jīntiān zài nàr kàn shū	WHO IS READING A BOOK THERE TODAY?
14. tā shénme shíhou zài zhèr kàn shū	WHEN IS HE READING A BOOK HERE?
15. tā jīntiān zài nàr kàn shū	WHERE IS HE READING A BOOK TODAY?
16. tā jīntiān zài nàr kàn shénme	WHAT IS HE READING THERE TODAY?

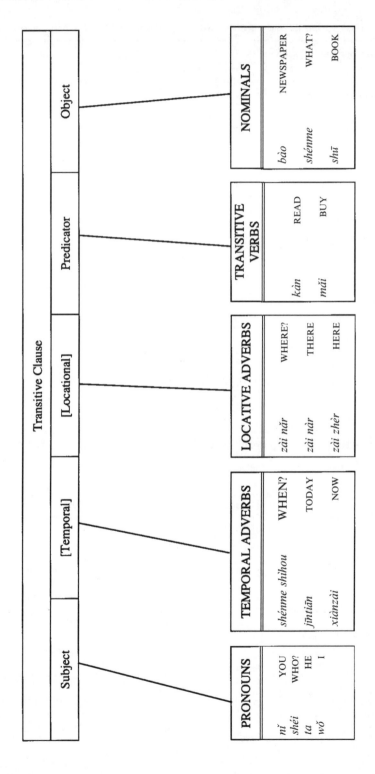

Figure 13.7 Solution to declaratives and supplement interrogatives in Mandarin Chinese

different model which would allow one to say that constituents "start out" in one position and then "move" to their actual positions. In this case, such an approach might begin with the interrogative words *who, what, where*, and *when* in positions typical for their non-interrogative counterparts and then subject the result to a special movement process which puts them in the initial position. On the one hand, such a process is rather unrealistic because there is no reason to believe that speakers actually produce the wrong combinations first and change them in the way suggested. On the other hand, many linguists have endorsed this kind of approach because it did seem to allow us to deal with the obvious generalization that interrogated constituents come initially in examples like these in a way that would not be captured with the use of several different constructions as suggested in Table 13.10.

Table 13.10 Some varieties of supplement interrogative transitive clauses in English

SUBJECT-INTERROGATIVE TRANSITIVE CLAUSE S_Q AUX P O [L] [T]	*Who is buying a book?* *Who is buying a newspaper now?* *Who is reading a newspaper here?* *Who is reading a book there today?*
OBJECT-INTERROGATIVE TRANSITIVE CLAUSE O_Q AUX S P [L] [T]	*What are you buying?* *What is he buying now?* *What am I reading now?* *What is he reading there today?*
TEMPORAL-INTERROGATIVE TRANSITIVE CLAUSE T_Q AUX P O [L]	*When is he buying a newspaper?* *When is he reading a book here?*
LOCATOR-INTERROGATIVE TRANSITIVE CLAUSE L_Q AUX P O [T]	*Where am I reading a newspaper?* *Where is he reading a book today?*

What would be desirable, of course, is an approach that would allow the generalization to be treated without the unrealistic implications of moving constituents. To begin an approach to this matter, consider what the four different formulas in Table 13.10 have in common. It can be summarized in the following schema:

$$\text{Theme}_Q \text{ Auxiliary [Subject] Predicator [Object] [Locational] [Temporal]}$$

They all begin with the interrogative word, whose function is here termed "Question Theme", and the Auxiliary follows. Then the remaining constituents include an obligatory Predicator preceded in some cases by a Subject and followed by an Object, Locational, and Temporal, all optional, in that order. As suggested above, however, this kind of statement would not be adequate by itself, because it misses the correlation between the fact that a particular one of the "optional" functions is impossible in each type. It further fails to indicate the specific nature of the Question Theme, which varies from one type to another. If we assume that a syntactic model must handle these relations in terms of a single level, we are forced to surrender to reality and postulate a multiplicity of supplement-question constructions so that the facts can be correctly accounted for.

If, on the other hand, we allow the syntax to operate, as it were, under the control of a more abstract level, it might be possible to use a more generalized construction such as that in Figure 13.8, which incorporates the schema shown above. This will work if it is assumed that the more abstract level, the SEMOLOGY, will specify that one of the elements ordinarily realized as Subject, Object, Locational or Temporal may involve an interrogative element, and this element will be realized in the Question Theme position initial in the clause. Then it will not be possible to realize that element again in the later position provided for it. Also, though Locational and Temporal are genuinely optional in these clauses, the more abstract structures will require both Subject and Object, with the proviso that one may be realized in the Question Theme position. This means that the optionality of Subject and Object is not the same thing as the optionality of Locational and Temporal.

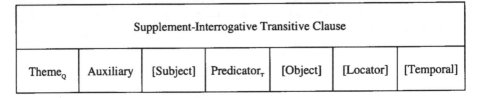

Figure 13.8 Generalized schema for some varieties of transitive supplement questions in English

Confirmatory questions

Many languages also have special varieties of both polarity questions and supplement questions which imply that the questioner knows the answer to his question, but is not completely sure of it. These can be termed CONFIRMATORY QUESTIONS. The form of confirmatory polarity questions often involves a special device at the end, termed a "tag", and so they are called "tag questions". Table 13.11 presents some examples of these questions in English and a few European languages. These examples illustrate that in English the form of the "tag" varies according to the Subject of the preceding statement and its polarity. Various other languages, including all those exemplified here, use fixed tags. In some regional forms of North American English, both Canadian and American, there is also a colloquial fixed tag of the form *eh?* In the proper dialect and style, this can be substituted for the variable tags shown here.

Table 13.11 Tag questions in various European languages

English
She works here, doesn't she?
He doesn't work here, does he?

French
Il parle français, n'est-ce pas?   HE SPEAKS FRENCH, DOESN'T HE?
Elle ne parle pas français, n'est-ce pas? SHE DOESN'T SPEAK FRENCH, DOES SHE?

German
Sie spricht Deutsch, nicht wahr?   SHE SPEAKS GERMAN, DOESN'T SHE?
Er spricht kein Deutsch, nicht wahr?   HE DOESN'T SPEAK GERMAN, DOES HE?

Russian
On govorit po-russki, ne tak li?   HE SPEAKS RUSSIAN, DOESN'T HE?
Ona ne govorit po-russki, ne tak li?   SHE DOESN'T SPEAK RUSSIAN, DOES SHE?

The agreement of the tag and the preceding "statement" in standard English involves several aspects, as follows:

1. The polarity of the tag shows anti-concord with that of the statement – negative if the statement is affirmative and affirmative if the statement is negative.
2. The Subject of the tag is always a pronoun, but it must agree in person, number, and (for the third-person singular) gender with the Subject of the statement.

3.   The verb in the tag can only be a form of *to be* or some kind of auxiliary, agreeing with the verb in the statement. *Do* is used as the default verb in the tag if no other eligible verb is used in the statement.

The schema in Figure 13.9 shows the basic structure of the English tag-type of confirmatory question, using superscripts as follows:

1.   *POLARITY ANTI-CONCORD*
2.   *GENDER CONCORD*
3.   *NUMBER CONCORD*
4.   *PERSON CONCORD*
5.   *VERB-STEM CONCORD*

For other languages and dialects with invariable tags, the same basic structure without the concord would be appropriate.

Confirmatory Polarity Interrogative Sentence	
Statement[1,2,3,4,5]	Tag[1,2,3,4,5]

Figure 13.9 Schema for Standard English confirmatory polarity interrogatives ("tag questions")

In English, confirmatory supplement questions differ from ordinary ones in that they use the special interrogative words with the syntactic order characteristic of statements. Some examples of these types, often termed "echo questions", are shown in Table 13.12. Their intonation patterns are of an interrogative type, and they center on the interrogative word, as suggested by the underlining.

Table 13.12 Confirmatory supplement ("echo") questions in English

He did <u>what</u>?	*He visited <u>who(m)</u>?*
They will arrive <u>when</u>?	*It works <u>how</u>?*
They're going <u>where</u>?	*You're reading <u>which</u> book?*

Formally, these questions can be treated in a way similar to the ordinary supplement questions (without a preposed question theme) in Mandarin, as solved in Figure 13.7. The important difference, of course, is that the more normal (unmarked) English supplement questions have the preposed question theme, while this device is simply not used in Mandarin.

Summary

While the details of interrogative structures, especially confirmatory types in general and the varieties of supplement questions, could be explored far more deeply, this chapter has presented the basic distinction between **POLARITY QUESTIONS** and **SUPPLEMENT QUESTIONS**, and the cross-cutting difference between ordinary types of these and the **CONFIRMATORY** varieties. It has been pointed out that there are several different ways of expressing polarity questions (using inflection, interrogative words, intonation, and/or element order) which may occur in different combinations in a given language. For supplement questions, there are subtypes in every language according to the nature of the supplemental information requested.

An interesting typological difference between languages involves the placement of the interrogative words used in supplement questions: in some languages, such as English, these are placed in the initial question-theme position, while in other languages like Mandarin Chinese they occur in the syntactic position usually reserved for their basic functions. The final typological difference illustrated involves the syntax of the tag questions used for confirmatory polarity interrogation: the tags may show degrees of agreement (fairly complex in standard English), or they may use a fixed particle or phrase for this purpose.

Exercises

A.   Interpretation problems

1. *Kusaiean declaratives and interrogatives*

The diagram on the next page shows some of the syntax of declarative and interrrogative sentences in Kusaiean, the language of the island of Kusaie in the western Caroline Islands in the Pacific. On the basis of this material, translate the following English sentences into Kusaiean.

Notes:

1.   This is based on Kee-dong Lee's grammar (1975) and dictionary (1976), as listed in the references: the transcription system was devised by the present author. It leaves out phonemic vowel length because this information cannot be consistently deduced from the available reference materials.

2.   For the purpose of easy glossing, the archaic English YON has been used for THAT OVER THERE, while THAT is used for THAT (NEAR THE HEARER).

1.   THIS LITTLE CAT WILL LIKE THE LIZARD.

_____

2.   WILL THAT CHILD POISON THE THIN CAT?

_____

3.   YON BIG MAN SAW THE CHILD.

_____

4.   DID THE YOUNG MAN STAY?

_____

5.   THIS OLD LIZARD WILL GO.

_____

6.   WILL YON YOUNG CHILD LIE DOWN?

_____

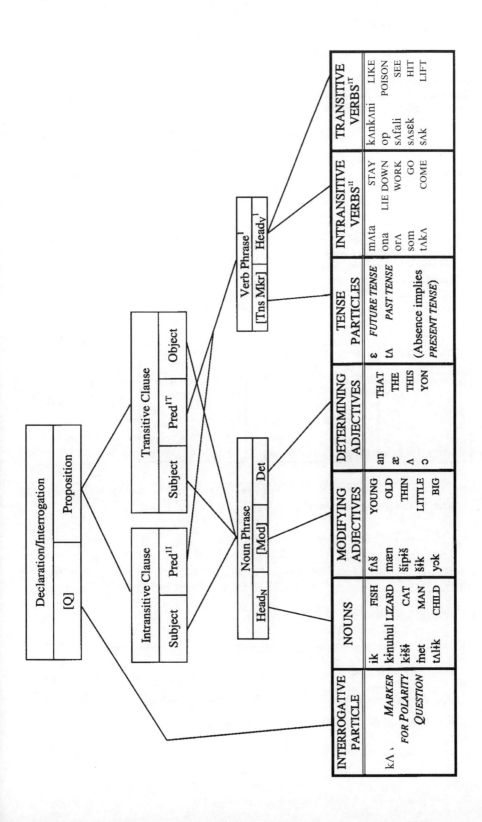

2. *Chrau statements and questions*

The following diagram deals with some kinds of statements and questions in Chrau, a Mon-Khmer language of southern Viet-Nam. Use this account as a basis for answering the questions below.

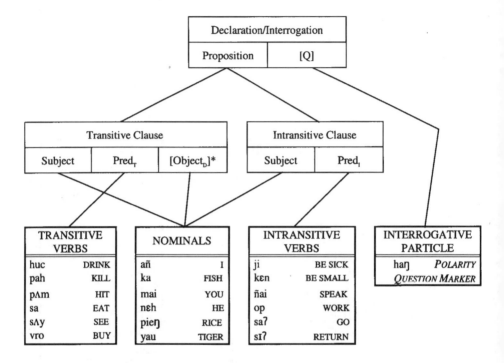

Note: *When a transitive verb occurs with no overt object, an inexplicit object like "it", "something", "someone" is implied.

a.   On the understanding that Chrau has no verbal tense or articles, use the above description to translate the following English sentences into the language.

1.   DO YOU BUY RICE?

_____

2.   THE TIGER EATS FISH.

_____

3.   IS THE FISH SMALL?

_____

4.   DOES HE GO?

_____

5.   I DRINK (SOMETHING).

_____

6.   YOU WORK.

_____

b.   In a brief prose statement, describe the relation between a statement and a corresponding polarity question in this language.

3. Statements and polarity questions in Modern Greek

The diagram on the next page shows the essentials of a structure accounting for declarative and polarity-interrogative transitive clauses in Modern Greek. Use this account to answer the following questions.

a.   Make an objective statement comparing the form of these statements and questions with those seen in the Dutch data of Table 13.3. It should be understood that an objective statement would speak directly of the differences in ordering to be observed in statements *versus* questions, and would not speak of unobservable "changes" deriving one from the other.

b.   Use this account to determine the edited forms in Modern Greek for the following meanings.

1.   THE MOTHERS WASH THE SISTERS.

_____

2.   IS THE NEIGHBOR WAITING FOR THE MOTHER?

_____

3.   THE SISTER PAYS THE WORKERS.

_____

4.   ARE THE MOTHERS CALLING THE MAN?

_____

c.   Use this account to generate one statement and one question of your own, presenting each one in a full boxed form.

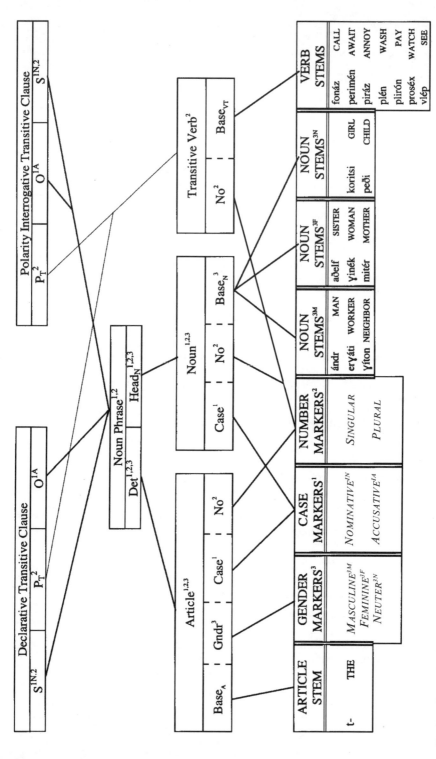

Declarative and polarity-interrogative transitive clauses in modern Greek

B. Analysis problems

1. Polarity questions in Chamorro

The following data set indicates the patterns for statements and polarity questions in Chamorro, a language of the Marianas Islands in the Western Pacific. Determine the pattern and solve the data set. No editing is needed, since no inflection is evident in this material.

1a. mačočoʔčoʔ hao giya guam	YOU ARE WORKING ON GUAM.
1b. kao mačočoʔčoʔ hao giya guam	ARE YOU WORKING ON GUAM?
2a. pumipiknik ham gi tasi	WE ARE PICNICKING AT THE BEACH.
2b. kao pumipiknik ham gi tasi	ARE WE PICNICKING AT THE BEACH?
3a. gumigimen hamyo gi restaurant	YOU ARE DRINKING AT THE RESTAURANT.
3b. kao gumigimen hamyo gi restaurant	ARE YOU DRINKING AT THE RESTAURANT?
4a. bumobola hamyo gi plasa	YOU ARE PLAYING BALL AT THE PLAZA.
4b. kao bumobola hamyo gi plasa	ARE YOU PLAYING BALL AT THE PLAZA?
5a. mačočoʔčoʔ gueʔ gi tenda	HE IS WORKING AT THE STORE.
5b. kao mačočoʔčoʔ gueʔ gi tenda	IS HE WORKING AT THE STORE?
6a. simasaga yoʔ giya guam	I AM STAYING ON GUAM.
6b. kao simasaga yoʔ giya guam	AM I STAYING ON GUAM?
7a. humahanao ham	WE (EXCL) ARE GOING.
7b. kao humahanao ham	ARE WE (EXCL) GOING?
8a. bumolbola yoʔ	I AM PLAYING BALL.
8b. kao bumolbola yoʔ	AM I PLAYING BALL?
9a. gumigimen gueʔ gi tenda	HE IS DRINKING AT THE STORE.
9b. kao gumigimen gueʔ gi tenda	IS HE DRINKING AT THE STORE?
10a. ñumañaɦu ham	WE (EXCL) ARE SWIMMING.
10b. kao ñumañaɦu ham	ARE WE (EXCL) SWIMMING?

Note: Based on Donald Topping. *Spoken Chamorro*. Honolulu: University of Hawaii Press, 1980.

2. Polarity questions in Hindi

The following data set illustrates two alternative ways of framing a polarity question in Hindi, using square brackets for an optional constituent. First describe in prose the relation between these questions and the corresponding statements, and then prepare an account of the edited data, including gender concord. It should be noted that the various tense forms of the verb TO BE are used as the main verb in copular clauses and as auxiliary verbs in intransitive clauses.

1. aˑdmiˑ accʰaˑ hɛ↓	THE MAN IS GOOD.
1a [kyaˑ] aˑdmiˑ accʰaˑ hɛ↑	IS THE MAN GOOD?
2. laṛkiˑ caltiˑ hɛ↓	THE GIRL GOES.
2a. [kyaˑ] laṛkiˑ caltiˑ hɛ↑	DOES THE GIRL GO?
3. ɔrat accʰiˑ hɛ↓	THE WOMAN IS GOOD.
3a. [kyaˑ] ɔrat accʰiˑ hɛ↑	IS THE WOMAN GOOD?
4. guru caltaˑ hɛ↓	THE TEACHER GOES.
4a. [kyaˑ] guru caltaˑ hɛ↑	DOES THE TEACHER GO?
5. aˑdmiˑ sundar tʰaˑ↓	THE MAN WAS HANDSOME.
5a. [kyaˑ] aˑdmiˑ sundar tʰaˑ↑	WAS THE MAN HANDSOME?
6. laṛkiˑ accʰiˑ tʰiˑ↓	THE GIRL WAS GOOD.
6a. [kyaˑ] laṛkiˑ accʰiˑ tʰiˑ↑	WAS THE GIRL GOOD?
7. šahar baṛaˑ tʰaˑ↓	THE CITY WAS LARGE.

7a. [kyaˑ] šahar baṛaˑ tʰaˑ↑   WAS THE CITY LARGE?
8.   ɔrat sundar tʰiˑ↓   THE WOMAN WAS BEAUTIFUL.
8a. [kyaˑ] ɔrat sundar tʰiˑ↑   WAS THE WOMAN BEAUTIFUL?
9.   guru boltaˑ tʰaˑ↓   THE TEACHER SPOKE.
9a. [kyaˑ] guru boltaˑ tʰaˑ↑   DID THE TEACHER SPEAK?
10. raˑjaˑ caltaˑ tʰaˑ↓   THE PRINCE WENT.
10a. [kyaˑ] raˑjaˑ caltaˑ tʰaˑ↑   DID THE PRINCE GO?

3. Supplement questions in Hindi

The following data set illustrates the relation between statements and some kinds of supplement questions in Hindi. Determine the pattern and solve, using as few distinct constructions as seems feasible. Verb forms will need to be edited to some extent.

1a. ɔrat yahãˑ hɛ   THE WOMAN IS HERE.
1b. makaˑn vahãˑ hɛ   THE HOUSE IS THERE.
1c. makaˑn vahãˑ tʰaˑ   THE HOUSE WAS THERE.
1d. laṛkiˑ kahãˑ hɛ   WHERE IS THE GIRL?
2a. ye pustak hɛ   THIS IS A BOOK.
2b. vo kursiˑ hɛ   THAT IS A CHAIR.
2c. ye kyaˑ hɛ   WHAT IS THIS?
2d. vo kyaˑ hɛ   WHAT IS THAT?
2e. vo kyaˑ tʰaˑ   WHAT WAS THAT?
3a. ɔrat accʰiˑhɛ   THE WOMAN IS GOOD.
3b. aˑdmiˑ accʰaˑ hɛ   THE MAN IS GOOD.
3c. ɔrat accʰiˑ tʰiˑ   THE WOMAN WAS GOOD.
3d. aˑdmiˑ kɛsaˑ hɛ   HOW IS THE MAN?
3e. ɔrat kɛsiˑ hɛ   HOW IS THE WOMAN?
3f. aˑdmiˑ kɛsaˑ tʰaˑ   HOW WAS THE MAN?
4a. vo raˑm hɛ   THAT IS RAM.
4b. vo raˑm tʰaˑ   THAT WAS RAM.
4c. ye raˑdʰaˑ hɛ   THIS IS RADHA.
4d. ye raˑdʰaˑ tʰiˑ   THIS WAS RADHA.
4e. vo kɔn hɛ   WHO IS THAT?
4f. ye kɔn hɛ   WHO IS THIS?
4g. vo kɔn tʰaˑ   WHO WAS THAT?
5a. raˑm aˑj caltaˑ tʰaˑ   RAM WENT AWAY TODAY.
5b. raˑdʰaˑ roz caltiˑ tʰiˑ   RADHA WENT AWAY DAILY.
5c. laṛkiˑ kab caltiˑ tʰiˑ   WHEN DID THE GIRL GO AWAY?
5d. aˑdmiˑ kab caltaˑ tʰa   WHEN DID THE MAN GO AWAY?
5e. kɔn roz caltaˑ tʰaˑ   WHO WENT AWAY DAILY?
6a. ɔrat yahãˑ boltiˑ hɛ   THE WOMAN SPEAKS HERE.
6b. aˑdmiˑ vahãˑ boltaˑ hɛ   THE MAN SPEAKS THERE.
6c. laṛkiˑ kahãˑ boltiˑ hɛ   WHERE DOES THE GIRL SPEAK?
6d. kɔn vahãˑ boltaˑ hɛ   WHO SPEAKS THERE?
6e. ɔrat roz vahãˑ boltiˑ tʰiˑ   THE WOMAN SPOKE THERE DAILY.
6f. laṛkiˑ roz yahãˑ boltiˑ tʰiˑ   THE GIRL SPOKE HERE DAILY.
6g. kɔn kal vahãˑ boltaˑ tʰaˑ   WHO SPOKE THERE YESTERDAY?
6h. ɔrat kab yahãˑ boltiˑ tʰiˑ   WHEN DID THE WOMAN SPEAK HERE?
6i. aˑdmiˑ aˑj kahãˑ boltaˑ hɛ   WHERE DOES THE MAN SPEAK TODAY?

4. Interrogatives in Japanese

The following data set shows the formation of polarity questions in relation to that of statements in Japanese. Prepare an account of this data. (Unlike most other Japanese data sets in the book, this problem uses the polite style of verbs, characterized by the affix / mas / rather than the plain form. This is because the pattern of interrogation shown is generally characteristic of the polite rather than the plain style.)

1.	ken wa hon o kaimasita	KEN BOUGHT A/THE BOOK.
2.	ken wa hon o kaimasita ka	DID KEN BUY A/THE BOOK?
3.	kare hon o yomimasita	HE READ A/THE BOOK.
4.	kare hon o yomimasita ka	DID HE READ A/THE BOOK?
5.	ken wa tokei o kaimasita	KEN BOUGHT A/THE CLOCK.
6.	ken wa tokei o kaimasita ka	DID KEN BUY A/THE CLOCK?
7.	kare wa zassi o yomimasita	HE/SHE READ A/THE MAGAZINE.
8.	kare wa zassi o yomimasita ka	DID HE READ A/THE MAGAZINE?
9.	karre wa asoko ni sakana o tabemasita	HE ATE FISH OVER THERE.
10.	kare koko ni sakana o tabemasita ka	DID HE EAT FISH HERE?

The following additional data shows the formation of several kinds of supplement questions. In what way do these resemble the polarity questions seen above? What is the major difference as regards these supplement questions in Japanese in comparison with their equivalents in English and other typical European languages? Prepare an account that will deal with all the data in 1–20.

11.	kanozyo wa nani o kaimasita ka	WHAT DID SHE BUY?
12.	ken wa nani o yomimasita ka	WHAT DID KEN READ?
13.	dare ga sakana o tabemasita ka	WHO ATE FISH?
14.	ken wa doko de sakana o tabemasita ka	WHERE DID KEN EAT FISH?
15.	kanozyo wa doko de hon o kaimasita ka	WHERE DID SHE BUY THE BOOK?
16.	nani ga asoko de sakana o tabemasita ka	WHAT ATE FISH THERE?
17.	dare ga koko de zassi o yomimasita ka	WHO READ THE MAGAZINE HERE?
18.	ken wa asoko de dare o mimasita ka	WHOM DID KEN SEE THERE?
19.	kanozyo wa kyooto de nani kaimasita ka	WHAT DID SHE BUY IN KYOTO?
20.	ken wa tookyoo ni dare o mimasita ka	WHOM DID KEN SEE IN TOKYO?

5. Polarity questions in Latin

The following data illustrates the formation of simple polarity questions in Classical Latin. The item /-ne/ should be treated as an enclitic, though this data is insufficient to demonstrate that analysis conclusively. Prepare a solution for this data set. Editing will be required for both nouns and verbs.

1.	*Vir vestem facit.*	THE MAN MAKES CLOTHING.
1a.	*Facit-ne vir vestem?*	DOES THE MAN MAKE CLOTHING?
2.	*Vir amphoram videt.*	THE MAN SEES THE JAR.
2a.	*Videt-ne vir amphoram?*	DOES THE MAN SEE THE JAR?
3.	*Fēmina amphoram lavat.*	THE WOMAN WASHES THE JAR.
3a.	*Lavat-ne fēmina amphoram?*	DOES THE WOMAN WASH THE JAR?
4.	*Lupus fēminam videt.*	THE WOLF SEES THE WOMAN.
4a.	*Videt-ne lupus fēminam?*	DOES THE WOLF SEE THE WOMAN?
5.	*Agnus lupum videt.*	THE LAMB SEES THE WOLF.
5a.	*Videt-ne agnus lupum?*	DOES THE LAMB SEE THE WOLF?
6.	*Lupus agnum quaerit.*	THE WOLF SEEKS THE LAMB.

6a. *Quaerit-ne lupus agnum?*	DOES THE WOLF SEEK THE LAMB?
7. *Fēmina laudem quaerit.*	THE WOMAN SEEKS PRAISE.
7a. *Quaerit-ne fēmina laudem?*	DOES THE WOMAN SEEK PRAISE?
8. *Vestis virum facit.*	CLOTHING MAKES THE MAN.
8a. *Facit-ne vestis virum?*	DOES CLOTHING MAKE THE MAN?
9. *Pater fīlium amat.*	THE FATHER LOVES THE SON.
9a. *Amat-ne pater fīlium?*	DOES THE FATHER LOVE THE SON?
10. *Fīlius patrem amat.*	THE SON LOVES THE FATHER.
10a. *Amat-ne fīlius patrem?*	DOES THE SON LOVE THE FATHER?

The following data set shows evidence for some additional types of Latin polarity questions, related to those above. On the basis of this evidence, elaborate your solution to the above problem so that these types can be included.

11. *Vir-ne vestem facit?*	DOES <u>THE MAN</u> MAKE CLOTHING?
11a. *Vestem-ne vir facit?*	DOES THE MAN MAKE <u>CLOTHING</u>?
11b. *Num vir vestem facit?*	THE MAN DOESN'T MAKE CLOTHING, DOES HE?
11c. *Nōnne vir vestem facit?*	THE MAN MAKES CLOTHING, DOESN'T HE?
12. *Fēmina-ne amphoram lavat?*	DOES <u>THE WOMAN</u> WASH THE JAR?
12a. *Num fēmina amphoram lavat?*	THE WOMAN DOESN'T WASH THE JAR, DOES SHE?
13. *Fēminam-ne lupus videt?*	DOES THE WOLF SEE <u>THE WOMAN</u>?
13a. *Nōnne lupus fēminam videt?*	THE WOLF SEES THE WOMAN, DOESN'T IT?
14. *Fēmina-ne laudem quaerit?*	DOES <u>THE WOMAN</u> SEEK PRAISE?
14a. *Num fēmina laudem quaeit?*	THE WOMAN DOESN'T SEEK PRAISE, DOES SHE?
15. *Fīlium-ne pater amat?*	DOES THE FATHER LOVE <u>THE SON</u>?
15a. *Nōnne pater fīlium amat?*	THE FATHER LOVES THE SON, DOESN'T HE?
16. *Vir-ne amphoram portat?*	DOES <u>THE MAN</u> CARRY THE JAR?
16a. *Num vir amphoram portat?*	THE MAN DOESN'T CARRY THE JAR, DOES HE?
17. *Lupum-ne agnus videt?*	DOES THE LAMB SEE <u>THE WOLF</u>?
17a. *Nōnne agnus lupum videt?*	THE LAMB SEES THE WOLF, DOESN'T IT?
18. *Fīlius-ne fēminam amat?*	DOES <u>THE SON</u> LOVE THE WOMAN?
18a. *Num fīlius fēminam amat?*	THE SON DOESN'T LOVE THE WOMAN, DOES HE?

Terminology

CONFIRMATORY QUESTIONS	LEXICAL INTERROGATIVE
ECHO QUESTIONS	POLARITY QUESTIONS
TAG QUESTIONS	POSITIONAL INTERROGATIVE
DISJUNCTIVE INTERROGATIVE	SUPPLEMENT QUESTIONS
INFLECTIONAL INTERROGATIVE	
INTONATIONAL INTERROGATIVE	

14

Subordinate clauses and clausoidal phrases

In Chapter 12, the idea of the complex sentence was presented, characterized as containing at least one subordinate clause in addition to a main clause. In this chapter, more details about the form and function of subordinate clauses will be investigated. Also to be considered here are some constructions traditionally treated as kinds of phrases, but which share some, but not all, of the characteristics of clauses.

English subordinate clauses

To begin our consideration, we can look at some of the kinds of subordinate clauses that can be found in English. As a first example, let us consider the data in Table 14.1, which shows subordinate clauses functioning in the role of Object. In the first six examples, the subordinate clause is marked by the word *that* at the beginning, but is otherwise like an ordinary declarative clause. This overt marker is in fact optional in English, as is indicated by the square brackets around each instance of it. The variant without *that* is more colloquial, but is very common in spoken English. In the second part of the table, we see subordinated interrogatives marked by *whether*. This word indicates that what follows is a subordinated polarity question. Here there is also a common colloquial variant marked by *if* instead of *whether,* and for some speakers this may be the only variant in use. In all of the examples with the marker *that,* the sentence as a whole is declarative. In such a case, of course, we can also make the sentence interrogative without affecting the nature or form of the subordinate clause. So corresponding to item no. 5 we can get the question *Did he say that Barbara likes them?* The examples with *whether* are shown as statements in some instances and questions in others, but again we can get either one, as in the declarative counterpart to item no. 11: *She can find out whether they are coming,* or the interrogative counterpart to item no. 8: *Did he hear whether Ivan was there?*

Table 14.1 Examples of *that*-clauses and *whether*-clauses as Objects with verbs of communication and perception

---

1. *I know [that] John speaks Spanish.*
2. *We understand [that] Selma gets up early.*
3. *They heard [that] Egbert works there.*
4. *She insisted [that] Irma speaks French with them.*
5. *He said [that] Barbara likes them.*
6. *You can see [that] Alvin is not busy.*
7. *Do you know whether she is busy?*
8. *He didn't hear whether Ivan was there.*
9. *Didn't they see whether the men were working?*
10. *I'm not sure whether we will be going.*
11. *Can she find out whether they will be coming?*
12. *I'm uncertain whether they are telling the truth.*

The structure of these examples, like that of many other subordinate clauses, and indeed marked coordinate clauses, involves a Relator-Axis structure where the Relator is manifested by a **SUBORDINATING CONJUNCTION** – in these examples *that, whether,* and *if* are used in this role. The Axis, it will be noted, is manifested by a simple declarative clause, even if the whole is shown to be a subordinated interrogative by the use of the appropriate conjunctions. The subordinating structure involved is sketched in Figure 14.1.

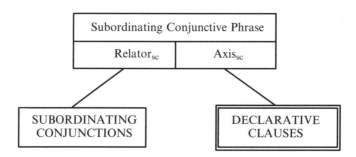

Figure 14.1   The general structure for the subordinating conjunctive phrase

Table 14.2 shows examples of another common use of simple *that*-clauses, namely as Subjects of various main clauses. These are essentially the same structures as those used for Objects, except for the fact that it is not possible to omit the conjunction *that* in this case. Clauses introduced by *whether* can similarly be used as Subjects, as shown in Table 14.3. Again the structure is the same as what we see in Object function, but we can never substitute *if* for *whether* in such a case. In all of these examples, we can say that the subordinate clauses occur in nominal function, since Subjects and Objects are typical functions for noun phrases.

Table 14.2   Subordinate declarative clauses as Subjects

1. ***That John refused to come*** *is not surprising.*
2. ***That he can do such precise work quickly*** *is amazing.*
3. ***That they failed so completely*** *is regrettable.*
4. ***That you happened to be in*** *was a great stroke of luck.*
5. ***That Sylvester met them there*** *was a pure accident.*
6. ***That Aunt Polly has been hospitalized*** *is a shame.*
7. ***That he spoke English so well*** *impressed us.*
8. ***That they behaved so awkwardly*** *embarrassed us all.*
9. ***That Anna will be coming tomorrow*** *astonished me.*
10. ***That the team lost so badly*** *disappointed us all.*

Table 14.3   Subordinate interrogative clauses as Subjects

1. ***Whether we live or die*** *is not the point.*
2. ***Whether I am successful in that*** *is a side issue.*
3. ***Whether they can get it finished*** *is an important question.*
4. ***Whether the cat catches mice*** *is hardly crucial.*
5. ***Whether she received the notice*** *is very important.*
6. ***Whether they live there the year round*** *is really unclear.*

Another very common function for a subordinate clause is that of adjunct in a noun phrase, as seen in the examples of Table 14.4, which are all noun phrases with a RELATIVE CLAUSE in the function of Qualifier. The structure of such clauses involves considerably more intricacy than that of the subordinate nominal clauses seen above. Generally speaking, such clauses are marked with one of several special words (*who*[*m*], *which, that*). These words can be said to fulfill a dual function: (1) as a marker of the subordination of the clause; and (2) as an indicator of function within the clause. The function in this second sense for each relative marker is indicated at the end of each item in the table. The form taken by the marker further depends on the person or thing to which it refers, which is always the same as the referent of the head of the noun phrase involved, with some further stylistic choices. One choice involved is between the more formal type with *who* or *which* and the more colloquial type with *that*. Within the former, *who*(*m*) will be used for a person and *which* for a thing. In the case of pets, at least for mammals like cats, dogs, and horses, we have the option of personifying them by choosing *who*(*m*) instead of *which*. In some cases, furthermore, the use of *that* in the colloquial style is optional. Observation of these examples will show that an occurrence of *that* in the function of Subject within its clause is never optional, but it is optional in Object or Axis functions.

Table 14.4   Examples of English relative clauses

1. *the old man who lives across the street* ∼ *the old man that lives across the street*	SUBJECT
2. *these people with whom I live* ∼ *these people [that] I live with*	AXIS
3. *the man whom I saw* ∼ *the man [that] I saw*	DIRECT OBJECT
4. *a little boy to whom I spoke* ∼ *a little boy [that] I spoke to*	AXIS
5. *this woman for whom I work* ∼ *this woman [that] I work for*	AXIS
6. *the new idea which amazed me* ∼ *the new idea that amazed me*	SUBJECT
7. *the camera which we liked* ∼ *the camera [that] we liked*	DIRECT OBJECT
8. *the book for which I traded* ∼ *the book [that] I traded for*	AXIS
9. *the store in which we were shopping* ∼ *the store [that] we were shopping in*	AXIS
10. *a stock for which I paid a lot* ∼ *a stock [that] I paid a lot for*	AXIS
11. *a dog who/which/that seemed to like me*	SUBJECT
12. *this cat [whom/which/that] I am feeding*	INDIRECT OBJECT
13. *the horse for whom/which I bought oats* ∼ *the horse [that] I bought oats for*	AXIS
14. *the canary which/that is singing right now*	SUBJECT

English grammars also make another important distinction regarding relative clauses, namely that between those that are RESTRICTIVE and those that are NON-RESTRICTIVE. The examples in Table 14.5 illustrate this distinction, showing cases that differ only in this matter. The basis for these contrasting terms lies in the meaning: a restrictive relative has the effect of narrowing down the meaning of the head to the one or ones that have the characteristic indicated by the relative clause. So in the first example, 1r indicates that the speaker is talking about one specific uncle, the one who lives in Philadelphia. Its non-restrictive counterpart 1n, on the other hand, adds the fact that the uncle lives in Philadelphia only as a bit of extra information.

Formal differences between the two kinds of clauses are as follows:

1.   non-restrictive relatives are set off by intonation breaks, indicated by commas in written English;
2.   most non-restrictive examples use *who/whom* or *which* (1n–4n), but the corresponding restrictives may alternatively use *that*, which is usually favored in colloquial forms (1r–4r);
3.   in some cases it is further possible to omit the relative pronoun altogether in restrictive use, namely when it is an object (2r, 4r) rather than a subject (1r, 3r) in a relative clause.

Table 14.5   Some examples of corresponding restrictive and non-restrictive relative clauses in English noun phrases

---

1r.   *my uncle who lives in Philadelphia* ∼ *my uncle that lives in Philadelphia*
1n.   *my uncle, who lives in Philadelphia*
2r.   *the city which I visited last summer* ∼ *the city that I visited last summer* ∼ *the city I visited last summer*
2n.   *the city, which I visited last summer*
3r.   *those employees who receive regular paychecks* ∼ *those employees that receive regular paychecks*
3n.   *those employees, who receive regular paychecks*
4r.   *the new sofa which we bought last year* ∼ *the new sofa that we bought last year* ∼ *the new sofa we bought last year*
4n.   *the new sofa, which we bought last year*
5r.   *my aunt whose son teaches physics*
5n.   *my aunt, whose son teaches physics*

Another important function for subordinate clauses can be described as adverbial, as illustrated in the examples in Table 14.6. These examples fall into five different types, as indicated by the labeling of the various sections. The functions of the first three have been discussed in previous chapters, and it is easy to think of single words or non-clausal structures that could occur in the same function, such as *there* for Locational, *now* for Temporal, or *like this* for Manner. Of the other two, Reason should be fairly obvious, and it is a function that can alternatively be expressed by a prepositional phrase, like *on account of their problems.* Concessives suggest information that seems to run contrary to what is reported in the main clause. They can also sometimes be expressed by a prepositional phrase, as in *despite the difficulties,* or *regardless of the dire consequences.*

Table 14.6   Some examples of adverbial subordinate clauses in English

---

LOCATIONAL
1.   *I expect to stay **where you are**.*
2.   *She followed **wherever they went**.*

TEMPORAL
3.   *I left the party **just after she arrived**.*
4.   *Let's get the job done **before the boss gets back**.*
5.   *I was still working **when she got in**.*
6.   *We'll be glad to leave **whenever you give the order**.*
7.   *We were getting some rest **while they prepared dinner**.*
8.   *Phone me **as soon as you get the information**.*

MANNER
9.   *We will design them **exactly as you want**.*
10.   *She does beautiful work **just like her mother always did**.*

REASON
11.   *They decided to stay at home **because it was so cold**.*
12.   ***Since he is so difficult to work with**, I decided against taking the job.*
13.   ***Inasmuch as the room wasn't ready for us**, we decided not to stay there.*

CONCESSIVE
14.   ***Although he enjoys gambling**, he passed up the trip to Las Vegas.*
15.   *I decided to accept the report, **even though I was not completely happy**.*
16.   ***While they seemed to be calm**, we could sense an underlying tension.*

The internal structure of these various subordinate clauses varies, in that it is sometimes more comparable to that of relative clauses, and in other cases it is more like the simpler Relator-Axis structure seen in nominal clauses, as in Tables 14.1–4. The simpler structure is seen in the examples of manner, reason, and concessive clauses, which have subordinating conjunctions as Relators in combination with a declarative clause in the role of Axis. The structure of the Locational and Temporal examples, on the other hand, is sometimes more like what we see in relative clauses.

This is true for both of the Locational examples given, in that *where* and *wherever* can be seen as subordinating conjunctions further indicating that location is involved. Among the temporal examples, those with *when* and *whenever* are exactly parallel, but others, like *before, after*, and *while*, are more similar to prepositions. Their meaning includes an element of anteriority (*before*), posteriority (*after*), or simultaneity (*while*) in addition to the more general idea of reference to time. Similarly, *as soon as* may be considered a compound temporal subordinating conjunction, indicating that the event reported in the main clause directly followed that in the subordinate clause.

Yet another kind of common subordinate clause usage in English is shown in the data of Table 14.7. The Objects in items 1–9 and the Subjects in items 10–18 all have forms reminiscent of English supplement ("wh") questions and of some relative clauses. Those examples using forms of *who* (5, 9, 15, 18), however, are the only ones that could also be used as relatives. Most would also have to be altered in one or more ways to be used as simple supplement questions. The only exceptions are those with *who* (5, 15) or *what* (8, 13) as their Subject. To be questions, the others would need a different word order, and in most cases a form of the auxiliary *do* would have to be introduced.

Table 14.7 Examples of *"wh"* clauses as Objects and Subjects

---

1. *Do you know **what they did?***
2. *I wonder **how they accomplished the feat**.*
3. *They're not sure **when their friends will get here**.*
4. *We have decided **where we are going**.*
5. *I told you **who was coming**.*
6. *He knows **why they made the decision**.*
7. *She doesn't know **which course they will take**.*
8. *I can't quite imagine **what happened**.*
9. *Do you remember **who[m] you saw?***
10. ***Where John vacationed** amazed us.*
11. ***Why they did it** is a real mystery.*
12. ***What she bought** was a real surprise.*
13. ***What attacked us** is not yet known.*
14. ***When we will leave** is still uncertain.*
15. ***Who will be coming** is not clear.*
16. ***How he did it so quickly** left us baffled.*
17. ***Which route we will use** is still being debated.*
18. ***Who[m] she will support** will be announced tomorrow.*

One more kind of subordination involves the use of special verb forms in some kinds of subordinate clauses. This is not particularly common in English, but can be found more often in some other languages. The best examples in a form of English still regarded as standard can be seen in the data of Table 14.8. These examples are very much like the Object clauses seen earlier in Table 14.1, but with one important exception: the verbs in these examples do not seem to show the expected agreement with the third-person singular Subjects of these clauses. The reason for this is that these examples show the one remaining remnant of the PRESENT SUBJUNCTIVE mood in standard English, though there are many younger speakers of otherwise standard English who avoid even that remnant. We can see the difference outside the third-person singular only if the verb *to be* is involved, and the use of *be* in all persons and numbers here differentiates this subjunctive from the ordinary suffixless present indicative. Some verbs, such as *insist*, can occur with either kind of *that*-clause, with a difference of meaning. Such a contrast can be seen by comparing item no. 4 in Table 14.1 with item no. 1 here. In the former example, *insist* means something like FIRMLY ASSERT THAT, while in the latter example the meaning is rather FIRMLY REQUIRE THAT.

Table 14.8   Examples of subjunctive *that*-clauses as Objects with verbs of suggestion, requirement and the like

 1. *She insisted **that Irma speak French with them**.*
 2. *I demand **that Zach work hard**.*
 3. *They require **that everybody tell the truth**.*
 4. *They stipulated **that the servant arrive before 8 am**.*
 5. *He ordered **that she complete the work by noon**.*
 6. *We urge **that you be patient**.*
 7. *The doctor prescribed **that she take the medicine every morning**.*
 8. *We suggested **that she come to live with us**.*
 9. *He advised **that Marcus work with our group**.*
10. *They directed **that Julie deliver all the packages**.*
11. *I must ask **that everyone be quiet**.*
12. *Did you request **that the butler wake us by 7 am?***

In a formal treatment of these examples, it is appropriate to attribute the mood difference to government by verbs of different classes. So the verbs seen in Table 14.1 would require the indicative mood, while those here would require the subjunctive. These kinds of things are much more frequent in some European languages, including French, Spanish, German and various Slavic languages. It can be formalized as sketched in Figure 14.2.

Clausoids in English: infinitive, participial, and gerund phrases

In addition to subordinate clauses of the various kinds discussed above, English has some other constructions that are often similar to them in function or meaning, but differ from them in form. One of these is traditionally termed an **INFINITIVE PHRASE**, and is illustrated in the data of Table 14.9.

Table 14.9   Examples of infinitive phrases in English

 1. *Would you like **me to show you my collection?***
 2. *They prefer **us to come after dinner**.*
 3. *I require **the servants to remain silent during our meals**.*
 4. *Susan asked **everyone to suggest a gift**.*
 5. *You expect **John to come into the city tomorrow**.*
 6. *Arthur just loved **to go fishing during the summer months**.*
 7. *I would hate **to go out on a night like this**.*
 8. *We want **to visit Philadelphia**.*
 9. *They all plan **to visit you next year**.*
10. *She has **to take her husband to the airport tomorrow**.*

Another kind of phrase that can, like these infinitive phrases, be used in various noun-like functions, such as Subject and Direct Object, is the **GERUND PHRASE**, as illustrated in Table 14.10. Examples 1–5 are functioning as Subjects, while 6–10 are Direct Objects and 11–15 are

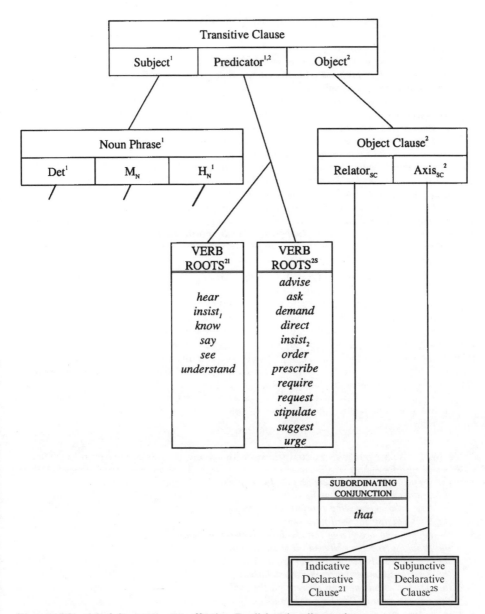

Figure 14.2   Modal government affecting English subordinate clauses

Axes in prepositional phrases. The verb form in *-ing* is used to indicate this function, which amounts to a verbal noun. While this form may occur alone, it is often accompanied by expressions that can be related to other clause functions beyond the Predicator. These include Direct Objects (e.g. *the newspaper* in no. 2, *math* in no. 3), Temporals (e.g. *during breakfast* in no. 2), and Locationals (e.g. *in high school* in no. 3, *in the ocean* in no. 9). In items 2, 4, 8, and 10–12 there is also an expression corresponding to the Subject, expressed by a possessive. These differ from Subjects in ordinary clauses in the way they are expressed, as well as in the fact that they are not obligatorily expressed.

Table 14.10   Examples of gerund phrases in English

1. ***Working for that guy*** *is no picnic!*
2. ***His reading the newspaper during breakfast*** *bothers his wife.*
3. ***Teaching math in high school*** *is my career aim.*
4. ***John's hunting moose*** *surprised us all.*
5. ***Singing in the shower*** *is the extent of his musical talent.*
6. *Tom would not suggest* ***abandoning the effort right away.***
7. *I would prefer* ***working for someone more friendly and considerate.***
8. *Did you like* ***her speaking her mind the way she did?***
9. *She really enjoys* ***swimming in the ocean.***
10. *I really cannot imagine* ***your wearing your hair so short.***
11. *I was upset about* ***her leaving so suddenly.***
12. *Can you object to* ***my holding another job?***
13. *We need to get away from* ***automatically opposing his ideas.***
14. *By* ***suggesting that course****, he redirected the discussion.*
15. *We would like to join you in* ***supporting the alternative plan.***

Two other functions of the English verb form in *-ing* are illustrated in Table 14.11, which compares the use of the form with an auxiliary verb in a relative clause with an essentially synonymous expression traditionally termed a **PRESENT-PARTICIPLE PHRASE**. These are like gerund phrases in the verb form they use, but are different in that they cannot include any expression corresponding to the Subject, which must necessarily be coreferrent with the Head of the noun phrase where they function. It should be noted that the corresponding relative clauses here have *who* as their Subjects, referring to the same person. Under the right circumstances, *that* or *which* may be used instead, but only if they are Subjects can we substitute a present-participle phrase. So we can have a gerund phrase such as *Her bringing them the milk* and we can speak of *The woman (who is) bringing them the milk,* but we cannot use a present-participle phrase to paraphrase *The people to whom she is bringing the milk.*

Table 14.11   Relative clauses in comparison with present-participle phrases in English

1. *the women* ***who are working in that factory*** ~
   the women ***working in that factory***
2. *the boys* ***who are playing football over there*** ~
   the boys ***playing football over there***
3. *the people* ***who are giving the children all those presents*** ~
   the people ***giving the children all those presents***
4. *those* ***who are always borrowing from their relatives*** ~
   those ***always borrowing from their relatives***
5. *the servant* ***who is putting flowers on the table*** ~
   the servant ***putting flowers on the table***

English does, however, have another phrase which can sometimes paraphrase relative clauses where the relative corresponds to an Object. This is the past-participle phrase, as illustrated in comparison with passive relative clauses in Table 14.12. In verb constructions in main clauses, the meaning of the past participle may be either active (as in *She has watered the garden*) or passive (as in *The garden was watered*), depending on whether the auxiliary *have* or *be* is used in most immediate relation to it. In such phrases as these here, however, it will always be passive, so that such a phrase as *The person injured in the fight* always speaks of someone who was injured, not someone doing the injuring.

Table 14.12 Passive relative clauses in comparison with past-participle phrases in English

1. *everyone **that was promised a fair hearing yesterday** ~*
    *everyone **promised a fair hearing yesterday***
2. *everything **that was given to the winners** ~*
    *everything **given to the winners***
3. *all the secretaries **that were trained by their agency** ~*
    *all the secretaries **trained by their agency***
4. *the dogs **which were groomed at their kennel** ~*
    *the dogs **groomed at their kennel***
5. *the slaves **who were tortured by the Romans** ~*
    *the slaves **tortured by the Romans***

In reference to pure morphology, it should be noted, modern English does not have a distinction between the present participle and the gerund, nor between an active and passive version of the past participle. So it would be a mistake to introduce different terms for them in a discussion of morphology. In syntax, on the other hand, we can and should distinguish the distinct functions and constructions involved by different labels. The English morphological "present participle" has essentially three functions: (1) occurrence with an auxiliary *be* in forming various progressive-aspect tense forms; (2) occurrence in gerund phrases, which have nominal functions; and (3) occurrence in present-participial phrases, which have adjunct functions. The past participle has no function corresponding to the gerund, but it still has three functions: (1) occurrence with an auxiliary *have* in forming various perfect aspect tense forms; (2) occurrence with an auxiliary *be* in forming passives; and (3) occurrence in past-participial phrases, where its meaning must be passive. These functions are illustrated by the examples in Table 14.13.

Table 14.13 Summary of the functions of the English morphological participles

	FORMS	
FUNCTIONAL TYPES	*PRESENT PARTICIPLE*	*PAST PARTICIPLE*
VERBAL		
ACTIVE	*They **were speaking** French.*	*They **had spoken** often.*
PASSIVE	————————————	*It **was spoken** there.*
NOMINAL		
(GERUND)	***Speaking frankly** was difficult.*	————————————
ADJUNCTIVE	*people **speaking French***	*languages **spoken here***

Grammarians disagree on how to classify the nominal and adjunctive constructions exemplified here, both those with participles and those with infinitives. The most traditional classification, as already suggested, considers the constructions in question to be phrases. A number of modern scholars, however, have been strongly influenced by the similarity of these constructions to full clauses, and the fact that they often have similar functions to relative clauses or other types of undoubted subordinate clauses. Based on this, they have departed from tradition and classified them as special types of subordinate clauses. The view adopted in this book takes something from both of these alternatives. It does not treat them as clauses in the full sense, but recognizes the kinship that they seem to share with true clauses by terming them CLAUSOIDAL PHRASES, or CLAUSOIDS. In English and many other languages, the difference between a clause and a clausoid is that a clause contains a FINITE VERB, that is a verb that can appear in an independent clause, one that can stand as a sentence by itself. In classical languages like Latin and Greek, a finite verb was defined as one that showed inflection for person and number. This definition also works for many other languages of Europe, but would have to be stretched considerably to apply to modern English, because only present indicatives of most verbs show any reflection of person and number, in the form of the special *-s* suffix on the third-person singular. We see person more fully reflected only in forms of *to be*, and comparison with these can perhaps be seen as justifying the use of this definition for the present and past tenses of other verbs.

Clausoids in other European languages

Other languages of the Indo-European family often show fuller and clearer evidence for clausoids than English does. One example is seen in the participial phrases illustrated in the Old Church Slavic data of Tables 14.14 and 14.15. Each example in these tables begins with a simple transitive clause; the indented examples below the clause are all noun phrases related to it, with Qualifiers manifested either by a relative clause or a participial phrase. The first and third phrases in each example involve relative clauses beginning with various forms of the Old Church Slavic relative pronoun /iže/ WHO/WHICH. The different forms assumed by

Table 14.14 Some Old Church Slavic present-tense clauses and participial paraphrases

1. žena xoštetŭ xlěbŭ	THE WOMAN WANTS THE BREAD.
žena jaže xoštetŭ xlěbŭ	THE WOMAN WHO WANTS THE BREAD
žena xotęšti xlěbŭ	THE WOMAN WANTING THE BREAD
xlěbŭ iže žena xoštetŭ	THE BREAD THAT THE WOMAN WANTS
xlěbŭ xoštěmŭ ženojǫ	THE BREAD BEING WANTED BY THE WOMAN
2. žena xoštetŭ rybǫ	THE WOMAN WANTS THE FISH.
žena jaže xoštetŭ rybǫ	THE WOMAN WHO WANTS THE FISH
žena xotęšti rybǫ	THE WOMAN WANTING THE FISH
ryba jǫže žena xoštetŭ	THE FISH THAT THE WOMAN WANTS
ryba xoštěma ženojǫ	THE FISH BEING WANTED BY THE WOMAN
3. žena xoštetŭ męso	THE WOMAN WANTS THE MEAT.
žena jaže xoštetŭ męso	THE WOMAN WHO WANTS THE MEAT
žena xotęšti męso	THE WOMAN WANTING THE MEAT
męso ježe žena xoštetŭ	THE MEAT THAT THE WOMAN WANTS
męso xoštěmo ženojǫ	THE MEAT BEING WANTED BY THE WOMAN
4. kŭnęʒĭ xoštetŭ xlěbŭ	THE PRINCE WANTS THE BREAD.
kŭnęʒĭ iže xoštetŭ xlěbŭ	THE PRINCE WHO WANTS THE BREAD
kŭnęʒĭ xotę xlěbŭ	THE PRINCE WANTING THE BREAD
xlebŭ iže kŭnęʒĭ xoštětŭ	THE BREAD THAT THE PRINCE WANTS
xlěbŭ xotěmŭ kŭnęʒemĭ	THE BREAD BEING WANTED BY THE PRINCE
5. kŭnęʒĭ xoštetŭ rybǫ	THE PRINCE WANTS THE FISH.
kŭnęʒĭ iže xoštetŭ rybǫ	THE PRINCE WHO WANTS THE FISH
kŭnęʒĭ xotę rybǫ	THE PRINCE WANTING THE FISH
ryba jǫže kŭnęʒĭ xoštetŭ	THE FISH THAT THE PRINCE WANTS
ryba xotěma kŭnęʒemĭ	THE FISH BEING WANTED BY THE PRINCE
6. kŭnęʒĭ xoštetŭ męso	THE PRINCE WANTS THE MEAT.
kŭnęʒĭ iže xoštetŭ męso	THE PRINCE WHO WANTS THE MEAT
kŭnęʒĭ xotę męso	THE PRINCE WANTING THE MEAT
męso ježe kŭnęʒĭ xoštetŭ	THE MEAT THAT THE PRINCE WANTS
męso xotěmo kŭnęʒemĭ	THE MEAT BEING WANTED BY THE PRINCE

this word reflect case and number. All the examples here are singular, but both dual and plural forms can also be found where appropriate. Turning to the second and fourth phrases, each of these paraphrases the phrase right above it, using a clausoid rather than a relative clause. In each case the first two phrases have the noun that serves as Subject of the corresponding independent clause as Head, while the other two are headed by the Direct Object noun. As suggested by the English glosses, the participles used in connection with the Subject nouns are active, while those used with the Object-nouns are passive. The difference between the examples in Tables 14.14 and 14.15 is a matter of tense, which, for the participial examples, can only be suggested in the glosses, because English does not have as full a complement of participles as this language does. Adjectives in this language are subject to inflection for three genders, three numbers, and seven cases, and they also have definite and indefinite forms. The four participles shown differ from one another in tense (past vs. present) and voice (active vs. passive), and each one can have 126 logically distinct inflectional forms. In addition, Old Church Slavic also had three other kinds of non-finite verbs, a verbal noun similar in function to the English gerund, an infinitive and another closely related form known as the SUPINE. Some examples of these are shown in Table 14.16. The examples in a involve the infinitive (in /ti/) as an Object with the verb /xoštetŭ/ WANTS. The b examples involve the supine (in /tŭ/), whose function is to indicate purpose after a verb of motion, here /pride/ CAME. The c examples are verbal-noun phrases (parallel to English gerund phrases), based on a verbal noun (in /nĭje/), with the Object expressed in the genitive case and the agent in the instrumental case.

Table 14.15   Some Old Church Slavic past-tense clauses and participial paraphrases

1a. žena xotě xlěbŭ — THE WOMAN WANTED THE BREAD.
  žena jaže xotě xlěbŭ — THE WOMAN THAT WANTED THE BREAD
  žena xotěvŭši xlěbŭ — THE WOMAN HAVING WANTED THE BREAD
  xlěbŭ iže žena xotě — THE BREAD THAT THE WOMAN WANTED
  xlěbŭ xotěnŭ ženojǫ — THE BREAD WANTED BY THE WOMAN

2a. žena xotě rybǫ — THE WOMAN WANTED THE FISH.
  žena jaže xotě rybǫ — THE WOMAN THAT WANTED THE FISH
  žena xotěvŭši rybǫ — THE WOMAN HAVING WANTED THE FISH
  ryba jǫže žena xotě — THE FISH THAT THE WOMAN WANTED
  ryba xotěna ženojǫ — THE FISH WANTED BY THE WOMAN

3a. žena xotě męso — THE WOMAN WANTED THE MEAT.
  žena jaže xotě męso — THE WOMAN THAT WANTED THE MEAT
  žena xotěvŭši męso — THE WOMAN HAVING WANTED THE MEAT
  męso ježe žena xotě — THE MEAT THAT THE WOMAN WANTED
  męso xotěno ženojǫ — THE MEAT WANTED BY THE WOMAN

4a. kŭnęʒĭ xotě xlěbŭ — THE PRINCE WANTED THE BREAD.
  kŭnęʒĭ iže xotě xlěbŭ — THE PRINCE THAT WANTED THE BREAD
  kŭnęʒĭ xotevŭ xlěbŭ — THE PRINCE HAVING WANTED THE BREAD
  xlěbŭ iže kŭnęʒĭ xotě — THE BREAD THAT THE PRINCE WANTED
  xlěbŭ xotěnŭ kŭnęʒemĭ — THE BREAD WANTED BY THE PRINCE

5a. kŭnęʒĭ xotě rybǫ — THE PRINCE WANTED THE FISH.
  kŭnęʒĭ iže xotě rybǫ — THE PRINCE THAT WANTED THE FISH
  kŭnęʒĭ xotěvŭ rybǫ — THE PRINCE HAVING WANTED THE FISH
  ryba jǫže kŭnęʒĭ xotě — THE FISH THAT THE PRINCE WANTED
  ryba xotěna kŭnęʒemĭ — THE FISH WANTED BY THE PRINCE

6a. kŭnęʒĭ xotě męso — THE PRINCE WANTED THE MEAT.
  kŭnęʒĭ iže xotě męso — THE PRINCE THAT WANTED THE MEAT
  kŭnęʒĭ xotěvŭ męso — THE PRINCE HAVING WANTED THE MEAT
  męso ježe kŭnęʒĭ xotě — THE MEAT THAT THE PRINCE WANTED
  męso xotěno kŭnęʒemĭ — THE MEAT WANTED BY THE PRINCE

Table 14.16 Non-participial clausoids (boldface) in Old Church Slavic

1.	petrŭ lovitŭ ryby	PETER CATCHES FISH.
1a.	petrŭ xoštetŭ **loviti ryby**	PETER WANTS TO CATCH FISH.
1b.	petrŭ pride **lovitŭ ryby**	PETER CAME TO CATCH FISH.
1c.	**lovljenĭje rybŭ petromĭ**	THE CATCHING OF FISH BY PETER
2.	děva čĭtetŭ bukŭvi	THE GIRL READS THE WRITINGS.
2a.	děva xoštetŭ **čisti bukŭvi**	THE GIRL WANTS TO READ THE WRITINGS.
2b.	děva pride **čistŭ bukŭvi**	THE GIRL CAME TO READ THE WRITINGS.
2c.	**čitenĭje bukŭvĭjĭ děvojǫ**	THE READING OF THE WRITINGS BY THE GIRL
3.	sǫdĭji rečetŭ istinǫ	THE JUDGE SPEAKS THE TRUTH.
3a.	sǫdĭji xoštetŭ **rešti istinǫ**	THE JUDGE WANTS TO SPEAK THE TRUTH.
3b.	sǫdĭji pride **reštĭ istinǫ**	THE JUDGE CAME TO SPEAK THE TRUTH.
3c.	**rečenĭje istiny sǫdĭjejǫ**	THE SPEAKING OF THE TRUTH BY THE JUDGE
4.	kŭnęʒĭ viditŭ plŭkŭ	THE PRINCE SEES THE REGIMENT.
4a.	kŭnęʒĭ xoštetu **viděti plŭkŭ**	THE PRINCE WANTS TO SEE THE REGIMENT.
4b.	kŭnęʒĭ pride **vidětŭ plŭkŭ**	THE PRINCE CAME TO SEE THE REGIMENT.
4c.	**viděnĭje plŭka kŭnęʒemĭ**	THE SEEING OF THE REGIMENT BY THE PRINCE

While both English and Old Church Slavic allow a choice between a subordinate clause and a clausoid in many situations, there are some languages that only use clausoids to translate English relative clauses, and can thus be said to lack relative clauses in the sense of the term adopted here. One such language is Turkish, as exemplified in the data of Table 14.17. Out of context, the forms *gelen* and *oynan* can best be translated as COMING and PLAYING, respectively, so the Subject of example 3 more literally means THE COMING MAN, and that of example 4 means THE PLAYING MAN. When there is an Object with the participle, as in examples 13–16, a literal translation of the subject would be THE CAT-SEEING MAN (13), or THE MAN-SEEING CAT (14). This material shows just a small sample of what can be done in this language, which has further participles and participial constructions to deal with different tenses and to handle different relations of the modified noun to the clausoid. Essentially, it illustrates a language where clausoids appear to take the place of genuine relative clauses.

Table 4.17 Examples of the use of present participles in Turkish

1.	*adam geliyor*	THE MAN IS COMING.
2.	*adam oynıyor*	THE MAN IS PLAYING.
3.	*gelen adam oynıyor*	THE MAN WHO IS COMING IS PLAYING.
4.	*oynan adam geliyor*	THE MAN WHO IS PLAYING IS COMING.
5.	*adam geldi*	THE MAN CAME.
6.	*adam oynadı*	THE MAN PLAYED.
7.	*gelen adam oynadı*	THE MAN WHO CAME PLAYED.
8.	*oynan adam geldi*	THE MAN WHO PLAYED CAME.
9.	*oynan çocuk geldi*	THE CHILD WHO PLAYED CAME.
10.	*gelen çocuk oynadı*	THE CHILD WHO CAME PLAYED.
11.	*adam kediyi gördü*	THE MAN SAW THE CAT.
12.	*kedi adamı görüyor*	THE CAT SEES THE MAN.
13.	*kediyi gören adam geldi*	THE MAN THAT SAW THE CAT CAME.
14.	*adamı gören kedi oynuyor*	THE CAT THAT SEES THE MAN IS PLAYING.
15.	*adam kediyi gören çocuğı gördü*	THE MAN SAW THE CHILD THAT SAW THE CAT.
16.	*çocuk adamı gören kediyi görüyor*	THE CHILD SEES THE CAT THAT SEES THE MAN.

Note: The above material is presented in Turkish orthography, which uses an undotted < i > (< ı >) for a high back unrounded vowel.

The non-universality of clausoids

While languages like English and Old Church Slavic have a clear distinction between subordinate clauses and clausoidal phrases, the same cannot be said of all languages. In these two languages, it is a part of the Indo-European heritage, and in languages of other families it may or may not occur. In languages such as Chinese and Thai, which have no verbal morphology, such a distinction would be out of the question. In other languages, as exemplified by the Turkish material just discussed, there may be clausoids which occur in place of subordinate clauses of at least some kinds rather than as alternatives to them. With respect to the Qualifier function in a noun phrase where we can find relative clauses in English, we can divide languages into those that use relative clauses only (Chinese), clausoidal phrases only (Turkish) and both (English, Old Church Slavic). Languages also differ with respect to the position of these adjuncts relative to the Head (compare the pre-head participial phrases of Turkish with their post-head counterparts in English), and with respect to the grammatical functions involved in the adjunct clauses or clausoids. This latter point can be illustrated with English data, as in Table 14.18.

Table 14.18   Roles associated with types of nominal qualifying clauses and participial clausoids in English

1.	*I see the dog* **that is biting Sally**. *I see the dog* **which is biting Sally**. *I see the dog* **biting Sally**.	SUBJECT (ACTIVE)
2.	*I see the woman* **[that] the dog bit**. *I see the woman* **whom the dog bit**. *I see the woman* **bitten by the dog**.	DIRECT OBJECT (PASSIVE)
3.	*I see the dog* **[that] the woman gave the toy to**. *I see the dog* **which the woman gave the toy to**. *I see the dog* **given the toy by the woman**.	INDIRECT OBJECT (PASSIVE)
4.	*I see the pony* **[that] Sally rode on**. *I see the pony* **which Sally rode on**. *I see the* pony **ridden on by Sally**.	$AXIS_{LOC}$ (PASSIVE)
5.	*I see the dog* **that our cat is bigger than**. *I see the dog* **which our cat is bigger than**.	$AXIS_{COMP}$
6.	*I see the lamb* **whose fleece is white as snow**.	POSSESSOR

Exercises

A. Interpretation problems

1. German principal and subordinate clauses

Answer the questions on the next page based on the following account of the structure of some German clauses.

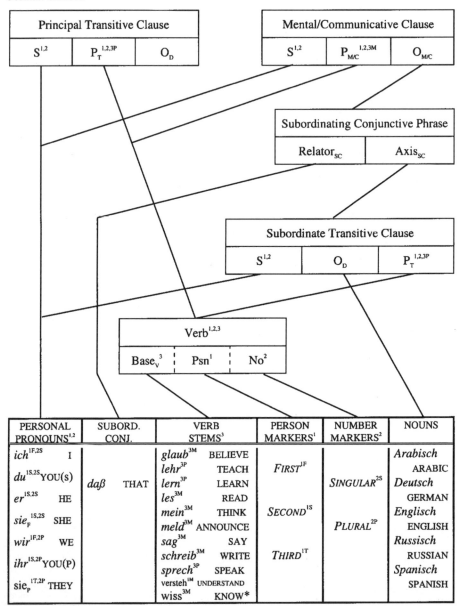

a. Show the edited versions of the German sentences with the following meanings:

1. YOU UNDERSTAND ENGLISH.

_____

2. I THINK THAT HE SPEAKS GERMAN.

_____

3. SHE BELIEVES THAT WE TEACH SPANISH.

_____

4. THEY KNOW THAT I AM LEARNING* RUSSIAN.

_____

*Note that this language makes no distinction between the simple present tense and the present-progressive.

b. Succinctly describe the difference of word order in German main and subordinate clauses based on this account.

2. Latin infinitive phrases in indirect speech

The diagram on page 304 provides for a use of infinitive phrases in Classical Latin. Use this account to answer the following questions. Assume the English past is translated via the Latin *PERFECT* and that any kind of English present (including the progressive) corresponds to the Latin *PRESENT*. English articles require no Latin translations, and the meaning of the English conjunction that is carried here by the Latin infinitive.

a. Show the edited versions of the Latin sentences with the following meanings:

1. THE POET WROTE THAT THE BOY IS RECITING.

_____

2. THE WOMAN BELIEVES THAT THE SOLDIER WORKED.

_____

3. THE SAILOR SAYS THAT THE FARMERS STAYED.

_____

4. THE LEADERS ARE DRINKING.

_____

b. Given the general translation of infinitives with "to" in English, can you suggest a more literal way of translating the Latin sentences produced for 1–3 into English?

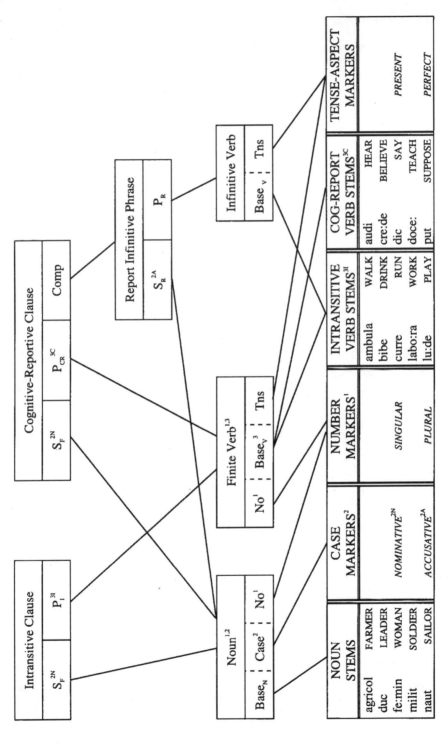

Use of infinitive phrases in Classical Latin

B. Analysis problems

1. Object clauses in colloquial Israeli Hebrew

Edit and account for the following data, which illustrates the expression of declarative object clauses in Hebrew.

1.	hem olxim habayta	THEY ARE GOING HOME.
2.	hu olex habayta	HE IS GOING HOME.
3.	hu ohev musika	HE LIKES MUSIC.
4.	hi ohevet matematika	SHE LIKES MATHEMATICS.
5.	hi yaševet po	SHE SITS HERE.
6.	hasefer nimca po	THE BOOK IS LOCATED HERE.
7.	habayit nimca karov	THE HOUSE IS LOCATED NEARBY.
8.	haxanut nimcet po	THE STORE IS LOCATED HERE.
9.	ha?universita nimcet karov	THE UNIVERSITY IS LOCATED NEARBY.
10.	raxel yaševet po	RACHEL IS SITTING HERE.
11.	dan yašev karov	DAN IS SITTING NEARBY.
12.	hi yoda?at šedan yašev karov	SHE KNOWS THAT DAN IS SITTING NEARBY.
13.	hu yode?a šeha?universita nimcet po	HE KNOWS THE UNIVERSITY IS LOCATED HERE.
14.	hem yod?im šehaxanut nimcet po	THEY KNOW THAT THE STORE IS LOCATED HERE.
15.	dan xošev šehem olxim habayta	DAN THINKS THAT THEY ARE GOING HOME.
16.	raxel xoševet šehu ohev musika	RACHEL THINKS THAT HE LIKES MUSIC.
17.	hem xoševim šeha?universita nimcet karov	THEY THINK THAT THE UNIVERSITY IS LOCATED NEARBY.
18.	hu ?omer šeraxel yaševet po	HE SAYS THAT RACHEL IS SITTING HERE.
19.	hi ?omeret šedan yašev karov	SHE SAYS THAT DAN IS SITTING NEARBY.
20.	dan ?omer šehabayit nimca karov	DAN SAYS THAT THE HOUSE IS LOCATED NEARBY.
21.	hem ?omerim šehaxanut nimcet po	THEY SAY THAT THE STORE IS LOCATED HERE.
22.	raxel ?omeret šedan xošev šehem olxim habayta	RACHEL SAYS THAT DAN THINKS THAT THEY ARE GOING HOME.
23.	dan xošev šeraxel yoda?at šehem ohevim matematika	DAN THINKS THAT RACHEL KNOWS THAT THEY LIKE MATHEMATICS.
24.	hem yod?im šedan xošev šehi olxet habayta	THEY KNOW THAT DAN THINKS THAT SHE IS GOING HOME.

2. Embedded questions in Russian

Prepare a syntactic account based on an edited version of the following data, which is designed to show how embedded questions equivalent to English "whether" clauses are expressed in Russian. All material is presented in a transliteration of the Cyrillic orthography.

1.	*On uezžaet.*	HE IS LEAVING.
2.	*Oni uezžajut.*	THEY ARE LEAVING.
3.	*Ona spit.*	SHE IS SLEEPING.
4.	*Oni spjat.*	THEY ARE SLEEPING.
5.	*On putešestvuet.*	HE IS TRAVELING.
6.	*Oni putešestvujut.*	THEY ARE TRAVELING.
7.	*Ona rabotaet.*	SHE IS WORKING.
8.	*Oni rabotajut.*	THEY ARE WORKING.
9.	*On boitsja.*	HE IS AFRAID.

10. *Oni bojatsja.*	THEY ARE AFRAID.
11. *Ona begaet.*	SHE IS RUNNING.
12. *Oni begajut.*	THEY ARE RUNNING.
13. *On znaet, spit li ona.*	HE KNOWS WHETHER SHE IS SLEEPING.
14. *Oni znajut, uezžaet li on.*	THEY KNOW WHETHER HE IS LEAVING.
15. *Ona sprašivaet, boitsja li on.*	SHE ASKS WHETHER HE IS AFRAID.
16. *Oni sprašivajut, putešestvuet li ona.*	THEY ASK WHETHER SHE IS TRAVELING.
17. *On obsuždaet, rabotajut li oni.*	HE IS DISCUSSING WHETHER THEY ARE WORKING.
18. *Oni obsuždajut, rabotaet li ona.*	THEY ARE DISCUSSING WHETHER SHE IS WORKING.
19. *Ona interesuetsja, begaet li on.*	SHE WONDERS WHETHER HE IS RUNNING.
20. *Oni interesujutsja, begaet li ona.*	THEY WONDER WHETHER SHE IS RUNNING.
21. *On sprašivaet, putešestvujut li oni.*	HE ASKS WHETHER THEY ARE TRAVELING.
22. *Oni sprašivajut, uezžaet li ona.*	THEY ASK WHETHER SHE IS LEAVING.
23. *Ona znaet, spjat li oni.*	SHE KNOWS WHERE THEY ARE SLEEPING.
24. *Oni znajut, spit li on.*	THEY KNOW WHETHER HE IS SLEEPING.

The following additional examples show further varities of embedded questions, with differences involving a kind of highlighting. Modify your initial solution to reflect these additional possibilities.

25. *Ona znaet, uezžaet li on segodnja*	SHE KNOWS WHETHER HE IS LEAVING TODAY.
26. *Oni znajut, on li uezžaet segodnja*	THEY KNOW WHETHER **HE** IS LEAVING TODAY.
27. *On sprašivaet, segodnja li on uezžaet*	HE ASKS WHETHER HE IS LEAVING **TODAY**.
28. *Oni sprašivajut, spit li ona sejčas*	THEY ASK WHETHER SHE IS SLEEPING RIGHT NOW.
29. *On obsuždaet, ona li spit sejčas*	HE IS DISCUSSING WHETHER SHE IS SLEEPING RIGHT NOW.
30. *Oni obsuždajut, sejčas li on spit*	THEY ARE DISCUSSING WHETHER HE IS SLEEPING **RIGHT NOW.**
31. *Ona znaet, on li spit sejčas*	SHE KNOWS WHETHER **HE** IS SLEEPING RIGHT NOW.
32. *Oni znajut, rabotaet li ona zdes'*	THEY KNOW WHETHER SHE IS WORKING HERE.
33. *On interesuetsja, zdes' li ona rabotaet*	HE WONDERS WHETHER SHE IS WORKING **HERE**.
34. *Oni interesujutsja, ona li rabotaet zdes'*	THEY WONDER WHETHER **SHE** IS WORKING HERE.

3. Subordination in Central Alaskan Yup'ik Eskimo

In some languages, the kind of subordination indicated by subordinating conjunctions in English may be indicated inflectionally, by the form of the verb. Yup'ik is a language of this sort, as illustrated by this data set. Although there are further types, all the examples used here function as expression of a Temporal function in the main clause. Special forms of the verb indicating BEFORE are said to be in the *PRECESSIVE* mood, those that indicate WHENEVER are in the *CONTINGENT* mood, those translated with WHILE are in the *DURATIVE-CONTEMPORA-TIVE*, and those meaning when are in the *PUNCTUAL-CONTEMPORATIVE*. Since tense distinctions are not reflected in the subordinate clauses given, it is most expedient to posit separate word-constructions for the principal and subordinated verbs.

1. niʁiɬχuuŋa	I ATE.
2. iʁmiɬχuuŋa	I WASHED MY FACE.
3. niʁiɬχuuŋa iʁmixpailiɣma	I ATE BEFORE I WASHED MY FACE.
4. caliɬχuutɨn	YOU WORKED.
5. iʁmiɬχuutɨn	YOU WASHED YOUR FACE.

6. caliɨ⁺χuutɨn ɨʁmixpailɨxpɨt   YOU WORKED BEFORE YOU WASHED YOUR FACE.
7. inaχtɨ⁺χuuq   HE/SHE LAY DOWN.
8. ɨʁmi⁺χuuq   HE/SHE WASHED HIS/HER FACE.
9. inaχtɨ⁺χuuq ɨʁmixpailɨɣmi   HE/SHE LAY DOWN BEFORE HE/SHE WASHED HIS/HER FACE.
10. inaχtɨ⁺χuuq ɨʁmixpailɨɣma   HE/SHE LAY DOWN BEFORE I WASHED MY FACE.
11. ɨʁmiuŋa   I WASH MY FACE.
12. ɨʁmiuŋa nɨʁʁaqama   I WASH MY FACE WHENEVER I EAT.
13. caliutɨn   YOU WORK.
14. ɨ⁺aɨχtuq   IT IS RAINING.
15. caliutɨn ɨ⁺aɨʁaqan   YOU WORK WHENEVER IT RAINS.
16. inaχtɨ⁺χuuq caliinanʁamni   HE LAY DOWN WHILE I WORKED.
17. ɨʁmi⁺χuutɨn qavainanʁani   YOU WASHED YOUR FACE WHILE HE WAS SLEEPING.
18. nɨʁɨ⁺χuuŋa qavainanʁapɨni   I ATE WHILE YOU WERE SLEEPING.
19. aya⁺χuuq   HE LEFT.
20. aya⁺χuuq caliinanʁani   HE LEFT WHILE YOU WERE WORKING.
21. qava⁺χuuŋa   I SLEPT.
22. qava⁺χuuŋa aya⁺χani   I SLEPT WHEN HE LEFT.
23. caliɨ⁺χuutɨn qava⁺ɨmni   YOU WORKED WHEN I SLEPT.
24. aya⁺χuuq qava⁺ɨχpɨni   HE LEFT WHEN YOU SLEPT.

4. Indicative vs. subjunctive clauses in Classical Latin

In Classical Latin, the indicative and subjunctive moods contrast in independent clauses, with the subjunctive indicating a wish, while in subordinate clauses, different conjunctions introducing the clause govern different moods. Account for the following data, which has all the verbs in the present tense. For purposes of this solution, the subordinate clauses can be treated as examples of a single construction manifesting an optional sentence-rank element labeled "Condition".

1. *dux dormit*   THE LEADER IS SLEEPING.
2. *rēx dormiat*   LET THE KING SLEEP.
3. *servī currunt*   THE SLAVES ARE RUNNING.
4. *servus curriat*   LET THE SLAVE RUN.
5. *servus currit*   THE SLAVE IS RUNNING.
6. *puerī dormiunt*   THE BOYS ARE SLEEPING.
7. *puer dormiat*   LET THE BOY SLEEP.
8. *puerī tacent*   THE BOYS ARE QUIET.
9. *puer tacet ut rēx dormiat*   THE BOY IS QUIET SO THAT THE KING SLEEPS.
10. *servus labōrat dum rēx dormit*   THE SLAVE IS WORKING WHILE THE KING SLEEPS.
11. *servī tacent nē magister audiat*   THE SLAVES ARE QUIET LEST THE MASTER HEAR.
12. *puer rīdet quod puella lūdit*   THE BOY LAUGHS BECAUSE THE GIRL PLAYS.
13. *puellae tacent nē puerī rīdeant*   THE GIRLS ARE QUIET LEST THE BOYS LAUGH.
14. *militēs taceant quod dux dormit*   LET THE SOLDIERS BE QUIET, BECAUSE THE LEADER IS SLEEPING.
15. *miles labōret dum ducēs lūdunt*   LET THE SOLDIER WORK WHILE THE LEADERS PLAY.
16. *puellae lūdunt ut rēgēs rīdeant*   THE GIRLS ARE PLAYING SO THAT THE KINGS LAUGH.
17. *militēs dormiunt quod populus tacet*   THE SOLDIERS ARE SLEEPING BECAUSE THE POPULATION IS QUIET.
18. *servī rīdeant dum populus lūdit*   LET THE SLAVES LAUGH WHILE THE POPULATION IS PLAYING.
19. *puerī taceant nē militēs audiant*   LET THE BOYS BE QUIET LEST THE SOLDIERS HEAR.
20. *magistrī dormiant quod servī tacent*   LET THE MASTERS SLEEP BECAUSE THE SLAVES ARE QUIET.

5. Japanese relative clause

Prepare an account of the following material, which illustrates two types of principal clause and one variety of relative clause in Japanese. Only the verbs will require editing. It should be noted that one tense (we may term it the "non-past") can express either present or future time, according to context. Account for the edited data and briefly explain the difference between the relative clauses of Japanese and their English counterparts.

1a. hon wa koko ni aru	THE BOOK IS HERE.
1b. watasi wa hon o yonda	I READ THE BOOK (*PAST*).
1c. watasi no yonda hon wa koko ni aru	THE BOOK I READ IS HERE.
2a. hoteru wa asoko ni atta	THE HOTEL WAS OVER THERE.
2b. anata wa hoteru o katta	YOU BOUGHT THE HOTEL.
2c. anata no katta hoteru wa asoko ni atta	THE HOTEL YOU BOUGHT WAS OVER THERE.
3a. resutoran wa soko ni atta	THE RESTAURANT WAS THERE.
3b. kare wa resutoran o miru	HE SEES A RESTAURANT.
3c. kare no miru resutoran wa soko ni atta	THE RESTAURANT HE SEES WAS THERE.
4a. kimono wa soko ni aru	THE KIMONO IS THERE.
4b. watasi wa kimono o kau	I (WILL) BUY THE KIMONO.
4c. watasi no kau kimono wa soko ni aru	THE KIMONO I (WILL) BUY IS THERE.
5a. biiru wa asoko ni aru	THE BEER IS OVER THERE.
5b. kare wa biiru o konomu	HE LIKES THE BEER.
5c. kare no konomu biiru wa asoko ni aru	THE BEER HE LIKES IS OVER THERE.
6a. mise wa koko ni atta	THE SHOP WAS HERE.
6b. anata wa mise o kononda	YOU LIKED THE SHOP.
6c. anata no kononda mise wa koko ni atta	THE SHOP YOU LIKED WAS HERE.
7a. hon wa asoko ni atta	THE BOOK WAS OVER THERE.
7b. watasi wa hon o kaita	I WROTE THE BOOK.
7c. watasi no kaita hon wa asoko ni atta	THE BOOK I WROTE WAS OVER THERE.
8a. sinbun wa soko ni aru	THE NEWSPAPER IS THERE.
8b. kare wa sinbun o yomu	HE READS THE NEWSPAPER.
8c. kare no yomu sinbun wa soko ni aru	THE NEWSPAPER HE READS IS THERE.
9a. sukiyaki wa koko ni atta	THE SUKIYAKI WAS HERE.
9b. watasi wa sukiyaki o taberu	I WILL EAT THE SUKIYAKI.
9c. watasi no taberu sukiyaki wa koko ni atta	THE SUKIYAKI I WILL EAT WAS HERE.
10a. kimono wa asoko ni atta	THE KIMONO WAS OVER THERE.
10b. anata wa kimono o aratta	YOU WASHED THE KIIMONO.
10c. anata no aratta kimono wa asoko ni atta	THE KIMONO YOU WASHED WAS OVER THERE.

Terminology

CLAUSOIDAL PHRASE	SUBJECT CLAUSE
GERUND PHRASE	SUBORDINATE CLAUSE
	CONCESSIVE
INFINITIVE PHRASE	LOCATIONAL
	MANNER
OBJECT CLAUSE	REASON
	TEMPORAL
PARTICIPIAL PHRASE	
	SUBORDINATING CONJUNCTIVE
RELATIVE CLAUSE	PHRASE
NON-RESTRICTIVE	
RESTRICTIVE	SUPINE

15

Syntax and semology

Examples of semological effects on syntax

In the very first chapter of this book, a model was presented (Figure 1.1) which depicted the relationships between syntax proper and adjacent areas of linguistic structure, especially morphology and semology. Since we have to deal directly with aspects of morphology as a preliminary to syntactic analysis, at least in most languages, its treatment via editing was presented in detail in Chapter 2, and has generally been assumed since then.

Up to this point, there has been only occasional reference to the phenomena of semology. One thing that has been left implicit, however, is that the syntax does not have to rule out anomalies based on meaning rather than grammar. Consider, for example, the English data of Table 15.1. The nouns in these examples are either proper names or abstractions, though some could be either. (Consistent capitalization is used for all examples so that the proper-vs.-abstract nature of a given example will be no clearer in writing than in speech.) In the first group, items 1 and 2, clear proper names are used for both Subject and Object with the verb *ADMIRE*. Examples 3 and 4 show that abstractions can equally well function as Objects of this verb. Then in 5 and 6, nouns usually used for abstractions are used as Subjects, and the nature of this verb forces the interpretation that *HOPE* and *CHARITY* are the names of people, and indeed there is a tradition of using nouns designating certain virtuous qualities as the names of women in particular. So we cannot understand *HOPE* and *CHARITY* as abstract nouns and make any sense out of these examples. Moving on to 7 and 8, these can be seen as ambiguous between a reading in which the Object nouns indicate qualities or people, since *FAITH* and *CHASTITY* can also be used as names. Then in 9 and 10 we have a case where the Subject nouns must be understood to name people rather than qualities. Finally, the last four examples would seem anomalous under normal circumstances, because the nouns in

Table 15.1 Various English examples with the verb ADMIRE

---

 1. *JANE ADMIRES REGGIE*
 2. *REGGIE ADMIRES JANE*
 3. *REGGIE ADMIRES SINCERITY*
 4. *JANE ADMIRES DEPRAVITY*
 5. *HOPE ADMIRES JANE*
 6. *CHARITY ADMIRES REGGIE*
 7. *REGGIE ADMIRES FAITH*
 8. *JANE ADMIRES CHASTITY*
 9. *FAITH ADMIRES OBESITY*
10. *CHASTITY ADMIRES HONESTY*
11. *HONESTY ADMIRES OBESITY*
12. *SINCERITY ADMIRES DEPRAVITY*
13. *DEPRAVITY ADMIRES JANE*
14. *OBESITY ADMIRES REGGIE*

Subject position would not normally be used to name people or other personifiable beings, and it is in the nature of the verb *ADMIRE* that it requires such an entity as its Subject. Of these, 11 and 12 would be easier to construe, because the subject-nouns indicate positive qualities which one might use for names, while the last two are even more difficult, since negative qualities are highly unlikely to be used as names.

The point about these and many other examples that could be given is that syntax should not be seen as having any responsibility for ruling out anomalies like those in 11–14. The ill-formedness of these is not a matter of syntax at all, but of semology. So our syntactic description should equally permit all of these examples, and only the semology should be sensitive to the fact that some verbs require certain meaning-based properties to be associated with the Subject and/or Objects. Table 15.2 provides some further examples of semologically based ill-formedness. In examples 1–6 the anomaly concerned is centered on the semological incompatibility of the Subject with the verb, while in others it is the Object that is incompatible with the verb. (These differences are highlighted by the use of boldface.) The third column provides an explanation for each of the particular anomalies.

Table 15.2 Examples of semologically anomalous grammatical sentences in English

1.	*Their **unreliability swam** in the river.*	ABSTRACTIONS CANNOT SWIM
2.	*My **astonishment fell** into the well.*	ABSTRACTIONS CANNOT FALL
3.	*Mary's **dog** will **explain** everything.*	NON-RATIONAL ANIMALS CANNOT EXPLAIN
4.	*The **goldfish conversed** with the farmers.*	NON-HUMANS CANNOT CONVERSE
5.	*Their **water supply burned** to a crisp.*	LIQUIDS DO NOT BURN
6.	*Our **wooden bookcase melted** in the heat.*	WOODEN OBJECTS DO NOT MELT
7.	*The children **amused** our **honesty**.*	ABSTRACTIONS CANNOT BE AMUSED
8.	*It all **amazed** their **hatred**.*	ABSTRACTIONS CANNOT BE AMAZED
9.	*We need to **entertain** the **oak tree**.*	INANIMATES CANNOT BE ENTERTAINED
10.	*The bad news **shocked** those **cucumbers**.*	INANIMATES CANNOT BE SHOCKED
11.	*They will **insert amazement** into the bread.*	ABSTRACTIONS CANNOT BE INSERTED
12.	*We **packed** the **atmosphere** in the bag.*	GASEOUS MATERIAL CANNOT BE PACKED

In the past, there were some linguists who in fact treated these anomalies as matters of ungrammaticality, but now it is generally recognized that the problems with them reside in the meaning structure, and have nothing to do with grammar. It should be noted, furthermore, that the expectations involved here are based on a "normal" universe of discourse, and there are some circumstances where one might expect to find them violated. One of the more obvious of these is in stories of science fiction and fantasy, where it is part of the expectation of the genre that norms of our ordinary world are often routinely violated. So many of these apparent violations might well be attested in the writings of one or more authors involved with these genres. To understand them, however, we normally require at least minimal preparation of our minds to accept the situations that would be described. In effect, our minds have to be made to switch from the normal universe of everyday experience to a special universe of discourse where such violations of normal expectations can be found. Some similar violations may also be found in the realm of poetic imagery.

Another kind of semological relation to grammar is found when syntactically relevant classifications are rooted at least partly in semology. This is often seen in relation to systems of grammatical gender, for instance. It is certainly a mistake to view grammatical gender classifications as totally arbitrary, but, as mentioned earlier, it would also be a mistake to see them as necessarily reflecting cultural beliefs in any precise way. For example, most continental European languages have a system of two or more genders that have some basis in semology but also have arbitrary aspects. Typically, words referring to persons and higher animals will show natural gender, in European languages being assigned to the masculine or feminine gender according to the sex of their referents. But then the remaining nouns are assigned to the masculine, feminine, and sometimes neuter genders in a way that has little, if

Table 15.3 Examples of gender assignment in languages with traditional two- and three-gender systems

	French	Hebrew	German	Russian
HOUSE	*maison* FEM	bayít MASC	*Haus* NEUTER	*dom* MASC
SUN	*soleil* MASC	šémeš FEM	*Sonne* FEM	*solnce* NEUT
WINDOW	*fenêtre* FEM	xalón MASC	*Fenster* NEUT	*okno* NEUT
ROOF	*toit* MASC	gag MASC	*Dach* NEUT	*kryša* FEM
SEA	*mer* FEM	yam MASC	*See* FEM	*more* NEUT
MEAT	*viande* FEM	basar MASC	*Fleisch* NEUT	*mjaso* NEUT
SALT	*sel* MASC	mélax MASC	*Salz* NEUT	*sol'* FEM
BOOK	*livre* MASC	séfer MASC	*Buch* NEUT	*kniga* FEM
LIGHT	*lumière* FEM	ʔor MASC	*Licht* NEUT	*cvet* MASC
MILK	*lait* MASC	xalav MASC	*Milch* FEM	*moloko* NEUT
EYE	*œil* MASC	ʔáyin FEM	*Auge* NEUT	*glaz* MASC
ROOM	*chambre* FEM	xéder MASC	*Zimmer* NEUT	*komnata* FEM

anything, to do with their meanings. Consider, for instance, the data in Table 15.3, which illustrates the distribution of genders for nouns referring to a few commonly found objects in four languages. In two of these, French and Hebrew, there are just two genders, called Masculine and Feminine, based on the typical assignment of nouns referring to males and females. In the other two, German and Russian, there is also a Neuter gender, so called because its nouns almost all refer to inanimate objects.

While there are often historical and cultural explanations for these gender assignments, it is a misunderstanding to think that speakers of French, for example, believe that books, knives and feet are somehow "male" because the words belong to the masculine gender, while houses, hands, and forks are somehow "female". We need to make a distinction between semological categories like male/female and grammatical genders. At the same time, there are in every known gender system *some* correlations between particular semological categories and gender assignments, but typically there are also factors of a morphological and arbitrary nature which are involved in the overall question of grammatical genders.

Agnation and semology

Another area where semology relates to syntax involves situations where syntactically distinct constructions nevertheless share a great deal of their meaning, typically referring to the same state or event in different ways. Many such cases were the subject of preceding chapters in this book. Examples are actives and corresponding passives (Chapter 11), affirmatives and corresponding negatives (Chapter 9), statements and corresponding questions, particularly polarity questions (Chapter 13), and relations between independent clauses and corresponding subordinate clauses and/or clausoidal phrases (Chapter 14). In the view of many specialists in syntax, it is part of the aim of syntax to provide an account (and possibly an explanation) for these kinds of relations. In the view adopted here, it is understood that they must be accounted for in the overall linguistic model. The place to treat them, however, is not in the syntax proper, but rather in the relation of syntactic constructions to their semological counterparts.

As already mentioned in the discussion of highlighting in Chapter 11, Gleason suggested the term AGNATE to cover syntactic constructions that share a core of meaning while differing in other ways. Besides applying to matters like the relation between an active and a corresponding passive, the notion of AGNATION can also be used to relate affirmative vs. negative versions of the same assertion, corresponding questions and statements, and so on. Dealing with the relations between such structures involves identifying a common core in their meaning while pointing out the additional differences in their meanings that still exist. Typically, agnate structures show greater differences in their syntax than in their semology, but details of this will generally vary from language to language. So for negation, we saw in Chapter 9 that some languages show very minor differences between corresponding affirmatives and negatives, while others show special syntactic constructions involving such phenomena as special auxiliary verbs and/or differences of constituent order. Similarly for polarity questions (Chapter 13), some languages simply mark the difference between these and statements by a different intonation, an inflectional distinction, or an extra interrogative word, while others show more complicated distinctions of order or other special properties. In all such cases, the semology of the corresponding agnate structures would be highly similar, but the syntax would often introduce additional complications, depending on the language.

In the history of twentieth-century linguistics, matters described here as involving agnation began to engage the attention of linguists in the 1950s. One group of linguists in that era proposed that linguistics accept a notion of "derivation", according to which simple affirmative statements as expressed in simple sentences constituted "kernel sentences" from which more complex types were produced via a set of operations called "transformations". This basic idea was refined and altered in many ways, but the Chomskyan school which grew out of this group continued to take pseudo-mathematical operations as fundamental ingredients of their model of language structure. The school represented by Gleason, in contrast, recognized the need to treat such relations, but saw them in terms of relation rather than operation. So rather than saying that questions derive from statements or negatives from affirmatives, they suggested that the relation between them is a matter of both connecting to a more abstract structure than syntax, the semology, where the organization of meanings is more fully reflected. The discussion of semology in this book follows the same approach, saying that various agnate structures share a common semological core. Their corresponding syntactic expressions may also differ only minimally, but in other cases we may find more complex differences involved in their syntax.

Markedness and semology

The distinctions between agnate structures often involve an element in semology which is present in one of the agnate structures but lacking in its counterpart. This is fairly clear in the case of negation, for instance, where the negative has an explicit negating element of meaning that is not present in its affirmative counterpart. An extra element present in this way is sometimes called a MARKED ELEMENT or MARK, and semological analysis often proceeds in such a way that as many differences as possible correspond to the presence or absence of such a marked element. In deciding what is marked and what, by virtue of lacking a mark, is termed UNMARKED, one is usually guided by considerations of meaning as well as formal expression. The unmarked situation is normally to be equated with the circumstance that occurs most commonly, and which is also seen as a kind of "default" situation. So typically a marked situation involves some kind of special circumstance. It may not be truly rare by any means, as grammatical negation certainly is not, but it is generally less frequent than its unmarked counterpart. This characterization seems to treat not only affirmatives as unmarked in contrast to negatives, but statements in contrast to either questions or commands, main clauses as opposed to subordinate clauses or clausoids. Indeed it could be extended much further into the realms more often expressed via morphology than via syntax.

Proponents of "operational" views of language sometimes argue that their methodology has a great advantage in being able to treat unmarked or default situations as lacking a special "operation" (for example "negativization" or "relativization") which is required for the more marked situations. Non-operational views such as the one sketched here, however, are able to handle such facts readily without positing such "operational" mechanisms. Alternative syntactic constructions related via agnation can, as appropriate, be ranked as to relative markedness, and a default choice can still be left as the one that would be entered in the absence of special circumstances.

Semological control of syntax

The essential assumption relating syntax with semology is that syntax normally operates under the control of the semology of the language. This means that the phrases, clauses, and sentences produced by the syntax will have to obey not only the constraints imposed by the syntactic description, but also those imposed by the semology. This allows the syntax to ignore semologically based restrictions and concentrate on those involving sequence, congruence, and determination.

With such an assumption we can, in fact, combine some syntactic patterns such as those for clause types discussed previously in terms of separate constructions. Consider, for instance, the six types of clauses first introduced for English in Table 6.1 and treated by the construction schemas in Figure 6.1. Although these have a good deal in common, we need to treat them as six separate types, as long as we assume that the syntax is not controlled by any more abstract factors. We can combine them into a single schema along the lines suggested in Figure 15.1, however, if we assume that the six types reflect different types of semological EVENT CLUSTERS rather than obeying restrictions specific to the syntax. These clusters are semological constructions that will account for necessary restrictions dealing with how many and what kinds of PARTICIPANT SEMEMES (the semological counterparts of grammatical Subjects and Objects – though the counterparts of nouns are appropriately termed ENTITY SEMEMES) occur obligatorily or optionally with different types of EVENT SEMEMES (the semological counterparts of typical verbs). If this matter is handled in the semology, a syntactic description under semological control will automatically reflect it, so that syntactic description can be correspondingly simplified. The semological subclassification for the event sememes reflected in Table 6.1 is summarized in Table 15.4. The primary names listed for each type are based on their semotactic properties, but the corresponding grammatical type for each is also listed in a contrasting typeface. It is better to use distinct terms for sememic and syntactic units. One reason for this is that they do not always correspond across the different levels. A simple example can be seen when passives are considered. So in English the semological role of ACTOR corresponds to an active Subject, but to a *by*-phrase when it is expressed in the passive. UNDERGOER and RECIPIENT will be expressed as Direct or Indirect Objects, respectively, in the active, but in a passive, one of them will be the grammatical Subject.

Verbal Clause			
Subject	Predicator	[Object$_i$]	[Object$_D$]

Figure 15.1   A generalized schema covering six English clause types

Syntactically discontinuous expressions of grammatical categories are another instance where semological control can simplify syntactic description and frequently allow data to be treated with fewer distinct syntactic constructions. For example, the discontinuous negation in French, as originally shown in Table 9.4, requires a degree of complication in the solution originally shown in Figure 9.4. If semological control makes it clear that the two negative markers are co-manifestations of the same negative sememic element, its solution can now be revised as shown in Figure 15.2, which makes both negative markers optional and relies on semology to disallow combinations with only one of the two negative words.

A somewhat more complex instance of the same thing is provided by the example of negation in Afrikaans, as originally shown in Table 9.5 and solved in Figure 9.5. Figure 15.3 shows a revised treatment of this material based on the assumption of semological control. This assumption allows us to dispense with the separate accounts of negation for present tense (with a simple verb) and non-present tenses (with an auxiliary combined with a verb inflected for a non-finite category). Here the obligatory verb is termed the "Finite". When the present tense is chosen, the verb occurs in this position. Otherwise there is an auxiliary verb in this

Table 15.4 Six types of event sememes reflected in the data of Table 6.1

Type	Examples	Undergoer?	Recipient?
Actor-only	*die*	NO	NO
	sleep		
INTRANSITIVE	*weep*		
± Undergoer	*unpack*	OPTIONAL	NO
	kill		
SEMI-TRANSITIVE	*wash*		
+ Undergoer	*time*	YES	NO
	seal		
TRANSITIVE	*damage*		
±(± Recipient	*sing*	OPTIONAL	OPTIONAL, but not
+ Undergoer)	*read*		without Undergoer
SEMI-BITRANSITIVE	*draw*		
± Recipient	*tell*	OPTIONAL	OPTIONAL
± Undergoer	*serve*		
PSEUDO-BITRANSITIVE	*write*		
± Recipient	*send*	YES	OPTIONAL
+ Undergoer	*bring*		
BITRANSITIVE	*cut*		

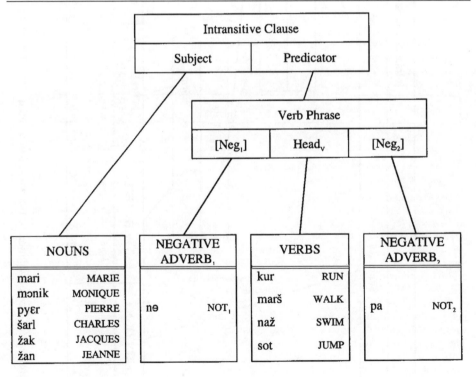

Figure 15.2 Revised solution to the French negation data

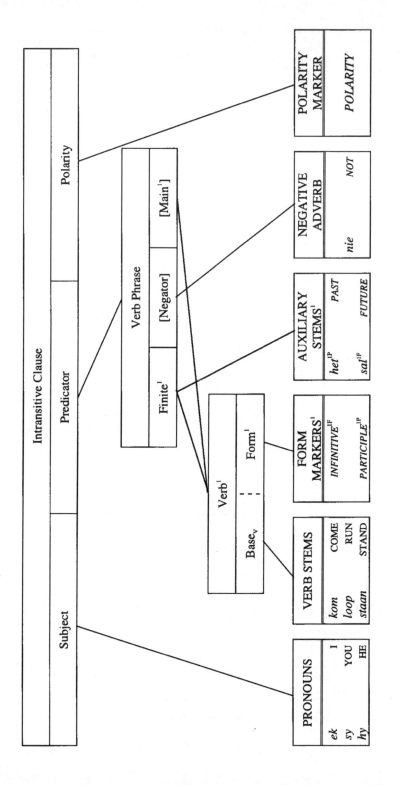

Figure 15.3 A revised solution to the Afrikaans negation data (Table 9.5)

position and the main verb occurs in the "Principal" position with an inflection appropriate to the tense chosen. Besides just the general assumption of semological control, this diagram includes an indication of precedence for the choices for "Finite". For this purpose, the alternative choices under the "Finite" function are connected one after the other rather than from a single point of origin. This means that an AUXILIARY occurs here if one is called for (by virtue of the selection of a non-present tense), but if none is called for one puts the main verb in this position. The main verb must occur in the "Principal" function when the "Finite" is occupied by an AUXILIARY. Semological control allows only one main verb, so this precludes the occurrence of such verbs in both positions, which would be possible when the syntax alone is considered.

English is characterized by many verb + adverb combinations like those in Table 15.5. Syntactically, the position of the adverb may vary in the presence of a nominal Object, but it can only follow a pronoun Object. It should be noted that items 1 and 2 are literal, in that the meaning of the combination involves the ordinary meaning of the verb with the ordinary meaning of the adverb. Items 3 and 4, however, are idiomatic because the meaning of the combination cannot be fully predicted from the meanings of the parts. In the tradition that allows "movement" as a part of syntactic description, these are commonly generated in the Predicator (verb) + Adjunct (adverb) + Object order, with obligatory "movement" of the adverb to a position following the pronominal Object and an optional "movement" in the case of a noun Object. In the approach used here, the syntactic facts can be handled with two alternative constructions, as illustrated in Figure 15.4. The constructions involved differ in (1) the order of Adjunct in relation to Object and (2) in the class of words/constructions that can appear as Objects. To deal with the synonymy of 1/1a, 2/2a, and so on, it is not necessary to derive one from the other, but only to relate them to an identical semological configuration.

In terms of semology, *put over* SUCCESSFULLY PROMOTED and *took in* DECEIVED should be regarded as unitary, since their meanings are not appropriately characterized in terms of the sum of the meanings of their parts. In the other examples, however, the adverbial particles show meanings that are simply added to the meanings of the verbs they combine with, with *in* meaning TOWARD THE INTERIOR, and *over* meaning VIA A PATH ACROSS SOMETHING.

The uses of various German verb forms provide another example of data that can be treated more readily when semological control of the syntactic system is assumed. The data in Table 15.6 is actually relatively simple, but it provides evidence for several syntactic characteristics related to declarative clauses in this language. For one thing, it provides

---

Table 15.5 English examples for the syntax of verb + particle combinations

1.	*John carried in the suitcase.*
1a.	*John carried the suitcase in.*
1b.	*John carried it in.*
1c.	**John carried in it.*
2.	*Elvira brought over the magazine.*
2a.	*Elvira brought the magazine over.*
2b.	*Elvira brought it over.*
2c.	**Elvira brought over it.*
3.	*The swindler took in his victims.*
3a.	*The swindler took his victims in.*
3b.	*The swindler took them in.*
3c.	**The swindler took in them.*
4.	*Jerry put over his ideas.*
4a.	*Jerry put his ideas over.*
4b.	*Jerry put them over.*
4c.	**Jerry put over them.*

Figure 15.4 Two constructions with English verbs and particles

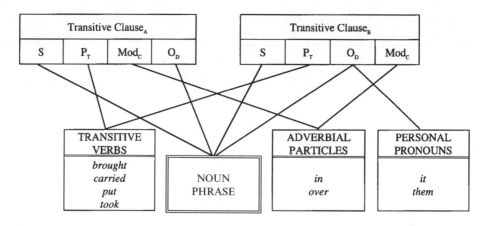

Table 15.6   Some clauses in modified German orthography

1. *Hans spricht das Wort aus.*	HANS PRONOUNCES THE WORD.
1a. *Hans wird das Wort aus sprechen.*	HANS WILL PRONOUNCE THE WORD.
2. *Anna sieht das Buch an.*	ANNA LOOKS AT THE BOOK.
2a. *Anna wird das Buch an sehen.*	ANNA WILL LOOK AT THE BOOK.
3. *Fritz hört die Musik zu.*	FRITZ LISTENS TO THE MUSIC.
3a. *Maria wird die Musik zu hören.*	MARIA WILL LISTEN TO THE MUSIC.
4. *Greta gibt den Brief auf.*	GRETA MAILS THE LETTER.
4a. *Wilhelm wird den Brief auf geben.*	WILLIAM WILL MAIL THE LETTER.
5. *Otto macht die Tür auf.*	OTTO OPENS THE DOOR.
5a. *Klara wird das Fenster auf machen.*	CLARA WILL OPEN THE WINDOW.
6. *Rosa gibt das Geld aus.*	ROSA SPENDS THE MONEY.
6a. *Heinz wird das Geld aus geben.*	HEINZ WILL SPEND THE MONEY.
7. *Fritz nimmt das Geld an.*	FRITZ ACCEPTS THE MONEY.
7a. *Greta wird das Geld an nehmen.*	GRETA WILL ACCEPT THE MONEY.
8. *Klara macht das Fenster zu.*	CLARA CLOSES THE WINDOW.
8a. *Otto wird die Tür zu machen.*	OTTO WILL CLOSE THE DOOR.
9. *Heinz sieht die Tür.*	HEINZ SEES THE DOOR.
9a. *Rosa wird das Geld sehen.*	ROSA WILL SEE THE MONEY.
10. *Hans nimmt das Hemd.*	HANS TAKES THE SHIRT.
10a. *Heidi wird das Kleid nehmen.*	HEIDI WILL TAKE THE DRESS.
11. *Heidi arbeitet.*	HEIDI IS WORKING/WORKS.
11a. *Fritz wird arbeiten.*	FRITZ WILL WORK.
12. *Ludwig läuft.*	LUDWIG RUNS/IS RUNNING.
12a. *Berthe wird laufen.*	BERTHA WILL RUN.
13. *Erika fährt ab.*	ERICA LEAVES/IS LEAVING.
13a. *Franz wird ab fahren.*	FRANZ WILL LEAVE.
14. *Max kommt an.*	MAX ARRIVES/IS ARRIVING.
14a. *Irene wird an kommen.*	IRENE WILL ARRIVE.

evidence of transitive verbs, taking Objects, versus intransitives without Objects, as in many other languages. Also there are two tenses shown, but their difference is not a simple matter of inflection. The presents are inflected (and actually show different persons and numbers not in evidence here), but for the future tense the auxiliary verb *wird* (also fully inflected for person and number) is used in combination with a different form of the verb, the infinitive. This infinitive, furthermore, regularly comes at the end of the clause, which is not necessarily right after the auxiliary. Finally, the transitive and intransitive verbs shown are sometimes simple, but in other cases there are adverbs (here *ab, an, auf, aus,* and *zu*), which make an essential contribution to the meaning of the whole. In the present-tense forms, these adverbs come at the end, after any Object that may be present, but in the future they still come after any possible Object but before the infinitive. In traditional German grammar, these adverbs are called "separable prefixes". (This nomenclature is related to the fact that they are traditionally written attached like prefixes to infinitives and other verbs they precede.)

If no control from semology is assumed, the treatment of this data could be seen as requiring eight distinct constructions to account for the differences involving the presence or absence of the auxiliary, presence or absence of Objects, and the occurrence or non-occurrence of an adverb. The essence of its arrangement could be captured, however, with a more generalized schema with two obligatory constituents and three others that occur or not, according to the type, as in Figure 15.5. This schema includes superscripts for Subject-Predicator concord in person and number, though evidence for this is not shown in this material.

Pseudo-Transitive Clause				
$S^{1,2}$	$P_F^{1,2}$	$[O_D]$	$[M_V]$	$[P_N]$

Figure 15.5 Generalized schema for some German clauses

By itself, however, this account, in combination with vocabulary we could extract from the data, would fail to deal with most of the details correctly. It would fail to distinguish precisely the types mentioned above as requiring distinct constructions. In addition, it would not restrict the verb + adverb combinations to those that actually occur, and would make it difficult to connect those that do show up to the meanings involved.

Suppose, however, that we assume that the semology tells us the following things about the event sememes related to various verbs:

1. Which ones occur with "Objects" (semological UNDERGOERS) and which do not.
2. Which combinations of verb and adverb occur with which meanings.

The specific information needed is given in Table 15.7. It will also be necessary to specify that the finite verb position will be manifested by the future auxiliary *wird* when this tense is required, but otherwise it will contain the main verb. The clause-final position will be filled by the infinitive of the main verb only under the former circumstances.

Table 15.7 Semological controls regarding event sememes in the German data

NO UNDERGOER		REQUIRES UNDERGOER	
ab ~ fahr	LEAVE	*an ~ hör*	LISTEN TO
an ~ komm	ARRIVE	*an ~ nehm*	ACCEPT
arbeit	WORK	*an ~ seh*	LOOK AT
komm	COME	*auf ~ geb*	MAIL
lauf	RUN	*auf ~ mach*	OPEN
		aus ~ geb	SPEND
		aus ~ sprech	PRONOUNCE
		nehm	TAKE
		seh	SEE
		zu ~ mach	CLOSE

These are just a few examples of how the syntax can be simplified if it is controlled by the semology. This view can be seen as a different interpretation of the facts which led many linguists starting in the 1950s and 1960s to insist that syntax ought to include "transformational" operations in addition to syntactic constructions. Their basic point was that the postulation of such operations allows more economical treatments of a whole range of phenomena. Implicit in such a view is that there is a level that is "deeper" or more abstract than the level of surface syntax. The viewpoint adopted in this book is that those linguists were partly right and partly wrong. They were right in insisting on the recognition of such a more abstract level, but their way of relating that level to the surface syntax is inappropriate. Rather than positing rules of derivation such as are found in some branches of mathematics, it is more appropriate to state relationships between levels more directly, as relationships between representations on different levels. This section has attempted to suggest a few ways in which this can be done.

Classifying semo-syntactic relations

One of the reasons that it is useful to think of a semology as existing as a separate level of language from syntax is that the two kinds of structure do not generally match up in an exact one-to-one manner. This concluding section of the chapter is intended to explore some of the basic kinds of difference that can be found between the meaning structure found in semology and the syntactic structure found in language as it is spoken. When we find that structures do not match perfectly, linguists viewing language in terms of the relation of different structural levels sometimes speak of a DISCREPANCY. Though this same term is also found in ordinary language, its linguistic use does not carry the implication that something is "wrong" the way the ordinary usage does. Rather, it just refers to a lack of one-to-one correspondence, which is very common as a part of the organization of language.

One very frequent discrepancy is called DIVERSIFICATION, which means that a semological unit can be manifested or realized in alternative ways in the same linguistic system. Simple lexical examples of this discrepancy are very common – take, for instance, English *little* and *small*, traditionally considered synonyms, which can be seen as alternative ways of saying the same thing, and thus as diversified realizations of a single semological unit or SEMEME. For a syntactic example, we can go back to the discussion of polarity questions in Chapter 13, where it was noted that languages often have alternative ways to signal that kind of question, such as using different element orders or differences of intonation, or a special word signaling a polarity question all by itself. Another excellent example of diversification involving syntax concerns the expression of approximate enumeration in modern Russian. Consider the following examples:

1.   *U nego pjat' karandašej*   HE HAS FIVE PENCILS
2a. *U nego karandašej pjat'*   HE HAS ABOUT FIVE PENCILS
2b. *U nego okolo pjati karandašej*   HE HAS ABOUT FIVE PENCILS

These examples all begin with the prepositional phrase *u nego*, literally meaning BY/AT HIM, which is an example of the standard expression of possession in Russian. In (1), one simply says *pjat'* FIVE and then *karandašej* PENCILS, much as in English except that the noun is inflected in the *GENITIVE PLURAL*. Examples (2a) and (2b) indicate two different ways of signaling the meaning that English expresses via the preposition *about*: in (2a) it is expressed by simply reversing the order of the noun and the numeral, but in (2b) the expression is more like what we find in English, with *okolo* being a preposition. The difference in form of the numeral involves the fact that this preposition governs the genitive case, and Russian numerals have case inflection, so *pjati* is simply the genitive of *pjat'*. In this situation, then, a sememe we can label APPROXIMATIVE is alternatively manifested by a preposition *okolo* or by a syntactic construction in which the numeral comes after the noun instead of before it.

Another frequent discrepancy comes when the same expression corresponds to alternative meanings. This is called SYNCRETIZATION. In simple lexical terms it can be seen as occurring both where traditional treatments speak of homonyms like *pail* BUCKET and *pale* LIGHT-COMPLEXIONED and where one speaks of a polysemous lexical item like *plain*, meaning UNADORNED in *a plain dress* but CLEAR in *the plain meaning*. (The traditional difference between polysemy and homonymy is usually more connected to spelling and/or history than to structural distinctness.) In syntax proper we can find this phenomenon when the same syntactic device can carry more than one alternative meaning. One example of this in English involves the meaning of the structure in which a finite verb is placed before the Subject either to signal a question, as in *Had she returned by noon?* or to indicate a hypothetical condition, as discussed in Chapter 12, seen in *Had she returned by noon, she would have phoned us*.

There are also many examples where neither conventional speech nor writing signals differences of meaning, and linguists have been interested in these as cases of ambiguity. Table 15.8 provides a few examples, many of them long-discussed. The type labeled "lexical" is essentially of the same kind as the *pail/pale* and *plain*, as mentioned above, though they are sometimes also discussed in terms of syntactic paraphrases. As suggested by the boldface representation, these ambiguities center on the prepositions. As displayed in Figure 15.6, *by* can indicate either agency or proximal location, *on* can refer to either location or subject-matter, and *of* can indicate either actor or undergoer (among other things).

Table 15.8 English sentences showing different sorts of ambiguities

---

LEXICAL AMBIGUITY
1. *The hobo was killed **by** the river.*
2. *We found a book **on** Long Island.*
3. *The shooting **of** the hunters was terrible.*

CONSTITUENCY AMBIGUITY
4. ***Old men and women** can stay at home.*
5. *Sally spotted the man **with a telescope**.*
6. *They **are hunting dogs**.*
7. *She enrolled at **Leland Stanford Junior University**.*
8. *They were studying **Dutch elm disease**.*

CONSTRUCTIONAL AMBIGUITY
9. ***Flying planes** can be dangerous.*
10. ***Visiting relatives** can be a nuisance.*

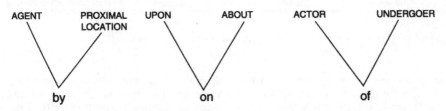

Figure 15.6 Lexical ambiguities as cases of semo-grammatical syncretization

The second type of ambiguity in Table 15.8 involves differences of constituent structure, so it is undoubtedly a syntactic matter. Example 4 is a classic, and its two interpretations are shown in Figure 15.7: it centers around whether one is coordinating complete noun phrases (*old men* with *women*) or just Heads (*men* with *women*). The ambiguity in example 5 centers around whether the phrase *with the telescope* refers to an accompaniment of the man who was spotted or to the means of spotting him. In the former case, it would be a noun phrase constituent, in the latter it would be a clause constituent indicating means. The ambiguity in example 6 centers around the function of *hunting*: this participle may have a verbal function as

(a)   Coordinate noun-phrase heads

old men and women			
old	men and women		
	men	and women	
		and	women
old	men	and	women

(b)   Coordinate noun phrases

old men and women			
old men		and women	
old	men	and	women
old	men	and	women

Figure 15.7   Alternative constituencies for *old men and women*

(a)   The official name of a world-renowned California university

Leland Stanford Junior University			
Leland Stanford Junior			University
Leland Stanford		Junior	
Leland	Stanford		
Leland	Stanford	Junior	University

(b)   The older name of a lesser-known college in Jacksonville, Florida

Edward Waters Junior College			
Edward Waters		Junior College	
Edward	Waters	Junior	College
Edward	Waters	Junior	College

Figure 15.8   Some institutional names with contrasting constituencies

Principal, leaving *dogs* to manifest the Object; alternatively, it may be a Modifier in a noun phrase with the Head *dogs*, such that the whole phrase serves as Complement in a copular clause. Figure 15.8 compares the correct constituency of example 7, with that for the former name of another institution in Jacksonville, Florida. *Leland Stanford Junior University* is the official full name of the California institution more usually called simply *Stanford University*. It was founded by Leland Stanford, Sr., a railroad magnate, California governor, and U.S. senator. He did not name it for himself, but in memory of his son Leland Stanford, Jr., who had died as a teenager. The word *Junior* thus belongs with *Leland Stanford*, and not with *University*. The correct constituency of the other institutional name, however, places *Junior* with *College*. (The term "junior college" is still familiar to many Americans, though it fell out of favor in the latter part of the twentieth century. In the case of public institutions, it has frequently been replaced with the term "community college". Edward Waters College still exists, but it dropped the "Junior" upon expanding to a four-year institution.)

The ambiguity seen in the last class of examples does not center around their constituency, but involves the syntactic function of the morphological participles. In the cases that can be paraphrased as *the flying of planes* and *paying visits to relatives*, we are dealing with gerund phrases with *planes* and *relatives* as their respective Objects. In the other understanding, the participles function as Modifiers and the nouns as Heads.

Another kind of discrepancy involves the manifestation of a single element of meaning by a combination of grammatical elements. This is termed COMPOSITE REALIZATION. We saw some examples of this in the discussion of negation in Chapter 9 (as well as in the previous section of this current chapter), as in standard French where separate words /nə/ and /pa/ combine to indicate negation. It is also possible to look at various situations of simple concord in this fashion, at least when there is a clear element of meaning that an inflectional category serves to manifest. So when there is number concord this means that the PLURAL sememe is (at least potentially) subject to multiple manifestation in the grammar, as in the Spanish phrase *los viejos abogados mexicanos* THE OLD MEXICAN LAWYERS, where each word is marked as plural by the terminal suffix *-s*. Another example is frequently found in the signaling of polarity questions by a combination of factors, as when it is signaled by both a special order and the selection of a rising intonation pattern.

We can also identify situations where a single grammatical element manifests more than one element of meaning in combination, in such a way that it makes no sense to break the expression down into different parts that manifest one or the other aspect of the meaning. This is called PORTMANTEAU REALIZATION. Again, it is not uncommon to find lexical examples of this. So in some cases where English has separate words for the female of animals we can identify a specific suffix that marks this, as with such words as *lioness*, *tigress*, and *leopardess*. The same suffix *-ess* occurs with the same female meaning in the names of some ranks of royalty and nobility: *empress, princess, duchess, countess*, and *baroness* and in more broadly occupational terms like *waitress* and *actress*. In both of these realms, however, there are other words that carry the same female meaning without any distinctive affix: *cow, mare, doe*, and *queen*, for instance. So with relation to semology, we can see the latter words as manifesting the FEMALE sememe along with a more general sememe for the animal type or rank/occupation involved. More purely syntactic examples of this phenomenon can be seen when we consider some of the highlighting phenomena discussed in Chapter 11. The grammatical passive in English, for instance, involves the FOCUS element in a portmanteau combination with either the marker of UNDERGOER (as in *Tom was slapped*) or of RECIPIENT (as in *Tom was given the prize*). This passive portmanteau can further be seen as involving composite realization, in that the focused element is Subject, the verb form is different, and the potential ACTOR is realized in a prepositional phrase with *by* as its Relator.

Some kinds of discrepancy involve an element on one level of abstraction corresponding to no element on an adjacent level. In morphology, for instance, linguists often posit a morpheme with overt manifestations under some circumstances but no manifestation at all in other cases. This phenomenon is called ZERO REALIZATION, and it is neatly illustrated by the lack of an overt suffix for the plural in such English words as *sheep* and *deer*, whereas most English plural nouns have a suffix. A fuller consideration of semology could reveal further elements that are sometimes overtly realized, but not always. In English, for instance, the accusative case of personal pronouns (e.g. *me, him, her, us, them*) can be seen as manifesting the role of either UNDERGOER or RECIPIENT, but with other nominals there is no overt difference to mark this.

It is also possible to find instances where a grammatical element is merely required by the grammar, and does not correspond to anything in the semology. Some governmental functions of cases, for instance, can be seen in this way, and the same is true of at least some instances of determination. The general name for this phenomenon is EMPTY REALIZATION: calling an element "empty" suggests that it does not contribute to the meaning. The Hebrew preposition marking definite objects, for instance, may be of this type. (It was illustrated in Exercise B.6 in Chapter 7.) It does not mark either definiteness or Direct Object status exclusively, but the grammar simply requires it to occur when these two things come together.

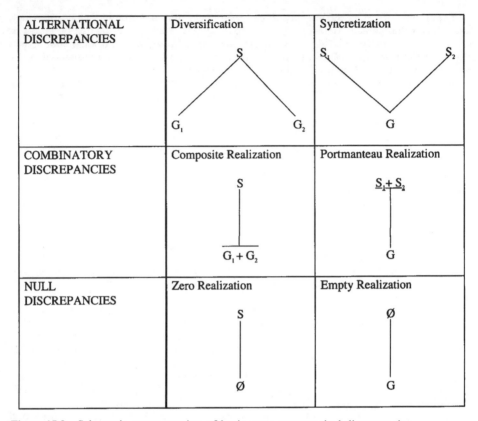

ALTERNATIONAL DISCREPANCIES	Diversification	Syncretization
COMBINATORY DISCREPANCIES	Composite Realization	Portmanteau Realization
NULL DISCREPANCIES	Zero Realization	Empty Realization

Figure 15.9   Schematic representation of basic semo-grammatical discrepancies

The six discrepancies discussed so far may be neatly represented diagramatically as shown in Figure 15.9. Here the letter S stands for "semological unit" and G for "grammatical unit". This diagram also shows a classification of the six discrepancies into three groups. Diversification and syncretization are grouped as ALTERNATIONAL DISCREPANCIES because both involve alternation, whether of sememes or grammatical units. Composite and portmanteau realization are called COMBINATORY DISCREPANCIES because combinations are regularly involved. And since null (zero) elements figure in both zero and empty realization, they are termed NULL DISCREPANCIES.

Another discrepancy that is sometimes found is a difference of ordering between elements of different levels. This can be termed ANATAXIS. Between semology and syntax as conceived here, the important kind of anataxis relates to the fact words are necessarily in some linear order in syntax, whereas it is not necessary to attribute any linear order to the sememes. So the imposition of a linear order down to the rank of the grammatical word is one of the most basic functions of a system of syntax. Semologically, we need to see certain associations between sememes, so in the example *Mary slapped Tom* from Chapter 10 the sememe for *Mary* will be associated with ACTOR, the sememe for *Tom* with UNDERGOER, and the event sememe *slap* will be associated with PAST TIME and related to the other elements, but it is the syntax that imposes a linear on the grammatical elements that realize these, and different languages may impose different orders, as we saw beginning in Chapter 1.

One other syntactically important kind of discrepancy has actually been implicit in much of the previous discussion in this section. It is involved in situations where a sememe is not realized by some particular word or morpheme, but rather as a direction to the syntax to select some particular construction that carries the meaning. A useful term for this phenomenon is SPECIFICATIONAL REALIZATION. We have seen examples of this in the use of particular constructions to signal polarity questions in many languages, and as an alternative way to signal hypothetical conditions in English or approximate enumeration in Russian. Prior examples have usually combined with diversification, but specificational realization can be recognized whether or not it combines with some other discrepancy, in the fact that the manifestation of a semological unit lies in the selection of a construction. The name comes from the fact that we can say the sememe **specifies** that selection.

Although these concepts have generally been illustrated here in terms of the relation between semology and grammar, usually syntax, they are in fact applicable as well, to one extent or another, to other areas of language, such as morphology and phonology.

Exercises

1. *Semological anomalies*

Explain the anomaly in each of the following grammatical English sentences, assuming a normal universe of discourse.

1. *We drank a porterhouse steak.*
2. *John will marry the old millpond.*
3. *The bookcase ate my ice cream.*
4. *Our goldfish will lecture on ichthyology.*
5. *John's cat flew up into the tree.*
6. *We will subsist on ridicule and hilarity.*
7. *Erma's sweater is broken.*
8. *The rosebush jumped across the road.*
9. *Their thoughts are either white or purple.*
10. *It was so cold I literally froze to death.*
11. *The table lamp was sleeping in a corner.*
12. *My car elapsed in Thursday.*

2. *Ambiguities in English*

Each of the following English sentences is ambiguous in one way or another. Explain each of the ambiguities as clearly as you can, providing paraphrases and indicating whether the ambiguity involves syntactic constituency or something else. For two of those which do show constituent ambiguity, show diagrams for the alternatives along the lines of Figures 15.7 and 15.8.

1. *The rabbits are ready to eat.*
2. *We met a Canadian bacon processor.*
3. *They are cooking apples.*
4. *They all can fish.*
5. *Those who saw the movie frequently praised it.*
6. *The idea that they studied is ridiculous.*
7. *Miriam told her daughter that she would have to go home at the end of the summer.*
8. *She defended the man she loved with all her heart.*
9. *Children who misbehave sometimes should be reprimanded.*
10. *Bill knew Peter and Tom knew Rob.*

3. *Verb tense in Tahitian*

In Polynesian languages like Tahitian, there is no inflection for tense, but different tenses are indicated by particles placed before, and sometimes after, the verb. Examine the data and fill in the appropriate particles in the table shown below. Without attention to semological connection, the generalization we could make here would be limited. How many verb-phrase constructions would be needed to account for all and only these combinations of particles with verbs in general? What simplification could be achieved if one assumes each tense that cannot be further analysed in meaning has a single sememe, connecting to one or two particles? Show the simplified structure for the verb phrase and briefly explain how control from the semology would allow only permissible combinations of tense particles.

1. *te tāmā'a nei Vau*   I AM EATING.
2. *te tāmā'a nei 'oe*   YOU (Sg) ARE EATING.
3. *te tāmā'a nei rātou*   THEY ARE EATING.
4. *te 'āu nei Vau*   I AM SWIMMING.
5. *te 'āu ra Vau*   I WAS SWIMMING.
6. *te 'āu ra 'oe*   YOU (Sg) WERE SWIMMING.
7. *'ua tāmā'a 'oe*   YOU (Sg) ATE.
8. *'ua tāmā'a 'ōrua*   YOU TWO ATE.
9. *'ua tāmā'a rātou*   THEY ATE.
10. *'ua 'āu 'ōrua*   YOU TWO SWAM.
11. *'i 'āu na Vau*   I SWAM JUST NOW.
12. *'i tāmā'a na rātou*   THEY ATE JUST NOW.
13. *'e 'āu Vau*   I WILL SWIM.
14. *'e tāmā'a 'ōrua*   YOU TWO WILL EAT.
15. *mai tāmā'a roa Vau*   I ALMOST ATE.
16. *mai tāmā'a rua 'oe*   YOU (Sg) ALMOST ATE.
17. *mai 'āu roa rātou*   THEY ALMOST SWAM.

Tense	Preverbal Particle	Postverbal Particle
PRESENT CONTINUOUS		
PAST CONTINUOUS		
GENERAL PAST		
RECENT PAST (JUST DID)		
FRUSTRATIVE (ALMOST DID)		
FUTURE		

4. *Standard Kannada gender*

The following data provides evidence for gender distinctions in Kannada, a Dravidian language from southern India. Determine the number of genders required and then explain the semantic basis which seems apparent. Then edit the data as usual and provide the usual kind of account.

1. hensu bandidḷu   THE WOMAN CAME.
2. hudigi wo·didḷu   THE GIRL RAN.
3. hudiga bandidda·ne   THE BOY CAME.

4. male bandittu	THE RAIN CAME.
5. hudigi biddidḷu	THE GIRL FELL.
6. pustaka biddittu	THE BOOK FELL.
7. gandassu biddidda·ne	THE MAN FELL.
8. heⁿsu nittidḷu	THE WOMAN STOOD.
9. pra·ni nittittu	THE ANIMAL STOOD.
10. gandassu nittidda·ne	THE MAN STOOD.
11. na·i wo·dittu	THE DOG RAN.
12. tamma wo·didda·ne	THE YOUNGER BROTHER RAN.
13. tamma kutkondidda·ne	THE YOUNGER BROTHER SAT.
14. pra·ni kutkondittu	THE ANIMAL SAT.
15. amma kutkondidda·le	THE MOTHER SAT.
16. na·i hogittu	THE DOG WENT.
17. amma hogidda·le	THE MOTHER WENT.
18. appa hogidda·ne	THE FATHER WENT.
19. akka nittidḷu	THE OLDER SISTER STOOD.
20. akka hogidda·le	THE OLDER SISTER WENT.
21. yemme hogittu	THE SHE-BUFFALO WENT.
22. ko·na wo·dittu	THE HE-BUFFALO RAN.

5. Simplification of syntax under semological control

This chapter has provided a number of illustrations of how more complicated syntactic situations can sometimes be given simpler descriptions if control of various factors from the semology is assumed. Examples included French and Afrikaans negation, English clause types, and aspects of German "separable prefixes". Applying similar ideas, it is possible to simplify the description of Kalagan which formed the basis for the interpretation problem 2 in Chapter 11. Reduce the four clause constructions to just one under the following assumptions:

a. Semological considerations will assure that the role of the Subject (ACTOR, UNDERGOER, INSTRUMENT, or LOCATION) will be in accord with the voice of the Predicator (Active, Undergoer-Passive, Instrument-Passive or Location-Passive, respectively).

b. Semological control will also assure that nothing can occur in the position of Agent, Object, Instrument, or Location when the voice demands that the corresponding role be reflected in the Subject. In other words, a role reflected in Subject position cannot also occur elsewhere in the clause.

c. Other matters relating to the optional/obligatory nature of constituents reflect semological requirements involved in the various events involved, and do not have to be repeated in the syntax.

Terminology

DISCREPANCY	ENTITY SEMEME
ALTERNATIONAL DISCREPANCY	
DIVERSIFICATION	EVENT CLUSTER
SYNCRETIZATION	
ANATAXIS	EVENT SEMEME
COMBINATORY DISCREPANCY	
COMPOSITE REALIZATION	MARKEDNESS
PORTMANTEAU REALIZATION	MARKED ELEMENT
NULL DISCREPANCY	UNMARKED ELEMENT
EMPTY REALIZATION	
ZERO REALIZATION	PARTICIPANT SEMEME
SPECIFICATIONAL REALIZATION	

Appendix

Adaptations of the boxed notation

The primary notation used for presenting solutions to syntactic problems in this book may be termed the **BOXED NOTATION**. As has been illustrated beginning with Chapter 1, this notation involves construction boxes, presenting constructions that combine two or more functionally defined constituents, and vocabulary boxes listing vocabulary items which may be full words, word-stems, or inflectional categories abstracted in the process of editing. This notation was devised as a way of presenting solutions to short data sets for classes in basic syntax. For this purpose, one of its distinct advantages is that it allows us to clearly distinguish functions like Subject, Object, and Predicator from constructions like Noun Phrase and Verb Phrase. It makes it clear that both of these matters are involved in syntax and that they are different. It has the further advantage of easily leading the reader's eye through the steps involved in generating sentences, clauses, and/or phrases as desired. Consider, for instance, the Hindi solution originally presented as Figure 7.9, as shown in Figure A.1.

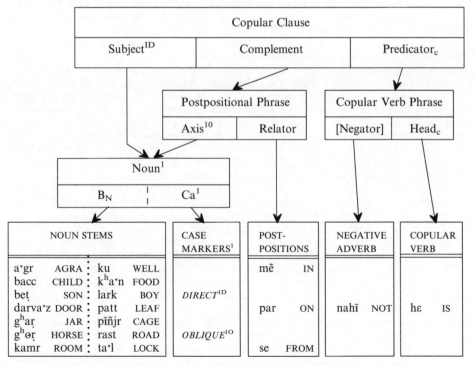

Figure A.1 Solution to Hindi data from Chapter 7 with arrowhead connecting lines

In this version, the connecting lines have been shown ending in arrowheads to emphasize that the diagrams can be used to generate representations of sentences. In actual fact, of course, the connections shown by the lines are bidirectional. So the functions Subject and Axis not only lead "down" to the noun construction, but this construction alternatively leads "up" to those functions. The plain solid connecting lines normally used imply this, though one could also use lines with arrows in both directions to give greater emphasis to the bidirectionality of the connections they depict.

While the notation has these advantages, it sometimes runs into practical problems, particularly with larger and more complex sets of data. If the complication is concerned mainly with vocabulary, it may be solvable by the simple expedient of restricting the vocabulary boxes to just the class names and providing lists of indefinite size to represent the actual vocabulary choices. One then simply has to refer to these correlated lists for specific choices after one reaches the vocabulary class in the process of using the description as a generating device. Exercise A.2 in Chapter 7, based on Hindi intransitive clauses, provides an illustration of the kinds of restricted vocabulary boxes involved. In that case, the classes were simply listed on the next page using a modified form of vocabulary boxes, each with a heading tied via its name to the abbreviated vocabulary boxes in the diagram. For most of the classes shown there, that would be adequate, but the open classes, such as noun stems of the different genders and the intransitive verb stems, consideration of further data would give long lists which could not practically be represented on a single page, let alone in a single box. So in such cases more extensive lexical listings of indefinite length could be given, keyed to same kinds of class labels.

Eventually one might consider assembling a glossary or lexicon in place of such lists. In order to be readily correlated with the syntax proper, such a listing would have to include the same classes indicated in the syntactic description. In addition, we would expect for each entry an indication of both the form and meaning/function for each item entered. For problems like we have considered, the representation of forms could be either orthographic or in some kind of transcription. Data sets presented in this book have sometimes involved transcriptions and have sometimes used orthography, whether original or transliterated.

When it comes to setting up such a glossary, it is necessary to make decisions about its arrangement, which can be different depending on the intended use of the listing. The most expedient organization for the purposes of generating phrases, clauses, and/or sentences in connection with syntactic description would be to line up things under the syntactic class label, as in the headings of vocabulary boxes. For other purposes, obviously, that kind of line-up would be difficult to use – such as for finding particular words and learning their meanings and classifications. The most usual arrangement in ordinary glossaries and dictionaries, of course, is alphabetical arrangement according to orthographic representation (or possibly according to transcriptions, especially in works by linguists for languages with no established orthography). For doing interpretation exercises such as those found in some chapters of this book, it would be naturally desirable to have the material alphabetized according to glosses. In effect, an ordinary bilingual dictionary that goes both ways provides both of these kinds of alphabetization, each in its own section of the overall book. Tables A.1, A.2, and A.3 provide examples of the three different alphabetizations of a Hindi glossary based on the material from exercise A.2 in Chapter 7. A second example, in Table A.4, is based on the Central Alaskan Yup'ik solution in Figure 11.6. It is arranged so as to add an orthographic representation which was not provided in the original data set or its solution, but has been regularly used for publications in the language since the mid-1970s. The arrangement here is according to orthography to illustrate the other possibility not seen in the previous tabular examples, but the other three arrangements, as shown with the Hindi, could also be used here, depending on one's needs and purposes.

Other expedients may become necessary when the number of constructions and/or vocabulary classes exceeds what can reasonably be presented on a page with enough space to clearly show the necessary connections. With moderate complexity, it may be enough to just introduce some diversity in the way connections are shown, so as to make it easier for a reader to follow the different lines. When technologically feasible, contrasting colors may be

Table A.1 Tabular glossary for Hindi arranged by class

Class	Form	Meaning
AUXILIARY STEM	h	*AUXILIARY*
AUXILIARY TENSE MARKER	*PAST-TENSE*	
AUXILIARY TENSE MARKER	*PRESENT-TENSE*	
GENDER MARKER^{1F}	*FEMININE*	
GENDER MARKER^{1M}	*MASCULINE*	
INTRANSITIVE VERB STEM	aˑ	COME
INTRANSITIVE VERB STEM	bol	SPEAK
INTRANSITIVE VERB STEM	cal	GO
INTRANSITIVE VERB STEM	gaˑ	SING
INTRANSITIVE VERB STEM	piˑ	DRINK
INTRANSITIVE VERB STEM	rah	STAY
INTRANSITIVE VERB STEM	soˑ	SLEEP
NEGATIVE ADVERB	nahĩˑ	NOT
NOUN STEM^{1F}	bahin	SISTER
NOUN STEM^{1F}	beṭiˑ	DAUGHTER
NOUN STEM^{1F}	gaˑy	COW
NOUN STEM^{1F}	laṛkiˑ	GIRL
NOUN STEM^{1F}	patniˑ	WIFE
NOUN STEM^{1F}	savaˑriˑ	PASSENGER
NOUN STEM^{1M}	aˑdmiˑ	MAN
NOUN STEM^{1M}	dost	FRIEND
NOUN STEM^{1M}	g^{h}oraˑ	HORSE
NOUN STEM^{1M}	haˑt^{h}iˑ	ELEPHANT
NOUN STEM^{1M}	mantriˑ	SECRETARY
NOUN STEM^{1M}	vidyart^{h}iˑ	STUDENT
NUMBER MARKER	*PLURAL*	
NUMBER MARKER	*SINGULAR*	
PARTICIPIAL ASPECT MARKER	*IMPERFECT-PARTICIPLE*	
PARTICIPIAL ASPECT MARKER	*PERFECT-PARTICIPLE*	
POSSESSIVE ADJECTIVE STEM	hamaˑr	OUR
POSSESSIVE ADJECTIVE STEM	mer	MY
POSSESSIVE ADJECTIVE STEM	ter	YOUR

Table A.2 Tabular glossary for Hindi arranged by form

Form	Class	Meaning
aˑ	INTRANSITIVE VERB STEM	COME
aˑdmiˑ	NOUN STEM^{1M}	MAN
bahin	NOUN STEM^{1F}	SISTER
beṭiˑ	NOUN STEM^{1F}	DAUGHTER
bol	INTRANSITIVE VERB STEM	SPEAK
cal	INTRANSITIVE VERB STEM	GO
dost	NOUN STEM^{1M}	FRIEND
FEMININE	GENDER MARKER	
gaˑ	INTRANSITIVE VERB STEM	SING
gaˑy	NOUN STEM^{1F}	COW
g^{h}oraˑ	NOUN STEM^{1M}	HORSE
h	AUXILIARY STEM	*AUXILIARY*
hamaˑr	POSSESSIVE ADJECTIVE STEM	OUR
haˑt^{h}iˑ	NOUN STEM^{1M}	ELEPHANT

Form	Class	Meaning
IMPERFECT-PARTICIPLE	Participial Aspect Marker	
laṛki	Noun Stem[1F]	GIRL
mantri·	Noun Stem[1M]	SECRETARY
MASCULINE	Gender Marker	
mer	Possessive Adjective Stem	MY
nahi·	Negative Adverb	NOT
PAST-TENSE	Auxiliary Tense Marker	
patni·	Noun Stem[1F]	WIFE
PERFECT-PARTICIPLE	Participial Aspect Marker	
pi·	Intransitive Verb Stem	DRINK
PLURAL	Number Marker	
PRESENT TENSE	Auxiliary Tense Marker	
rah	Intransitive Verb Stem	STAY
sava·ri·	Noun Stem[1F]	PASSENGER
SINGULAR	Number Marker	
so·	Intransitive Verb Stem	SLEEP
ter	Possessive Adjective Stem	YOUR
vidyart^{h}i·	Noun Stem[1M]	STUDENT

Table A.3 Tabular glossary for Hindi arranged by meaning

Meaning	Class	Form
	Auxiliary Tense Marker	*PAST-TENSE*
	Auxiliary Tense Marker	*PRESENT-TENSE*
	Gender Marker	*MASCULINE*
	Gender Marker	*FEMININE*
	Number Marker	*SINGULAR*
	Number Marker	*PLURAL*
	Participial Aspect Marker	*PERFECT-PARTICIPLE*
	Participial Aspect Marker	*IMPERFECT-PARTICIPLE*
AUXILIARY	Auxiliary Stem	h
COME	Intransitive Verb Stem	a·
COW	Noun Stem[1F]	ga·y
DAUGHTER	Noun Stem[1F]	beti·
DRINK	Intransitive Verb Stem	pi·
ELEPHANT	Noun Stem[1M]	ha·t^{h}i·
FRIEND	Noun Stem[1M]	dost
GIRL	Noun Stem[1F]	laṛki·
GO	Intransitive Verb Stem	cal
HORSE	Noun Stem[1M]	g^{h}ora·
MAN	Noun Stem[1M]	a·dmi·
MY	Possessive Adjective Stem	mer
NOT	Negative Adverb	nahĩ·
OUR	Possessive Adjective Stem	hama·r
PASSENGER	Noun Stem[1F]	sava·ri·
SECRETARY	Noun Stem[1M]	mantri·
SING	Intransitive Verb Stem	ga·
SISTER	Noun Stem[1F]	bahin
SLEEP	Intransitive Verb Stem	so·
SPEAK	Intransitive Verb Stem	bol
STAY	Intransitive Verb Stem	rah
STUDENT	Noun Stem[1M]	vidyart^{h}i·
WIFE	Noun Stem[1F]	patni·
YOUR	Possessive Adjective Stem	ter

Table A.4 A tabular glossary for the Central Alaskan Yup'ik data solved in Figure 11.7 arranged according to orthographic representation

Orthography	Transcription	Class	Meaning
	ABSOLUTIVE[1A]	CASE MARKER	
	ABLATIVE[1B]	CASE MARKER	
	RELATIVE[1R]	CASE MARKER	
	PAST	TENSE MARKER	
	PRESENT	TENSE MARKER	
	TRANSITIVE[2T]	TYPE MARKER	
	INTRANSITIVE[2T]	TYPE MARKER	
angute	aŋuti	NOUN STEM	MAN
arnaq	aʁnaʀ	NOUN STEM	WOMAN
kemeg	kɨmɨɣ	NOUN STEM	MEAT
kener	kɨniʁ	VERB STEM	COOK
neqe	nɨqɨ	NOUN STEM	FISH
nere	niʁɨ	VERB STEM	EAT
nunur	nunuʁ	VERB STEM	SCOLD
piste	pistɨ	NOUN STEM	SERVANT
qilug	qiluɣ	VERB STEM	BARK (AT)
qimugte	qimuxtɨ	NOUN STEM	DOG
tangerr	taŋɨχ	VERB STEM	SEE
tuntuvag	tuntuvaɣ	NOUN STEM	MOOSE

assigned to different sorts of connections, or we can use different sorts of lines, such as dotted/ dashed vs. solid and/or differences of thickness. The latter set of possibilities has been used in some cases in the course of this book, and this is quite easy to do with modern computer software. (Examples of this use are seen in Figure 5.9 [English], Figure 11.3 [English], and Figure 11.8 [German] and also in the diagrams accompanying Exercises 4.A.1 [Gothic] and 13.A.3 [Modern Greek].) Some English constructions considered in various chapters, but never integrated into a whole will be used to illustrate some further possibilities. Consider Figure A.2, which shows eight of the English clause constructions exemplified in Chapter 6, along with three phrase constructions and four word constructions needed to elaborate these. These approach any reasonable limit of complexity for the diagrams in the boxed notation. Certainly the addition of vocabulary boxes and full connections to these would place it beyond the limit, if it is not already there. Though complex, however, this diagram is somewhat easier to read because of the use of different kinds of lines. A total of four are used: (1) hyphenated lines show connections between Predicators and the verb construction; (2) broken lines with larger solid segments are used for connections to the prepositional phrase; (3) thick solid lines indicate connections to vocabulary classes, in effect pointing outside this diagram; and (4) all other connections are shown by thin solid lines. Alternatively, different colors could be used for these, which is feasible either for hand-drawn lines or for computer-generated ones, depending on available printing resources.

To complete this description, making up for the absence of vocabulary boxes, two additions are needed: some kind of lexicon or glossary along the lines already illustrated, and some indication of how the various thick lines connect to the classes of the glossary. One way to do the latter is in a table such as Table A.5, which lists each of the functions involved alphabetically by its assigned label, and then relates this to a manifestation class. Here each class is given a label in full capitals.

This can then be further related to a lexicon or glossary. An example of an alphabetized tabular glossary for this English material is present over several pages in the form of Table A.6. Instead of meanings, each of the lexical stems and unanalysed words is associated with a phonemicization representing a fairly conservative style in the author's midwestern American pronunciation. Taken together, this information from Tables A.5 and A.6 combines with that in Figure A.2 to represent the complete description of a fragment of English syntax.

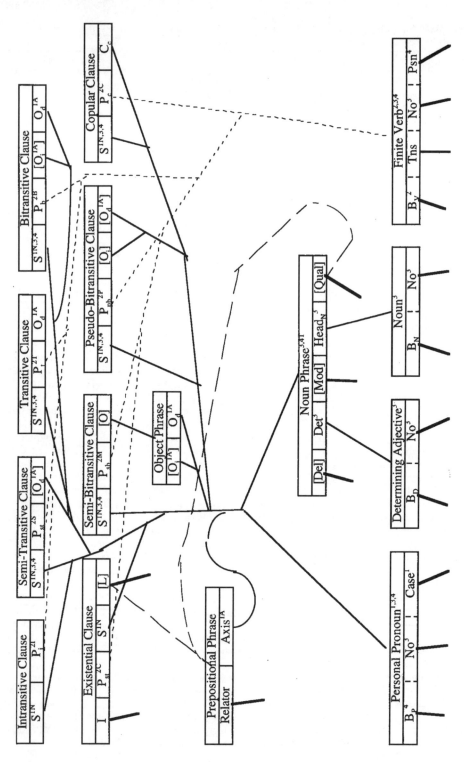

Figure A.2 Some English constructions at the ranks of clause, phrase, and word

Table A.5 Table of functions relating directly to vocabulary classes, supplementing Figure A.2

Function symbol	CLASS NAME
B_D	DETERMINING ADJECTIVE STEMS
B_N	NOUN STEMS
$B_P{}^4$	PRONOUN STEMS[4]
$B_V{}^2$	VERB STEMS[2]
Case[1]	CASE MARKERS[1]
Del	DELIMITING ADJECTIVES
I	EXISTENTIAL PARTICLE
L	LOCATIVE ADVERBS
Mod	ORDINARY ADJECTIVES
No[3]	NUMBER MARKERS[3]
Psn[4]	PERSON MARKERS[4]
Qual	LOCATIVE ADVERBS
Relator	PREPOSITIONS
Tns	TENSE MARKERS

Table A.6 Tabular lexicon for some English clause data

Orthography	Phonemic form	Class
a	/ə/	DETERMINING ADJECTIVE STEM
above	/əbə́v/	PREPOSITION
academic	/ǽkədémik/	ORDINARY ADJECTIVE
accident	/ǽksədənt/	NOUN STEM
ACCUSATIVE[1A]		CASE MARKER[1]
all	/ól/	DELIMITING ADJECTIVE
at	/ǽt/	PREPOSITION
attorney	/ətə́rniy/	NOUN STEM
aunt	/ǽnt/	NOUN STEM
award	/əwórd/	VERB STEM[2B]
be	/bíy/	VERB STEM[2C]
beautiful	/byúwtəfəl/	ORDINARY ADJECTIVE
behind	/bəháynd/	PREPOSITION
big	/bíg/	ORDINARY ADJECTIVE
bird	/bə́rd/	NOUN STEM
book	/búk/	NOUN STEM
bouquet	/buwkéy/	NOUN STEM
bread	/bréd/	NOUN STEM
bring	/bríŋ/	VERB STEM[2B]
child	/čáyld/	NOUN STEM
choose	/čúwz/	VERB STEM[2B]
cook	/kúk/	VERB STEM[2B]
cousin	/kə́zən/	NOUN STEM
curtain	/kə́rtən/	NOUN STEM
cut	/kə́t/	VERB STEM[2B]
damage	/dǽmiǰ/	VERB STEM[2T]
daughter	/dótər/	NOUN STEM
desk	/désk/	NOUN STEM
dessert	/dəzə́rt/	NOUN STEM
die	/dáy/	VERB STEM[2I]
difference	/dífərəns/	NOUN STEM

table continues

Table A.6 – *continued*

Orthography	Phonemic form	Class
dinner	/dínər/	NOUN STEM
dish	/díš/	NOUN STEM
dog	/dóg/	NOUN STEM
draw	/dró/	VERB STEM[2P]
drug	/drə́g/	NOUN STEM
employee	/implóyiy/	NOUN STEM
excellent	/éksələnt/	ORDINARY ADJECTIVE
famous	/féyməs/	ORDINARY ADJECTIVE
favor	/féyvər/	NOUN STEM
fine	/fáyn/	ORDINARY ADJECTIVE
FIRST[4F]		PERSON MARKER[4]
friend	/frénd/	NOUN STEM
give	/gív/	VERB STEM[2B]
good	/gúd/	ORDINARY ADJECTIVE
governor	/gə́vərnər/	NOUN STEM
grant	/grǽnt/	NOUN STEM
great	/gréyt/	ORDINARY ADJECTIVE
he[4T]	/híy/	PRONOUN STEM[4]
her	/hə́r/	DETERMINING ADJECTIVE STEM
here	/hír/	LOCATIVE ADVERB
his	/híz/	DETERMINING ADJECTIVE STEM
husband	/hə́zbənd/	NOUN STEM
I[1F]	/áy/	PRONOUN STEM[4]
important	/impórtənt/	ORDINARY ADJECTIVE
in	/ín/	PREPOSITION
issue	/íšuw/	NOUN STEM
it[4T]	/ít/	PRONOUN STEM[4]
its	/íts/	DETERMINING ADJECTIVE STEM
judge	/ǰə́ǰ/	NOUN STEM
just	/ǰə́st/	DELIMITING ADJECTIVE
kill	/kíl/	VERB STEM[2S]
lawyer	/ló + yər/	NOUN STEM
letter	/létər/	NOUN STEM
linen	/línən/	NOUN STEM
loyal	/lóyəl/	ORDINARY ADJECTIVE
make	/méyk/	VERB STEM[2B]
man	/mǽn/	NOUN STEM
meal	/míyl/	NOUN STEM
mother	/mə́ðər/	NOUN STEM
my	/máy/	DETERMINING ADJECTIVE STEM
neighbour	/néybər/	NOUN STEM
new	/núw/	ORDINARY ADJECTIVE
nice	/náys/	ORDINARY ADJECTIVE
NOMINATIVE[1N]		CASE MARKER[1]
notebook	/nówt + bùk/	NOUN STEM
on	/án/	PREPOSITION
only	/ównliy/	DELIMITING ADJECTIVE
our	/áwr/	DETERMINING ADJECTIVE STEM
over	/ówvər/	PREPOSITION

table continues

Table A.6 – *continued*

Orthography	Phonemic form	Class
paper	/péypər/	NOUN STEM
PAST		TENSE MARKER
person	/pə́rsən/	NOUN STEM
philosopher	/fəlásəfər/	NOUN STEM
picture	/píkčər/	NOUN STEM
PLURAL		NUMBER MARKER[3]
pound	/páwnd/	NOUN STEM
present	/prézənt/	NOUN STEM
PRESENT		TENSE MARKER
prize	/práyz/	NOUN STEM
professor	/prəfésər/	NOUN STEM
provide	/prəváyd/	VERB STEM[2B]
read	/ríyd/	VERB STEM[2P]
salami	/səlámiy/	NOUN STEM
seal	/síyl/	VERB STEM[2T]
SECOND[4S]		PERSON MARKER[4]
send	/sénd/	VERB STEM[2B]
serve	/sə́rv/	VERB STEM[2M]
she[4T]	/šíy/	PRONOUN STEM[4]
sheep	/šíyp/	NOUN STEM
sing	/síŋ/	VERB STEM[2P]
SINGULAR		NUMBER MARKER[3]
sister	/sístər/	NOUN STEM
sleep	/slíyp/	VERB STEM[2I]
some	/səm/	DET ADJ STEM
son	/sə́n/	NOUN STEM
song	/sóŋ/	NOUN STEM
story	/stóriy/	NOUN STEM
suitcase	/súwt+kèys/	NOUN STEM
supper	/sə́pər/	NOUN STEM
sweater	/swétər/	NOUN STEM
table	/téybəl/	NOUN STEM
tell	/tél/	VERB STEM[2M]
that	/ðǽt/	DETERMINING ADJECTIVE STEM
the	/ðə/	DETERMINING ADJECTIVE STEM
their	/ðér/	DETERMINING ADJECTIVE STEM
there[L]	/ðér/	LOCATIVE ADVERB
there[X]	/ðér/	EXISTENTIAL PARTICLE
THIRD[4T]		PERSON MARKER[4]
this	/ðis/	DETERMINING ADJECTIVE STEM
time	/táym/	VERB STEM[2T]
treasurer	/tréžərər/	NOUN STEM
uncle	/ə́ŋkəl/	NOUN STEM
under	/ə́ndər/	PREPOSITION
unpack	/ənpǽk/	VERB STEM[2S]
valet	/vǽlət/	NOUN STEM

The next possibility to consider involves separating the description into sections, interrelated as well as can be done. That kind of separation inevitably makes it harder for the reader to see the whole picture, but it may sometimes be the best expedient, because numerous connections can make the diagram tangled and therefore difficult to follow. Figures A.3, A.4, and A.5 represent an attempt to make Figure A.2 more understandable by breaking it down in such a way that each diagram has only what is needed for two or three of the eight clause types represented. It is necessary then to repeat the connected phrase- and word-constructions that relate to more than one group. The use of different styles of lines shown in Figure A.2 is continued. This description will relate to Tables A.5 and A.6 in exactly the same way as the more elaborate Figure A.2 does.

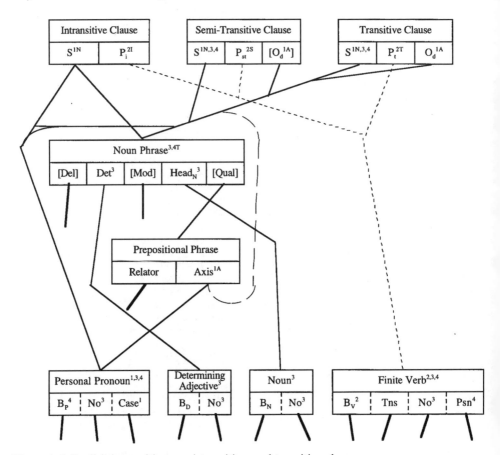

Figure A.3 English intransitive, semi-transitive, and transitive clauses

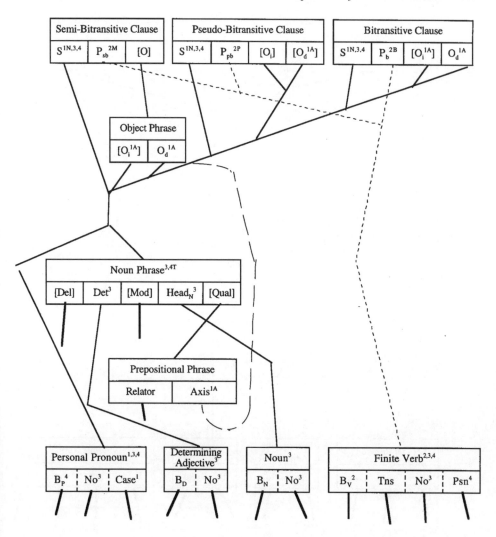

Figure A.4 English semi-bitransitive, pseudo-bitransitive, and bitransitive clauses

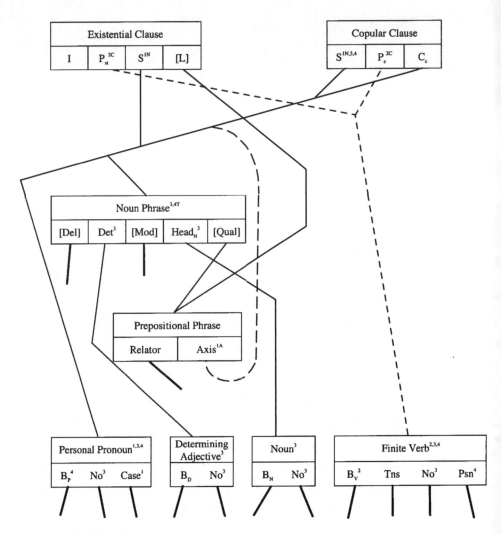

Figure A.5 English existential and copular clauses

Finally, it is also possible to represent this description entirely in terms of formulas to be related to the lexical table. Two kinds of formulas are involved: (1) those which show the relation between a construction and its functional constituents are CONSTRUCTION FORMULAS; and (2) those which show connections between constructional functions and either other constructions or vocabulary classes are MANIFESTATION FORMULAS. The construction formulas use an equals sign (=) to link the name of the construction with the names of its functional constituents. Table A.7 presents the formulas needed for constructions on the rank of the clause (a), phrase (b), and word (c). Linearly arranged constituents such as those characteristic of clauses and phrases have their constituents separated by a space, while the non-linear associated constituents found in word structures are separated by a raised dot (·).

Table A.7 English constructions in formulas

(a) CONSTRUCTION FORMULAS: CLAUSES

Intransitive Clause $= S^{1N,3,4} P_i^{2I,3,4}$

Transitive Clause $= S^{1N,3,4} P_t^{2T,3,4} O_d^{1A}$

Semi-Transitive Clause $= S^{1N,3,4} P_{st}^{2S,3,4} [O_d^{1A}]$

Bitransitive Clause $= S^{1N,3,4} P_b^{2B,3,4} [O_i^{1A}] O_d^{1A}$

Semi-Bitransitive Clause $= S^{1N,3,4} P_{sb}^{2M,3,4} [O]$

Pseudo-Bitransitive Clause $= S^{1N,3,4} P_{pb}^{2P,3,4} [O_i^{1A}] [O_d^{1A}]$

Existential Clause $= I\ S^{1N,3,4} P_c^{2C,3,4}$

Copular Clause $= S^{1N,3,4} P_c^{2C,3,4} C_c$

(b) CONSTRUCTION FORMULAS: PHRASES

Noun Phrase^{4T} $= [Del]\ Det^3\ [M]\ Head_N^3\ [Q]$

Object Phrase $= [O_i^{1A}]\ O_d^{1A}$

Prepositional Phrase $= Relator\ Axis^{1A}$

(c) CONSTRUCTION FORMULAS: WORDS

Determining Adjective^3 $= B_D \cdot No^3 \cdot Psn^4$

Finite Verb^2 $= B_V^2 \cdot Tns \cdot No^3 \cdot Psn^4$

Noun^3 $= B_N \cdot No^3$

Personal Pronoun^{1,3,4} $= B_P^4 \cdot No^3 \cdot Case^1$

   Manifestation formulas use a colon (:) to separate the functional constituent symbol from the labels for the classes and/or constructions involved in its manifestation. In the simplest form, this gives a formula for every individual function with a distinct label, as shown in Table A.8 for this English description. The actual formula is shown in the first column, and the second column spells out the name of the function in full. The latter is not essential for the mechanical use of the formulas, but it can be of aid to human readers trying to understand the description. In some instances, there are alternative manifestations, and their labels are separated by a comma (,). Labels for classes listed in the lexical table are in CAPITALS, while the other manifestations are the names of other constructions.

   This algebraic system, incorporating the construction formulas of Table A.7 and the manifestation formulas of Table A.8 with the lexical information in Table A.6 allows all of the description to be indicated without the use of boxes or connecting lines between them. One advantage to this manner of presentation is that it allows the indefinite expansion of the number of constructions, classes, and individual lexical items, as would be required in larger-scale descriptions of more extensive sets of data. It also may be considered an advantage to have the ability to represent the description without resort to the special graphic devices required with boxes and lines. On the other hand, the mind generally has to make a greater effort to understand the connections in the algebraic formulas, and some readers might even use them as a set of directions for producing the more explicitly connected boxed description. The lines are particularly useful in showing the interrelations of constructions and classes up to a point where they become too numerous and tangled.

   In summary, there are various ways of representing descriptions equivalent to what we have been showing here, and anyone using this system to show descriptions has to exercise judgement about breaking up a description into multiple overlapping diagrams, organization of related lexical listings and other matters of practical presentation.

Table A.8 Manifestation formulas for the English description

Formula	Function name
Axis[1A]: Pronoun, Noun Phrase	Axis
B_D: DETERMINING ADJECTIVE STEM	Determining Adjective Base
B_N: NOUN STEM	Nominal Base
$B_P{}^4$: PRONOUN STEM[4]	Pronominal Base
$B_V{}^2$: VERB STEM[2]	Verbal Base
Case[1]: CASE MARKER[1]	Case
C_c: Pronoun[1], Noun Phrase[1]	Copular Complement
Del: DELIMITING ADJECTIVE	Delimiter
Det[3]: Determining Adjective[3]	Determiner
$Head_N{}^3$: Noun[3]	Nominal Head
I: EXISTENTIAL PARTICLE	Introducer
L: Prep. Phrase, LOCATIVE ADVERB	Locational
M: ORDINARY ADJECTIVE	Modifier
No[3]: NUMBER MARKER[3]	Number
O: Object Phrase	Object
$O_d{}^{1A}$: Pronoun[1], Noun Phrase[1]	Direct Object
$O_i{}^{1A}$: Pronoun[1], Noun Phrase[1]	Indirect Object
$P_b{}^{2B,3,4}$: Finite Verb[2,3,4]	Bitransitive Predicator
$P_c{}^{2C,3,4}$: Finite Verb[2,3,4]	Copular Predicator
$P_i{}^{2I,3,4}$: Finite Verb[2,3,4]	Intransitive Predicator
$P_{pb}{}^{2P,3,4}$: Finite Verb[2,3,4]	Pseudo-Bitransitive Predicator
$P_{sb}{}^{2M,3,4}$: Finite Verb[2,3,4]	Semi-Transitive Predicator
$P_{st}{}^{2S,3,4}$: Finite Verb[2,3,4]	Semi-Transitive Predicator
$P_t{}^{2T,3,4}$: Finite Verb[2,3,4]	Transitive Predicator
Psn[4]: PERSON MARKER[4]	Person
Q: LOCATIVE ADVERB	Qualifier
Relator: PREPOSITION	Relator
$S^{1N,3,4}$: Pronoun[1], Noun Phrase[1]	Subject
Tns: TENSE MARKER	Tense

Glossary

Introduction

This section is presented as an aid to students and other readers in mastering the technical terms presented in this book. It is not intended to be a guide to the usages of other writers. Where possible, traditional terms and usages are followed, and where this is not done, some discussion of the traditional terms and their shortcomings is included. It is based on the terms listed at the end of each chapter.

In the alphabetical listing, each term is followed by the number of the chapter where it is introduced. This is intended as a direction to further explanation and examples. For some terms, the actual definition has sometimes been incorporated into the discussion of a more basic related term, and in these cases an explict cross-reference is provided. Terms in small italic capitals in the definitions indicate a separate entry in the Glossary. These cross-references should further aid the reader to gain an appreciation of the degree to which many of the terms are interrelated.

ABSOLUTIVE CASE (10)   See **ERGATIVE SYSTEM**.

ACCUSATIVE SYSTEM (10)   One of the kinds of clause organization in which the doer of an action, whether expressed by a transitive or an intransitive verb, is placed in the nominative case, while the one seen as somehow acted upon is in the accusative case. We say that English has a system like this because it has pronouns with different case forms functioning this way. Other languages such as German and Russian have different forms for their nouns as well. This is to be distinguished from various other kinds of system, such as the *ERGATIVE, AGENTIVE, UNIPARTITE* and *TRIPARTITE* systems.

ACTIVE VOICE (11)   In English and many other languages, the voice in which the clause Subject is seen as the *ACTOR*, the "doer" of the action, as in *Bill gave Tim the book*, where Bill is the person who did the giving. This is opposed to examples of the *PASSIVE VOICE*, which may occur in one or more varieties in a language.

ACTOR (11)   The participant in an event seen as a "doer" of the action. In unmarked cases, it will coincide with the *SUBJECT*, but in passives it will be expressed (if at all) by a non-subject, as in the English example *He was kidnapped by the giant,* where a prepositional phrase is used to express the actor.

ADJUNCT (3)   A general term used in this book for any kind of subordinate (non-head) element in an *ENDOCENTRIC* construction. In school grammar "modifier" is often used for this meaning, but here that term is reserved for a special subtype of adjunct. So in the phrase *all my green books over there*, *books* is the head, and each of the words preceding it is an adjunct of a different kind, and the final phrase *over there* has still another adjunct function.

ADPOSITION (3)   A generic term for a Relator analogous to the English preposition. The two basic varieties of adpositions are **PREPOSITIONS** placed before their related axes, and

POSTPOSITIONS placed after. Most often, a language will have one or the other of these types but not both. Exceptions to this include Finnish, which has a number of both kinds, and English, which predominantly has prepositions, but has a few postpositions which have developed from adverbs (arguably *ago*) and from affixes (the possessive enclitic -*'s*).

ADVERSATIVE SENTENCE (12)   In English and many other languages, a special type of sentence in which one principal constituent contains a qualification that is treated as antithetical to the idea(s) expressed in the main clause. *I'll go, but it won't help* is a simple example, with the antithetic aspect expressed by *but*. *However* and *nevertheless* are other ways of expressing similar ideas in English. See also *ANTITHESIS* and *THESIS*.

AFFIRMATIVE (9)   The preferred grammatical term for the opposite of NEGATIVE, as when we say that *He did it* is affirmative as opposed to the negative *He didn't do it*. In non-linguistic contexts "positive" is the usual term, as when we speak of the positive and negative poles of a magnet. In linguistic tradition, however, POSITIVE is normally used in relation to the comparison of adjectives and some kinds of adverbs, in contrast to comparative and superlative, and it is confusing to use the same term for both. There are some linguists, especially semanticists, who favor "positive" because not all non-negatives necessarily affirm. If and when such a fine distinction is needed, however, one could resort to other derivatives of *affirm*, such as affirmatory. There is no obvious alternative, however, to POSITIVE in the more traditional sense of neither comparative nor superlative.

AFTERBRANCHING (5)   A pattern of constituency that frequently shows up in the treatment of grammatical coordination, with potentially deep branching at the end of a construction, *after* the first constituent. The source of the name suggested here is rather obvious, but the more common name found in the literature is "right-branching". This term is rejected here because it is based on the conventions of writing European languages from left to right. Spoken languages cannot have a "left" or a "right", only a "before" and "after" in their linear order. Contrast *FOREBRANCHING*.

AGENT (11)   In the usage suggested here, the name for the optional constituent allowing mention of the ACTOR in a passive clause. In English, this *FUNCTION* is generally filled by a prepositional phrase with *by* as *RELATOR*. (In semantics and some views of *SEMOLOGY*, this term is often used in a way roughly similar to *ACTOR* here, but often with further restrictions.)

AGENTIVE CASE (10)   See **TRIPARTITE SYSTEM**.

AGENTIVE SYSTEM (10)   An alternative to either an *ACCUSATIVE* or an *ERGATIVE* system according to which the case of the intransitive Subject will be identical to that of the transitive Subject or the transitive Object according to the nature of the event involved. When an active, though intransitive, process like running or walking is involved, the AGENTIVE CASE will be used for its Subject, as it is also used for transitive Subject. For other events like sleeping or dying, the PATIENTIVE CASE, also used for transitive Objects, will be used. (The term "agentive" is also suggested for the case of the transitive Subject in a *TRIPARTITE SYSTEM*.)

AGNATE (11)   Two or more linguistic forms may be said to be agnate when they share a common core of their meaning. Corresponding active and passive clauses such as *Harry saw the book* and *The book was seen by Harry* are prime examples of the phenomenon. Typically agnate structures will pass logicians' tests for "synonymy" based on truth conditions, but will differ in the overall meaning in more subtle ways. The difference in this example centers on the fact that the first clause is about Harry and something that he experienced, while the second is about some known book and Harry's experience in relation to it.

ALTERNATIONAL DISCREPANCY (15)   See **DISCREPANCY**.

ANATAXIS (15)   See **DISCREPANCY**.

ANTIPASSIVE VOICE (11)   In a language with an *ERGATIVE SYSTEM*, a special marked voice which is in some ways the counterpart of the *PASSIVE VOICE* in a typical language with a *NOMINATIVE-ACCUSATIVE SYSTEM*. While in the latter types the use of the passive makes something other than *ACTOR* the Subject, the use of the antipassive in some ergative-absolutive systems allows something other than the *UNDERGOER* to be in the absolutive case and thus (in some views) the Subject. Not all languages of the ergative-absolutive type have constructions of this kind. Some which do have it include Australian languages such as Dyirbal and Eskimo languages such as Yup'ik.

ANTITHESIS (12)   This term is suggested here for one functional part of an *ADVERSATIVE* sentence type, as typically introduced in English by *but* or a synonym. So in the example *Jack lives here, but his sister has moved to Alaska*, the portion beginning with *but* is the antithesis, while the rest is the *THESIS*.

APODOSIS (12)   This term has been taken from Greek rhetoric and applied to the function of the "*then*-clause" in a conditional sentence. So in *If it rains, we'll stay home*, the clause *we'll stay home* manifests the apodosis. (The "*if*-clause" manifests the *PROTASIS*.)

ASPECT (2)   An inflectional category associated with verbs in many languages which relates to the nature of an event itself rather than its relation to time. Among the more common aspects found in various languages are the "durative" which indicates that the action involved is seen as continuing over time and "perfective", which indicates an action seen as completed (to be completed). Aspect combines with TENSE in many languages (such as Russian) though in others verbs may indicate aspect alone and exclude tense. By itself, aspect may be purely morphological rather than syntactic, but it may be expressed by separate particles in a verb phrase, and it may have effects on aspects of the structure of phrases and/or clauses, making it syntactically relevant.

ASYNDETIC COORDINATION (= **ASYNDETON**) (5)   Coordination of syntactic constituents accomplished without an overt conjunction. This is common in some languages like Chinese. In English, it exists as in *We visited Aunt Sally, Uncle Morey, Cousin Jack...*, where it usually leaves the implication that the enumeration involved is not complete. Contrast *SYNDETIC COORDINATION*.

AUGMENTED SUPERSCRIPT (4)   An aspect of the notation introduced in this book for formalizing some kinds of congruence. This term is applied specifically to cases where a letter is added to the numerical superscript, as in ^{1M}, ^{2P}, and so on. This device is first introduced in Chapter 4 to allow a classification of nouns to correlate with an inflection of their associated adjuncts. In Chapter 7, another usage for these kinds of superscript is introduced to allow the ready description of *DETERMINATION*. The letters used in setting up these superscripts are most useful for human readers when they have mnemonic references, as with M/F/N for masculine, feminine, and neuter genders. More arbitrary assignments are possible, however, when one is not certain how to label a given category, and the mechanics of the matter will work just as well.

AUXILIARY (3)   A kind of dependent verb which combines with a primary verb in a given language to express verbal categories that might in some other language be expressed by inflectional affixes in the verb itself. Auxiliary verbs are generally quite prominent in the verbal systems of modern European languages like English, but are at least less prominent in classical languages like Latin and Ancient Greek and may be entirely lacking in some languages. In English, some auxiliary verbs like *be*, *do*, and *have* may also be used as primary verbs: compare the auxiliary uses in *She **was** frightened by the bat*, *They **did** not work*, and *He **has** read all the books* with primary uses in *It **was** over there*, *Tom **did** most of the work*, and *Harriet **has** the new* *reports.* Another subclass of English auxiliaries, modal auxiliaries such as *can*, *will*, and *may*, are generally used with a primary verb or at least imply one in cases of ellipsis. Compare *He can easily finish the work, She **will** fit that project in*, and *They **may** not complete their investigation.*

AXIS (3)   A constituent characterizing, together with a RELATOR, one major subtype of EXOCENTRIC CONSTRUCTION. While the relator indicates some relation to further structure outside this construction, the AXIS indicates what it relates. So in the exocentric construction called the prepositional phrase, e.g. *in books*, the axis function is indicated by the simple noun phrase *books*, and the relator (*in*) shows a specific relation we might label INTERIORITY. In another common exocentric construction, the conjunctive phrase, e.g. *and Mary*, the proper noun phrase *Mary* functions as axis, while the relator *and* indicates a relation we might term SIMPLE ADDITION (or perhaps CONJUNCTION).

BITRANSITIVE CLAUSE (6)   A clause that has two Objects rather than just one, as typically with the verb *give* in English taking both a Direct Object and an Indirect Object: *Sam gave Sue the answers.* Strictly speaking, a full bitransitive verb should be one that requires both of these Objects, and a clause containing it would be bitransitive. English, however, also has some verbs capable of taking both kinds of Objects, but not always requiring both. In this book the terms SEMI-BITRANSITIVE and PSEUDO-BITRANSITIVE are suggested for such cases. The former term is proposed for verbs like *sing*, *read*, and *draw*, which can occur either with no Object, with both Objects or with just a Direct Object. The latter term applies to verbs like *sell*, *serve*, and *write*, which can have either of the Objects, or both or none at all. Since English does not seem to have any verbs that actually require both kinds of Object, the term "bitransitive" is applied to verbs like *send*, *bring*, and *cut*, which require a Direct Object and may also have an Indirect Object.

CASE (2)   An inflectional categorial dimension applying to nominal words in relation to their grammatical function. Case can relate either to purely grammatical functions (such as Subject, Direct Object, Indirect Object, or Instrument), which is termed grammatical case, or to relations of locus such as would be expressed by prepositions in a language like English, which is termed local case.

   In this book, this term is used only for an inflectionally signaled distinction. In recent years, however, many linguists have come to use the term in an extended sense, applying to the meaning relation involved in case, regardless of whether it is expressed morphologically or syntactically. While the functional similarities lying behind these usages are worthy of note, it is felt better here not to overextend the traditional term.

CASE GOVERNMENT (7)   A variety of the more general phenomenon of grammatical GOVERNMENT in which the governed category is CASE. The most frequent governing classifications found are associated with ADPOSITIONS (in adpositional phrases, affecting case in the AXIS) or with verbs in clauses (affecting case in associated Objects). Neither of these phenomena is seen in modern English, but they are frequent in more highly inflected languages.

CIRCUMSTANTIAL (6)   In the semological treatment of events, this term is used by some linguists to refer to an aspect of the situation that is less central than those assigned the contrasting label PARTICIPANT. Typical circumstantials include those indicating time and location.

CLASSIFIER (4)   A kind of word found in some languages which in effect signals a kind of gender concord. This differs from the more common forms of gender in that a word rather than an affix is used to signal it. The congruence involved is most commonly associated with either (1) numerals or other quantifiers or (2) demonstratives. Some accounts of these words compare their function to that of *head* in such an English expression as *ten head of cattle*, and some traditions, particularly that found for Chinese, speak of them as "measure words", suggesting they are used to individuate when nouns are not inflected for number. This characterization seems to work better for the use with quantifiers than for that with demonstratives, however.

CLAUSE (1)   Traditionally understood as a construction involving a finite verb related to expressions of the *PARTICIPANTS* involved with it and possibly also some *CIRCUMSTANTIALS*. One way clauses can be subclassified is into **INDEPENDENT CLAUSES** like *There was a fire over there* and *Aunt Matilda and Uncle Fred left for Hawaii yesterday*, as opposed to **DEPENDENT CLAUSES** like the relative clause in *That's the man **who tried to sell us a new vacuum**, or the subject clause in **Whether we will go** is still not certain*. These are differentiated on the basis of their ability to stand as sentences by themselves, or not.

CLAUSOIDAL PHRASE (14)   A term suggested here for what traditional grammar treats as special phrases with non-finite verbs and which some more modern grammatical traditions regard as non-finite clauses. Examples include the *GERUND PHRASE, PARTICIPIAL PHRASE, INFINITIVE PHRASE*, and *SUPINE PHRASE*. The term suggested here recognizes their similarity to clauses, while at the same time following the traditional distinction.

CLITIC (8)   A grammatical entity which behaves like a word syntactically, but like an affix phonologically, being attached to a preceding or following word. The primary criteria for the recognition of clitics include *SEPARABILITY, COMEMBERSHIP*, and *DIFFERENTIAL LINKAGE*, any one of which is sufficient to establish its status. A word that can occur in both clitic and non-clitic forms (like *'s* in *John's here* [beside the more formal *John is here*]) is termed a **VARIANT CLITIC**. A clitic that does not have a non-clitic form (like the possessive *'s* in *John's books*) is a **CONSTANT CLITIC**. Another way to classify clitics is according to their position in relation to the word they attach to. One that attaches to a preceding word (like both the examples cited above) is an **ENCLITIC**, which is named for the Greek for "leaning back"; one that attaches to a following word, like the unstressed forms of many English articles and prepositions, is a **PROCLITIC**, named for the Greek for "leaning forward". In some languages, enclitics have been found that automatically attach to the end of the first word in a longer phrase. These are here called **POSTINITIAL ENCLITICS**, as illustrated by the Bulgarian articles in Table 8.8 and the Amharic articles in Table 8.9.

COMBINATORY DISCREPANCY (15)   See **DISCREPANCY**.

COMEMBERSHIP (8)   One major criterion for the identification of clitics, on the basis of the fact that their syntactic position allows them to be considered alternatives to other units which are obviously words rather than affixes. In English, this criterion helps in the identification of the articles and some prepositions as clitics rather than affixes. So the articles *the* and *a/an* are usually unaccented, superficially like prefixes, but they occur as alternatives to accented words like *this* and *that*, and this makes them members of the same syntactic class as undoubtedly accented words, inviting us to see them as proclitic words. A similar reasoning applies to the usually unaccented prepositions *of, to, for, from* which have the same general syntactic behavior as accented prepositions like *behind, over*, and *under*.

COMPLEX SENTENCE (12)   In traditional school grammar, a sentence containing both an independent clause and one or more subordinate clauses, not capable of being an independent sentence. For example, *The man that lives across the street knows that I am interested in buying his car* is a complex sentence with two subordinate clauses: the relative clause *that lives across the street* functions as a Qualifier in the noun phrase that is the Subject in its main clause, and the clause *that I am interested in buying his car* serves as Object in the main clause. While the distinctions are fairly easy to recognize and apply to examples, they do not correspond to what we would treat as separate sentence types according to the approach presented in this book, because the complex type merely involves particular choice(s) made to manifest certain clause or phrase functions such as Subject, Object, Qualifier, and so on.

COMPOSITE REALIZATION (15)   See **DISCREPANCY**.

COMPOUND SENTENCE (12)   In traditional school grammar, a sentence containing at least two clauses, any of which could stand in isolation as a sentence, joined by conjunctions or a functionally equivalent grammatical device. Examples would be *Tom lives next-door and Sally has settled in Florida,* whose parts joined by *and* are both capable of being complete sentences. While the distinctions are fairly easy to recognize and apply to examples, they do not correspond to what we would treat as separate sentence types according to the approach presented in this book, because the compound type merely involves a choice to extend a one-clause sentence by joining on one or more additional clauses.

COMPOUND-COMPLEX SENTENCE (12)   In traditional school grammar, a sentence that combines the properties attributed to a *COMPOUND SENTENCE* (at least two independent clauses) with those found in a *COMPLEX SENTENCE.* An example, expanded from that given for the compound type, would be *Tom lives next-door and Sally, who was always his favorite sister, has settled in Florida.* While the distinctions are fairly easy to recognize and apply to examples, they do not correspond to what we would treat as separate sentence types according to the approach presented in this book, because the compound-complex type merely involves exercising both the choice to extend a one-clause sentence by joining on one or more additional clauses and to manifest at least one function within one of these clauses (or its constituent phrases) in a particular way.

CONCESSIVE CLAUSE (14)   See **SUBORDINATE CLAUSE**.

CONCORD (4)   A general term for a situation seen when two or more co-constituents in a grammatical construction must agree in inflection for some particular grammatical category, such as *NUMBER, DEFINITENESS,* or *CASE.* It may alternatively be termed either **CONCORDIAL CONGRUENCE** or **SIMPLE CONCORD**. The latter term clearly distinguishes it from the governmental type of concord, seen especially in *GENDER CONCORD.*

CONCORDIAL CONGRUENCE (4)   See **CONCORD**.

CONFIRMATORY QUESTION (13)   A term suggested here for a question that seeks confirmation of a state of affairs already presumed by the speaker rather than asking for fully new information. In English, confirmatory polarity questions (like *He's coming, isn't he?)* are commonly termed **TAG QUESTIONS**, while confirmatory *SUPPLEMENT QUESTIONS* (like *He's going where?)* are called **ECHO QUESTIONS**. In English, the latter type are signaled by the fact that the interrogative word occurs in its usual place rather than at the beginning, as would be found with the more usual types.

CONJUNCTIVE COORDINATION (5)   Coordination using conjunctions that indicate that the coordinated elements function together in combination, as opposed to *DISJUNCTIVE COORDINATION.* For example **Both Sally and Emily** love basketball or **They and their relatives** *enjoyed a wonderful picnic last evening.*

CONJUNCTIVE SENTENCE (12)   A sentence containing two or more clauses intended as a combination, as would be indicated by the conjunction *and* or the correlative pair *both ... and.* For example *It's raining outside and so she has decided to stay at home.* Compare *DISJUNCTIVE SENTENCE.*

CONSTANT CLITIC (8)   See **CLITIC**.

CONSTRUCTION (1)   As understood in this book, a construction is a recurrent pattern of syntactic combination associated with some rank of syntactic structure in some particular language. It is described as a combination of constituent functional elements, each either obligatory or optional for it. The construction will also have properties of arrangement and potentially may show one or more kinds of congruence between co-constituents.

CONSTRUCTION BOX (1)   In the notation introduced in this book, one of the two fundamental types of boxes indicating the properties of some particular *CONSTRUCTION* postulated to help account for the syntactic patterns of the language. In the upper part of such a box, each construction is assigned a name, preferably one which is mnemonically useful and different from that assigned to any distinct construction in the same language. The lower part of each box is then divided into two or more sub-boxes, each indicating the name of the functional element of the construction.

CONTINUATION (5)   A term suggested in this book for the function of an optional part of a Continuation Phrase construction involved in accounting for *COORDINATION*, its obligatory co-constituent being the *MAIN*.

COORDINATION (5)   The grammatical device(s) used to combine two or more diverse but functionally similar expressions into one syntactic unit, whether a phrase, clause, or sentence. One possible way of treating this is here termed the **LOGIC-BASED FORMALIZATION**. It is founded on the idea that the expressions being coordinate are co-equal from a logical point of view. It sees each of them as equally central to a unitary construction, with the conjunctions linking them as markers of their relation. So in *Mary, Martha, and Ann*, this view sees each of the personal names as co-equal, with the conjunction *and* and the intonation breaks as signals. Here a different treatment, termed the **PRODUCTION-BASED FORMALIZATION**, is preferred. It is founded on the fact that a speaker begins with one constituent and adds on the others as necessary to complete the expression. This would require a choice to continue the construction each time, with the break or the conjunction as relators in a conjunctive phrase with *RELATOR* and *AXIS*.

COPULAR CLAUSE (6)   A generic term for a clause involving a link verb like English *to be* often termed a "copula" or "copular verb". In English, we can recognize five different subtypes of this construction based on meaning and functional relations, associated with different formal kinds of expression of the **COMPLEMENT** function. One of these is the **DESCRIPTIVE CLAUSE**, characterized by an adjective phrase as Complement, with the function of indicating qualities describing the referent of the Subject, as in *Arthur is **very handsome***. Another is the **EQUATIVE CLAUSE**, characterized by a definite noun phrase as Complement, with the function of equating the referent of the Subject with that of the phrase, as in *Maria is **the teacher***. Another is the **IDENTIFICATIONAL CLAUSE**, characterized by an indefinite noun phrase as Complement, with the function of indicating that the referent of the Subject is a member of the class designated by the Complement, as in *Philip is **a ditchdigger***. Still another is the **LOCATIVE CLAUSE**, which has a locational expression of the Complement, functioning to indicate the locus of the referent of the Subject, as in *Elvira is **over there***. Finally, there is the **POSSESSIVE CLAUSE**, which uses an expression of possession as the Complement, intending to indicate the "ownership" (in one or another sense) of the Subject's referent, as in *Timmy is **ours***. In English these can all be seen as varieties of a single construction because the only formal differences among them involve the different manifestations of Complement. In other languages, however, we may find further differences – involving such matters as the verb or constituent presence or order – to justify the recognition of more than one construction.

CORRELATIVE COORDINATION (5)   A form of grammatical coordination in which a pair of distinct conjunctions function together to signal some relation. English examples include *Both Mary and Sue*, *either the butler or the gardener*, and *neither fast nor slow*.

DECLARATIVE SENTENCE (12)   A kind of sentence used to make a statement rather than to ask a question (see *INTERROGATIVE SENTENCE*) or give a command (see *IMPERATIVE SENTENCE*). For example, *This is a declarative sentence*.

DEFINITENESS (2)   An inflectional category of the noun and some adjuncts in some languages. The term *DEFINITE* generally implies the item is known to the hearer, while the contrasting *INDEFINITE* suggests that it is not, though details of usage can vary considerably from one language to another. The category is of special syntactic relevance when it affects some kind of concordial or governmental relationship. Definiteness may also be expressed by separate words rather than via morphology, and there are many languages in the world that do not express it in either of these ways.

DEFINITENESS GOVERNMENT (7)   A term suggested here for the situation seen in languages like German, where ordinary adjectives have different inflectional forms depending on the definiteness of determiners. In German, for instance, one finds the nominative noun phrases *der gute Mann* THE GOOD MAN and *ein guter Mann* A GOOD MAN, with the definite article *der* calling forth a different inflectional form of the word meaning GOOD than the indefinite *ein*. For the German case, at least, it must be admitted that the term is potentially misleading, because it is not simply definite vs. indefinite in a purely semantic sense. However, like the use of simple designations based on some forms for grammatical genders, it is convenient.

DEGREE (2)   A grammatical categorial dimension applicable to adjectives and adverbs, as in English *fast, faster, fastest* illustrating the terms *POSITIVE, COMPARATIVE,* and *SUPERLATIVE*. While many textbooks treat this as a matter of inflection, it is probably best viewed as a matter of stem-formation. It can, like other categories, relate to syntax in that it can alternatively be expressed with a minor syntactic construction, as seen in English *quickly, more quickly, most quickly*.

DEIXIS (2)   Literally a "pointing out", but the term is used here for degrees of distance as commonly reflected by either determining words or in some languages by inflectional affixes. When inflectional deixis occurs, it often involves a system of two terms *PROXIMAL* (for something close by) vs. *DISTAL* (for something further removed). In English, this distinction is represented by the determiners *this* and *that*. Many other languages, and even some old-fashioned varieties of English, show a three-term system, with an intermediate term which can be termed *MEDIAL* often associated with location near the addressee – *this, that, yon* for *PROXIMAL, MEDIAL,* and *DISTAL* respectively.

DELIMITER (3)   A term used by some linguists for the function of an adjunct such as English *all*, which precedes the *DETERMINER*.

DEPENDENT CLAUSE (6)   See **CLAUSE**.

DESCRIPTIVE CLAUSE (6)   See **COPULAR CLAUSE**.

DETERMINATION (7)   A term suggested in this book for a situation where the function of some construction within a larger structure is grammatically related to the selection of some inflectional category or vocabulary choice. For example, if such a syntactic function as Subject, Direct Object, or Indirect Object is correlated with some particular case of a nominal or adpositional selection, we can speak of the function **determining** the inflection or adposition. This contrasts with *GOVERNMENT*, which will always involve a classification within the governing element.

DETERMINER (1)   A term used rather commonly in linguists' grammars for the generalized function of certain types of traditional adjectives, often including articles, demonstratives, and/or possessives. In English, it has been applied to a class including all three of these plus further the -'*s* possessive construction.

DIFFERENTIAL LINKAGE (8)   A criterion for the recognition of clitics via distinctions between the grammatical relations of an element and its phonological linkage, such that it is linked grammatically to a constituent on one side, while it is linked phonologically in the other direction. For example, we sometimes find prepositions obviously relating to a following AXIS, but phonologically linked to a preceding word. The cases where this criterion applies seem to be distinctly less frequent than those for the other criteria for clitic status. One case of its applicability in English may be seen in forms like *wanna*, seen as a reduced form of *want to*, where the reduced *to* relates grammatically to the following verb (as in *wanna go*) but is phonologically linked to the preceding word.

DIRECT OBJECT (6)   See **OBJECT**.

DIRECT TRANSITIVE CLAUSE (11)   A term suggested in this book for the variety of transitive clause that is not *ANTIPASSIVE* in a language such as Yup'ik, which distinguishes the antipassive within an *ERGATIVE* system. So the distinction *DIRECT/ANTIPASSIVE* would be the counterpart of the *ACTIVE/PASSIVE* distinction in a language of the *ACCUSATIVE* type.

DISCREPANCY (15)   A general term for a situation in which there is not just a simple one-to-one correspondence between two levels of linguistic structure. In syntax the most interesting aspect of this has to do with semology vs. grammar. Eight types of discrepancy are exemplified here. There are two kinds of **ALTERNATIONAL DISCREPANCY**: in the one called **DIVERSIFICATION** a more abstract element (such as a sememe) is realized grammatically in alternative ways; in **SYNCRETIZATION** a less abstract unit realizes alternate ones on the more abstract level. There are also two types of **COMBINATORY DISCREPANCY**: in **COMPOSITE REALIZATION** a more abstract unit is manifested by a combination of two or more less abstract units, while in **PORTMANTEAU REALIZATION** a single less abstract unit serves to manifest a combination of two or more more abstract ones. And there are two types of **NULL DISCREPANCY**, so called because both involve zero elements: under **ZERO REALIZATION**, a more abstract unit is at least sometimes manifested as zero, while under **EMPTY REALIZATION** an overt element on the less abstract level corresponds to nothing on the more abstract, and is simply predictable on the basis of what does occur. The term **ANATAXIS** refers to a difference of ordering between levels, which between semology and grammar commonly involves a semology without linear order manifested syntactically in a particular order. Finally, there are many cases where an element of meaning is manifested as a specification to the grammar to select some particular construction: this is called **SPECIFICATIONAL REALIZATION**.

DISJUNCTIVE COORDINATION (5)   Coordination using conjunctions that indicate that the coordinated elements function as alternatives, as opposed to *CONJUNCTIVE COORDINATION*. For example, *She will **either move overseas or go to her daughter's to live**,* or ***Bill or John** should be able to fix that*.

DISJUNCTIVE INTERROGATIVE (13)   In general, any question which lists alternative answers, such as *Are you going or not?* or *Will you buy your baked goods at Wilson's, DuPont's or DiMarco's?* In some languages, such as Chinese, a variety involving a negative versus an affirmative has become a very frequent kind of *POLARITY QUESTION*.

DISJUNCTIVE SENTENCE (12)   A sentence containing two or more clauses intended as alternatives, as would be indicated by the conjunction *or* or the correlative pair *either ... or*. For example, *John will give me a loan or I will have to sell the property to pay my debts.* Compare *CONJUNCTIVE SENTENCE*.

DISTANCE (2)   An inflectional category subordinated to TENSE in some languages. Specifically, it helps to distinguish varieties of non-present tenses in terms of their removal from the present or other basic reference point in time. Most often, degrees of distance are used to break down past time into two or more actual tenses, but some languages have distinctions in the future as well, distinguishing, for instance, an immediate future from a more general one.

DIVERSIFICATION (15)   See **DISCREPANCY**.

ECHO QUESTIONS (13)   See **CONFIRMATORY QUESTIONS.**

EMPHASIS (11)   A term suggested in this book for a variety of *HIGHLIGHTING* that involves placing the major accent in a clause on a different word to draw special attention to it, often to contrast it with some other possibility.

EMPTY REALIZATION (15)   See **DISCREPANCY**.

ENCLITIC (8)   See **CLITIC**.

ENDOCENTRIC (3)   A term for any *CONSTRUCTION* seen as having a "center" or *HEAD* within it, with non-head constituents being *ADJUNCTS* to this head.

ENTITY SEMEME (15)   A sememe roughly corresponding to a grammatical noun. It may be marked as fulfilling some role as a *PARTICIPANT* in an event, but it may also function as a *CIRCUMSTANTIAL* (as in *in the house*) or it may occur as a verb, especially in languages that regularly use verbs of existence from any noun, such as Yup'ik Eskimo.

EQUATIVE CLAUSE (6)   See **COPULAR CLAUSE**.

ERGATIVE CASE (10)   See **ERGATIVE SYSTEM**.

ERGATIVE SYSTEM (10)   One of the kinds of clause organization in which the noun (or pronoun) referring to the person or thing affected by an action, whether expressed by a transitive or an intransitive verb, is placed in the *ABSOLUTIVE CASE*, while the one indicating the doer of a transitive act is in a different case termed the *ERGATIVE.* This kind of system is less frequent than the *ACCUSATIVE SYSTEM* found in most European languages and many others elsewhere as well, but it is found in Basque, varieties of Eskimo, and many Australian Aboriginal languages, among others. This is to be distinguished not only from the *ACCUSATIVE* but also from various other kinds of system, such as the *AGENTIVE, UNIPARTITE* and *TRIPARTITE* systems.

EVENT (11)   The semological category most obviously associated with a grammatical verb, though some verbs (like *remain* or *ail*) may represent states and events may be represented in other ways, such as by nouns like *running* or *competition*.

EVENT CLUSTER (15)   See **EVENT SEMEME.**

EVENT SEMEME (15)   A unit in the semology of a language corresponding to a happening. It will most typically be grammatically manifested as a verb, but under other circumstances it may occur as a noun such as *washing* or *legalization,* or as still another part of speech. In the semotactic patterns of a language, the various event sememes would be associated with kinds of *PARTICIPANTS* in **EVENT CLUSTERS**, corresponding roughly to logical propositions. Such a cluster, for instance, would associate an event such as hitting with John as actor and Harry as undergoer, to produce the semological representation which could variously be expressed by the clauses *John hit Harry, Harry was hit by John,* or the clausoidal phrases *John's hitting Harry, Harry's being hit by John.* These different forms of manifestation would depend on grammatical context and the presence or absence of additional sememes.

EXHAUSTIVE CONJUNCTIVE (5)   A special kind of conjunctive in such languages as Japanese, used to indicate that the speaker believes a given list is complete rather than just partial. This contrasts with the *SELECTIVE CONJUNCTIVE.*

EXISTENTIAL CLAUSE (6)   A special kind of clause which predicates the existence (or non-existence) of whatever is named by its Subject. In English, this can be seen as a special clause type introduced by *there*, as in *There are fish in the pond*.

EXOCENTRIC (3)   A term for any CONSTRUCTION seen as lacking a "center" or HEAD characterizing the ENDOCENTRIC type of construction. There are two major sorts of such constructions that are widespread. One of these is the RELATOR/AXIS type, including adpositional and conjunctive phrases. Another is the predicative type of construction, as typically seen in clause structures.

EXTENDABLE PHRASE (5)   A general structure suggested for the formalization of COORDINATION. Such a phrase typically has a structure of an obligatory constituent accompanied by an optional one, generally Initial plus Addition in AFTERBRANCHING (or alternatively Addition plus Terminal if the possibility of FOREBRANCHING coordination is accepted for some languages).

EXTENDED SUPERSCRIPTS (7)   A notational device used in this book to aid in dealing with situations in which a PREDICATOR agrees regarding the same grammatical categories with more than one PARTICIPANT in a clause. The extension of the superscript number standing for a categorial dimension (such as GENDER, NUMBER, or PERSON) uses a decimal point followed by a second number standing for the relevant participant. (For instance 1.1 might stand for NUMBER related to SUBJECT while 1.2 stands for NUMBER related to the DIRECT OBJECT.)

FOCUS (11)   A term suggested in this book for the semological element that lies behind the selection of the Subject in a clause. So the Subjects of actives and passives alike are seen as being focused. This usage is historically derived from the traditional treatment of voice in the Philippine languages. It should not be confused with the use of the same term by other linguists for what is here termed EMPHASIS.

FOREBRANCHING (5)   A pattern of constituency that sometimes shows up in the treatment of grammatical coordination and elsewhere, with potentially deep branching at the beginning of a construction, **before** the first constituent. The source of the name suggested here is rather obvious, but the more common name found in the literature is "left-branching". This term is rejected here because it is based on the conventions of writing European languages from left to right. Spoken languages cannot have a "left" or a "right", only a "before" and "after" in their linear order. Contrast AFTERBRANCHING.

FUNCTION (1)   An indication of what some syntactic constituent **does**, as contrasted with what it **is**. According to the general approach to syntactic constructions used in this book, each position in a construction requires mention of both its function and the class of words or other constructions that manifest that function. So in characterizing the Transitive Clause construction involved with such an English example as *These dogs chase cats*, it is not adequate to characterize it in terms of Noun Phrase + Verb + Noun Phrase. Rather, the more complete and accurate characterization requires the mention of both the function and its manifestation, so Subject manifested by Noun Phrase, Transitive Predicator manifested by Transitive Verb, and Direct Object manifested by Noun Phrase. This already illustrates the fact that different functions can be manifested by the same structure (Noun Phrase). Further consideration of the manifestations of these two functions would also show that a distinct structure, the Nominative Pronoun Phrase, can manifest Subject, and the Accusative Pronoun Phrase can serve as an alternative manifestation of Direct Object.

GENDER (2)   A grammatical classification imposed by the grammars of some languages upon noun phrases and/or pronouns with an effect on the forms of co-constituents or syntactic constructions. As understood in linguistics, gender may or may not have a relation to biological sex. In most languages that have it, gender typically has some relation to semantic classification and some relatively arbitrary aspects as well. Besides sex, however, gender may relate to semantic properties of animateness and shape, among others. For syntactic purposes, genders are recognized as classifications of lexical items which have an effect on some or all of their co-constituents, as expressed via GENDER CONCORD.

GENDER CONCORD (4)   Agreement of certain adjuncts with a head or of a verb with expressions of associated participants for the category of GENDER. While this kind of concord is often treated in the same breath as simple concord, such as is found for number, person, or definiteness in various languages, it has more in common with GOVERNMENT because gender is inflectional in the adjective or verb, but is essentially a classification in the governing nominal.

GERUND PHRASE (14)   A kind of CLAUSOID involving a gerund, which is a kind of verbal noun. In English the gerund always coincides morphologically with the present participle, involving the suffix -*ing*. Examples of gerund phrases in the role of Subject in English are ***Entertaining friends*** *can be a nuisance* and ***Always having to defer to her brother*** *made her angry*. Used after *She hated,* either of these could be a Direct Object, and after *She talked about* either would be Axis in a prepositional phrase.

GLOSS (1)   A rough translation commonly given to identify a morpheme, word, phrase, or longer passage cited from a foreign language in linguistic discussion. Most commonly, linguists identify glosses by enclosing them in single quotes: Spanish *la mesa* 'the table'. In this work, small capitals with no quotes are used instead: THE TABLE.

GOVERNED (4)   See **GOVERNMENT.**

GOVERNMENT (= **GOVERNMENTAL CONGRUENCE**) (4)   A kind of dependence between co-constituents in a construction such that a classification applying to one of these, termed the **GOVERNOR**, affects the morphological form of the other, called the **GOVERNED**. In more conservative Indo-European languages the prime examples of this phenomenon involve the *CASE* of governed nominals related to classifications of verbs of which they serve as Objects (in predicative constructions) or to classifications of prepositions with which they serve as axes in relator-axis constructions. Neither of these relations is present in modern English. A genuine English example of government involves verbs governing the mood of subordinate clauses, as in the difference between the indicative in *I know that she* **works** *hard* and the subjunctive in *I require that she* **work** *hard* in standard American English.

GOVERNOR (4)   See **GOVERNMENT.**

GRAMMAR (1)   In this book "grammar" is used for the central part of linguistic description, excluding both semology and phonology. This includes both syntax and morphology. In some alternative usages the term is used as a synonym for what is here termed "linguistic description", therefore including phonology, morphology, syntax, and semology.

HEAD (1)   The central constituent of an *ENDOCENTRIC CONSTRUCTION* whose co-constituents are all kinds of *ADJUNCTS*. In the understanding followed here, the common kinds of heads are found in noun phrases, verb phrases, adjective phrases and adverbial phrases. In more recent years, some linguists have adopted a more expansive conception, seeing even adpositional phrases as having heads, but this view is not followed here.

HIGHLIGHTING (11)   A term suggested here to cover various kinds of phenomena involving the selection of certain *PARTICIPANTS* or *CIRCUMSTANTIALS* for special attention marked by various linguistic devices. *VOICE* is one widespread example of the phenomenon, involving the selection of some *PARTICIPANT* (in some languages even a *CIRCUMSTANTIAL*) as the Subject. Other varieties involve placement of major accent or selection of special constructions.

HYPOTHETICAL CONDITIONAL SENTENCE (12)   A sentence that involves a condition contrary to the known (or assumed) fact. For example, *If he had come, he would have let us know*. In many languages these have one or more differences of form setting them apart from *REAL CONDITIONAL SENTENCES.*

IDENTIFICATIONAL CLAUSE (6)   See **COPULAR CLAUSE**.

IMPERATIVE SENTENCE (12)   A kind of sentence which gives a command, typically implicitly second person, with Subject pronouns optional even in languages like English where they are normally obligatory. Many languages (e.g. Latin and Russian) have a distinctive verbal mode for imperatives. This is opposed to a sentence which makes a statement (see DECLARATIVE SENTENCE) or asks a question (see *INTERROGATIVE SENTENCE*).

INCLUSION (2)   A categorial dimension relevant to non-singular pronouns of the first person in some languages, distinguishing whether the "we" includes the addressee (*INCLUSIVE*) or not (*EXCLUSIVE*).

INDEPENDENT CLAUSE (6)   See **CLAUSE**.

INDIRECT OBJECT (6)   In a *BITRANSITIVE CLAUSE*, a second Object that indicates the recipient or beneficiary involved in an action: *I gave **him** a book, They will fix **her** a good dinner, Father will tell **us** a story.*

INFINITIVE PHRASE (14)   A kind of *CLAUSOID* in which the main verb is expressed in an inflectional form called the infinitive, characterized in the classical languages by lacking inflection for person and number. Examples in English include *you to visit Aunt Myrtle, to bravely go where no man has gone before* and *to dispense with the formalities*, any of which could occur as Object after *They wanted*. (In English these infinitives are "marked" by the word *to* with the unaffixed form of the verb, but this latter has a special form only in *to be*, [with *be* also functioning as the imperative] otherwise coinciding in form with the present tense outside the *THIRD-PERSON SINGULAR*.)

INFLECTIONAL INTERROGATIVE (13)   A type of interrogative signaled by inflection of the verb rather than by other devices like word order, particles, or intonation. This phenomenon is not generally found in European languages, but can be found in various parts of the world, as, for instance, in Turkish, Eskimo, and some languages of India.

INSTRUMENT-PASSIVE (11)   See **PASSIVE VOICE**.

INTERROGATIVE SENTENCE (12)   A kind of sentence used to ask a question rather than to make a statement (see *DECLARATIVE SENTENCE*) or give a command (see *IMPERATIVE SENTENCE*). For example, *Is this a declarative sentence?*

INTONATIONAL INTERROGATIVE (13)   In the purest sense, a polarity question that differs from a corresponding statement only in the kind of intonation it shows (usually a rising pattern, though the precise description can vary). There are also many interrogatives which can be marked by intonation in combination with other devices like special particles or word order differences.

INTRANSITIVE CLAUSE (6)   In traditional grammatical terminology, a clause without any Objects, so expressing only one *PARTICIPANT.* Such clauses often express motion like *He is going* or states like *She is sleeping*. In the present usage, it does not cover all non-transitives, excluding *COPULAR* and *EXISTENTIAL* clauses, for instance.

INTRODUCER (6)   A functional term suggested in this book for the function of *there* in an English existential clause such as *There is a book on the table*. While in some traditions this is treated as the SUBJECT, the approach used here would assign that role to *a book* in this example.

LEXICAL INTERROGATIVE (13)   A kind of *POLARITY QUESTION* indicated by the occurrence of a particular item of vocabulary which has the function of indicating a question all by itself.

LOCATION-PASSIVE (11)   See **PASSIVE VOICE**.

LOCATIONAL (1)   A functional term for a clause element indicating the place where some event occurs or state exists. For example, the final expression in each of the following can be taken to manifest this function: *He will complete the work **over there***; *Her children often misbehave **in elegant restaurants***.

LOCATIONAL CLAUSE (14)   See **SUBORDINATE CLAUSE.**

LOCATIVE CLAUSE (6)   See **COPULAR CLAUSE**.

MAIN (5)   A term suggested in this book for the function of the obligatory part of a continuation phrase construction involved in accounting for *COORDINATION*, its obligatory co-constituent being the *CONTINUATION*.

MANIFESTATION CLASS (1)   The class of words or other constructions that serve to manifest a given syntactic function. In practice, such a class may be limited to a single morpheme or indefinitely large, depending on the circumstances.

MANNER CLAUSE (4)   See **SUBORDINATE CLAUSE.**

MARKED ELEMENT (15)   See **MARKEDNESS**.

MARKEDNESS (15)   The general notion that many choices involved in language are profitably seen as involving a more special, typically rarer, choice termed the MARKED ELEMENT as contrasted with a more usual, default choice termed the UNMARKED ELEMENT. So the difference between Singular and Plural is usually seen with Plural as marked vs. Singular as unmarked. There may be more than one marked term, so with Dual added, this would also be viewed as marked. The notion of "transformational operation" is sometimes seen as an appropriate way to distinguish the marked from the unmarked, but the extra idea of a derivational process is not necessary to capture the idea that some terms or constructions are more marked than others.

MODE (2)   A form of verbal inflection seen in some languages, most usually distinguishing at least some of such categorial terms as *DECLARATIVE*, *INTERROGATIVE*, and/or *IMPERATIVE*. In this book, it is treated as distinct from *MOOD*, but some grammatical traditions conflate these two.

MODIFIER (1)   Used here for the function of an ordinary descriptive adjective as in an example like *the **big** horse*, and for parallel functions manifested by adverbs, as in ***completely** explicit*. In more traditional grammar, this same term is used more generally for what may be termed an *ADJUNCT*.

MONOSYNDETON (= **MONOSYNDETIC COORDINATION**) (5)   A term suggested in this book for the pattern of coordination of three or more elements according to which an overt conjunction is found only in construction with the final element, as in the phrase *the books, the magazines, and the pamphlets*. Compare *POLYSYNDETON*.

MOOD (2)   A form of verbal inflection seen in some languages, most usually distinguishing at least some of such categorial terms as *INDICATIVE*, *SUBJUNCTIVE*, *OPTATIVE* and/or *CONJUNCTIVE*. In this book, it is treated as distinct from *MODE*, but some grammatical traditions conflate these two.

MORPHOLOGY (1)   The study and description of the internal grammatical structure of words. Together with *SYNTAX*, it makes up *GRAMMAR*. Unlike syntax, however, morphology is not found in all languages, though it is found to some degree in most languages. Furthermore, its role in a given language may be larger or smaller.

MULTIPLE COORDINATION (5)   A term suggested for the case where instead of the *CORRELATIVE CONJUNCTIONS* found in English, we find rather a repetition of the same conjunction over and over again. So in Russian, for instance, we find *ili Petr ili Pavel* EITHER PETER OR PAUL with the same word *ili* used for both of the correlatives *either* and *or* of English.

NEGATIVE ANTI-CONCORD (9)   The situation in standard English, where the presence of a negative word like *nothing*, *never*, *nobody* precludes the use of another of these or a negated Predicator in the same clause. This is the opposite of the *NEGATIVE CONCORD* seen in non-standard English and both standard and non-standard forms of various other languages.

NEGATIVE AUXILIARY (9)   A special kind of *AUXILIARY* verb used in some languages (e.g. Finnish) to signal negation.

NEGATIVE CONCORD (9)   A requirement found in some languages requiring negation to be multiply expressed under some circumstances.

NEGATIVE COORDINATION (5)   The special type of coordination that involves the *CORRELATIVE* pair *neither … nor* in English. In other languages, the expression of this may involve the *MULTIPLE* rather than the correlative type of coordination.

NOMINAL-TYPE-BASED SYSTEM (of split ergativity) (10)   See **SPLIT ERGATIVITY**.

NON-RESTRICTIVE RELATIVE CLAUSE (14)   See **RELATIVE CLAUSE.**

NULL DISCREPANCY (15)   See **DISCREPANCY.**

NUMBER (2)   A frequent inflectional category for nouns, pronouns, verbs, and adjectives relating, as a minimum, to the terms *SINGULAR* and *PLURAL*. In some languages, more detailed terms such as *DUAL* may also figure. In many cases this category may be involved in concord, as within noun phrases or between Subjects (and some Objects) and associated Predicators. In conjunction with nouns in particular, number may be expressed by separate words, thus syntactically rather than morphologically, in some languages.

OBJECT (1)   In general, the grammatical expression of certain non-Subject participants in a clause, usually either *UNDERGOERS* or **RECIPIENTS**. An Object expressing the former is traditionally termed a **DIRECT OBJECT** (*She took **the book***), and one expressing the latter is an *INDIRECT OBJECT* (*They awarded **them** first prize*).

OBJECT CLAUSE (14)   A clause that fulfills the function of *OBJECT* in a larger clause, as in *I know **that he cannot finish the work*** or *Can you tell me **whether your project will be finished on schedule***?

OBJECTIVE CASE (10)   See **TRIPARTITE SYSTEM.**

OBJECTIVE-TRANSITIVE CLAUSE (6)   See **TRANSITIVE CLAUSE.**

PARTICIPANT (6)   In *SEMOLOGY*, a general term referring to a person or thing that plays a central role in some event, most usually including at least the *ACTOR, UNDERGOER*, and **RECIPIENT**. Compare *CIRCUMSTANTIAL*.

PARTICIPANT SEMEME (15)   An *ENTITY SEMEME* marked with the role of some *PARTICIPANT* in conjunction with some state or event.

PARTICIPIAL PHRASE (14)   A variety of *CLAUSOIDAL PHRASE*, typically with the function of an *ADJUNCT*. English examples would be *the books **written by Irish authors*** or *all people **working at this location.***

PASSIVE VOICE (11)   A frequent *HIGHLIGHTING* device which treats some *PARTICIPANT* other than the one that does the action as the grammatical SUBJECT, often further associated with differences in the way the *PREDICATOR* is expressed. The most commonly found subtype of this is the **UNDERGOER-PASSIVE**, where the participant that undergoes the action is the Subject (e.g. *Ron was injured*). English also has a **RECIPIENT-PASSIVE** (e.g. *Helen was given the prize*) with the recipient expressed as Subject, though this is lacking in many other European languages. Some languages, especially Austronesian languages of the Philippines, have other passives like the **INSTRUMENT-PASSIVE** (instrument as passive Subject) and **LOCATION-PASSIVE** (location as passive Subject).

PATIENTIVE CASE (10)   See **AGENTIVE SYSTEM**.

PERSON (2)   A traditional grammatical category associated with personal pronouns and verbs in various languages. The terms involved are quite standard with *FIRST PERSON* referring to the speaker(s) or groups including them, the *SECOND PERSON* to the addressee, and the *THIRD PERSON* to all other persons or things.

PHONOLOGY (1)   The part of linguistic description that treats the linguistic organization of sound, along with *GRAMMAR* and *SEMOLOGY*. It includes the identification of the basic signaling units, the phonemes, and the description of their manifestations in different environments. It also includes the study of the arrangement patterns of these phonemes, the **PHONOTACTICS**, which can show considerable difference from one language to another. Morphophonemics, the study of how phonemes can alternate in the manifestation of grammatical units, can also be seen as part of phonology in the broad sense, but its study requires considerable attention to the phonology. Any spoken language, by definition, has a phonology as its system of expression. Languages expressed in other media have their own kinds of expression systems, and it is not appropriate to extend the term "phonology" to these. So for the sign languages widely used in various deaf communities, the system corresponding to a phonology is best given a distinctive name – "cheirology" has sometimes been used – though some linguists dealing with it have spoken of "phonology" in this regard. In a study of syntax, phonology is of peripheral interest, though in practical terms it is often necessary to penetrate alternations of the morphophonemic sort in the editing of data for syntactic analysis. Also, phonological aspects such as the study of accent and intonation are intimately connected to syntax as well as phonology.

PHONOTACTICS (1)   See **PHONOLOGY**.

PHRASE (1)   A relatively low *RANK* of syntactic structure typically involving patterns of word-combination of units smaller than the *CLAUSE*. According to the approach adopted here, a minimal phrase may sometimes be a single word, provided this could be expandable by the addition of other words. So in both *They greeted **visitors*** and *They greeted **visitors from Mars*** boldface items would exemplify the noun phrase, while *visitors* would not be a phrase by itself in *They greeted **the visitors*** because the entire phrase would have to include the definite article there.

POLARITY (2)   A traditional grammatical category distinguishing the terms *AFFIRMATIVE* and *NEGATIVE*. Every language has a way of expressing such distinctions. In some, such as Turkish and various Eskimo languages, it may be part of the verbal inflections, but in others it may be syntactic, using special particles or auxiliary verbs.

POLARITY QUESTION (13)   A basic kind of question, found in every language, which involves asking someone to indicate the truth of a proposition (via an affirmative answer) or its falsity (via a negative answer). Often these are also called "yes-no questions".

POLYSYNDETON (= **POLYSYNDETIC COORDINATION**) (5)   A term suggested in this book for the pattern of coordination of three or more elements according to which an overt conjunction is found in construction with each associated element after the first one, as in the phrase *the books, and the magazines, and the pamphlets*. Compare MONOSYNDETON.

PORTMANTEAU REALIZATION (15)   See **DISCREPANCY**.

POSITIONAL INTERROGATIVE (13)   A widely found pattern for forming *POLARITY QUESTIONS* by using a special order of clausal elements. This is seen in such English examples as *Is he here?* (vs. the statement *He is here*) and *Can she dance?* (vs. *She can dance*). While this pattern is quite normal for examples like these, it is much more restricted in modern English than it was at the time of Shakespeare, when it was in general use and *Know you the way?* and *Speak they good English?* would have been normal polarity questions. This more general use is still common in many languages of continental Europe and elsewhere.

POSITIONAL NOUN (3)   One of a class of nouns referring to physical location which may be used to augment a more rudimentary system of local cases or locational adpositions. Yup'ik Eskimo, for instance, has just four local cases indicating (1) position at/in; (2) motion toward/into; (3) motion from; and (4) motion through. It has no further local cases and no adpositions at all, but it has a rather large class of positional nouns. So while English would use a preposition like *over it* or *under it*, a Yup'ik speaker would use an expression literally translatable as AT ITS AREA-ABOVE or AT ITS AREA-BELOW. In some languages such expressions may evolve into adpositions, and there is sometimes uncertainty as to how to treat some of them. In English, for instance, we usually treat *in front of* and *in back of* as "compound prepositions" even though their structure is quite transparent, and we could view *front* and *back* as positional nouns here. The quite frozen nature of these expressions undoubtedly has a great deal to do with this traditional treatment, whereas we would be more likely to give a fuller syntactic analysis to otherwise similar expressions like *at the front of* and *at the back of*.

POSSESSION (2)   In some languages, an inflectional category for nouns, though of course every language has some way or other of expressing possession, whether inflectional or syntactic. In some instances of such inflection, we may find a noun simply inflected to indicate the presence or absence of possession, while in other cases, the specific *PERSON* and *NUMBER* of a possessor will be inflectionally indicated.

POSSESSIVE CLAUSE (6)   See **COPULAR CLAUSE**.

POSTINITIAL ENCLITIC (8)   See **CLITIC**.

POSTPOSED CONJUNCTION (5)   A conjunction placed after the word, phrase or other expression to which it relates most closely. This is clearly different from the typical English pattern, but can be found in many languages.

POSTPOSITION (3)   See **ADPOSITION**.

PREDICATOR (1)   A functional term for a function most typically indicated by a verb or verb phrase. The terms verb and Predicator are far from synonyms, however, because in some languages other kinds of words (such as adjectives, nouns, or locative adverbs) may sometimes function as Predicators. In addition, a verb may sometimes have a function other than that of Predicator, such as a Nominal Head or an adjunct of some kind.

PREPOSED CONJUNCTION (5)   A conjunction placed before the word, phrase or other expression to which it relates most closely. Typical English conjunctions like *and, or, but* are all of this type.

PREPOSITION (3)   See **ADPOSITION**.

PRINCIPAL (3)   A term suggested in this book to refer to the function of a "main verb" used in connection with an auxiliary. Therefore, in English examples like *They can **do** it, Does she **work** nights?* and *You have been **fighting*** the boldface forms can be seen as fulfilling the function of Principal.

PROCLITIC (8)   See **CLITIC**.

PROTASIS (12)   In traditional Greek rhetorical terms, the clause (or subsentence) expressing a condition, sometimes termed an "*if*-clause". For example, protasis would be the function of the boldface part in the sentence *I will do it **if I can find the time***.

PSEUDO-BITRANSITIVE CLAUSE (7)   See **BITRANSITIVE CLAUSE**.

QUALIFIER (3)   A term used by some linguists for a certain kind of adjunct coming after the HEAD in languages like English. In English, this function is often associated with relative clauses and some prepositional phrases, as shown in bold in such examples as in the noun phrases *the people **who refuse to understand*** and *the gentleman **from across the street***. In other languages, qualifiers may not share the same characteristics of position, so some judgment needs to be exercised in generalizing the term.

QUANTIFIER (3)   A general term for a kind of noun phrase Adjunct expressing quantity, whether precisely as in ***twelve** famous novels* or more vaguely as in ***several** broken windows* or ***many** old dogs*.

RANK (12)   A scale of size-difference reflecting a hierarchical arrangement of syntactic constructions. The ranks usually recognized, taken from the lowest up, are those of *WORD, PHRASE, CLAUSE,* and *SENTENCE*. It is also necessary to recognize that some constructions depart from simple rankings, especially when phrases or clauses occur within other phrases.

REAL CONDITIONAL SENTENCE (12)   A sentence that involves a condition in line with the known (or assumed) reality, though it may be seen as only possible or probable rather than actual. For example, *If he is ready, he will greet us shortly.* In many languages these have one or more differences of form setting them apart from *HYPOTHETICAL CONDITIONAL SENTENCES*.

REASON CLAUSE (14)   See **SUBORDINATE CLAUSE**.

RECIPIENT-PASSIVE (11)   See **PASSIVE VOICE**.

RELATIVE CLAUSE (14)   A kind of subordinate, dependent clause which typically serves as an adjunct within a noun phrase. English relative clauses are typically marked with *which, that,* or forms of *who* as in such examples as *the book there, **which I have yet to finish**, everything **that he touched**,* and *the man **whose dog I was feeding***. In English and many other languages, a distinction is observed between NON-RESTRICTIVE examples like the first one and RESTRICTIVE types like the other two. The former types are used to simply fill in some additional information, whereas the others help to indicate the identity of the referent of the fuller noun phrase.

RELATOR (3) A functional name used for one of the elements of such an *EXOCENTRIC CONSTRUCTION* as an adpositional phrase or a conjunctive phrase, specifically for the element that indicates the relation of the phrase to something else in its context. So in an English prepositional phrase, the Relator is manifested by the preposition, which typically indicates some particular relation of its phrase to some larger structure. And similarly a conjunction, filling the role of Relator in a conjunctive phrase, indicates such a relation as "addition" (*and*) or "alternative" (*or*).

RELATOR-FINAL CONJUNCTIVE PHRASE (5) A *CONJUNCTIVE PHRASE* of the sort found typically in some languages like Yup'ik Eskimo, in which the *RELATOR*, manifested by the conjunction, follows the associated AXIS rather than preceding it. To combine *kuskaq* CAT with *qimugta* DOG in Yup'ik, for instance, one says *kuskaq qimugta-llu*. Compare *RELATOR-INITIAL CONJUNCTIVE PHRASE*.

RELATOR-INITIAL CONJUNCTIVE PHRASE (5) A *CONJUNCTIVE PHRASE* of the sort found typically in languages like English, in which the *RELATOR*, manifested by the conjunction, precedes the associated *AXIS*, as in *John **and** Martha*. Compare *RELATOR-FINAL CONJUNCTIVE PHRASE*.

REPETITIVE COORDINATION (5) A phenomenon found in some languages in place of the correlative coordination found in English for meanings such as BOTH/AND, EITHER/OR, and NEITHER/NOR. It involves the use of the same word to translate both members of each pair. So in Russian *i* can mean either BOTH or AND, *ili* can mean EITHER or OR, and *ni* can mean either NEITHER or NOR.

RESTRICTIVE RELATIVE CLAUSE (14) See **RELATIVE CLAUSE**.

SELECTIVE CONJUNCTIVE (5) In some languages, a kind of conjunctive word that carries the implication that the enumerated possibilities in a list of conjuncts is a representative selection rather than an exhaustive enumeration. This contrasts with the *EXHAUSTIVE CONJUNCTIVE*.

SEMI-BITRANSITIVE CLAUSE (6) See **BITRANSITIVE CLAUSE**.

SEMI-TRANSITIVE CLAUSE (6) See **TRANSITIVE CLAUSE**.

SEMOLOGY (1) The linguistically based study of the organization of meaning, including the identification of meaning units called "sememes" and the study of their possible combinations in each language, termed **SEMOTACTICS**. Some treatments of syntax seek to include certain aspects of what is here seen as semology. The approach taken here, however, tries to distinguish them rather strictly. Two matters are worthy of special note in this regard. For one thing, syntax is responsible for **grammatical** compatibility, but not meaning compatibility, which is the domain of semology. So the fact that we can get *The man was here* and *The men were here,* but not either *The man were here* or *The men was here* in standard English is a matter of syntax, and an adequate syntactic description would have to provide for the first two while excluding the others. Such a description would not be responsible, however, for disallowing adjective–noun combinations like *energetic lake* or *married batchelor* or Subject–Predicator combinations like *The book froze* or *My pen ran away*. Those matters would be left to semology. Furthermore, syntax as such does not have the responsibility of relating *AGNATE* structures like *Sam prepared the report, The report was prepared by Sam,* and *the preparation of the report by Sam*. These are a matter of relations between syntax and semology, despite the attempts to treat them via forms of "deep syntax" in other models.

SEMOTACTICS (1)   See **SEMOLOGY**.

SENTENCE (1, 12)   The rank of syntactic structure conventionally understood as its upper limit. According to the usual understanding, a sentence must as a minimum incorporate at least one clause, but grammatical devices may be used to allow a single sentence to incorporate more than one clause in various ways. In spoken English, a single sentence is generally unified intonationally, while in the written language it is marked by its final punctuation via a period < . >, question mark < ? > or exclamation point < ! >.

SEPARABILITY (8)   A major criterion for the identification of *CLITICS*, and probably the one that is most frequently applicable in practice. According to this criterion, we recognize a clitic when an element looks like an affix phonologically, but can be more readily characterized by a particular syntactic position within a phrase, clause, or sentence than by a position in the morphological structure of words. This results in pseudo-affixes attaching to different kinds of words in different circumstances, as when the unaccented English definite article looks like a prefix to a numeral in *the-ten books*, to an adverb in *the-very old idea*, to an adjective in *the-good carpets*, but to a noun in *the-receipts*. This element has a readily statable syntactic position in relation to the noun phrase, but an insistence on treating it as a morphological prefix instead of a word would result in unnecessary complication.

SIMPLE CONCORD (4)   See **CONCORD**.

SIMPLE SENTENCE (14)   In traditional school grammar, a sentence containing just a single clause which can stand in isolation. For example *Tom lives next door to Sally in Florida.* While the distinctions made in this tradition are fairly easy to recognize and apply to examples, they do not correspond to what we would treat as separate sentence types according to the approach presented in this book, because the compound type merely involves a choice to extend a one-clause sentence by joining on one or more additional clauses.

SPECIFICATIONAL REALIZATION (15)   See **DISCREPANCY**.

SPLIT ERGATIVITY (10)   A name used for either of two kinds of systems which combine aspects of an *ACCUSATIVE SYSTEM* and an *ERGATIVE SYSTEM*. One subtype is a **TENSE-BASED SYSTEM**, in which some tenses (aspects, moods) seem to operate with one of the more basic types while others seem to operate with the other. This is often found in various languages of the Caucasus and in India. The other subtype, found in many languages of Australia, is the **NOMINAL-TYPE-BASED SYSTEM**. In this kind of system, the inflection of pronouns typically follows one basic type, while that of common nouns follows the other. Proper nouns, especially personal names, may work either way depending on the language.

STATIVE CLAUSE (6)   A convenient term to use for clauses involving verbs that express being along with an adjectival quality, which occur in many non-European languages such as Japanese and Yup'ik Eskimo.

SUBJECT (1)   In a clause, the grammatical element indicating what that clause is taken to be about. In many, but far from all, languages, this element may show agreement (regarding *PERSON*, *NUMBER*, and/or *GENDER*) with the *PREDICATOR*, but Objects, whether Direct or Indirect, may also show this in some languages. Across languages, it is not always easy to apply this notion, especially in languages of the *ERGATIVE TYPE*, where it is not clear whether the **ABSOLUTIVE** or the **ERGATIVE** element should be viewed as the grammatical Subject.

SUBJECT CLAUSE (14)   A clause that fulfills the function of Subject in a larger clause, as in ***Whether she arrives on time*** *is not important* or ***That he would dare to attack you*** *astounded me.*

SUBJECTIVE CASE (10)   See **TRIPARTITE SYSTEM**.

SUBJECTIVE-TRANSITIVE CLAUSE (6)   See **TRANSITIVE CLAUSE.**

SUBORDINATE CLAUSE (14)   A traditional name for any clause that functions in a phrase or another clause rather than standing as a sentence by itself or as one of two or more clauses coordinated in a *COMPOUND SENTENCE.* One obvious type would be a *RELATIVE CLAUSE,* and others would be a *SUBJECT CLAUSE* and an *OBJECT CLAUSE.* Another would be the *CONCESSIVE CLAUSE* like *although she will arrive tomorrow* which has the function of indicating a potentially contrasting fact. Others, named according to the clause or sentence functions that they manifest, include the **LOCATIONAL CLAUSE** like *where his brothers live* (manifesting Locational), the **MANNER CLAUSE** such as *just like all her friends do* (manifesting Manner), the **REASON CLAUSE** like *because they don't think that's right* (manifesting Reason), and the **TEMPORAL CLAUSE,** such as *when the rain started* (manifesting Temporal). (This listing should by no means be seen as exhaustive.) While in some languages like Yup'ik Eskimo at least some such clauses may be signaled by special modal inflections of the verb, in English and other languages many of the structures usually called subordinate clauses are in fact examples of the *SUBORDINATING CONJUNCTIVE PHRASE.*

SUBORDINATING CONJUNCTIVE PHRASE (14)   A generic term for a kind of *RELATOR-AXIS CONSTRUCTION* combining a clause as Axis with a subordinating conjunction as Relator. In less precise terms, the result is often termed a *SUBORDINATE CLAUSE* by itself.

SUPERSENTENCE (12)   A term suggested here as a possible name for a structure which can have a full sentence as a constituent. In a traditional (*REAL* or *HYPOTHETICAL*) *CONDITIONAL SENTENCE,* for example, we can easily find a *COMPOUND* (or *COMPOUND-COMPLEX*) *SENTENCE* as one of the syntactic constituents, as in *If she really returned and they were remarried, I am surprised that we did not find out sooner and I would think you would be shocked at all that secrecy.* The need for a separate term here, at the same time, is really debatable, since one can also get phrases in phrases and clauses within clauses, so the occurrence of sentences within sentences should not seem surprising.

SUPINE (14)   In some languages, a non-finite verb structure distinct from the infinitive which can form the basis for *CLAUSOIDAL PHRASES.* The term is actually used for forms of rather different functions in the grammars of various Indo-European languages. The Old Church Slavic supine, exemplified in some of the data of Table 14.16, is used solely to indicate purpose in combination with a verb of motion. In Latin grammar, there is one very similar usage of the accusative supine, but there is also a different ablative-case supine used in combination with other verbs and some adjectives. In Swedish grammar, the term is applied to a special verb form used in forming perfect compound tenses, which in Swedish (unlike English) is distinct from the past participle.

SUPPLEMENT QUESTIONS (13)   A term suggested by Leonard Bloomfield and adopted here for the general kinds of questions that ask the listener to supply more specific information than is found with a *POLARITY QUESTION.* Examples include *Who is it?, Where is she going?* English grammars have sometimes called these "wh-questions" based on the written form of most of the English words which signal them. This term is acceptable in discussions of English, but its extension to equivalents in other languages, though often encountered, is not appropriate.

SUPERSCRIPTS (4)   A notational device introduced in this book to formalize various kinds of grammatical congruence and determination. In general, the occurrence of the same numerical superscript on two or more co-constituents in some construction indicates at least a potential grammatical tie (such as *CONCORD* or *GOVERNMENT*) between or among them. A numerical suprascript augmented with a letter, on the other hand, indicates that the associated syntactic function specifies some grammatical selection via *DETERMINATION.*

SYNCRETIZATION (15)   See **DISCREPANCY**.

SYNDETIC COORDINATION (5)   Coordination of syntactic constituents accomplished with at least one overt conjunction. This is the most common pattern in languages like English, and occurs widely in various languages. It is applicable to either a pattern like *John, Tom, and Bill* or the alternative *John, and Tom, and Bill.* Compare *ASYNDETIC COORDINATION (= ASYNDETON).*

SYNTAX (1)   Generically, the study and description of arrangements in language. In linguistics, the usual use is applied more specifically to the study and description of how words are arranged into phrases, clauses, and sentences.

TAG QUESTIONS (13)   See **CONFIRMATORY QUESTIONS**.

TEMPORAL CLAUSE (14)   See **SUBORDINATE CLAUSE.**

TENSE (2)   A very common inflectional category for verbs, based on the time of an action relative to the moment of speech (or other possible temporal reference point). Basically, this allows one to distinguish past, present, and future. In some languages, some or all such distinctions may be indicated syntactically, via particles or auxiliaries, rather than morphologically.

TENSE-BASED SYSTEM (of split ergativity) (10)   See **SPLIT ERGATIVITY**.

THEMATIC TOPIC (11)   See **TOPIC.**

THEME (11)   A term used especially by M. A. K. Halliday (but dating originally to linguists of the Prague School in the period before World War II) for the element of a clause used as a starting point of a message, generally placed initially. In the most usual, unmarked, examples, the theme coincides with the grammatical Subject, as in *John visited his daughter in Chicago yesterday.* But in possible variants, used in different communicative circumstances, we may have other elements as theme, as in *His daughter, John visited in Chicago yesterday* or *In Chicago, John visited his daughter yesterday,* or *Yesterday, John visited his daughter in Chicago.* According to the treatment sketched in this volume, the choice of a non-Subject as theme is a matter of *HIGHLIGHTING.*

THESIS (12)   This term is suggested here for the functional part of an *ADVERSATIVE SENTENCE* type, which precedes what is introduced in English by *but* or a synonym. So in the example *Jack lives here, but his sister has moved to Alaska,* the portion preceding *but* is the thesis, while the rest is the *ANTITHESIS.*

TOPIC (11)   A term suggested in this book for the kind of *HIGHLIGHTING* signaled in English by the "pseudo-cleft construction" as in *What the cat catches is **the mouse**.* The term is far from standard, and the same word may be used by other writers for different kinds of highlighting. A related term, **THEMATIC TOPIC**, is suggested for the highlighting signaled by the "cleft construction", as in *It is **the mouse** that the cat catches.*

TRANSITIVE CLAUSE (6)   In traditional grammar, any clause where the verb is seen as taking an *OBJECT* as opposed to an intransitive without one. In English, one can distinguish a fully transitive type where an Object obligatorily occurs from a **SEMI-TRANSITIVE CLAUSE** where the Object is optional rather than obligatory (e.g. *We see* [*the book*]). In some languages, however, the Object is regularly omissible because its person and number are coded in the verb or are contextually predictable. Other subtypes of transitives seen in English include the **OBJECTIVE-TRANSITIVE CLAUSE** with two co-referential objects (e.g. *They appointed him Secretary of State*) and the **SUBJECTIVE-TRANSITIVE CLAUSE** with an Object co-referential with the subject (e.g. *He will make a fine valet*).

TRIPARTITE SYSTEM (10) A variety of clausal organization in which intransitive Subjects, transitive Subjects, and Objects are all always expressed in different ways, whether by different morphological cases or with distinct adpositional markers. When different morphological cases are involved, the terms *SUBJECTIVE CASE, AGENTIVE CASE*, and *OBJECTIVE CASE*, respectively, are suggested.

UNDERGOER (11) The *PARTICIPANT* seen as subjected to a process, whether expressed as the grammatical Subject, Object, or in some other way. So in both *John caressed Susan* and *Susan was caressed by John*, the word *Susan* expresses the undergoer, as Object in the first example, but as Subject in the second.

UNDERGOER-PASSIVE (10) See **PASSIVE VOICE.**

UNIPARTITE SYSTEM (10) A variety of clausal organization in which there is no formal case distinction involved in the expression of intransitive Subjects, transitive Subjects, and Objects – all are always expressed the same way. This phenomenon is found in Chinese, and it would be seen in English if all pronouns were without case differences, like *you* and *it*. It is to be expected in a language which is either without case inflection entirely (as Chinese is) or at least with no case distinctions in this area. It is contrasted to several kinds of *BIPARTITE SYSTEMS* and a *TRIPARTITE SYSTEM.*

UNMARKED ELEMENT (15) See **MARKEDNESS**.

VARIANT CLITIC (8) See **CLITIC**.

VOCABULARY BOX (1) In the primary notation system used to show solutions to data sets in this book, a box which lists vocabulary items of a particular syntactic class. Such a box is divided into two sub-boxes: the upper sub-box indicates the name assigned to the class involved, while the lower sub-box indicates the particular vocabulary items, with their glosses. In the instance of inflections, categorial-term labels (like *SINGULAR* and *PLURAL*) are used rather than the individual morphemic expressions, which have been abstracted out as a result of editing.

VOICE (2, 11) The grammatical category most commonly involving terms like *ACTIVE* and *PASSIVE*. indicating the different roles associated with Subjects. In a simple active/passive system the active voice has the *ACTOR* functioning as the grammatical Subject, while the corresponding passive has the *UNDERGOER* as Subject. Voice may be expressed morphologically in verbs, as in Latin and Classical Greek, or it may be expressed via syntactic constructions using auxiliary verbs, as in English. While some languages do not have voice as a grammatical category at all, others have more than just two voices, as in typical Philippine languages. Even English has two types of passives, as in *He was given the book* vs. *The book was given to him*.

WORD CONSTRUCTION (2) A grammatical construction internal to the structure of a particular word. In full detail, such constructions belong to morphology rather than syntax. Many languages have, however, inflectional properties that are of importance for syntax, so they need to be represented in edited forms in a word-construction box. These boxes differ from the construction boxes used for phrases, clauses, and sentences in not specifying a linear order of constituents, since word-internal matters of order are treated in morphology.

ZERO REALIZATION (15) See **DISCREPANCY**.

References

Textbooks and other works on syntax

Blake, Barry J. (1994) *Case*. Cambridge: Cambridge University Press.
Comrie, Bernard (1976) *Aspect*. Cambridge: Cambridge University Press.
Comrie, Bernard (1987) *Tense*. Cambridge: Cambridge University Press.
Comrie, Bernard (1989) *Language Universals and Linguistic Typology: Syntax and Morphology*. 2nd edn. Chicago: University of Chicago Press.
Corbett, Greville G. (1991) *Gender*. Cambridge: Cambridge University Press.
Corbett, Greville G. (2000) *Number*. Cambridge: Cambridge University Press.
Croft, William (1990) *Typology and Universals*. Cambridge: Cambridge University Press.
Dixon, R. M. W. (1994) *Ergativity*. Cambridge: Cambridge University Press.
Elson, Benjamin and Pickett, Velma (1988) *Beginning Morphology and Syntax*. Dallas: Summer Institute of Linguistics.
Gleason, H. A., Jr. (1961) *An Introduction to Descriptive Linguistics*, 2nd edn. New York: Holt, Rinehart and Winston. [Especially Chapters 10–14.]
Gleason, H. A., Jr. (1964) The organization of language: a stratificational view. *Georgetown University Round Table* 15:75–95.
Gleason, H. A., Jr. (1968) Contrastive analysis in discourse structure. *Georgetown University Round Table* 19:258–76.
Greenberg, Joseph H. (ed.) (1978) *Universals of Human Language*, vol. 4, *Syntax*. Stanford: Stanford University Press.
Hall, Robert A., Jr. (1964) *Introductory Linguistics*. Philadelphia: Chilton. [Especially Chapters 31–7.]
Halliday, M. A. K. (1967–8) Notes on transitivity and theme in English. *Journal of Linguistics* 3:37–81, 199–244; 4:179–215.
Halliday, M. A. K. (1994) *Introduction to Functional Grammar*. 2nd edn. London: Arnold.
Hockett, Charles F. (1958) *A Course in Modern Linguistics*. New York: Macmillan. [Especially Chapters 17–31.]
Klavans, Judith (1979) On clitics as words. *Chicago Linguistic Society Papers* 15:68–80.
Klavans, Judith (1982) *Some Problems in a Theory of Clitics*. Bloomington: Indiana University Linguistics Club.
Klavans, Judith (1985) The independence of syntax and phonology in cliticization. *Language* 61:95–129.
Koutsoudas, Andreas (1964) *Writing Transformational Grammars: An Introduction*. New York: McGraw-Hill.
Lamb, Sydney M. (1966) *Outline of Stratificational Grammar*. Washington, DC: Georgetown University Press.
Lamb, Sydney M. (1999) *Pathways of the Brain*. Amsterdam and Philadelphia: John Benjamins.
Lockwood, David G. (1972) *Introduction to Stratificational Linguistics*. New York: Harcourt Brace Jovanovich.
Lockwood, David G. (1980) Principles for a box-diagram notation for syntactic solutions. *LACUS Forum* VI:292–301.

Lockwood, David G. (1987) Clitics in a stratificational model of language. *LACUS Forum XIII*: 236–45.
Lockwood, David G. (1993) *Morphological Analysis and Description: A Realizational Approach*. Tokyo: International Language Sciences Publishers.
Lockwood, David G. (1996) Syntactic Specification of Morphological Categories: Government vs. Determination. *LACUS Forum XXII*: 133–43.
Longacre, Robert E. (1960) String constituent analysis. *Language* 36:63–88.
Longacre, Robert E. (1964a) *Grammar Discovery Procedures: A Field Manual* (Janua Linguarum, Series Minor, No. 33). The Hague: Mouton.
Longacre, Robert E. (1964b) Prolegomena to lexical structure. *Linguistics* 5:5–24.
Lyons, Christopher (1999) *Definiteness*. Cambridge: Cambridge University Press.
Matthews, P. H. (1981) *Syntax*. Cambridge: Cambridge University Press.
Merrifield, William, *et al.* (eds) (1987) *Laboratory Manual for Morphology and Syntax*. Dallas: Summer Institute of Linguistics.
Palmer, F. R. (1986) *Mode and Modality*. Cambridge: Cambridge University Press.
Palmer, F. R. (1994) *Grammatical Roles and Relations*. Cambridge: Cambridge University Press.
Pickett, Velma B. (1987) Clitics – to be or not to be words. *LACUS Forum XIII*: 246–53.
Pike, Kenneth L. (1967) *Language in Relation to a Unified Theory of the Structure of Human Behavior*. The Hague: Mouton.
Pike, Kenneth L. and Pike, Evelyn G. (1981) *Grammatical Analysis*, 2nd edn. Dallas: Summer Institute of Linguistics.
Wells, Rulon S. (1947) Immediate constituents. *Language* 23:71–117.

Sources consulted for language data

Abraham, R. C. (1959) *The Language of the Hausa People*. London: University of London Press.
Appleyard, David (1995) *Colloquial Amharic: A Complete Language Course*. London: Routledge.
Aronson, Howard I. (1982) *Georgian: A Reading Grammar*. Columbus, Ohio: Slavica Publishers.
Atmosumarto, Sutanto (1994) *Colloquial Indonesian*. London: Routledge.
Austin, Peter (1981) *A Grammar of Diyari (South Australia)*. Cambridge: Cambridge University Press.
Backhouse, A. E. (1993) *The Japanese Language: An Introduction*. Oxford: Oxford University Press.
Ballhatchet, H. J. and Kaiser, S. K. (1992) *Teach Yourself Japanese*. Lincolnwood, Illinois: NTC Publishing.
Bánhidi, Zoltán, Jókay, Zoltán and Szabó, Dénes (1965) *Learn Hungarian*, 2nd edn. Budapest: Publishing House for Textbooks.
Bennett, William H. (1980) *An Introduction to the Gothic Language*. New York: Modern Language Association.
Betts, Gavin (1992) *Teach Yourself Latin: A Complete Course*. Lincolnwood, Illinois: NTC Publishing.
Bhatia, Tej K. (1997) *Colloquial Hindi*. London: Routledge.
Bielec, Dana (1998) *Polish: An Essential Grammar*. London: Routledge.
Burgers, M. P. O. (1957) *Teach Yourself Afrikaans*. Hertford: English Universities Press.
Clarke, H. D. B. and Hamamura, Motoko (1981) *Colloquial Japanese*. London: Routledge and Kegan Paul.
Couro, Ted and Hutcheson, Christina (1973) *Dictionary of Mesa Grande Diegueño*. Banning, California: Malki Museum Press.
Couro, Ted and Langdon, Margaret (1975) *Let's Talk 'Iipay Aa: An Introduction to the Mesa Grande Diegueño Language*. Banning, California: Malki Museum Press, and Ramona, California: Ballena Press.

Dambriunas, Leonardas, Klimas, Antanas and Schmalstieg, William (1966) *Introduction to Modern Lithuanian*. New York: Franciscan Fathers Press.

Derbyshire, Desmond C. (1985) *Hixkaryana and Linguistic Typology*. Dallas: Summer Institute of Linguistics, and University of Texas at Arlington.

Dixon, R. M. W. (1972) *The Dyirbal Language of North Queensland* (Cambridge Studies in Linguistics 9). Cambridge: Cambridge University Press.

Donaldson, Bruce (1997) *Dutch: A Comprehensive Grammar*. London: Routledge.

Dunn, C. J. and Yanada, S. (1958) *Teach Yourself Japanese*. London: English Universities Press.

Durrell, Martin (1996) *Hammer's German Grammar and Usage*, 3rd edn. Lincolnwood, Ilinois: NTC Publishing.

Fairbanks, Gordon H. and Govind Misra, Bal (1966) *Spoken and Written Hindi*. Ithaca, New York: Cornell University Press.

Griffin, Robin M. (1992) *A Student's Latin Grammar*, North American edn. (revised and supplemented by Ed Phinney). Cambridge: Cambridge University Press.

Hayon, Yehiel (1970) *Modern Hebrew I*. Columbus: Ohio State University Bookstores.

Herrity, Peter (2000) *Slovene: A Comprehensive Grammar*. London: Routledge.

Hewitt, George (1996) *Georgian: A Learner's Grammar*. London: Routledge.

Holton, David, Mackridge, Peter and Philippaki-Warburton, Irene (1997) *Greek: A Comprehensive Grammar of the Modern Language*. London: Routledge.

Hyde, Villiana (1971) *An Introduction to the Luiseño Language*. Banning, California: Malki Museum Press.

Jacobson, Steven A. (1977) *A Grammatical Sketch of Siberian Yupik Eskimo, as Spoken on St. Lawrence Island, Alaska*. Fairbanks: Alaska Native Language Center, University of Alaska.

Jacobson, Steven A. (1984) *Yup'ik Eskimo Dictionary*. Fairbanks: Alaska Native Language Center, University of Alaska.

Jacobson, Steven A. (1990) *A Practical Grammar of the St. Lawrence Island/Siberian Yupik Eskimo Language*, Preliminary edn. Fairbanks: Alaska Native Language Center, University of Alaska.

Jacobson, Steven A. (1995) *A Practical Grammar of the Central Alaskan Yup'ik Eskimo Language*. Fairbanks: Alaska Native Language Center, University of Alaska.

Karlsson, Fred (1999) *Finnish: An Essential Grammar*. London: Routledge.

Kim, In-Seok (1996) *Colloquial Korean: A Complete Language Course*. London: Routledge.

King, Alan R. (1994) *The Basque Language: A Practical Introduction*. Reno: University of Nevada Press.

King, Alan R. and Olaizola Elordi, Begotxu (1996) *Colloquial Basque: A Complete Language Course*. London: Routledge.

Kraft, Charles H. and Kirk-Greene, A. M. H. (1973) *Teach Yourself Hausa*. Lincolnwood, Illinois: NTC Publishing.

Kraft, Charles H. and Kraft, Marguerite G. (1973) *Introductory Hausa*. Berkeley and Los Angeles: University of California Press.

Kramer, Christina E. (1999) *Macedonian: A Course for Beginning and Intermediate Students*. Madison: University of Wisconsin Press.

Kwee, John B. (1976) *Teach Yourself Indonesian*, rev. edn. Sevenoaks: Hodder & Stoughton.

Lazdiņa, Terēza Budiņa (1966) *Teach Yourself Latvian*. London: English Universities Press.

Lederer, Herbert (1969) *Reference Grammar of the German Language*. New York: Charles Scribner's Sons.

Lee, Kee-dong (1975) *Kusaiean Reference Grammar*. Honolulu: University Press of Hawaii.

Lee, Kee-dong (1976) *Kusaiean-English Dictionary*. Honolulu: University Press of Hawaii.

Leslau, Wolf (1968) *Amharic Textbook*. Berkeley: University of California Press.

Lewis, M. B. (1968) *Teach Yourself Malay,* 2nd edn. London: English Universities Press.

Li, Charles N. and Thompson, Sandra A. (1981) *Mandarin Chinese: A Functional Reference Grammar*. Berkeley: University of California Press.

Lukoff, Fred (1982) *An Introductory Course in Korean*. Seoul: Yonsei University Press.

Lunt, Horace G. (1952) *A Grammar of the Macedonian Literary Language*. Skopje: Državno Knigoizdatelstvo.

Lunt, Horace G. (1974) *Old Church Slavonic Grammar*, 6th edn. The Hague: Mouton.

Martin, Samuel E. and Lee, Young-Sook C. (1986) *Beginning Korean*. Rutland, Vermont: Tuttle.

Mathiassen, Terje (1996a) *A Short Grammar of Latvian*. Columbus, Ohio: Slavica Publishers.

Mathiassen, Terje (1996b) *A Short Grammar of Lithuanian*. Columbus, Ohio: Slavica Publishers.

McGregor, R. S. (1977) *Outline of Hindi Grammar with Exercises*, 2nd edn. Delhi: Oxford University Press.

McLendon, Sally (1978) Ergativity, case, and transitivity in Eastern Pomo. *International Journal of American Linguistics* 44:1–9.

Mithun, Marianne (1991) Active/agentive case marking and its motivations. *Language* 67:510–46.

Moseley, Christopher (1994) *Colloquial Estonian: A Complete Language Course*. London: Routledge.

Moseley, Christopher (1996) *Colloquial Latvian: The Complete Course for Beginners*. London: Routledge.

Othman, Zaharah and Atmosumarto, Sutanto (1995) *Colloquial Malay: A Complete Language Course*. London: Routledge.

Payne, Jerry (1987) *Colloquial Hungarian*. London: Routledge and Kegan Paul.

Pontifex, Zauzsa (1993) *Teach Yourself Hungarian: A Complete Course for Beginners*. Lincolnwood, Illinois: NTC Publishers.

Proudfoot, Anna and Cardo, Francesco (1997) *Modern Italian Grammar: A Practical Guide*. London: Routledge.

Ramoniene, Meilute and Press, Ian (1996) *Colloquial Lithuanian: The Complete Course for Beginners*. London: Routledge.

Reed, Irene, Miyaoka, Osahito, Jacobson, Steven, Afcan, Paschal and Krauss, Michael (1977) *Yup'ik Eskimo Grammar*. Fairbanks: Alaska Native Language Center, University of Alaska.

Reid, Lawrence Andrew (1966) *An Ivatan Syntax* (Oceanic Linguistics Special Publication No. 2). Honolulu: Pacific and Asian Linguistics Institute, University of Hawaii.

Reif, Joseph A. and Levinson, Hanna (1965) *Hebrew Basic Course*. Washington, DC: Foreign Service Institute, U.S. Department of State.

Rogers, Michael C., You, Clare and Richards, Kyungnyun K. (1992) *College Korean*. Berkeley: University of California Press.

Sadler, J. D. (1973/74) *Modern Latin* (Books One and Two). Norman: University of Oklahoma Press.

Scatton, Ernest A. (1984) *Bulgarian Reference Grammar*. Columbus, Ohio: Slavica Publishers.

Snell, Rupert and Weightman, Simon (1989) *Teach Yourself Hindi*. New York: Random House.

Thomas, David D. (1971) *Chrau Grammar* (Oceanic Linguistics Special Publication No. 7). Honolulu: University of Hawaii Press.

Topping, Donald M. (1973) *Chamorro Reference Grammar*. Honolulu: University of Hawaii Press.

Topping, Donald M. (1980) *Spoken Chamorro*, 2nd edn. Honolulu: University of Hawaii Press.

T'ung, Ping-cheng and Pollard, D. E. (1982) *Colloquial Chinese*. London: Routledge & Kegan Paul.

Van Schalkwyk, H. (1992) *Teach Yourself Afrikaans*. Lincolnwood, Illinois: NTC Publishing.

Vincent, Mark and Yeon, Jaehoon (1997) *Teach Yourself Korean*. Lincolnwood, Illinois: NTC Publishing.

Wade, Terence (1992) *A Comprehensive Russian Grammar*. Oxford: Basil Blackwell.

Wheelock, Frederic M. (1995) *Wheelock's Latin*, 5th edn. (revised under the editorship of R. A. LaFleur) New York: HarperCollins.

Wright, Joseph (1954) *Grammar of the Gothic Language*, 2nd edn. London: Oxford University Press.

Index of Languages

Note: There are references to various aspects of the analysis of English syntax in every chapter, so it has not been deemed necessary to include in this index the long list of pages where English is treated.

Index of Names and Terms

References to pages 342–64 are in the Glossary.